FROM GUNS TO GAVELS

FROM

GUNS

TO

GAVELS

HOW JUSTICE GREW UP
IN THE OUTLAW WEST

BILL NEAL

TEXAS TECH
UNIVERSITY PRESS

This book is typeset in Monotype Perrywood. The paper used in this book meets
the minimum requirements of ANSI/NISO Z39.48-1992 (R1997). ∞

Designed by Lindsay Starr

Library of Congress Cataloging-in-Publication Data
Neal, Bill, 1936-
  From guns to gavels : how justice grew up in the outlaw West / Bill Neal.
      p. cm.
  Includes bibliographical references and index.
  Summary: "Linked accounts of frontier crimes and trials from 1885 to 1929 across
West Texas, Indian and New Mexico Territories, and Montana trace the evolution of
criminal justice in the American West"—Provided by publisher.
  ISBN 978-0-89672-637-6 (hardcover : alk. paper) 1. Criminal justice, Administration
of—West (U.S.)—History. 2. Crime—West (U.S.)—History. 3. Trials—West (U.S.)—
History. I. Title.
  HV9955.W4N43 2008
  364.97809'041—dc22   2008030351

Printed in the United States of America
08 09 10 11 12 13 14 15 16 / 9 8 7 6 5 4 3 2 1

Texas Tech University Press
Box 41037, Lubbock, Texas 79409-1037 USA
800.832.4042 | ttup@ttu.edu | www.ttup.ttu.edu

In memory of my granddad,

Will Neal (1874–1952):

Oklahoma Territory cowboy and pioneer Texas rancher—

A man of few words

with a lot of character, courage, and determination.

A man who would do to ride the river with.

CONTENTS

5

Introduction

10

CHAPTER ONE

Duels of the Lawmen

The Volatile Motley County War and the Outlaw Sheriff

64

CHAPTER TWO

Wichita Falls Justice: Judge Lynch Presiding

Oklahoma Territory Outlaws "Dangle Twixt Heaven and Earth"

108

CHAPTER THREE

High Noon in Paducah

"I Kilt Him Purty . . . Real Purty"

ILLUSTRATIONS

ILLUSTRATIONS

MAPS

PREFACE

HARDLY AN ISSUE OF ANY POPULAR WESTERN NONFICTION MAGAZINE
hits the stands nowadays without a rehash of at least one of the celebrated gunfights on the frontier. Such shoot-'em-up confrontations
between outlaws and lawmen, soldiers and Indians, Indians and settlers, and cattle barons and sheepherders have become standard fare.
But precious little has been written about another kind of frontier
combat—courtroom confrontations that, in a larger sense, tell us
much about the beginnings and development of our criminal justice system. Indeed, the rich lodes of frontier legal history have only
been surface-mined by either grassroots historians or storytellers—
or even by scholars.

Such noted academics as Gordon Morris Bakken and John Phillip Reid have commented on the paucity of research on the subject.[1]
Reid wrote that "in the vast unresearched reaches of North American legal history, there may be no area neglected more than that of
what some have started to call western legal history."[2] It appears
that no serious legal history of the frontier was even contemplated
until the late 1980s. General historians seemed to have neglected
law in the history of the West even more than legal historians have
neglected the West in the history of the law.

That's not to say that "western" legal history is synonymous with
"frontier" legal history. Geographically, western legal history covers

all the western states. It begins with the arrival of the first settlers and extends to the present. Frontier legal history, on the other hand, is not the history of a fixed region, but rather a borderland, and a moving borderland at that.[3] Under that broad definition, the North American "frontier" could be located anywhere between the Atlantic and the Pacific, depending on the point in time the settlers passed there as they pressed ever westward across the continent. However, we will confine our discussion to the frontiers on the western states. Although the frontier experience varied from state to state (and, to refine it further, from region to region within a state), still in each frontier a similar evolution in the establishment of the law occurred: no law in the beginning, then self-help redressal of wrongs (usually called "Winchester law"), then law enforcement by private groups (e.g., vigilante committees, stockmen's protective organizations such as the "anti-horse thief association" plus lynch mobs spontaneously formed to mete out punishment for specific crimes deemed to have been particularly egregious by the local community), and finally the beginnings of a crude court-administered justice system that struggled to gain ascendancy over the earlier self-help forms of reining in outlawry. In that sense at least the Texas frontier experience was quite similar to the frontier experience in other states. And so, when we narrate the story of the frontier legal history of West Texas we are also telling in a broader sense the story of the coming of the law to frontiers in the rest of the West.

The story of the coming of the law to any frontier can be told in more than one way. In my first book on the subject, *Getting Away with Murder on the Texas Frontier*,[4] I explored the concept of narrating frontier legal history by telling stories of individual crimes and trials. Through that experience, I came to believe that thoroughly researched and well-documented individual stories anchored in the place and time under scrutiny and enhanced by a trial lawyer's insight into the workings of our legal machinery could make some serious contributions to our quest. My overall strategy for this book remains basically the same, although refined and more focused this time. My approach is not intended to replace or diminish the importance of traditional scholars' analytical commentaries but rather to enhance and complement their work—to engraft flesh, face, and features on the academic skeleton while capturing a flavor of the times. Admittedly my storytelling concept is not original. In *A Vast Amount of Trouble: A History of the Spring Creek Raid*,[5] attorney John W. Davis focused on a 1909 murder case in the Big Horn Basin to tell the dramatic story of how, and at what a dear price, the supremacy of the law was finally achieved on the Wyoming frontier. His later book, *Goodbye, Judge Lynch: The End of a Lawless Era in Wyoming's Big Horn Basis*,[6] further pursues the establishment of court-administered justice in that state. Again Davis concentrates on a single criminal case to dramatize and explain the end of a lawless era. Another book that explores the rise and fall of vigilante justice is Frederick Allen's *A Decent Orderly Lynching: The Montana Vigilantes*.[7] As a means of social control, Montana vigilantes made a mob decision to replace court justice with extralegal hangings. Between 1864 and 1879, they executed fifty men.

Another recent book not only recounts a sensational criminal trial but also affords the reader an in-depth understanding of the tumultuous times and the corrosive bitterness that permeated post-Civil War society in Missouri. Gerard S. Petrone examines in riveting detail the 1883 train-robbery trial of Frank James in *Judgment at Gallatin: The Trial of Frank James*.[8] A still more recent book proves that a well-told tale of a murder trial can be as gripping as the story of the underlying murder itself—even when that bloodletting resulted from the most sensational gunfight in the history of the West, that being no less than the shootout at the OK Corral. In *Murder in Tombstone: The Forgotten Trial of Wyatt Earp*,[9] lawyer-historian Steven Lubet, in prose cleansed of stilted legalese, guides us so skillfully through the 1881 Arizona Territory trial of Wyatt Earp that even nonlawyers will not only readily understand and appreciate the significance of the competing trial tactics but will also become vicariously caught up in the proceedings as the tale unfolds. Both of these books also provide a valuable analysis of the state of the developing criminal justice system of the 1880s in Missouri and the Arizona Territory, respectively.

Taking it one step further, I have not limited myself to the examination and interpretation of actual court documents and trial records. In addition, I relied heavily on contemporary news accounts of the crimes and trials. In this pursuit, frontier journalists have proved to be a godsend. The editors of that day never hesitated to inject their personal observations into objective reporting of events, and, in so doing, they unwittingly enriched their accounts with revealing insights not only into their personal views but also into the values and beliefs of their society. Again, I was not the first to take this approach. Richard F. Hamm, in his perceptive and reader-friendly work, *Murder, Honor, and Law: Four Virginia Homicides from Reconstruction to the Great Depression*, pointed out that criminal trials that received extensive press coverage functioned as "powerful teachers and preachers of conventional morality and customs."[10] As noted by legal historians Lawrence Friedman and Robert Percival, trials were "public theater, presenting the mores of society to an audience larger than that in the courtroom."[11] And, as Jake Lule shows in his study of the mythological elements of modern journalism, such trials and the accompanying news accounts "lay bare the soul of a given society."[12]

In both Petrone's *Judgment at Gallatin* and in Lubet's *Murder in Tombstone*, the authors, much to the enhancement of the quality of their books, make generous use of contemporary newspaper accounts of the trials and background events.

Blessed with markers blazed by able pioneers in the field, I too have set off down the trail of frontier legal history, collecting, researching, and committing to print my own stories.

ACKNOWLEDGMENTS

I AM INDEBTED TO MANY FOR THEIR ASSISTANCE, ADVICE, AND encouragement. Special thanks begin with my long-suffering wife, Gayla, who does most of the tedious detail work involved in producing a nonfiction book. Much gratitude also to my assistant researcher and mapmaker, the irrepressible Hanaba Munn Welch, "The Perfectionist"; to my longtime friend and college roommate, Dave McPherson, PhD, a retired English professor, who critiqued my first draft; to Texas Tech University Press editor-in-chief Judith Keeling for her patience, support, and encouragement; and to that tireless and ever-cheerful researcher Joy Wiley of the genealogical section of the Abilene Public Library. Also graciously extending me encouragement and the benefit of their experience were veteran western writers Bill O'Neal, Rick Miller, James I. Fenton, R. K. DeArment, and Bob Alexander, for which I am most appreciative. I especially appreciate the encouragement and constructive criticism given by professor Gordon Morris Bakken of California State University, Fullerton.

Local historians who have generously shared their stories and material with me include Marisue Burleson Potts Powell of Matador, Texas; Robert Kincaid and Clark Hitt of Crowell, Texas; Jack Jones of Seymour, Texas; Glenn Collier of Iowa Park, Texas; Jannis Hayers of Electra, Texas; Joe Hagy, former Oklahoma state geographer for research under Gov. David Walters; Richard Mize, Oklahoma historian and an editor of *The Daily Oklahoman*; Beth Railsback of the Carnegie City-County Library in Vernon, Texas; and Scarlett Daugherty of the QA&P Museum in Quanah, Texas.

To those others who were kind enough to grant interviews I am also much obliged: Frank McAuley of Knox City, Texas; Stanton Brown of Benjamin, Texas; A.C. "Arb" Piper and Waylon "Toar" Piper, both of Paducah, Texas; Ralph Powell of Matador, Texas; and George Webb of Canyon, Texas.

Thanks also to the court clerks in Wichita Falls, Vernon, Quanah, Childress, Crowell, Benjamin, Seymour, Matador, and Abilene, Texas, for assisting me in my research of court records, and to personnel at the *Wichita Falls Times Record News*, the *Vernon Daily Record*, the *Quanah Tribune-Chief*, the *Childress Index*, the *Paducah Post*, the *Matador Tribune*, and the *Baylor Banner* in Seymour, all of whom were most helpful.

Also appreciated are Tai Kreidler and his staff at the Southwest Collections Library at Texas Tech University in Lubbock; the Panhandle-Plains Archives Library in Canyon; the Texas State Archives Library in Austin; the University of Texas at Arlington Library; the Fort Worth Public Library; the Nita Stewart Haley Memorial Library and History Center in Midland; the QA&P Museum in Quanah; the Carnegie City-County Library in Vernon; the Texas Rangers Hall of Fame and Museum at Waco; *The Cattleman* magazine; the Wichita Falls Museum and Art Center; the Seminole Public Library and Heritage Center Museum in Seminole; and the Abilene Public Library, all of whom were unfailingly patient and helpful.

FROM GUNS TO GAVELS

★

The outlaw element of the [Texas] Panhandle [from the late
1870s through the 1880s] abhorred law. They had come here because
there were no officers within two hundred miles. They declared war
against officers. . . . Those officers knew that they were walking dangerous paths, that there were men who hoped to get them out alone. . . .
A member of the grand jury occupied a position of great service and
great danger. . . . The honest grand juror was a marked man during
the years when law was being slowly established. . . .

Courts were well established by 1894. [However,] they were
not always effective for it was sometimes difficult to get a conviction.
[Livestock thefts] were major crimes in that day, taking precedence in
the public mind over murder. Getting a jury was not easy for men were
readily biased in favor of friends who had "got in trouble," as they said
when a man yielded to temptation and had committed a theft. In some
counties the wrong-doers managed always to get a man on the jury
who would hang the jury when a case was tried.

Laura V. Hamner, Light 'n Hitch[1]

★

The [Texas] Pan-handle [*sic*] was full of bad men in the early nineties. Most of them had graduated from other schools of crime and found here a last resort. Some of them—a good many of them—had obtained official positions and were outlaws and deputies by turns. . . . Local authorities, even when conscientious, were poorly equipped to cope with such an element. . . . That was a wild epoch—chaotic and picturesque—a time of individual administration and untempered justice. It was also a time of mighty domain. Ranches there were as big as some kingdoms. . . . There was a grand [land] gobble. The big stockmen fenced everything with little regard for boundaries and less for the law. With such examples as these in high places, it is not strange that a general indifference for legal rights and possessions prevailed. Next to cattle-raising, cattle-stealing was the chief industry.

Capt. Bill McDonald, Texas Ranger[2]

INTRODUCTION

STRINGING THE BEADS TOGETHER

One bead, no matter how beautiful, does not a necklace make. To fashion a necklace the craftsman strings many beads together. Hopefully, what is crafted hereafter, story-wise, is a necklace and not merely a loose assortment of beads.

Geographically, the tales that follow take us from Mississippi to the frontiers of West Texas, the Indian Territory, the New Mexico Territory, and finally to the frozen Montana wilderness. The journey begins in 1885 when a thirteen-year-old lad strikes out on his own, leaving his Civil War-ravaged Mississippi homeland for the wild and outlaw-infested Red River borderland along the North Texas and Indian Territory boundary. The journey ends when the same lad—an outlaw now—dies by the gun in 1929, after a tempestuous career of nearly half a century, much longer than any western outlaw had any right to expect.

But this is not a book about the adventures—or misadventures—of a single outlaw. Instead, it is a series of connected stories each of which comfortably stands on its own as a fascinating tale about the taming of the Old West. Some of the characters in early stories reappear in one or more of the later stories. In this book I have attempted to refine the concept of narrating West Texas fron-

tier legal history by telling separate stories of actual crimes and trials—refining that concept by linking separate stories together not
only by theme and individual characters, but also by telling them
in chronological order—each story a freeze-frame depiction of the
state of the law and society at that particular time, thus revealing
how both the law and society had matured since the time of the previous tale. Meanwhile, we encounter plenty of outlaws and lawmen
(some of whom swap roles in midstream and others who play such
ambiguous roles that it is difficult to categorize them), plus a host of
colorful frontier trial lawyers and judges.

Drama abounds in each of these yarns of bygone days. Take,
for example, the story of the Main Street shootout between two
bitter enemies—a Texas Ranger captain and a county sheriff—or
the killings of three Texas sheriffs, two range detectives, and an
assortment of outlaws as well as a few innocent citizens. Another:
the abrupt demise of two Indian Territory outlaws who met their
respective ends at the end of a rope in a lynching so sensational that
it galvanized even the Texas Legislature into action. Then there is
the made-for-tabloid story of the murder trial of a famous cattle
baron who, together with an associate, cornered and killed a known
cow thief at high noon in front of witnesses in a West Texas hotel.
However, the most sensational southwestern courtroom battle of
the early twentieth century was the trial of two indicted cattle rustlers who ambushed and killed two brand inspectors who were
about to testify against them—again, the killings taking place in yet
another West Texas hotel and in front of witnesses. Also recounted
here are the heroics of two crusty and fearless old district judges.
One stood up, almost alone, unsuccessfully, against a lynch mob;
the other, with some backing from the Texas Rangers, refused to
be buffaloed by the two armed factions teetering on the brink of a
county-wide civil war over the organization of a new West Texas
county—thus preventing wholesale bloodshed. And there are stories
featuring the boisterous and bombastic trial lawyers of the era who
engaged in countless courtroom battles in murder cases, the prosecu-

tion demanding that the jury convict the defendant of murder under the clear provisions of the newly enacted statutory laws of the State of Texas while the defense attorney harangued the jury to acquit his man pursuant to the unwritten codes of the Old South and the violence-tolerant Old West.

These tales add up to more than the sum of their parts. An anecdotal textbook, they begin in a land beyond the law and take us down a trail of blood leading from the beginnings and the incipient struggles of our modern criminal justice system in the Southwest all the way through its development to a post-World War I time when the black-robed Judge Blackstone finally gained ascendancy over Judge Winchester and Judge Lynch—the trail from guns to gavels.

In our journey down that trail of frontier legal history, the following stories raise—and perhaps partially answer—some tantalizing issues. For instance, what are the dynamics of the complex relationship between popular culture and the law? It is a given that the mores and values of a specific society in large part are reflected in the content of its criminal statutes and the applicable sanctions provided for the violation of each. But how much does the law affect the cultural values of its subjects? And how much does a community's culture and beliefs affect the enforcement of criminal statutes? In one story, a mob in 1896 stormed a local jail and gained possession of two loathsome Indian Territory outlaws and proceeded to lynch them. Despite the fact that the leaders of the mob were well known (none wore masks), and despite the fact that the local district judge railed against the outrage, still no effective prosecution was sustained because popular sentiment fell heavily in favor of the lynching. There was, however, an outcry against this mob justice from reformers in other parts of Texas, including protests voiced in several influential newspapers. Finally the Texas Legislature was jarred into action and in 1897 enacted some sweeping antilynching laws. But no one was ever prosecuted under those statutes, again because popular culture supported the lynching of heinous criminals (and some not-so-heinous subjects whose skin pigmentation didn't meet mob approval). Local officials simply refused to enforce duly enacted statutes when their constituents were strongly supportive of Judge Lynch solutions. That is, until after World War I, when a sea change in society significantly eroded support for the use of lynching. The same was essentially true of what constituted "self-defense" under Texas' written law. Despite the explicit provisions of the written law, almost anything qualified as self-defense on the frontier, harking back to the unwritten laws imported from the Old South—a code that pervaded the frontier mind-set until the Texas frontier period ended with World War I.

THE LAWYER AS HISTORIAN AND STORYTELLER

When I was but a cub at the bar, a veteran trial lawyer once told me this: "You can make a point. Or you can tell a story. But the trick is to make a point by telling a story. That way," he continued, "a jury will not only understand your point, but they'll remember it. And, if you're good enough to *involve* them in your story, they'll not only remember and understand it, but they'll also give a damn."

In telling the stories of the criminal trials that follow, I have attempted first to amass all the available facts and then to present the reader with both the prosecution and defense positions before giving my take on the case.

The central question in most true-crime stories usually is not "who done it?" or even "how'd they do it?" but rather "*why* did they do it?"—a kind of psychological autopsy of the dead and the deadly, followed by a legal autopsy of the ensuing trial, its principals and their tactics, as well as its outcome and its aftermath.

Most interesting of all—most intriguing of all—is the acuity of the best of the frontier trial lawyers in perceiving the values, mores, and beliefs of their society plus their uncanny ability to read people. Depending on these skills, the lawyers selected jurors with whom their message would resonate, right down to the bone.

DUELS OF THE LAWMEN

The Volatile Motley County War and
the Outlaw Sheriff

It seemed as if you could almost see forever across those gently roll-ing, virtually treeless and wind-swept plains that sprawled south of the Red River and on north into the Oklahoma Territory. For certain there wasn't much that was manmade to get in the way—just one set of railroad tracks evidencing the creep of frontier settlement. But on this day, excited townsfolk watched intently as a small, sooty cloud of engine smoke appeared some six or eight miles down those railroad tracks. They watched as it billowed larger and larger. Final-ly, amidst much huffing and puffing and the tooting of whistles and the clanging of bells, the train labored into the station and screeched to a halt.

Despite the bone-chilling winter weather, a sizeable crowd had gathered at the Quanah, Texas, railroad depot that Saturday to wit-ness the arrival of the Fort Worth & Denver City train. Gathering there each evening at six o'clock was a community ritual for the set-tlers of this fledgling northwest Texas village. After all, the town—named for the famous Comanche Chief Quanah Parker—was just nine years old, and it had been only five years since the railroad tracks had linked it to the outside world. So the daily arrival of the train was still something of a novelty. In fact, the spectacle of the

Capt. W. J. "Bill" McDonald, com-
mander of Company B, Frontier
Battalion of the Texas Rangers.
*(Courtesy of the Texas Ranger Hall of
Fame and Museum, Waco, Texas)*

Childress County, Texas, Sheriff John
Pearce Matthews. *(From the* Childress
Index*)*

mighty iron monster in those horse-and-buggy days when nobody
had even seen an automobile (much less a radio or a television set)
was a great source of entertainment. And it freighted not only mun-
dane supplies but also hints of exotic and far-away places that common folks of that time could never hope to visit; plus there was
always the chance of glimpsing the face of some important traveler
through a curtain briefly parted.

However, this evening, December 9, 1893, the townsfolk were
about to witness a lot more drama than they ever could have imagined . . . or wanted.

THE PLAYERS

Lots of folks had been milling about downtown Quanah that Saturday, and the local saloons had done a brisk business. Few frontiersmen of the time frowned on a man having a sociable snort or two.

Or three. Even if the snorter happened to be a lawman. In fact, the local sheriff, Hardeman County Sheriff Dick Coffer, and a neighboring sheriff, Childress County Sheriff John Pearce Matthews, had spent a good part of that day socializing in watering holes along Main Street.

The county seat of Childress County is the town of Childress, some thirty miles to the west of Quanah. Sheriff Matthews and a couple of his cronies had caught the eastbound FW&DC passenger train early that morning in Childress and had detrained in Quanah, where they hooked up with Sheriff Coffer.

Another lawman happened to be in town that fateful day. He was Capt. William Jess "Bill" McDonald, age forty-one, commander of Company B of the Frontier Battalion of the Texas Rangers—a lawman legend in the making. And he looked the part: long, lean, and wiry, he stood about six feet tall, had steel blue-gray eyes, a Roman nose, and a weather-beaten face.[1]

Ranger McDonald and Sheriff Matthews, however, were not close friends.

Born in 1852 in Mississippi, McDonald had enjoyed an almost idyllic boyhood—for a time. His parents were moderately well-to-do, growing cotton on the rich, black loam of their plantation. Then came the devastation of the Civil War. After the mass slaughtering finally ended, the war left behind only a seared landscape, economic ruin, poverty, broken and scattered families, and a legacy of violence that corroded the psyche of the survivors and their progeny for a century to come. McDonald's father, Maj. Enoch McDonald, a Confederate soldier, was killed in 1862 in a battle at Corinth, Mississippi. Young Bill's childhood ended that day. At ten years of age he shouldered the mantle of being oldest male of the McDonald family. Some four years later, in 1866, he, his younger sister, Mary, and his mother, Eunice Durham McDonald, gathered the remnants of the family fortune and migrated westward, ending up in the East Texas town of Henderson. Scarcely two years after his arrival in Texas, sixteen-year-old McDonald got himself into a peck of trouble with the hated Radical Reconstruction authorities. A McDonald relative, one "Colonel Greene," was killed by a black man, apparently as a result of mistaken identity. The black man was jailed, but an irate mob, of which young Bill Jess McDonald was probably a member, stormed the jail, seized the prisoner, and lynched him.[2] Later, McDonald and Charles Greene, Colonel Greene's brother, got into a running gun battle with Union soldiers at Henderson. McDonald was arrested and court-martialed on a charge of treason.

When the case was called for trial, a folksy, disheveled country lawyer by the name of Dave Culberson arose and announced he represented young McDonald. His rustic appearance, however, belied his considerable lawyering skills and oratorical talents, and he was able to clear his client. David B. Culberson was a skilled politician as well and was later elected to the U.S. Congress. He also passed his talents along to his son, Charles A. Culberson, who was elected governor of Texas in 1909, and later elected to the U.S. Senate.

This judicial episode in young McDonald's life occurred at a critical juncture along the road to his future. He was a spirited, bold, and fearless youth no doubt much embittered by the trauma of the Civil War and the hated Yankees who had killed his father and who later attempted to imprison him and who now, with arrogance, ruled his adopted state. At that fork in the road he could easily have gone down the outlaw trail, as did the Youngers, the Jameses, John Wesley Hardin, and Bill Longley. Or, he could have gone down the road of those who wore a star and claimed to be lawmen, but whose conduct was scarcely more law-abiding than the outlaws they pursued. Yet, young Bill Jess McDonald, to his credit, reined his horse down the third fork in that road—the righteous one. Righteous, at least, according to his lights.

In the 1870s McDonald established a grocery business in the small town of Mineola in Wood County, Texas. His first law enforcement experience began in the early 1880s when he was appointed as a deputy sheriff of that county. In about 1885 McDonald moved to

Hardeman County in North Central Texas where he bought a section of school land just south of Quanah and began cattle ranching.

However, McDonald's peaceful life as a Texas cattleman didn't last long. One morning he discovered that four of his best horses and a fine Newfoundland dog had been stolen by a gang of livestock thieves called the Brooking gang. McDonald promptly applied to the sheriff of Hardeman County for a deputy's badge. It was granted, and not long thereafter the Brooking gang ceased to be a threat to law-abiding settlers. That was only the beginning of McDonald's war on outlaws along the frontier. However, his authority as a county deputy limited him to Hardeman County. Texas Gov. L. S. Ross remedied that by appointing him as a "special ranger," thus giving him statewide authority. Thieves, however, were not limited to plundering just within the state of Texas. Since the outlaw-infested Indian Territory lay just a few miles to the north, it was not a difficult task for outlaws to steal in Texas and then quickly drive their stolen livestock across the Red River to safety. McDonald's reputation as a lawman soon earned him an appointment as a U.S. Deputy Marshal of the Northern District of Texas with authority to operate in the southwestern part of the Indian Territory and also (at least according to McDonald's interpretation) in no-man's-land, an unassigned territory that is now the Oklahoma Panhandle. This was followed by an appointment as Deputy U.S. Marshal of the U.S. District of Kansas, which enabled him to operate in another outlaw-infested area: the northwest portion of the Indian Territory including the so-called Cherokee Strip or Cherokee Outlet, which lay just east of the Oklahoma Panhandle and just south of the Kansas line.[3] (In 1890 the U.S. Congress resolved some jurisdictional disputes when it opened up the western part of the Indian Territory for white settlement. Thereafter the western part of what is now Oklahoma was known as the Oklahoma Territory, while the eastern portion was still known as the Indian Territory. Such was the case until 1907 when the Oklahoma Territory and the Indian Territory were combined and admitted into the union as the state of Oklahoma.)

In the late 1880s, however, the rule of the outlaws went virtually unchallenged in no-man's-land and the Cherokee Strip in the Indian Territory—that is, until Bill McDonald decided to take up the challenge. Empowered by his newly acquired badges, he wandered unarmed into the territory disguised as, of all things, a humble peddler of fruit trees. Dressed in shabby clothes, he strapped a cheap saddle on an old paddle-footed, paint horse and, armed only with a fruit tree catalog, headed north into the land of the lawless. For several weeks he ambled leisurely through the countryside, stopping here and there to visit, whittle, gossip, and show his fruit tree catalog. Folks just naturally trusted this inoffensive tramp and shared all sorts of gossip with him—some of which proved to be most incriminating both to themselves and to their neighbors. When McDonald returned sometime later, it was to make deliveries all right—but they weren't deliveries of fruit trees. He delivered instead eight felony arrest warrants.

In addition to his law enforcement abilities, McDonald was a born showman who never missed an opportunity to embellish and then broadcast his exploits. He is responsible for one story that is probably more myth than reality but that stuck as a Texas Ranger legend. Supposedly a local official called ranger headquarters and demanded a company of rangers to quell an angry mob threatening to cause a riot. When a lone ranger (McDonald) detrained at the troubled town, the mayor, aghast, wailed in despair and demanded to know why they had sent only one ranger, to which Captain Bill shrugged: "Well, you ain't got but one riot, do you?"[4] Myth or not, nobody could doubt that McDonald was fearless and unflappable under pressure. He was famous for confronting angry mobs either alone or accompanied by one other lawman. Once when Captain Bill started out alone to talk down a mob of angry strikers, someone protested, pointing out the danger. Bill replied that he was "a pretty good single-handed talker." And he got the job done. Another time, with only one ranger backing him up, he faced down a contingent of twenty armed and hostile soldiers blocking his way. The commanding officer of that post later commented that "Bill McDonald would charge Hell with a bucket of water."

In 1891 Gov. James Stephen Hogg appointed McDonald to replace Samuel A. McMurry as captain of Company B of the Frontier Battalion of the Texas Rangers. As such he was in charge of the whole Texas Panhandle with Amarillo as his headquarters. However, he continued to live on his Hardeman County ranch on Wanderers Creek just south of Quanah.

Sheriff Matthews, age thirty-six, was handsome, bold, brash, egotistical, and volatile. He never hesitated to vent his spleen about rivals or to give tongue to the retaliation he intended. But his talk was not to be dismissed as mere braggadocio, for his reputation as a deadly opponent was not based on mere huff and puff. Matthews had already killed two men before becoming Childress County sheriff. In his native Louisiana, he had killed a man and then, to escape prosecution, fled to Texas and dropped his surname, introducing himself as "John Pierce." One account says that the victim was a riverboat captain; another holds that it was a black man. In the Texas Panhandle he cowboyed for the Laurel Leaf outfit and, in 1884, killed another cowboy, James Mankins, in Wheeler County, Texas. However, the Wheeler County coroner's inquest jury found that the death was "accidental," and therefore he was never indicted or tried for the killing. (According to Matthews's version, he and his friend Mankins were engaged in an innocent game of "mumble peg" when, in a bit of horseplay, he accidentally stabbed Mankins.)[5] Afterward he drifted south to the town of Childress where in 1892 he managed to get himself elected as the second sheriff of Childress County. Despite his overweening ego and mouth to match, he was a popular sheriff in his home county.

Matthews and McDonald, both fearless and equipped with Texas-size egos, shared another common trait: they let no criticism, however mild or constructive, go unchallenged. And each insisted on being portrayed as the star, and the only star, on any stage. McDonald grumbled to his superior, Texas Adjutant General W. H. Mabry, that

Matthews conceived himself to be the "District Sheriff" of the entire Texas Panhandle and all of the "Oklahoma country," a role McDonald obviously considered already occupied. And, in what has to be a textbook example of the pot calling the kettle black, McDonald went on to grouse that Matthews was "very domineering and when he fails to carry his point it makes him mad."[6] Meanwhile, an Amarillo real estate agent, complaining to Adj. Gen. Mabry about the "bad conduct" and "cruelty" of one of McDonald's men (Tom "Red" O'Hare), warned Mabry that it would be useless to assign McDonald the task of investigating the complaints, adding that McDonald "is so constituted that he thinks that a man who does not like the ranger force is a scoundrel and can't be too badly treated by them."[7]

It was common knowledge that there was bad blood between McDonald and Matthews, and therefore, when Matthews and his associates got off the train at Quanah the morning of December 9, 1893, word quickly spread that there might be big trouble before sundown.

The trouble between Matthews and the ranger force, in general, first started about 1890 when Matthews was still foreman of the Laurel Leaf Ranch in the Texas Panhandle. He and his men took a herd of cattle to Amarillo for shipment and, while in town, they (predictably) went on a spree that ended in a gambling dispute. Two Texas Rangers intervened and forcibly subdued Matthews and one of his men.[8] From that point on, Matthews held a grudge against any ranger. After Matthews was elected Childress County sheriff, he aggravated the animosity by provoking an incident at the 1892 annual Texas Sheriffs' Convention in Houston. Gov. James Hogg was a guest of the sheriffs and was preparing to speak when Matthews (who, for reasons unexplained, also bore a grudge against the governor) jumped to his feet and exclaimed: "Let Governor Hogg come forward and explain his treatment of the sheriffs." Hogg attempted to assuage Matthews, but Matthews, unappeased, again attempted to force the issue. McDonald, Hogg's longtime friend and champion, intervened. He stepped to the speaker's platform and shouted, "Stand your ground, Governor, these men are your friends!" Again the governor tried to smooth ruffled feathers by inviting Matthews to come to Austin later to discuss his concerns. Thinking he had quelled the storm, Governor Hogg left. But after the governor departed, Matthews accosted McDonald, and but for the intervention of other sheriffs, a showdown would likely have occurred. The convention ended without further confrontations, but the bad seed had been sown, and the ill will between the two took root and sprouted.[9] McDonald didn't help matters when he later blackballed Matthews's application to join a Wichita Falls Masonic Lodge in which McDonald was a member (the Hella Temple, Order of the Mystic Shrine).[10]

However, it would be a handsome and likeable young cow-puncher who would be the unlikely catalyst to precipitate the final showdown between McDonald and Matthews. His name was Joe Beckham, and he worked for the Matador Ranch. When Beckham was hired, the sprawling ranch had its headquarters in what is now Motley County, Texas, just southwest of the then newly formed counties of Childress (where Matthews was sheriff) and Hardeman (where Dick Coffer was sheriff and where McDonald lived). As a child, Joseph P. Beckham, orphaned by the death of his mother, Sally Bundy, and the desertion of his father, Rodric Carroll Beckham, grew up with a sister, Nancy T. Beckham McCarty, near the town of Ennis in East Texas. After one of Joe's older brothers, Buck (Rodric Carroll Beckham Jr.), was hired by the Matador Ranch, Joe and his brother Jim joined him as Matador cowboys in 1882.[11] For the next nine years, until Motley County was organized, Joe lived the uncomplicated life of a Matador cowhand.

THE MOTLEY COUNTY WAR

The tragic saga of Joe Beckham can best be understood in its context: take notice of the times and the place—more specifically, the origins and early development of the Matador Ranch and the extraordinarily violent birth pains of Motley County, the former contributing greatly to the violence of the latter.

Handsome young Joe Beckham was named the first sheriff of Motley County, Texas, in 1891. It all went downhill for Joe after that. *(Courtesy Nita Stewart Haley Memorial Library, Midland, Texas)*

The Matador Ranch—called the Matadors—was one of the vast West Texas outfits then being cobbled together by whatever means it took, fair or foul. As with many of the other big ranches, foreign capital financed the venture: a Scottish syndicate bought the Matador Land and Cattle Company. By 1888 the group had succeeded in putting under one fence nearly all of present-day Motley County, more than half of Dickens County to the south, and sizeable chunks of Cottle County to the east and Floyd County to the west.[12] The boundary fence enclosed some one million acres, give or take, known as the Matador pasture, and it included some lands owned outright by the syndicate. Most of the acreage, however, consisted of lands leased from the state or from private owners, lands claimed by right of first occupancy, or lands owned outright by settlers and not leased to the Matadors. By the late 1880s, a trickle of settlers began moving into the country and claiming preemptive homestead rights from the state to perfect title to one-section tracts of land consisting of 640 acres.

Unsurprisingly, the Scots took a dim view of this incursion into their domain. They realized that with the ever-increasing influx of "nesters" a higher price would be required for future land acquisitions, the annual lease rates would rise commensurately, and home-steaders would claim and occupy many choice tracts of grassland lying within the Matador pasture—tracts of land that the syndicate, until the mid-1880s, had grazed free of cost and thereafter had been able to lease from the state for a few cents per acre.[13] The Scots were also aware that the coming of these sod-busters foretold the organization of counties, and with that, ad valorem taxes would increase dramatically to finance county governments and schools.

Yet the settlers continued to come; the storm clouds continued to darken. Strangely enough, it was one of the founders of the vast Matador Ranch who championed the cause of the settlers and who was to figure prominently in the impending storms of violence then gathering—a series of eruptions that might well be described as the Motley County War. Henry H. Campbell, a thrice-wounded Confederate veteran, became a successful trail driver after the Civil War and was one of the principals of the original Matador Ranch, which, in 1882, was sold to the Scottish syndicate. The syndicate then hired him as ranch superintendent to ramrod what turned out to be a most successful enterprise, and which, fueled by generous helpings of foreign capital, began to grow by leaps and bounds during the 1880s. However, as time passed, Campbell chafed under what he considered "over-supervision" by foreigners who hadn't the faintest idea of how to run a West Texas cattle outfit. The Scots, in turn, became increasingly frustrated with Campbell's independent ways, including his failure to make frequent and detailed reports of ranch affairs. As one former Matador employee later remarked: "We never bought a hobble rope on the Matador but that they [the Scots] had to know about it in Dundee [Scotland]." With a chuckle, he recalled that once the Scots demanded a count of that year's calf crop. Of course the Matador cow herd was "scattered from Hell to breakfast" over nearly a million acres of rough range land. Nevertheless, the ranch superintendent dutifully wired back an estimate of ten thousand calves. Turned out he was right on the money, too. When the branding was finally completed at the annual fall roundup that year and the head counts were tallied, the boss was only twenty-seven calves short of

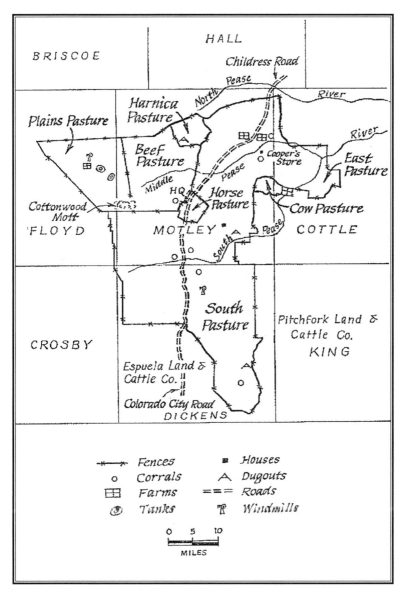

In 1888 the Matador Ranch sprawled over a huge range including nearly
all of Motley County, Texas, and parts of three other adjoining West Texas
counties, according to a survey by Sam L. Chalk.

(Courtesy of University of Oklahoma Press)

his estimate. But were the Scots pleased? Hardly. "We got a letter from them. . . . They wanted to know what happened to the other twenty-seven."[14] All this led to Campbell's resignation in late 1890, and both sides were much relieved to be rid of the other.[15]

Relations between the Scots and Campbell took another sharp turn for the worse when, immediately after his resignation, Campbell undertook, successfully, to organize Motley County. The county, named after a signer of the Texas Declaration of Independence and a casualty of the battle of San Jacinto, Dr. Junius William Mottley, became organized and independent on February 5, 1891. Henry H. Campbell became the first Motley County judge.[16]

The title of county judge is something of a misnomer since in Texas that official has but limited judicial duties. (He presides over misdemeanor criminal cases, minor civil disputes, and probate matters, although to this day in the state of Texas, there is no statute that provides that having a license to practice law is a necessary qualification for holding this office.) More important, the county judge serves as the county's chief executive officer, plus he presides over the county's legislative branch (the "commissioners' court"). Consequently, the office freighted considerable political clout to County Judge Campbell—a state of affairs not very much to the liking of the Matador Land & Cattle Company.

If all that weren't enough to cause major consternation in the boardroom across the Atlantic, what Campbell did next really brought the simmering pot to a boil. He hauled the Scots into the Matador County District Court, bringing an injunction suit against the ranch and all its employees on behalf of himself and other settlers owning or leasing small tracts located within the Matador pasture. He complained that the Matadors were driving the settlers' cattle off their small tracts and throwing them *outside* the distant Matador pasture boundary fence. Much to the chagrin of the Scots, he was successful in persuading District Judge W. T. "Billy" McGill to grant the injunction[17]—this during the month of December 1891, less than a year after Campbell's resignation from the Matadors and only ten months after Campbell had succeeded in organizing Mot-

Henry H. Campbell, Confederate
army veteran and pioneer Texas
cattleman, was one of the founders
of the legendary Matador Ranch
in West Texas. Later he became
the first county judge of Motley
County, Texas. *(Courtesy of Southwest
Collection/Special Collections Library,
Texas Tech University, Lubbock, Texas)*

ley County. In a lengthy letter to Governor Hogg, County Judge
Campbell detailed the history of the bitter struggle between the
factions—the settlers and the Matador Ranch—and congratulated
the governor for his appointment of Judge Billy McGill. Campbell
described McGill as a judge who could not be intimidated by the
cattle barons—or by anybody else. He also noted that before Judge
McGill granted the settlers' injunction against the Matador Ranch,
Matador cowboys had run more than 1,600 head of the settlers' cattle out of the fenced-off Matador pasture that also enclosed settlers'
tracts, adding that very few of those cattle had been recovered.[18]

Meanwhile, other brush fires were breaking out on the Motley
County political landscape. When the county became officially organized in February 1891, county officials (including County Judge
Campbell) were elected. It was not the Democrats versus the Repub-
licans when it came to Motley County politics; it was the Matadors
versus the settlers. Campbell was, as we have seen, the leader of the
settler ticket and was elected. But he was in the minority. The county
attorney, W. M. Smith, and three of the four county commissioners
were pro-ranch.[19] (One of these three pro-ranch commissioners was
George W. Cook, a Matador Ranch line rider. For reasons that are

not clear, Cook was determined to take an active hand in the play. We shall soon hear much more about the belligerent Cook.)

The joker in the political deck, however, was a most unlikely card: young Joe Beckham, age twenty-one. Although woefully innocent of life experiences and completely devoid of any law enforcement training (or, for that matter, training in the collection and management of tax revenues), the youthful Matador cowboy nevertheless tossed his Stetson into the ring in the sheriff and county tax collector race. He apparently was elected with the support of the ranch faction. Surprisingly, however, Joe soon found himself aligned with County Judge Campbell and the pro-settler clique. Quite possibly the ranch became disenchanted with Beckham when he began taking his office seriously and arresting Matador cowboys who came to town, got on a spree, and began shooting up the place.[20] In any event, political enmity escalated to a fever pitch, and the Motley County War was on.

Adding fuel to the fire was a showdown between Beckham and Jeff Davis Boone, a former Matador Ranch wagon boss. A bully some ten years older than Beckham, Boone may have gotten his ego bruised when young Beckham became sheriff. While they both cowboyed for the Matadors, Boone had hazed Beckham and, on one occasion, had repeatedly whipped Beckham over the head with his rope. After Joe became sheriff, Boone quit the Matador Ranch and bought the Dew Drop Saloon in the town of Matador, county seat of Motley County. On February 17, 1892, Boone, sufficiently fortified with his own brew, sauntered into the courthouse and taunted Beckham. But this time Beckham did not back down, and the fight began. Both drew their pistols. In the exchange of shots, Beckham shot Boone in the arm while Beckham himself was slightly wounded. Boone's wound did not appear to be serious, and he refused to see a doctor—a fatal mistake. On June 23, 1892, Boone died of blood poisoning. On September 21, 1892, a grand jury indicted Beckham for assault to commit the murder of Jeff Boone. The district judge moved the case to Floyd County (Floydada, Texas) on a change of venue. Beckham was tried there and acquitted.[21]

Former Matador Ranch cowboy Jeff Davis Boone was fatally wounded in the Motley County courthouse in 1892 when he picked a fight with new Motley County Sheriff Joe Beckham. *(From the* Matador Tribune*)*

Beckham's troubles were only beginning. Most (but not all) of his future problems were of his own doing. In the fall election (November 8, 1892), voters reelected Beckham sheriff. In addition to his law enforcement duties, it was also his duty to collect and account for the county's ad valorem taxes. Well, Joe collected . . . but he didn't account for or turn the funds over to the county treasurer. About this time he apparently got down to some serious drinking and gambling, and when he ran out of his own money, he stayed in the game—betting away some of Motley County's tax money. His friends made up the shortfall in his tax collections—once. But Beckham repeated his mistake, and this time his friends could not cover his shortages.[22] On January 15, 1893, Sheriff Beckham was arrested in Sheriff Matthews's bailiwick (Childress County) on a misdemeanor charge of "gaming," more specifically spelled out in the complaint as follows: "unlawfully playing a game with cards in a certain outhouse where people consort." He was fined ten dollars.[23] Just a week after this embarrassment, the newly constructed

Motley County courthouse mysteriously burned down. Speculation was rife that it was the result of arson and that Joe Beckham was the arsonist, his motive being obvious. However, if he did torch the courthouse and did so with the intention of destroying evidence, he was foiled as the county's tax collection records were locked up in a six-ton, fire-proof safe.[24]

From that point on, things went downhill for Beckham.[25]

On May 24, 1893, the Motley County Commissioners Court ordered Beckham to pay the missing 1892 tax collection funds. He failed to comply. Worse, only a few days later, on June 4, 1893, he was ambushed by Motley County Commissioner George Cook. That Beckham was not murdered on the spot was due solely to Cook's poor marksmanship. Cook had foreknowledge that Beckham would arrive by train at the Childress, Texas, depot on that date. When Beckham stepped off the train, Cook cut down on him with his Winchester rifle. After Cook missed him a couple of times, Beckham unlimbered his own Winchester and fired back, but also missed. The duel thus ended.

Although the shooting occurred in Childress, Texas, the editor of the neighboring weekly newspaper in Quanah, Texas, some thirty miles down the trail, took the opportunity to treat his readers to a classic example of late-nineteenth-century frontier journalism— "small-town style." The editor's take tells us much more about the culture of that time and place than it does of the incident under scrutiny. To begin with, the editor couldn't resist taking a dig at the next settlement down the road, dismissing rival Childress as a "rural village." (Actually in small-town journalism of that day, any opportunity to take a cheap shot at a neighboring town was considered a sacred and obligatory boosterism duty! Although Quanah was about the same size as Childress—neither community having more than a few hundred souls calling their village home—each local editor touted his burg as destined, inevitably, to become the next Chicago.) The editor's account of the shooting itself speaks volumes of frontier West Texans' nonchalant attitude toward violence even when it was lethal in scope. Then too there was a strained attempt at humor—the favored style of the day consisted of calling everything by a name other than that which it really was. It may sound contrived, corny, and juvenile today, but in those entertainment-starved and unsophisticated times, it undoubtedly passed as knee-slappin', belly-laughin' comedy. At any rate, under the headline of "Poor Shooting," the Quanah editor sniffed:

> Considerable excitement was caused at Childress last Sunday evening by a "shooting bee" which took place near the depot of that rural village a few minutes after the train pulled in. It seems that sheriff Beckham of Motley County, and one of the commissioners, Mr. Cook, had a disagreement. The sheriff was a passenger on Sunday evening's train and Mr. Cook was in Childress very anxious to "cook" Mr. Beckham's goose. As soon as the train stopped at the depot, Mr. Beckham alighted and started across to the hotel when, some 50 or 60 feet from the train, Cook began "pumping" hot lead at him from a Winchester. Mr. Beckham, taking the "lay of the land" at a glance, concluded that as he had his Winchester along, he would "ante" and take a hand in the game also, and immediately his "music box" began to grind. After some three or four shots apiece had been fired . . . no one, not even a looker on . . . [was] hit.[26]

Although it was clear that Cook was the aggressor and that Beckham returned fire only in self-defense, Childress Sheriff Matthews, a close friend and ally of Cook, arrested *both* Cook and Beckham, charging each with aggravated assault. Each made bond and was released. A Childress County grand jury later indicted both men.[27]

Beckham barely got out of the Childress County jail before he was again arrested, this time back home in Matador where he was ignominiously caged in his own jail. The three pro-ranch Motley County commissioners and the county attorney had waited until pro-settler County Judge Campbell was out of town. Then, on June 14, 1893 (only ten days after Beckham had narrowly escaped death by ambush in Childress), they met and ordered the county attorney to file a civil suit against Beckham for the 1892 tax collections, and without any legal authority whatsoever, they declared the office of sheriff vacant. The commissioners next voted to appoint one J. L. Moore, a pro-ranch man, as the new sheriff. Finally, they had an arrest warrant issued against Beckham for the felony offense of embezzlement of public funds. "Sheriff" Moore executed the warrant and jailed his predecessor—but not for long. With a little help from his friends (including Clarence Nugent, a local newspaper editor, George Bigham, and Joe's brother, Jim Beckham), Sheriff Beckham was sprung from his captivity and immediately proceeded to disarm and arrest "Sheriff" Moore and his deputies for unlawfully carrying firearms.[28]

The result was that Motley County teetered on the brink of civil war: two bitterly opposing armed factions faced off against each other with no law enforcement presence as a buffer. To make matters worse, Childress County Sheriff John Matthews (never one to be confined by the boundaries of his own county) decided to take an active hand in the dispute, siding, of course, with the pro-Cook and pro-Matador Ranch faction. He rode down to Matador and, with no apparent legal authority, proceeded to deputize and then lead a posse of fifty to seventy-five armed Matador Ranch cowboys in an effort to capture Beckham and his supporters.[29] But Beckham had disappeared again.

When Beckham could not be found, Matthews and Cook concluded (correctly, as it turned out) that he must have fled to the Oklahoma Territory, whereupon Matthews, pursuant to his self-appointed role as "sheriff of the entire Texas Panhandle and the Oklahoma Territory," set out with Cook to run Beckham to ground wherever he might be found. But first, Matthews and Cook stopped at Quanah and requested Bill McDonald to send one or more of his rangers with them. McDonald (somewhat reluctantly, it might be surmised) agreed to send Ranger Bob McClure along. McDonald later claimed that he instructed McClure not to cross over into Oklahoma Territory—orders that, if given, McClure promptly decided to ignore. Nevertheless, with McClure's aid, the posse soon captured Beckham near the present town of Frederick, Oklahoma.

At this point the story takes another strange twist. For reasons not recorded, Matthews and Cook turned on their fellow posseman, Ranger McClure, and instigated charges in the Oklahoma Territory against him for the attempted rape of an Indian girl. According to McDonald, "they were about to mob him." McDonald later related that he had to "drive a hundred miles on a bad night" into Oklahoma Territory to extricate McClure from this mess. His investigation indicated that the attempted rape charge was groundless, and McDonald succeeded in getting it dismissed.[30] McDonald related that he brought McClure home, "a wiser and better ranger."[31] But not, however, before more harsh words were directed at McDonald and his rangers by Matthews. In an ominous harbinger, McDonald sent a report to his boss, Adjutant General Mabry, noting that he was "getting rather sore" at Matthews and that "dirty little [news] paper" [in Childress] for "hammering away at us," but then went on to assure Mabry that he would "try and keep silent awhile longer."[32]

Leaving Beckham in an Oklahoma Territory jail, Matthews then set off for Austin to obtain requisition papers in an effort to extradite Beckham back to Texas. Meanwhile, however, Beckham filed a habeas corpus action alleging that his confinement was unlawful since Matthews and his Texas posse had no legal authority to arrest and imprison anybody beyond the borders of the state of Texas. Beckham succeeded and was freed. When Matthews returned to the Oklahoma Territory with his extradition documents, he was outraged to discover that his prey had flown the coop; Beckham was long gone.

Meanwhile, back in Motley County, a complete breakdown of law and order had taken place.

Fortunately, at this juncture, two dominant and determined characters were about to step onto this turbulent stage and restore order: Capt. Bill McDonald and District Judge Billy McGill, both of whom had been appointed to their respective posts by Gov. James Stephen Hogg in the same year—1891. The three men had become acquainted in the East Texas county of Wood. In the 1870s when McDonald was operating a grocery store in Mineola, Hogg was a justice of the peace in nearby Quitman, the county seat. By the time Hogg got himself elected county attorney, he and McDonald had become close friends. But in short order, their friendship was put to an acid test when Hogg, always a conscientious and impartial prosecutor, insisted on prosecuting McDonald on a misdemeanor charge of carrying a concealed weapon. McDonald, young and arrogant, wasn't inclined to accept his just deserts with grace. That incident, especially for McDonald, strained the relationship considerably.

But the two men later reconciled their differences and formed a lifelong friendship that ultimately led to Hogg's 1891 appointment of McDonald as a Texas Ranger captain. Meanwhile, before Hogg became governor, he was elected as district attorney of Wood County. While serving as such, he obtained a grand jury indictment against Billy McGill. The charge was murder. Hogg prosecuted McGill, but McGill was found not guilty. Even though Hogg had prosecuted McGill for the ultimate felony, he earned McGill's respect—an unlikely beginning for a lifelong friendship. In 1891, he appointed McGill as the first district judge of the 50th Judicial District. The jurisdiction was comprised of Motley and twelve other frontier West Texas counties, a monster district stretching across more than two hundred miles from Baylor County in the east all the way to the New Mexico line in the west.[33] But McGill's appointment didn't stick.

Hogg, a progressive populist governor, was definitely sympathetic to the settlers. During his administration, he opposed the monopolistic consumer-gouging practices of large corporations and railroads, and he championed passage of the Alien Land Law, which prohibited further land grants to foreign corporations in an effort to keep Texas lands in the hands of citizen settlers. Unsurprisingly, his policies earned the enmity of land barons, railroads, and large corporations.

Billy McGill was also a populist, and therefore, when Hogg appointed him as district judge, friends of the cattle barons in the Texas Senate blackballed McGill and blocked his confirmation. Hogg was thus forced to appoint an unknown, F. M. Perrill, to fill the office until the November 1892 election. But the irrepressible Billy

Judge W. R. "Billy" McGill was appointed in 1891 by Texas Gov. James Hogg as the first district judge of a newly formed 50th Judicial District of Texas, which consisted of thirteen West Texas counties including Motley County. *(Courtesy of Southwest Collection/Special Collections Library, Texas Tech University, Lubbock, Texas)*

McGill wasn't about to give up without a fight. He promptly tossed his hat into the ring and, in a bitterly fought campaign, defeated the cattle barons' candidate, J. T. Montgomery, by a razor-thin margin.[34]

After taking office, McGill promptly aggravated the insult to the cattle barons. He issued, at the behest of County Judge Campbell and the settlers, the previously noted injunction against the Matador Land and Cattle Company, which forbade the Matadors to run any more of the settlers' cattle off their properties or to chase them outside the Matador pasture boundary fence.[35]

In the midst of the Motley County War, District Judge McGill was scheduled to convene the Motley County District Court on August 15, 1893. Apparently, County Judge Campbell forewarned McGill about the volatile situation in Motley County, because McGill contacted Captain McDonald in advance of his arrival and requested his assistance in restoring and maintaining order. In compliance, McDonald left Quanah in early August 1893 and headed for Matador, taking with him Corporal (later Sergeant) W. J. L. Sullivan and several privates. (Conspicuously left behind in Quanah was the recently chastised Bob McClure.) McDonald, together with the intimidating six-foot, six-inch-tall, full-bearded Sullivan[36] and his men, set up headquarters in the Motley County jail and, in effect, placed the entire county under martial law. They restored order quickly, yet the fires of bitter resentment between the factions smoldered barely beneath the surface of the rolling prairie of Motley County.

Then, another weird thing happened. The renegade sheriff, Joe Beckham, showed up in Quanah and voluntarily surrendered himself to Bob McClure, begging for protection from Matthews and Cook.[37] Beckham told McClure that they had threatened to kill him on sight. And so, the next day, August 15, 1893, McClure set off for Matador with his prisoner, intending to jail him there on the Motley County embezzlement warrants. To get there, however, he had to cross Matthews's territory. McClure and Beckham rode the Fort Worth & Denver City passenger train from Quanah to Childress, detrained there, and then secured a horse and buggy to get from Childress to Matador. McClure, very much aware of Matthews's personal vendetta against Beckham, was understandably apprehensive about the prospect of getting himself and his prisoner through Childress with life and limb intact. Before the train arrived in Childress, he enlisted the aid of a fellow train passenger, Quanah livery stable owner R. A. Quisenberry (who was armed), and he also returned Beckham's rifle to him.

Sure enough, Matthews somehow got wind of the passage and confronted McClure, demanding that he surrender Beckham to him (apparently so Beckham could face the Childress County indictment against him for his alleged assault on Cook). McClure refused. A bloody confrontation was averted only by the intervention of Sheriff J. V. Cunningham of Abilene, Texas, who it seems had come to Childress on other business and happened to be with Matthews at the time. On discovering the facts underlying the encounter, Cunningham backed McClure. McClure then loaded Beckham into a buggy and departed for Matador, leaving Sheriff Matthews once more thwarted and enraged.[38]

Company B, Frontier Battalion of the Texas Rangers was commanded by Capt. W. J. "Bill" McDonald. This picture was made in 1893 in Amarillo. Front row (*left to right*) Billy McCauley, Bob McClure, Wes Carter and [first name unknown] Owens. Back row (*left to right*) Jack Harwell, Sgt. W. J. L. Sullivan, Bob Pease, Arthur Jones, Ed Connell, and Lee Queen. *(Courtesy Panhandle-Plains Historical Museum, Canyon, Texas)*

Back in Matador that same day, the awe-inspiring District Judge Billy McGill arrived to convene that term of the Motley County District Court. When McGill arrived, county attorney W. M. Smith, a Matador Ranch supporter, warned McGill that if he did not recognize the new, pro-ranch sheriff, J. L. Moore, when court convened, the Matadors "will have 100 armed men in town in less than two hours." McGill responded that if such occurred then "the jail will be fuller than the town in the next two hours." Nobody showed up to challenge McGill, and he went on about his judicial business.[39] Pioneer lawyer Charles Coombes recalled what happened next this way:

> Those were wild days. . . . Beckham and his deputies and Moore and his deputies took time about arresting and jailing one another for unlawfully carrying arms. It looked like a gen-

eral feud was brewing. When Judge McGill appeared to hold the next term of district court, both sets of sheriffs and deputies were on hand, claiming the right to wait on the court. The courtroom was jammed with armed officers. If Judge McGill had recognized either side officially, trouble was certain, and doubtless a wholesale killing would have followed. The Judge calmly took his seat, laid a .45 caliber six-shooter on the bench in front of him and announced: "By God, gentlemen, I have come here to hold court and I'll be damned if I ain't going to do it." He turned to Billy Moses, brother of celebrated lawyer, Dayton Moses, and said, "Mr. Moses, I appoint you Sheriff of Motley County. Open court!"

Billy opened court and Judge McGill, to relieve the tension, had his pet dog perform a trick he had taught him. He then announced, "All you other damn fellows stack arms and vacate the courtroom; it is time to transact business." The order was obeyed and the business of the court proceeded in regular order.[40]

Of course, Judge McGill had no more authority to remove an elected official on his own motion or to appoint another than did the commissioners court. But he made it stick.

While he was about the business of cleaning house, McGill decided to put the quietus on another source of annoyance. Lee Smith, the *Matador Maverick* newspaper editor, a pro-ranch and anti-Beckham man, incurred McGill's wrath by writing a scathing editorial that week wherein he portrayed Judge McGill as a "monarch to whom subjects must bend their knees" and then proceeded to attack the character of both McGill and Beckham. McGill ordered Deputy Ed E. Denny to bring forth and place before him the body of editor Smith. Deputy Denny soon reappeared with the protesting editor in tow. McGill waved the newspaper in his face and demanded to know whether he had written the offending words. The editor admitted that he had.

"Well, then, I am going to have you locked up in jail for contempt of court," McGill bellowed.

Smith sputtered something about the "U.S. Constitution" and "freedom of the press" and tried to explain that he was not criticizing the court but, as was within his rights, only criticizing the judge. But McGill was having none of it: "I *am* the court," he roared. With that, Deputy Denny hauled him off to jail. Next day McGill had the deputy haul Denny back before the court, and, after administering a very long, loud—and uninterrupted—tongue-lashing, McGill ordered the editor released.[41]

Having thus hacked away all the troubling underbrush, Judge McGill was ready to get down to the business of administering justice. First off, he convened a grand jury, which, on August 18, 1893, returned three indictments against Joe Beckham for embezzling Motley County's tax funds. McGill then, on his own motion, wisely changed the venue of these cases, transferring them out of Motley County to Seymour, the county seat of Baylor County, some one hundred miles to the southeast.[42]

Meanwhile, as soon as Judge McGill had opened that term of the district court, McDonald himself departed, leaving Sullivan and his men to keep the peace while court was in session. On his way back to Quanah, McDonald again encountered Sheriff Matthews in Childress. Matthews was still seething. First, Matthews demanded that McDonald fire McClure for arming his prisoner, Joe Beckham, and for refusing to release him to Matthews's custody. McDonald refused. Then Matthews demanded that McDonald employ a Childress County deputy, Percy Roberts, as a Texas Ranger, leaving him in Childress under Matthews's control. McDonald again refused.[43] The encounter further embittered both men and set the stage for their next encounter . . . their last encounter.

About three months later, in late November or early December 1893, the assault-with-intent-to-murder (George W. Cook) case pending against Beckham in Childress came up for trial. When Beckham failed to appear, the court issued another arrest warrant—

this one for his failure to appear—and placed it in the eager hands of Sheriff Matthews.[44] Beckham, meanwhile, had been released from the Matador jail after having posted an appearance bond in the embezzlement cases and had once again disappeared, presumably to hide out in the Oklahoma Territory. (Beckham's mother-in-law, Nanny Wray, lived near Taloga in the Oklahoma Territory, and he had a sister living in Altus.) Result: Matthews was once again frustrated in his grudge pursuit of Beckham.

During this time, McDonald kept hearing a disturbing rumor, to wit, that Matthews was telling various folks that as soon as he had a little leisure time, he intended to mosey down to Quanah and shoot Bill McDonald between the eyes. If McDonald had been "getting a little sore" before, it may only be imagined what kind of volcano was now a-bubblin' in McDonald's psyche. Such was the state of affairs when, on December 9, 1893, Matthews and two of his Childress buddies, Cal Dykes and D. V. Smith, got off the FW&DC passenger train at the Quanah depot about nine-thirty that morning.

SHOWDOWN ON MAIN STREET

The real reason for Matthews's excursion to Quanah that fateful day has long been a subject of debate. According to Matthews, he came to town to solicit Hardeman County Sheriff Dick Coffer's help in locating and arresting Beckham. Matthews did have a warrant for Beckham's arrest, and he did visit with Coffer when he arrived in Quanah. Still, it is difficult to imagine what real assistance a Quanah sheriff could have been to Matthews in capturing a renegade who'd fled to the Oklahoma Territory. Nobody had suggested that Beckham was hiding out in Hardeman County, Texas.

Meanwhile, more folks kept telling McDonald that Matthews was bragging at local saloons that he had come to town to shoot him "square 'tween the eyes." One salient fact tended to lend considerable credence to this street talk: Matthews, accompanied by two of his confederates, had chosen to invade McDonald's home turf on a day when all of McDonald's men happened to be on duty elsewhere. In a later report to Adjutant General Mabry, McDonald's ranger sergeant, J. W. Britton, related that he had been informed by "reliable parties" that Matthews and his buddies had spent the previous night on a drinking binge in Childress and, thus fortified, decided that this was just the right day to settle their score with Captain McDonald and that all three were drunk (and still drinking) when they arrived in Quanah that morning.[45] During the day Coffer and Matthews did patronize several saloons in Quanah. However, the tension-tightening day was winding down without incident, and it was about time for Matthews and his friends to catch the six o'clock westbound back to Childress.

But it was a train that Matthews would never board. Later on that chilly gray December afternoon, Matthews's path would cross McDonald's for the last time.

Matthews and his cohorts and Sheriff Coffer tipped a last one for the road and started walking down Main Street toward the depot. By chance, McDonald was just leaving the depot, having sent a telegram to his men in Amarillo. They met in the middle of Main Street between the depot and the Quanah Opera House a few minutes before six o'clock.

All accounts of the ensuing encounter are remarkably consistent— up to a point. Eyewitness statements given by the principals— McDonald[46] and Matthews[47] as well as bystanders Sheriff Dick Coffer[48] and "Uncle Dick" Crutcher[49]—all agreed that the parties came face-to-face on Main Street about two or three feet apart. McDonald confronted Matthews about the "hard things" he had heard Matthews was saying about him. All four remembered the conversation the same, almost word for word.

McDonald said, "I understand you have been making some pretty hard talk against me."

Matthews replied, "Yes, Bill, I have."

McDonald said, "I understand you said I was a damned cock-sucking son-of-a-bitch, and you said you were going to shoot me between the eyes."

Matthews, pointing his left index finger at McDonald, replied, "I didn't say that, Bill, but I'll tell you what I did say . . . Don't put your hand on your gun, Mack!"

Then the shooting began! Who drew first? That's where the stories diverge. Matthews in a *Dallas Morning News* interview a few days later said McDonald drew his pistol first and fired at him, leaving him with no alternative but to return the fire. Crutcher stated: "Then, both pulled their pistols and began shooting." Coffer recalled: "McDonald fired the first shot." McDonald, in a telegram forwarded to his boss, Adjutant General Mabry, the day after the shooting said, "We both got our guns about the same time." However, a month later and after mulling over the event, McDonald wrote Mabry this: "Matthews went after his gun. I, of course, *then* had to go after mine and then we went to shooting." Years later when McDonald retold the tale to his biographer, Albert Bigelow Paine, he embellished the account a bit more. He said that when Matthews pointed his left index finger at his face, he noticed that Matthews's right hand "slipped in the direction of his hip pocket." Only then, said McDonald, did he reach for his pistol. Matthews, he went on, stepped behind Coffer and fired the first shot (which, he says, missed) over Coffer's right shoulder. Then McDonald fired his first shot. (Coffer, meanwhile, wisely dropped to the ground where things were considerably quieter.) McDonald's biographical account then shades off into shameless self-aggrandizement.[50]

As for the shooting, a couple of things are beyond dispute. McDonald's first two shots were dead on—they both hit Matthews in his left chest within a space that could have been covered by a silver dollar. Trouble was, neither penetrated Matthews. He was carrying a thick plug of Star Navy chewing tobacco and a notebook in his left vest pocket, and both of McDonald's .44 slugs embedded in this virtual shield. (The pinpoint accuracy of McDonald's first two shots lends

Looking south on Main Street in Quanah, Texas, circa 1896. This is the scene of the December 9, 1893, shootout between Ranger Capt. Bill McDonald and Childress County Sheriff John Pearce Matthews. (*Courtesy of Hardeman County Historical Association Museum, Quanah, Texas*)

circumstantial credence to the theory that it was McDonald who fired the first shot—or shots—in this showdown.) Second, partisans on both sides joined in the gunfight, and both McDonald and Matthews were hit at least once (Matthews probably twice) by partisan bullets.

When the fierce firefight finally ended, both men had been shot twice. Both slumped to the ground seriously wounded, but neither was dead.

One slug hit McDonald in his right shoulder, the ball ranging upward before lodging in the left side of his neck, while the other slug hit him in his left shoulder, shattering his collarbone and puncturing a lung before exiting on his right side. Taking all the accounts into consideration, it seems most likely that it was Matthews's shot that hit McDonald in the left shoulder and that it was one of the Childress partisans who shot McDonald in the right shoulder.

Matthews took two slugs. One struck his right shoulder, passed through his esophagus, and lodged just behind his left collarbone;

another struck him in the small of his back just below his right kidney and lodged against his backbone, temporarily paralyzing him. The wounds appeared to have been made by different caliber weapons—the first by a .44 or .45 caliber and the second by a smaller caliber firearm. It seems obvious that the second wound was inflicted by a Quanah partisan.[51] McDonald claims his third shot caused Matthews's shoulder wound, and it is possible.[52] But, since it entered in the back part of Matthews's right shoulder, it seems at least as likely that it was fired by a Quanah partisan, albeit a different one.[53]

The identity of the McDonald partisan—or partisans—who shot Matthews was never revealed. Quanah native George Webb was sixteen years old when the shootout occurred. He was about a block from the site when he heard the gunshots, and by the time he reached the scene McDonald was already on his knees. Four years later, in 1897, Webb became a deputy sheriff at Quanah and served in that capacity for about four years. Webb was eighty-three years old and living in Canyon, Texas, when he was interviewed in 1960. "It came out later," Webb said, "that the shot that killed Matthews hit him in the back. It was fired by a Quanah partisan standing over by the railroad tracks." Webb, however, declined to speculate on the identity of the shooter.[54]

The shootout left both McDonald and Matthews in critical condition. The pair were taken to local drugstores where doctors attended them. Matthews was later taken back to his home in Childress. Both men, though gravely wounded, were expected to recover. The day after the shooting the indomitable Bill McDonald, even though his life was teetering on the brink, managed to fire off this telegram to his commander, Adj. Gen. W. H. Mabry:

> Matthews sheriff of Childress County came here yesterday with three others purposely to kill me as I was reliably informed. Called me hard names and threatened to shoot me. We both got our guns about the same time. I was shot through both shoulders. One ball lodging near my backbone which was cut out. I shot Matthews three times. While am badly

Form No. 290.

THE WESTERN UNION TELEGRAPH COMPANY.

This Company TRANSMITS and DELIVERS messages only on conditions limiting its liability, which have been assented to by the sender of the following message.
Errors can be guarded against only by repeating a message back to the sending station for comparison, and the Company will not hold itself liable for errors or delays in transmission or delivery of Unrepeated Messages, beyond the amount of tolls paid thereon, nor in any case where the claim is not presented in writing within ninety days after the message is filed with the Company for transmission.
This is an UNREPEATED MESSAGE, and is delivered by request of the sender, under the conditions named above.

THOS. T. ECKERT, General Manager. NORVIN GREEN, President.

NUMBER 170 | SENT BY Rot 9 | REC'D BY | 91 Collect | CHECK

RECEIVED at 10:30 a 12/10 189 3

Dated March X 10

To Genl W H. Mabry Austin

Matthews Sheriff of Childress County
Came here yesterday with three
others purposely to kill me
as I was reliably informed
called me hard names X
threatened to shoot me we

289-1

Both got our guns about
the same time I was
shot through both shoulders one
ball lodging near my backbone
which was cut out I
shot Matthews three times while

289-2

I am badly wounded think I
will pull through all right
he said everything he could
that was detrimental to the
ranger force & that he
ca-uld down etc.

W J McDonald

289-3

On December 10, 1893, the day after he was critically wounded in a gunfight with Childress Sheriff John Pearce Matthews, Texas Ranger Capt. Bill McDonald managed to fire off this telegram to his superior, Texas Adj. Gen. W. H. Mabry.

(Courtesy of Texas State Library and Archives Commission, Austin, Texas)

wounded think I will pull through all right. He said everything he could that was detrimental to the ranger force and
that he would down them.

W. J. McDonald[55]

The next day a *Dallas Morning News* reporter, in a bedside interview with Sheriff Matthews, reported Matthews's version:

I went to Quanah on business. I had no idea of trouble when
I went. I met Captain McDonald several times during the day,
but had no business with him. About train time I, in company
with Sheriff Coffer, started for the depot. When near the platform Captain McDonald came from the depot and met us. He
remarked that I had said certain things about him. I replied,
no, I had not said that but I would tell him what I did say, and
before I could speak, he fired upon me. Nothing was left for
me to do but protect myself. There were several shots fired
from behind me, two of which entered my flesh, and one hit
my pistol scabbard. McDonald's first shot missed my neck by
a hair's breadth; the other two that he fired went into a plug
of tobacco which saved my life. If the men arrested who were
from Childress [D. V. Smith and Cal Dykes] were armed I did
not know it, nor do I believe it.[56]

Although it was believed initially that Matthews would recover, he died of blood poisoning on December 30, 1893. McDonald
eventually recovered and lived another twenty-five years.

The *Quanah Chief* reported that Matthews's funeral was "the
largest ever witnessed in Childress County and that proved conclu-
sively that the deceased had many friends." The *Fort Worth Daily
Gazette* concluded on this somber note: "It all began as a studied insult
to the governor at Houston and ended in murder at Quanah."[57]

Sheriff Matthews's pals, D. V. Smith and Cal Dykes, were
arrested immediately after the fray but were subsequently released
on bond and were never prosecuted. Feeling was running high in

Childress against McDonald in particular and against the Quanah community in general. The powder-keg factor was apparently the reason Quanah prosecutors decided not to pursue Dykes and Smith. McDonald informed Adjutant General Mabry that "the cases of two of them were dismissed on account of not wanting to stir the thing any further."[58]

McDonald, however, was indicted for the murder of Matthews. He went to trial in Quanah on May 15, 1894. Most of the official Hardeman County records relating to this event have been either lost or destroyed, but Childress attorney A. J. Fires was present at the trial and gave an account of what happened. Fires stated that McDonald entered alternative defense pleas: first he alleged that he shot and killed Matthews but did so in self-defense. Alternatively, he pled that Matthews was shot and killed by somebody else. Whichever version the jury believed, it found McDonald not guilty.[59]

In a tantalizing head-scratcher, the Hardeman County grand jury *also indicted Sheriff Dick Coffer* for the murder of Matthews. Coffer was also tried in May 1894. However, after the prosecution had presented its case, the district judge instructed the jury to find Coffer not guilty.[60]

An examination of the official file in the case of *The State of Texas v. R. P. Coffer* for murdering Matthews reveals another interesting tidbit. A few days after the shooting (but *before* Matthews died), Coffer had given a sworn affidavit tending to confirm Matthews's claim that he had come to Quanah that day simply to solicit Coffer's help in arresting Beckham. In it he said nothing about Matthews making any threats against McDonald. However, in a later sworn document executed *after* Coffer was indicted (and *after* Matthews died), he told quite a different tale, apparently in an attempt to prove that he had no motive to shoot Matthews and to prove that the blood feud was solely between Matthews and McDonald. According to the later document, Coffer swore that he could produce witnesses (whom he named) to prove that Matthews had made "violent threats against the life of W. J. McDonald" and that Matthews "was a man likely to carry such threats into execution." Matthews, Coffer continued, had said that "he would do it [kill McDonald] before Christmas [1893]." He went on to swear that on a recent occasion when McDonald had gone to Childress, Matthews had made threatening gestures toward McDonald and had stalked McDonald from the railroad depot to his hotel and then back to the depot.[61]

Another interesting sidebar is found in McDonald's subsequent correspondence to his boss, Adjutant General Mabry. Apparently Mabry (or his superiors) questioned whether the State of Texas should pay McDonald's medical expenses. The decision hinged on whether McDonald's duel with Matthews was actually an act in the line of McDonald's official duty as a Texas Ranger or simply the result of a personal vendetta. McDonald used up a lot of ink arguing that it was a part of his official duty. "Had I not fought him after he continued to abuse me and hunt me up, I would have been branded as a coward and my usefulness as a ranger captain might not have amounted to anything," McDonald explained.[62]

AFTER MATTHEWS: THE MCDONALD LEGEND GROWS

Undoubtedly, the Joe Beckham matter, the centerpiece of the Motley County War, ultimately precipitated the 1893 shootout between McDonald and Matthews. But, as we shall soon discover, the former Motley County sheriff-turned-outlaw wasn't through precipitating bloodshed.

Meanwhile, McDonald's legend grew larger by the year. Over the next fourteen years he and the rangers under his command took part in a number of celebrated criminal episodes from the Panhandle to the Rio Grande. For instance, during those two pre-automobile years from September 1, 1902, to August 31, 1904, McDonald's Company B endlessly crisscrossed the huge state of Texas, logging an incredible 74,537 miles, all in the line of duty. His official report for that period shows that McDonald and the eleven rangers under his command made some 205 scouts, conducted numerous investigations, and made 344 arrests, including 31 for murder.[63] Meanwhile, his reputation as a troubleshooter continued to grow—the lawman who could quell riots, stop lynchings, solve frontier crimes, break up bloody feuds and vigilante groups, intimidate strikers as well as arrest, and bring back alive, desperate hard cases. Texas governors learned to rely on Bill McDonald whenever there was a breakdown of law and order anywhere in the state. On November 6, 1906, District Judge Stanley Welch was assassinated in Rio Grande City. Gov. S. W. T. Lanham ordered McDonald to investigate. McDonald and four of his men set out in a buggy for Rio Grande City, but before they arrived they were caught in a nighttime ambush on the banks of the Rio Grande. Although outnumbered, the rangers repelled the attack—killing four, wounding one, and capturing two. None of the rangers were killed, wounded, or captured. That proved to be McDonald's final ranger exploit.[64]

However, as we shall discover in the next chapter, McDonald played an important, though less heroic, role in a sensational 1896 case in Wichita Falls—one that involved a bank robbery, a murder, and a double lynching—and in the 1896 Fitzsimmons-Maher heavyweight fight in El Paso. Amazingly, in all these legal encounters only one ranger under McDonald lost his life—T. L. Fuller, a young lieutenant shot in a barbershop in Orange, Texas, by the brother of a man Fuller had killed in the line of duty.

Even after his retirement from the ranger force in 1907, McDonald continued an active and colorful career. That same year, Texas Gov. Thomas M. Campbell appointed him state revenue agent. McDonald, with typical vigor, tackled the thorny problem of obtaining full tax valuation of assets statewide. Despite howls of criticism from those adversely affected, he succeeded within two years in increasing the state tax valuation base by almost a billion dollars—one whopping sum in 1909 Texas.[65]

McDonald's fame reached the White House. While still with the rangers, he accompanied Pres. Theodore Roosevelt on an Oklahoma wolf-hunting expedition in the spring of 1905. In 1912, he became a bodyguard for presidential candidate Woodrow Wilson. Brash as ever, McDonald, sporting twin six-shooters, not only protected the candidate but greatly impressed Wilson's Yankee supporters. And he never lost his salty talent for coining a press-captivating quip. Once, in McDonald's presence, one of Wilson's staff told his credulous audience that Captain Bill could draw a six-gun and, firing from the hip, hit a mosquito in the eye from five hundred yards. Some wide-eyed soul (who doubtless hailed from somewhere way north of the Mason-Dixon line) turned to Bill and gasped, "Can you really?" To which Bill, without batting an eye, modestly inquired: "Which eye?" After Wilson was elected, he appointed Bill McDonald as U.S. Marshal of the Northern District of Texas.[66]

Along with John A. Brooks, John R. Hughes, and John H. Rogers, Bill McDonald was acclaimed as one of the "Four Great Captains" of the Texas Rangers. Although McDonald relished publicity and was a master of self-aggrandizement and self-promotion, he nevertheless was absolutely fearless, and even against the odds, he usually got the job done. In the end, whatever his shortcomings, he was a most effective champion of law and order in a violent and lawless land, and he really did earn that oft-repeated persona descripti: "the man who would charge Hell with a bucket of water."

When the ranger captain died of influenza in 1918, he was buried in the Quanah cemetery, and the epitaph they carved on his impressive tombstone was the motto he lived by. It reads: "No Man in the Wrong Can Stand Up Against a Fellow That's in the Right and Keep[s] on A Comin."

Meanwhile, just thirty miles to the west in the Childress cemetery stands another tombstone—this one marking the grave of Sheriff John Pearce Matthews. And carved on that tombstone is a cryptic epitaph, not nearly as lofty as McDonald's, but considerably more . . . well, ominous? It reads, simply: "We Shall Meet Again."[67]

TWO MORE SHERIFFS DIE BY THE GUN

Last we heard of young, handsome Joe Beckham, he was in big trouble with the law, facing three embezzlement indictments charging him with running away with a saddlebag full of Motley County's tax funds. (Or, more accurately, gambling away a saddlebag full of the

Childress County Sheriff John Pearce Matthews's tombstone is in the Childress County, Texas, cemetery. He was killed in an 1893 shootout with Capt. Bill McDonald. His epithet reads: "We Shall Meet Again." *(Author's Collection)*

Capt. Bill McDonald's tombstone in the Quanah, Texas, cemetery. The epithet, McDonald's motto, reads: "No Man in the Wrong Can Stand Up Against a Fellow That's in the Right and Keep on A Comin'." Capt. Bill McDonald, 1852–1918. *(Author's Collection)*

county's tax funds.) But, bad as all that was, Beckham still had more serious and immediate problems. One was the Childress sheriff, John Pearce Matthews, who had repeatedly threatened to kill him. But, of course, Ranger Capt. Bill McDonald and friends had solved that problem for Beckham in a cloud of gunsmoke on the Main Street of Quanah. That still left the George Cook problem. Not only had Cook threatened to kill Beckham, but he had almost done it when he ambushed Beckham at the Childress depot in June 1893—Beckham having escaped only due to Cook's poor marksmanship. Now Cook had succeeded Beckham as the Motley County sheriff and tax collector. However, just because Cook had pinned a lawman's badge on his vest didn't mean he had given up on nailing Joe Beckham. No, there remained bad blood aplenty between the two men.

Beckham was out of jail on bond when his embezzlement case was set for trial on May 28, 1895, in Seymour—District Judge Billy McGill having changed venues from Motley County to Baylor County. Presumably Beckham had been hiding out in the Indian Territory or the Oklahoma Territory, or both, pending his trial. But now Beckham had a big decision to make. He knew that Cook would appear as a witness against him in the upcoming trial. Cook, as sheriff and tax collector, was the official custodian of the Motley County tax records—key evidence against Beckham on the embezzlement charges. Plus, Cook would no doubt testify as to Beckham's hasty departure for the Oklahoma Territory when the funds were discovered to be missing. This "guilty flight" evidence would be admissible, tending to prove Beckham's culpability. Cook would also be allowed to testify that he and the other Motley County commissioners had filed a civil lawsuit against Beckham to recover these funds, and that Beckham had never repaid the deficit or even made any efforts in that direction. Or denied his guilt. (It will be recalled that Cook was one of the Motley County commissioners when Beckham fled the county.)

As the crow flies it is about 100 miles from Matador, the county seat of Motley County, to Seymour. Today's highway mileage between the towns is about 120 miles. But, of course, in 1895 there were no highways—no need for any, either, since there were no automobiles.

George Cook, when he set out for Seymour with the tax records and several "attached" witnesses in tow, elected to take a more circuitous (but interesting) route, covering approximately 210 miles. He first traveled northeast for fifty miles or so by horseback, going from Matador to Paducah and then on to Childress. There he swapped his cow horse for an iron horse—the Fort Worth & Denver City passenger train. Cook boarded that train at the same depot where, less than two years earlier, he had greeted Beckham with a .30-30 Winchester. From Childress he rode the FW&DC southeast 110 miles or so through the prairie villages of Quanah, Vernon, and Electra (then called Waggoner), and then on to Wichita Falls where he detrained and caught the Wichita Valley Railway Co. train heading back west toward Seymour, some fifty miles distant. When he finally arrived in Seymour on May 27, 1895, Cook stepped off the train carrying the tax records and escorting the "attached" witnesses who were also to testify at Beckham's trial. A crowd had gathered at the depot. The atmosphere was "pre-trial festive." Somebody exclaimed: "There's Sheriff Cook!"

But not everyone in the crowd was in a cordial mood. Joe Beckham was there, and his mood was way south of cordial. This time it was Beckham who greeted Cook with the business end of a gun.

In response to the crowd's greeting Beckham replied, "Yes, and he's bringing hell to me." Then to Cook he said, "So you have come, you son-of-a-bitch!" With that Beckham drew his pistol and shot Sheriff Cook dead—two shots at point-blank range. Before the stunned crowd, he mounted, put the steel to his horse, and raced north. (Actually it wasn't *his* horse; Beckham had stolen it from Henry Jones.) George Caylor gave chase, emptying his pistol, but with no effect. In the hail of bullets, Beckham rode hell-for-leather back to the Territories. Beckham had the better horse (thanks to Henry Jones) and eventually left Caylor in his dust.[68]

Beckham thus succeeded in settling an old score against an arrogant and dangerous bully. He also succeeded in putting a dent in the state's embezzlement case against him by removing a prime prosecution witness, although the lack of Cook as a witness would not be a fatal blow to the prosecution. He might have greatly weakened the state's embezzlement case, but at a terrible cost. Now the state also had a murder case against him buttressed by a host of credible eyewitnesses to the killing. Of course Beckham might have had at least a slim chance of beating the murder rap by entering a plea of self-defense and then proving up Cook's prior death threats and his previous attempt to carry them out. In the frontier mind-set, nurtured by popular Western folk law and the Old South's code of honor, simply proving up the deceased's prior threats to kill was often enough to support a self-defense plea. On the other hand, since the renegade ex-sheriff Beckham had by now already acquired a widespread reputation as a thief and embezzler, he most likely would have had an uphill battle in gaining much jury sympathy.

Thus, when Joe Beckham left George Cook lying dead in the cinders of the Seymour train yard and headed north to the Oklahoma and Indian Territories, he crossed more than the Red River—he crossed a Rubicon beyond which there would be no turning back. His future was now irrevocably cast with the fate of the Oklahoma outlaws, a brotherhood in which a man's life expectancy was exceedingly short. True enough for Beckham, as it turned out. He didn't live to see one sun in the year 1896.

In the "safe harbor" of the Territories—particularly in the Indian Territory, where law enforcement was next to nonexistent—Beckham proceeded to hook up with some hard cases, such as the infamous stone-killer, George "Red Buck" Weightman (often spelled "Waightman"), who had previously ridden with Bill Doolin's gang, Elmer "Kid" Lewis, and others—a gang that often made lightning raids into North Texas before streaking back across the Red River to sanctuary. Beckham and his new cohorts promptly went on a rampage of violence and looting during the fall of 1895, first north of the Red River in Greer County (at that time Texas claimed Greer County for its own while the United States claimed it was a part of the Oklahoma Territory), and then farther north into the Oklahoma Territory.

In October, Red Buck, Kid Lewis, and Beckham were identified as the trio that robbed the Charles E. Noyes general store in Arapahoe, Oklahoma Territory. Noyes and his wife, Alice, were closing up the store one evening when Red Buck, Beckham, and Lewis burst into the store undisguised but with guns drawn. Red Buck shoved his gun in Noyes's face and demanded to know where he kept the money. Noyes explained that all his cash had been shipped to an El Reno bank that morning. Disgusted, Red Buck relieved him of a fine gold watch. Then the gang sacked up all the merchandise they could carry, but before leaving, Red Buck grabbed Mrs. Noyes and demanded the diamond ring she wore.

"Take your hands off me!" the feisty Alice Noyes shouted. "The only way you'll get that ring is by cutting it off my finger!"

Red Buck put his gun down on the counter and began struggling with the uncooperative woman. She grabbed Red Buck's gun off the counter, but he wrenched it from her grasp and jammed the pistol to her chest, and with his other hand he seized her by the throat. Red Buck hissed, "I'll kill you, Alice."

Still not intimidated, Alice Noyes snarled: "You wouldn't have the nerve to kill a woman."

Red Buck paused, glared at her for a moment, then whirled around and stalked out of the store. Mrs. Noyes would later say that in that moment when they eyed each other she got a close look at the outlaw Red Buck—an image that was imprinted indelibly in her mind: his unusually bright auburn hair and moustache, and even more vividly, his eyes. "They were mean and cold," she later recalled. "Coyote eyes."[69]

On December 4, 1895, the same trio robbed the Shultise Store in Taloga, Oklahoma Territory, on the South Canadian River about thirty miles north of Arapahoe. In the process they also robbed fifteen store customers and made off with about a hundred dollars plus some items of clothing. When they wheeled and galloped away, about a dozen irate citizens gave pursuit.[70] These brazen robberies drew the attention of Oklahoma Territory lawmen, who, aided by citizen posses, put heat on the outlaws. The trio quit those parts and headed south.

About the middle of December 1895 the three were sighted on West Cache Creek near the Wichita Mountains in Oklahoma

Territory, not far north of the Red River. About that time they came across a young and impetuous Waggoner Ranch cowboy at a dugout along the North Fork of the Red River east of Navajoe Mountain and somewhere just north of the present town of Headrick, Oklahoma. His name was Hillary U. "Hill" Loftis, and he would later become well known under his alias, Tom Ross. Hill Loftis, age twenty-three, made a fateful decision that day: he allowed the three outlaws to persuade him to join their gang.[71]

Next report of the group was on December 22 when one of them—almost certainly the vicious Red Buck—for no reason other than for the fun of it, killed a Waggoner Ranch line rider—a black man named Brown.[72] (In the 1890s the legendary Waggoner Ranch ran approximately 60,000 head of cattle on a vast spread it owned in North Texas, plus thousands more acres it had leased just north of the Red River in the Oklahoma Territory. The ranch is still in existence, covering approximately 520,000 acres of land.)[73]

The following day, December 23, Red Buck and company attempted an armed robbery of the Hightower Brothers store in Altus, Oklahoma. C. C. Hightower, correctly sensing serious peril, broke and ran for it. One of the gang wounded him in the arm in midflight, but he escaped with his life. The outlaws fled without reaping a cent.[74]

Then they crossed the Red River and invaded Texas, still determined to live and profit by the gun. On Christmas Day the four desperadoes attempted to rob the D. Waggoner & Son General Merchandise Store (the Waggoner Ranch company store) on the FW&DC railroad line at a point where the present-day town of Electra, Texas, is located. In the process they "beat one of the clerks nearly to death," presumably for refusing to reveal the location of the store's money stash. The outlaws again left empty-handed.[75]

On the next day, December 26, the rampaging foursome moved south to a wide spot in the road called Ronda. Nothing remains of Ronda today, but it was located about six miles southwest of the Waggoner Store and about eighteen miles southeast of Vernon. At that time a man named Alf Bailey operated a small general merchandise store there. He was also the local postmaster, so he ran the post office out of the same building. It was there, on that date, that Red Buck, Kid Lewis, Beckham, and Hill Loftis appeared, guns drawn, and robbed Alf Bailey—this time succeeding in getting about seven hundred dollars' worth of merchandise, plus about seventy-five dollars in money and postage stamps.[76]

Meanwhile, Taylor Holt, bookkeeper at Waggoner Store, had wired Texas Ranger Sgt. W. J. L. Sullivan at Vernon, informing him of the attempted robbery of Waggoner Store and calling for help. In response, Captain McDonald sent five of his rangers under the command of Sergeant Sullivan to pursue the gang. The other rangers included McDonald's nephew, W. J. "Billy" McCauley, as well as Jack Harwell, Lee Queen, and Bob McClure, all of whom joined Dick Sanders, the Wilbarger County sheriff, and C. M. Moses, the Wichita County sheriff. The posse also included Wichita County Constable Tom Pickett; Bud Hardin, a special ranger from Harrold, Texas; Johnny Williams, deputy sheriff of Wilbarger County; and Charley Landers, city marshal of Vernon, Texas.[77] Doubtless expecting pursuit, the robbers mounted and raced back north across the Red River into the Oklahoma Territory. Ranger Sullivan's posse was in hot pursuit and had no intention of letting the river boundary stop them. Just before they crossed the river they met Dick Farrell, another Waggoner Ranch line rider who lived in a dugout on Suttle Creek in the Oklahoma Territory about twenty miles north of Red River.[78] Farrell told Sergeant Sullivan that there was nobody at his dugout when he left. There was, he added, plenty to eat and lots of horse feed at the camp.

About an hour before sundown, a whistling blue norther hit. "It was so cold the coyotes' howls froze in mid-air."[79] Still they pressed on. At dusk on December 27, 1895, they came in sight of Dick Farrell's camp, a half rock and half dirt dugout carved into the head of a draw on Suttle Creek.[80] A light was burning in the dugout. Sullivan then realized that there were either outlaws or hunters inside. Since six of his men had fallen behind, he told the other five that they had better wait for the stragglers to catch up before advancing. They waited, but the stragglers didn't come. Meanwhile, the temperature kept dropping. Finally Sullivan told his men they would try it without the others. Years later Sullivan described what happened next this way:

> We started toward the dugout in a gallop, getting a little faster all the time, and when we got within 75 yards of the dugout, the four desperadoes—Joe Beckham, Hill [Loftis], Red Buck [Weightman], and the kid, Elmore [*sic*] Lewis—ran out and opened fire on us, killing three horses. I was making every effort to get my Winchester out of the scabbard, with all four of the outlaws shooting at us, but my horse was rearing and plunging so much to get away from the flare of the guns that every time I would reach down to pull my gun out, he would rear, and the horn of my saddle would knock me away from it; but, after three trials, and after getting a rib broken, I succeeded in getting my gun, when I fell off my horse and faced the four men. Three of them were in a trench leading into the dugout, and the fourth, Redbuck [*sic*], was standing in the door of the dugout. I opened fire on them . . . and my first shot struck Redbuck just over the heart, and he fell backward into the dugout. The ball had only struck his breast-plate, however, and he fainted, but recovered in a few minutes and again joined in the fight. . . . The firing was kept up until we had emptied our Winchesters and reloaded them. Suddenly I heard a gunshot behind me, and I turned and discovered that Johnnie[*sic*] Williams, the deputy from Wilbarger County, had come to my assistance. His horse had been killed in the fight, and Johnnie returned to me at once. . . . Out of all the officers, Johnnie was the stayer.
>
> We fired several more shots at the three men, but they went into the dugout and fired at us from a window. I suggested to Johnnie that we dismount the [outlaws] by killing their horses, which we did, and every time we fired, a horse

fell. . . . I suggested to Johnnie that we crawl across the draw and get into the corral, behind those dead horses, and kill the men as they came to the door.[81]

However, the outlaws foiled Sullivan's plan. Every time the lawmen slipped out of the draw and started crawling up the ridge toward the horse lot, the outlaws "sky-lighted" them and opened fire, driving them back into the draw. Result: a stalemate. Finally, about eleven o'clock that night the rangers "got so cold we couldn't pull a cartridge from our belts, and couldn't work the levers of our Winchesters," so they had to quit. The weather worsened; snow began falling. On foot and in the midst of a blinding snowstorm, they struggled back to Waggoner's camp some twenty-five miles to the south across the icy Red River.

Later, when they returned after the storm, they found the dugout deserted—except for Joe Beckham. He lay dead, killed by a gunshot wound to the head.[82] (To trace the route of the four outlaws' December 1895 rampage in North Texas, old Greer County, and the Oklahoma Territory, see accompanying map on page 56.)

Sergeant Sullivan wounded Red Buck during the fight, and it appears likely that it was Sullivan who killed Beckham, although Sullivan, in his account of the fight, doesn't speculate. In any event, strange as it seems in view of the circumstances, the U.S. District Court in El Reno, Oklahoma Territory, indicted Sullivan for killing Beckham. To nobody's surprise, however, Sullivan was not convicted.[83]

With the slaying of Beckham, three sheriffs had been killed in shootouts with other lawmen—ex-sheriff Beckham, Sheriff Cook, and Sheriff Matthews. All three sheriffs had been major sources of agitation in the Motley County War, and all three deaths were directly related thereto. Now, with the removal of these three troublemakers from the scene, and with the settlers gaining firm control of the courthouse in the 1896 elections, peace was finally restored to strife-torn Motley County.[84]

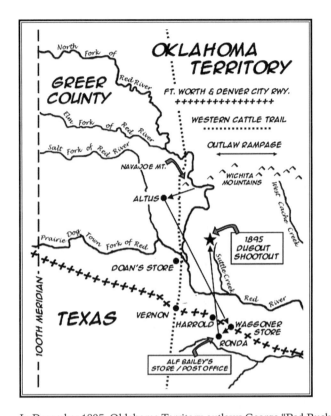

In December 1895, Oklahoma Territory outlaws George "Red Buck" Weightman, Elmer "Kid" Lewis, Joe Beckham, and Hill Loftis (alias Tom Ross) went
on a rampage, killing one man and looting stores along the way. This map
traces their path of mayhem, beginning near West Cache Creek in the Wichita
Mountains of the Oklahoma Territory, then to Altus, then turning south and
crossing the Red River into Texas, then to Waggoner Store (now Electra, Texas),
then to Ronda, where a posse led by Texas Ranger Sgt. W. J. L. Sullivan picked
up their trail and finally ran them to ground in a dugout on Suttle Creek back
in the Oklahoma Territory on December 27, 1895. The dugout was located near
present-day Frederick, Oklahoma. In the ensuing shootout, Joe Beckham was
killed and Red Buck was wounded, although he recovered and escaped. Lewis
and Loftis also escaped. Also depicted is Greer County, Oklahoma. At the time
both Texas and the United States claimed Greer County—the United States
claiming it was part of the Oklahoma Territory. The dispute was settled in 1896
when the U.S. Supreme Court denied Texas' claim and made it officially a part of
the Oklahoma Territory. Also shown is the Western Cattle Trail where between
the mid-1870s through the mid-1890s some three million to five million head of
Texas cattle were trailed to Dodge City, Kansas, crossing into Oklahoma Territory at the historic Doan's Crossing. *(Map by Hanaba Munn Welch, Author's Collection)*

Joe Beckham's brief life of crime ended with the Oklahoma Territory dugout battle, but his three cohorts remained at large: Hill Loftis, Elmer "Kid" Lewis, and George "Red Buck" Weightman. All three eventually met violent ends, either by gun or by rope, but not until each had shed more blood—the blood of law officers or innocent citizens or both. Meanwhile, all three had been identified as the bandits who had robbed Alf Bailey's store near Vernon, Texas, on December 26, 1895. Lawmen and prosecutors wasted little time in setting the wheels of the Texas judicial machinery in motion. A Wilbarger County, Texas, grand jury at Vernon returned armed robbery indictments against all three on February 12, 1896.[85] Swift as it was, the court wasn't swift enough to mete out its brand of justice for two of the three bandits. Frontier justice moved faster. The ink was hardly dry on the indictments before frontier justice assessed and imposed the ultimate sentence on Kid Lewis and Red Buck Weightman.

Of the four bandits, George "Red Buck" Weightman was without doubt the worst of the lot. Also without doubt, he was their leader. Long before the 1895 Christmastime crime spree in North Texas, Red Buck had been a member of Bill Doolin's infamous Oklahoma Territory train-robbing gang. But Red Buck proved to be so vile that even Bill Doolin couldn't stomach him.

Weightman was a powerful man, standing five feet, ten inches tall and weighing 180 pounds. He first came to the attention of Oklahoma Territory lawmen in 1890 when Deputy Marshal Heck Thomas arrested him for stealing horses and mules in the Cherokee Strip. He got a nine-year sentence and was shipped off to the pen. But he never got there. En route, he pulled a homemade saw from his boot, sawed through his shackles, and then leaped out of a window of the penitentiary-bound train. Guards fired at him, but missed.[86]

A couple of years later he joined a gang Bill Doolin was putting together. Doolin had ridden with the infamous Dalton gang until it was decimated in its disastrous attempt to rob two banks at once at Coffeyville, Kansas, in October 1892. Bob Dalton, brother Grat Dalton, Dick Broadwell, and Bill Powers were killed while brother Emmett Dalton was wounded, captured, and sentenced to prison. Gang members Bill Doolin, Bill Dalton, and Bitter Creek Newcomb were lucky enough to miss out on that party.[87]

Although Red Buck became a member of Doolin's gang, he was never popular with the other members, who considered him a "chain-harness horse thief." But that was the best thing that could have been said about Red Buck. In addition to being a sorry, low-life thief, he was a surly and vicious for-hire killer. His fee for bushwacking a man was fifty dollars up front, no questions asked, and he had already killed at least four men.[88] He was also suspected of being the hired gun who waylaid and killed D County Oklahoma Treasurer Fred Hoffman in January 1895 near Taloga. (D County was later renamed Dewey County.) Hoffman, in addition to his official duties for D County, was also employed as an undercover detective for the Santa Fe Railroad. He was apparently making so much progress in his investigation that some folks decided they were in dire need of Red Buck's services.[89] D County attorney George E. Black, writing his memoirs years later, commented that Red Buck was "the basest and most cruel outlaw to infest the area."[90] And that was certainly saying a lot. Finally, even Bill Doolin had had enough of Red Buck and expelled him from the gang. Some sources say the straw that broke the camel's back was Red Buck's wanton and unnecessary slaying of an old unarmed preacher named Godfrey, whose only transgression had been that he exhibited the temerity to protest the theft of his horse by the Doolin gang, a horse confiscated from the old man to replace a mount that had just been shot out from under one of the gang by a pursuing posse.[91]

The D. Waggoner & Son General Merchandise Store as it appeared in 1895. On Christmas Day of that year four Oklahoma Territory outlaws (Red Buck Weightman, Kid Lewis, Joe Beckham, and Hill Loftis, alias Tom Ross) made an unsuccessful attempt to rob the store. The store was the Waggoner Ranch company store and was located at the present-day site of Electra, Texas. *(Courtesy of Southwest Collection/Special Collections Library, Texas Tech University, Lubbock, Texas)*

Ronda, Texas, now a ghost town, was located approximately six and a half miles south of Harrold, Texas. All that is left now is the nearby weed-covered cemetery, pictured here. Founded in about 1881, the little frontier village prospered until 1885, when the westward-advancing Fort Worth and Denver City Railway bypassed the town to the north, laying its tracks instead through Electra, Harrold, and Vernon and then on to Amarillo and eventually to Denver, Colorado. Nevertheless, the town was still in existence on December 26, 1895, when four Oklahoma Territory outlaws—Red Buck Weightman, Kid Lewis, Joe Beckham, and Hill Loftis, alias Tom Ross, robbed Alf Bailey's general store and post office in Ronda. *(Author's Collection)*

When Red Buck, badly wounded and afoot in a December blizzard, managed to escape after the Oklahoma Territory dugout battle at Suttle Creek, he headed back northwest to Cheyenne country—Custer and D County in the Oklahoma Territory. There, within slightly more than two months, he engaged in three more "dugout battles" with lawmen. He survived the first two.

Three different dugouts, all located within a few miles of each other in the Custer and D County area, were to figure in the following sequence of violent events. The first dugout was a rock half-dugout located about five miles north of Canute in Custer County. It was occupied by Dolph Picklesimer, and we will call it the "Picklesimer" dugout. The second one we'll name the "Glover" dugout. It was located about five miles west of Arapahoe. W. W. Glover, an old bachelor, lived there. In early 1896, a Texas horse thief named George Miller was living there with him. The third dugout was a hideout used first by the Dalton gang and later by the Doolin gang as well as other outlaws. It was located along the rough breaks near the steep banks of the South Canadian River a few miles southwest of Taloga in D County. That hideout was a stone's throw from the site where, only a short year before, somebody—that somebody strongly believed to have been none other than Red Buck—had ambushed and murdered secret agent Hoffman, the Santa Fe Railroad investigator. The third dugout we will call the "Canadian River" hideout.[92]

In January 1896 Red Buck dragged himself into the Picklesimer dugout still suffering from the wound inflicted on him by Sullivan in the Suttle Creek dugout fight. George Miller just happened to be visiting at the Picklesimer dugout. After what must have been a most interesting preliminary exchange, Red Buck and Miller excused themselves and, after a brief conversation outside the dugout, departed together. Picklesimer must have been glad to see them go. Miller and Red Buck then holed up in the Canadian River hideout. But soon they needed supplies. Each fearing they would be recognized if they showed up in a town, they rode over to Glover's dugout on February 14 and persuaded Glover to go into Arapahoe for supplies. Glover agreed—but very reluctantly. He didn't want to

Wilbarger County, Texas, Deputy Sheriff (later sheriff) Johnny Williams was a member of Ranger Sgt. W. J. L. Sullivan's posse that ran four Oklahoma Territory outlaws to ground on December 27, 1895. In the ensuing shootout, Joe Beckham, ex-Motley County Sheriff-turned-outlaw, was killed. *(Courtesy of the Wilbarger County Historical Commission)*

The end of the line for Joe Beckham, ex-sheriff of Motley County, Texas— killed by lawmen in an Oklahoma Territory shootout on December 27, 1895. *(From the* Wichita Falls Times Record News*)*

cross the fearsome Red Buck but on the other hand, he had no desire to harbor that notorious outlaw or to get mixed up in his troubles with the law. So as soon as he got to Arapahoe, he went straight to the law. Some local (and, as we shall soon see, exceptionally inept) lawmen promptly rounded up a posse and accompanied Glover back to his dugout. The plan was for the lawmen to surround the dugout surreptitiously while Glover approached it openly and gave Red Buck and Miller the "all-clear" signal—a pistol shot in the air. Then Glover was to get out of the way and take cover.

The plan went badly awry. When Glover got near the front of the dugout, he fired the all-clear shot. Red Buck and Miller accordingly appeared in the doorway. That's when the posse jumped the gun and began firing before Glover could get out of harm's way. Worse yet, they all missed, which left the hapless Glover stranded in no-man's-land. The wily Red Buck immediately sensed a double-cross and fired one shot at Glover. He did not miss. Glover fell dead as Red Buck and Miller made a mad dash for their horses and escaped untouched in a hail of gunfire.

The outlaw pair retreated to the Canadian hideout, but D County deputy Joe Ventioner by this time suspected, or was tipped off, that the old gang hideout might be Red Buck's lair, and so, together with deputies Bill Quillen and William Holcomb, he attacked. But the outlaws were not surprised. They returned the fire and out-gunned the deputies. Once again Red Buck escaped.

The fugitives headed south for the Wichita Mountains with the officers in hot pursuit. The two separated and then doubled back and headed north, hoping to elude the posse. They reunited at Picklesim-er's dugout, but the officers were not fooled. Ventioner, Quillen, and Holcomb, now reinforced by G County constables T. L. Shahan and J. T. Duckworth, as well as Louis N. Williams of Washita County, surrounded Picklesimer's dugout during the night of March 3, 1896, and waited for daylight. The next morning George Miller and Pick-lesimer emerged and started for the horse lot. The officers called for them to surrender. Picklesimer took cover. Miller pulled a revolver but dropped it when a slug from the posse whistled past his head. He ran for the dugout, shouting the alarm. Red Buck appeared and loosed a volley at the officers. But Ventioner and Holcomb returned fire, and this time Red Buck finally got his. The officers' slugs found their mark, and Red Buck fell dead in the doorway of Picklesimer's dugout. Miller, however, recovered his pistol and began firing at Ventioner and Holcomb. Miller wounded Ventioner, the ball strik-ing the deputy in the lower abdomen and passing out just above his left hip, making a serious but not fatal wound. Holcomb returned the fire, and his bullet shattered Miller's right arm above the wrist. Another ripped into his left hand. Miller staggered back into the dugout, but he was totally disabled and finally yelled out to the offi-cers to come get him, saying he was "shot all to pieces."[93]

George "Red Buck" Weightman, Oklahoma Territory outlaw. He attended one too many dugout shootouts. *(From* West of Hell's Fringe: Crime, Criminals, and the Federal Peace Officer in Oklahoma Territory, 1889-1907, *by Glenn Shirley, University of Oklahoma Press, 1978)*

When the officers entered and captured Miller, they searched the dugout and there recovered the gold watch Red Buck had stolen from Charles Noyes in the October 1895 burglary of Noyes's store in Arapahoe.[94] On March 4, 1896, scarcely more than two months after the Christmastime shootout at Suttle Creek dugout in the Oklahoma Territory, Red Buck joined Joe Beckham in the Great Wherever to which such outlaws go for their final comeuppance.

In the end, only three positive things could be said about Red Buck Weightman: he was a total stranger to fear—the man simply had no "give up" in him; he was said to have been a tolerably good fiddle player who, on occasion, entertained those of the outlaw-sympathizer persuasion at country dances; and finally he was, at last, certifiably dead. That leaves us with the other two survivors of the Oklahoma Territory dugout battle to be accounted for: Hill Loftis (alias Tom Ross) and Elmer "Kid" Lewis.

WICHITA FALLS
JUSTICE, JUDGE LYNCH
PRESIDING

Oklahoma Territory Outlaws "Dangle
Twixt Heaven and Earth"

Everybody he talked to about his dream must have begun to wonder about Frank Dorsey's sanity. Frank Dorsey, of all people! He was a model citizen, a family man with a wife and three small children, a respected member of the community, a trusted employee (a cashier) of the Citizens National Bank in Wichita Falls, Texas. And, had you set about to find the most levelheaded man in town, Frank Dorsey would have been right up there among the finalists. Yet here he was going around telling folks that he wanted to quit his job at the bank because he had been plagued by a recurring nightmare that the bank would be robbed and that he would be killed during the holdup.[1] All this went on for some time during the first days of 1896: he told his wife; he told the bank president, J. A. Kemp; and he even told Texas Ranger Sgt. W. J. L. Sullivan. They all assured Dorsey that it was just a bad dream; that he had nothing to worry about.[2]

Truth be told, though, there was some legitimate concern about the threat of a bank robbery. For some time Wichitans had been hearing rumors that Oklahoma/Indian Territory outlaws were planning to rob a Wichita Falls bank. In an abundance of precaution, Kemp wired Texas Gov. Charles A. Culberson for ranger support, and, Cul-

Frank Dorsey, a cashier of the City National Bank in Wichita Falls, Texas, was killed by Oklahoma Territory bank robbers on February 25, 1896. *(From the* Wichita Falls Times Record News*)*

berson in turn ordered Ranger Capt. Bill McDonald to investigate the matter. McDonald dispatched Sergeant Sullivan and four of his men to Wichita Falls and told them to see what was afoot—and to safeguard the banks.[3] Sullivan and his men spent several uneventful days hanging around town and guarding the two banks. During this time Frank Dorsey related his premonition to Sullivan. Sullivan, of course, assured Dorsey that his fears were groundless. Besides, even if the bank were robbed it seemed quite a stretch to conclude that the murder of Frank Dorsey would be the inevitable, or even a likely, result. Finally McDonald concluded that all this talk about a bank robbery was just that—talk. And so Sullivan gathered up his troops and departed.

February 25, 1896, was the pivotal day. In the early morning hours Frank Dorsey had his last terror-filled presentiment. His wife once again attempted to calm him, but he was adamant and determined to resign from the bank. Later that morning, Dorsey tendered his resignation to bank president J. A. Kemp, but once again Kemp remonstrated with Dorsey and persuaded him to stay at his post. Then Kemp left the bank on other business.

It was the last time Kemp ever saw Frank Dorsey, age thirty-six, alive.[4]

CAPTAIN MCDONALD AND THE RANGERS VS. DAN STUART
AND JUDGE ROY BEAN

While Frank Dorsey was having his nightmares, Capt. Bill McDonald and his men were being dispatched to El Paso on an errand that turned out to be more of a Keystone Cop comedy than a heroic triumph in the annals of crime fighting. Dan Stuart of Dallas, a smooth, cool, and totally unflappable prizefight promoter, had signed Bob Fitzsimmons and Peter Maher for a world heavyweight championship boxing contest, and he proposed to hold it in El Paso.[5] However, religious leaders of the day denounced prizefighting as a transgression second only to the crucifixion of Jesus Christ. In the waves of righteous fervor that ensued, they proceeded to raise such a tub-thumping protest that intimidated legislators in Texas and surrounding states passed legislation prohibiting such egregious depravity. Yet as the announced time for the fight approached, Stuart never wavered. Amid nationwide publicity, Dan Stuart, nonchalance personified, calmly assured everyone that the fight would be held. The nation's newspapers couldn't get enough of this spicy unfolding drama. Unamused, Texas Governor Culberson pompously umbraged up and directed Adj. Gen. W. H. Mabry to bring on the Texas Rangers—all four companies—to occupy El Paso. Mabry himself arrived, took command, and solemnly assured one and all that under no circumstances would he allow such a flagrant display of pugilism to disgrace the great state of Texas during his watch. The territorial governors of New Mexico and Arizona followed suit. Then, amid fears that sly Dan Stuart might pull a fast one and stage the fight across the Rio Grande in Juarez, the governor of Chihuahua, Miguel Ahumada, was somehow persuaded to join the holy anti-fisticuffs crusade. He responded by sending a company or so of Mexican soldiers to Juarez. Everyone on both sides of the border believed they had Dan Stuart in a box. Mabry ordered McDonald to personally shadow Stuart day and night. And, of course, Bill McDonald being Bill McDonald, earnest and intense as ever, he was on him like a bloodhound, trailing him day and night. Yet Stuart—jovial and serene as ever—continued to reassure the nation's press that the fight would occur on Friday, February 21, 1896. No problem.

Texas Ranger Sgt. W. J. L. Sullivan led a posse that ran Oklahoma Territory outlaws to ground on December 27, 1895. Ex-Motley County Sheriff Joe Beckham was killed in that confrontation. Less than two months later Sullivan assured City National Bank cashier Frank Dorsey that his fears of being killed by bank robbers were unfounded. *(From* Twelve Years in the Saddle for Law and Order on the Frontiers of Texas *[originally copyrighted and published] by W. J. L. Sullivan, 1909)*

And so it did.

Turned out that Stuart had secretly enlisted the connivance of an effective, if not particularly scrupulous, ally—none other than old Judge Roy Bean, a saloonkeeper and justice of the peace at Langtry, Texas, who had already promoted himself for ages to come as "the Law West of the Pecos." Making up his own law as he went along, the judge was an irrepressible and unrepentant scoundrel. Sporting a long white beard, and with a malevolent glint of the eye, he looked for all the world like a degenerate Santa Claus. Langtry, like El Paso, is perched on the north bank—the Texas bank—of the Rio Grande, about 350 miles to the southeast of El Paso. The towns are linked to one another by the Southern Pacific Railway, and, in those days, unless you took it into your head to walk, ride your horse, or float down the Rio Grande, the only way you could get from El Paso to Langtry was via the Southern Pacific.

The day before the fight, Stuart gathered up the fighters, their supporters, and all the spectators and herded them aboard the east-bound Southern Pacific. He also hitched on a few boxcars filled with lumber and supplies as well as a small army of Mexican laborers and then loaded everything and everybody onto the train. Not to be left behind, all the Texas Rangers bought tickets and clambered aboard. Stuart disclosed his destination to no one. When the train finally got to Langtry, Stuart announced they had reached their destination. All the passengers disembarked and received hearty greetings from none other than the Honorable Judge Roy Bean himself, who graciously invited one and all to join in the spirit of this festive occasion and properly fortify themselves for the upcoming historic event at his saloon, the Jersey Lilly, which, conveniently, just happened to be the only watering hole in town. Meanwhile, the laborers piled off the train and *muy pronto* toted all the lumber and supplies down to the Rio Grande, where they hastily proceeded to tack together a make-shift boxing ring on a sandbar in the middle of the Rio Grande—in the state of Coahuila, Mexico.

The Texas Rangers, of course, had no authority to invade Mexico. Thus Adjutant General Mabry, Captain McDonald, and the other three Texas Ranger captains as well as their minions were reduced to fuming impotently from their cheap seats on the high bluffs on the north bank of the Rio Grande, watching from afar as Fitzsimmons punched out Maher in the first round. Meanwhile, the Mexican army, having been neatly outflanked by Stuart and Bean, was reduced to fuming impotently in distant Juarez.

Stuart returned to his hometown Dallas a conquering hero. And the amusing aspects of the governor calling out the entire Texas Ranger force in an unsuccessful effort to fight sin and crime did not

No fun and games allowed by this grim bunch! When boxing promoter Dan Stuart threatened to stage a heavyweight championship boxing match in El Paso in 1896, Texas Gov. Charles Culberson pulled out all the stops to prevent such blatant sinning from taking place within the state of Texas: he called out the above no-nonsense contingent of Texas Rangers to stop this threatened fistic carnival. Front row (*left to right*): Adj. Gen. W. H. Mabry, Texas Ranger Captains John Hughes, J. A. Brooks, Bill McDonald, and J. H. Rogers. (Courtesy Special Collections, University of Texas at Arlington Library, Arlington, Texas)

go unnoticed. *The Dallas Morning News* even poked some fun at the rangers: "It was amusing to see the flower of the frontier guard sitting on the crags above with their rifles resting lazily on their laps while that great and unpardonable crime, the big glove contest, was taking place a few hundred yards away."[6]

Predictably, those proud and puffed gladiators of the law, Adjutant General Mabry, Captain McDonald, and the Rangers of Texas, failed to see any humor in this farce. And, just as predictably, Mabry immediately fired off a long and detailed account of the heroics of the Texas Rangers to Governor Culberson, ending his report with an unqualified declaration of victory for the forces of law and order and righteous living. After all, Mabry triumphantly trumpeted, the

Texas Rangers had succeeded in ensuring that no unpardonable sin or fistic criminal offense had taken place on sacred Texas soil![7]

THE 1896 WICHITA FALLS BANK ROBBERY

The Fitzsimmons-Maher fight occurred on February 21, 1896. Afterward, McDonald put his men on a train headed back to the Panhandle. He followed a couple of days later. When Sergeant Sullivan got to Wichita Falls, however, he received a telegram from a federal marshal in the Oklahoma Territory ordering him to surrender himself to federal authorities in El Reno to be tried for the killing of former Motley County sheriff Joe Beckham in the December 1895 Suttle Creek dugout fight.[8] The telegram was no cause for alarm. Everyone expected, correctly as it turned out, the trial would be a mere formality, and the exoneration of Sullivan would be inevitable.

It was February 24, 1896, when Sullivan arrived in Wichita Falls and received the telegram. He and two of his men spent that night in Wichita Falls, and then boarded the Fort Worth & Denver City train about noon the next day and headed back southeast toward Fort Worth on the circuitous route to El Reno. A sizeable crowd of local folks was on hand to wave a hearty bon voyage to the rangers.

Legend has it that there were two men in that crowd who were especially delighted to wave good-bye to the rangers. One was the outlaw Elmer "Kid" Lewis, whose exploits we have been following. The other was Foster Crawford, Oklahoma/Indian Territory outlaw.[9] (Before statehood in 1907, Oklahoma was divided into two territories: Oklahoma Territory covering the western portion and Indian Territory covering the eastern portion. The north-south dividing line lay just north and slightly to the east of Wichita Falls. See the map on page 7. Outlaws in the 1890s roamed freely between the territories.) The pair apparently had been hanging around town for quite a spell waiting for the rangers to clear out. It also happened that Wichita County Sheriff C. M. Moses and his men were out of town that day. Ironically, they were over on Burk Burnett's lease in the Oklahoma Territory searching for Foster Crawford, whom they (correctly) suspected of stealing horses from Burnett.[10] Anyway, that left a jailer, Deputy Sheriff Frank Hardesty, and the Wichita Falls city marshal, Mage Davis, as the only lawmen in town. Which suited the outlaws just fine.

Elmer "Kid" Lewis, eighteen years old, was a native of Neosho, Missouri, the son of James Lewis, a mechanic who had served a term in the Missouri pen for highway robbery. The Kid stood five feet, seven inches tall, weighed in at about 145 pounds, had fair skin, and was clean shaven. He got off to an early start riding the owlhoot trail, first migrating to Montana where he quickly became a "person of interest" to lawmen there. Highway robbery, holding up poker games, getting into shooting scrapes, and other "strong-arm" misdeeds were credited to Kid Lewis by the Montana authorities.[11] Lewis therefore found it expedient to head south for the territories, where he found more than a few men of his ilk. For a brief time he worked as a cowhand for Burnett on his Oklahoma Territory lease, but turning an honest dollar was just not in the Kid's game book. It will be recalled that less than two months prior to this escapade, Kid Lewis, together with his cohorts Red Buck Weightman and Hill Loftis, had survived the Suttle Creek dugout gun battle with a ranger-led posse while his associate Joe Beckham had not been so fortunate.

Foster Crawford, thirty-five years of age, five feet, eight inches tall, and 145 pounds, was dark-complected and sported a mustache. Every bit as sorry as Kid Lewis, he nevertheless was a more complex character and, when sober, his IQ might even have hit the high double-digits. Born to a good family in McLennan County, Texas, near Waco, he appeared to be on the road to success and respectability until booze and bad companions derailed his career. After a whiskey-fueled knife fight he lit out for the territories. It was said he left a beautiful sweetheart behind and that her subsequent death drove Crawford further down the road to ruin. It was also said that during drinking bouts he sometimes began talking incoherently in Spanish and Comanche as well as English.[12]

Crawford worked as a cowhand for Burnett for a number of years before Burnett fired him. Burnett said that in the beginning Crawford was a "splendid hand" but that he had to fire him. "It was a case of too much whiskey and a gradual going from bad to worse."[13] Afterward, Crawford supposedly took up briefly with the notably unsuccessful Al Jennings gang in the Oklahoma/Indian Territory. Jennings would later claim that he had to get rid of Crawford because he was "too high-tempered and volatile."[14] Still later, Crawford roamed the territories with outlaw pals, but he also spent considerable time in Wichita Falls hanging out at saloons. About two years earlier, Crawford had been involved in an altercation at a local watering hole. His opponent brought that difficulty to an abrupt halt when he beaned Crawford on the head with a brick, a blow that apparently had a noticeable and lasting effect on the recipient. He got even more "peculiar"—some folks said downright crazy. Not long after that he had a nasty encounter with an area cattleman named Marion Potter. Crawford threatened to kill him. Potter took him seriously, gathered up his family, and moved away to avoid trouble.[15] However, as we shall soon see, Potter would eventually have his day.

Apparently, most of the rumors of an impending bank robbery originated in Crawford's loose saloon talk. He and Lewis had heard that the vault of the City National Bank was stuffed with cash—maybe even a half million dollars. Actually the bank vault usually held from $40,000 to $70,000.[16] Anyhow, the two would-be Jesse Jameses decided their nefarious careers were ready to be launched—that they had outgrown minor-league stuff like holding up country stores for a few bucks or stealing a couple of steers and an occasional horse from Burk Burnett.

After seeing the rangers depart at noon that day, February 25, 1896, the two aspiring robbers most likely retired to a local saloon where they spent the next couple of hours fortifying themselves for the upcoming task, meanwhile allowing plenty of time for the

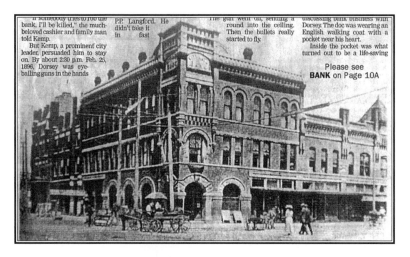

if somebody tries to rob the
bank, I'll be killed," the much-
beloved cashier and family man
told Kemp.
  But Kemp, a prominent city
leader, persuaded him to stay
on. By about 2:30 p.m. Feb. 25,
1896, Dorsey was eye-
balling guns in the hands

P.P. Langford. He
didn't take it
in   fast

The gun went off, sending a
round into the ceiling.
Then the bullets really
started to fly.

discussing bank business with
Dorsey. The doc was wearing an
English walking coat with a
pocket near his heart.
  Inside the pocket was what
turned out to be a life-saving

Please see
BANK on Page 10A

The City National Bank Building at the corner of Seventh and Ohio Streets in Wichita Falls as it appeared when it was robbed by Oklahoma Territory outlaws Elmer "Kid" Lewis and Foster Crawford on February 25, 1896. After being captured, the two were hanged by a mob at the scene of their crime. The telegraph poles shown were used as gallows. (From the *Wichita Falls Times Record News*)

The interior of the City National Bank in Wichita Falls as it appeared on February 25, 1896, when two Oklahoma Territory outlaws robbed it and killed cashier Frank Dorsey. (*left to right*) Wiley Robertson, an assistant cashier and later president of the bank; Lovik P. Webb, a collection clerk; an unidentified customer; P. P. Langford, the bookkeeper who was wounded during the robbery; and O. E. Cannon, a collection clerk. (From the *Wichita Falls Times Record News*)

rangers to clear the area. Or so they supposed—a supposition that would soon be proven erroneous. Shortly after two o'clock that afternoon, Crawford and Lewis tied their two stolen horses up behind the City National Bank. (One had been stolen from Burk Burnett, the other from a circuit-riding Methodist preacher.)[17]

They pulled their pistols and entered the bank. Then just about everything that could go wrong for them did go wrong.[18] Too much booze undoubtedly played a large part in the disaster, as did inexperience and ineptitude. They just didn't have the right stuff for this line of work. For one thing, although Foster Crawford was pretty well known about town, neither of the wannabes bothered to wear a mask.[19]

Local historians have since debated which robber did what and to whom during the hectic proceedings that followed. One of them, probably Crawford, approached the bookkeeper P. P. Langford with gun drawn. "Up! Up!" he commanded. But the studious bookkeeper was concentrating on a column of figures, and he didn't get it. Instead of explaining what he wanted, the nervous and booze -addled robber proceeded to crack Langford on the head with his pistol, which, in turn, caused him to accidentally pull the trigger and shoot a hole in the ceiling. Then all hell broke loose, and apparently both robbers began firing. Frank Dorsey, seeing his nightmare unfold, reached into the drawer of his desk and grabbed his pistol. But he was too slow. One of the robbers, most likely Kid Lewis, shot the clairvoyant cashier dead before he could fire off a shot. Then the trigger-happy bandits zeroed in on Dr. O. J. Kendall, a prominent physician and also a vice president and director of the bank. Didn't matter to the shooters that Kendall was unarmed and was not threatening them. They shot him in the heart—or so they thought. It was Dr. Kendall's lucky day, for he was carrying a metal hypodermic kit in his vest pocket, which absorbed the slug. Nevertheless, he wisely went down and played dead. Meanwhile, Langford regained semi-consciousness. The groggy accountant began crawling on all fours toward the door. He was shot in the buttocks but still he managed to make it through the door yelling, "Robbers! Robbers!" Fortunately,

FROM GUNS TO GAVELS

the wound, while most painful and embarrassing, proved not to be life-threatening.

(Much, much later, Wichitans would chuckle over two jests about the otherwise tragic episode: the embarrassing wound the heroic accountant P. P. Langford suffered, and the role of John L. Nichols, Wichita Falls city treasurer. Nichols was the only other person in the bank when the robbery occurred. A slight, small fellow, Nichols was not injured or even shot at during the robbery, apparently because neither Crawford nor Lewis noticed him. The jest: Nichols was so skinny that he hid by jumping into an ink well.)

With all the fireworks and the commotion going on, a good portion of the population was by this time aware that a bank robbery was in progress. But the inept duo had yet to sack up even one dollar of the bank's money. Finally, one of them found $410 in a teller's cash drawer. The next teller's drawer had about $1,000 in it, but neither bothered to open it. The vault was where the big bucks were kept, and the vault door was not locked. Still, even that task proved to be too much for their combined talents. Somehow they couldn't manage to get it open. So, amid the growing clamor as people gathered in the street outside, the pair made a dash for freedom.

As they went through the back door they ran headlong into the unarmed city marshal, Mage Davis, who demanded to know what they were up to. They simply shoved him aside and climbed aboard their horses. About this time, Deputy Hardesty, the jailer, arrived. Crawford shot at Hardesty and hit him. In the second miracle of the day, Crawford's shot, while true, did no damage. A silver watch in Hardesty's vest pocket saved his life. For his part, Hardesty managed to get off a shot aimed at Kid Lewis, but he missed. He did, however, hit and fatally wound the Kid's horse—a shot that would ultimately prove to be the undoing of the pair of thieves. A short distance down the getaway trail Lewis leaped off the dying animal and jumped on the back of Crawford's horse.

It didn't take long for the Wichitans to organize a citizens' posse. It was led by City Marshal Mage Davis and *Wichita Weekly Times* editor Will Skeen. Ironically, Skeen, at the time the gunfire interrupted his work, was sitting at his office a few doors away chewing on a pencil and composing an editorial entitled "The Peaceful Wichita Valley."[20] When Skeen heard the shooting, he raced to the scene and, on learning what had happened, borrowed a rifle, borrowed a horse, and helped City Marshal Mage Davis organize a posse.

Meanwhile, the robbers' transportation problems became critical. The one horse they were riding was tiring fast. It finally came down to a matter of obtaining fresh mounts. Everything depended on strong, speedy steeds to get them across the Red River ahead of the posse and far enough into Oklahoma or Indian Territory (where lawmen were scarce and Texas officers had no authority) to find another low-life who would hide and shelter them. In the end, they confiscated two plow horses from a farmer, unhooked them from the plow, and continued their desperate flight north. But the plow horses were not built for speed. Besides, they had been pulling a plow all day.

Finally, just before sundown, the citizens' posse, a hundred men strong now, hemmed the bandits up in a thicket just south of the Red River. Meanwhile, an alert citizen, C. K. Thomas, had raced to the depot and wired ahead, alerting Bill McDonald and his rangers. Fortunately, McDonald was not far away. He and a couple of his men were aboard the Fort Worth & Denver train returning from the Fitzsimmons-Maher circus, and the telegram reached them at Bellevue, only thirty-five miles southeast of Wichita Falls. McDonald was then able to intercept Sergeant Sullivan and his two men at that town, so McDonald, together with Rangers Sullivan, Lee Queen, Jack Harwell, Bob McClure, and W. J. "Billy" McCauley, commandeered a special car and engine, and they all chugged back toward Wichita Falls.[21] Fresh horses, saddled and ready, were waiting for them courtesy of old George A. Soule, an early-day stage driver and owner of a Wichita Falls livery stable.[22] They mounted up an hour or so before sundown, and by nine or ten o'clock that night—it was a bright full-moon night—they arrived at the thicket where the posse was holding the desperadoes at bay. Rightly fearing for their lives if captured by the enraged citizens, the pair agreed to surrender when they learned that the rangers had arrived, but they did so only on McDonald's promise to protect them.[23]

Lewis and Crawford were wagoned back to the Wichita County jail. Their pitifully trifling loot was recovered—all $410. Back in downtown Wichita Falls, mob fever was rising fast, and a crowd began to form at the jail. Captain McDonald and his rangers, however, succeeded in dispersing the mob. The threat of a lynching was over—for then, at least. But McDonald and his men kept watch that night in the Wichita jail.

A rather curious exchange occurred the next morning between the harried but genial jailer, Frank Hardesty, and the prisoners. Hardesty complimented Crawford on his marksmanship of the previous day, when he came close to killing the deputy.

"You were trying to kill my pal," explained Crawford, "and I had to shoot."

"You sure did ruin my watch," said Hardesty, exhibiting the battered silver timepiece that had saved his life.

"Well then, I'll give you mine," Crawford replied, handing Hardesty his gold watch. "I guess I won't be needing it any more."

"You might as well take mine too," shrugged Lewis, also handing over his watch to Hardesty.[24]

THE HANGING OF KID LEWIS AND FOSTER CRAWFORD

The next day, Tuesday, February 26, 1896, was a very long and eventful day. Citizens were enraged, not only in the town of Wichita Falls but all across North Central Texas. They were enraged over the bank robbery and the murder of the popular Frank Dorsey. They were also enraged at Oklahoma/Indian Territory outlaws in general— sick and tired of these sorry ne'er-do-wells who periodically crossed the Red River to rob, pillage, and kill and then to gaily skip back across the river to their outlaw sanctuary.

The Dallas Morning News explained the Texans' frustration as follows:

> To understand . . . the feelings of the [Texans] . . . it must be remembered that for years back outlaws in the territory have been depredating upon them. Bands of marauders have been crossing Red River into Texas, seizing stock, robbing stores and communities and committing other deviltry of an equally atrocious nature. The deed would be done and the guilty safely harbored in the territory before the luckless victim would learn [about it].[25]

That day the whole town was in a state of shock—galvanized. Tension increased moment by moment. Schools were dismissed, and several teachers escorted their classes to the jail where they were permitted to view the villains at close range. The emotional pitch was heightened further by Frank Dorsey's funeral that afternoon. The sight of Dorsey's widow and three small children grieving over his casket was heartwrenching. The First Baptist Church couldn't begin to accommodate the crowd that showed up. Afterward, nearly everybody in town joined the sorrowful procession of mourners who escorted Dorsey's remains to the Riverside Cemetery.[26] Then everything got quiet—deathly quiet. For a time.

Meanwhile scores of out-of-towners began pouring into the city. Every incoming train brought another crowd. Everybody, as *The Fort Worth Gazette* put it, was "eager to join the hanging bee." Sullen men, all armed, filled the streets of Wichita Falls, muttering violence.[27]

McDonald had promised the prisoners that he and the rangers would protect them if they surrendered. If ever the prisoners needed protection, it was now. But the rangers were long gone. That afternoon, despite the protests of District Judge George E. Miller, McDonald loaded his men on a westbound train and departed. More than a half century later, in an attempt to piece together the story, *Wichita Daily Times* reporter John Gould reflected on the events of that fateful day:

In the minds of many Wichitans, a question mark hung over the conduct of Bill McDonald that day. He must have known— no one could have failed to know—that the mob spirit was developing fast and that an attempt would be made to lynch the prisoners. In the face of that knowledge, he and his fellows left town, catching the afternoon train to Quanah.[28]

In 1909 when McDonald told the tale to his biographer, Albert Bigelowe Paine, he was still chafing from the criticism leveled at him more than a decade earlier for abandoning his prisoners. He explained it like this:

> McDonald informed him [Judge Miller] that it was impossible for his force to remain in Wichita Falls; that other work was waiting for them; . . . that they had been away from their head-quarters for two weeks. Besides being wet and cold and worn out from exposure and want of sleep . . . "I'm about used up, and likely to be sick. . . . I'm going to get out of here tonight [February 26, 1896] unless you get an order from Governor Culberson for me to stay."[29]

And so the proud lion "who would charge hell with a bucket of water" slouched off to Quanah.

At six o'clock that evening they laid Frank Dorsey to rest. At 8:45 the city's fire bell sounded and two shots rang out. That was the signal: the Bastille had fallen and the mob had its prisoners.[30] There was no turning back.

Between three hundred and five hundred mob members initially gathered to storm the jail. More joined. None were disguised. Many were leading citizens of the town. Meanwhile, Sheriff Moses and his men were still in the outback searching for Foster Crawford. Little did they guess that the horse thief-bank robber was locked up in the Wichita County jail where Deputy Hardesty alone manned the ramparts. When the mob arrived, Hardesty retreated inside and locked the doors. But it was useless.

Outside the jail, unarmed, District Judge Miller, county attorney C. D. Keys, and R. E. Huff, president of the First National Bank of Wichita Falls, tried to reason with the leaders of the mob. Huff warned the vigilantes that if they proceeded with their plan "they would have murder on their consciences for the rest of their lives." Judge Miller faced the mob on the steps of the jail and made a plea, eloquent and stentorian, that the law be allowed to take its course. He promised the mob that he would see that the robbers were brought to trial within eight weeks. He also told them that he had talked with Dorsey's widow and that it was her desire that there be no mob violence.[31]

But the mob was not in any mood to listen to that kind of talk—or any kind of talk. They taunted and jeered him, and one of them shouted: "Oh, yes. There will be a continuance, and then an appeal, and then a reversal, and then a bond, and finally liberty." Another mob member chimed in: "Boys, did you see that good woman and her three orphan children kissing the dead lips of Frank Dorsey today?" With that, the talking was over.[32]

Jailer Hardesty was grimly aware of what was about to happen. He hurried his wife and children to safety out of the family's jailhouse apartment and sent them to a friend's home. That left him alone to protect Crawford and Lewis. He retreated inside the jail and locked the door. But the mob, wielding a battering ram, broke into the jail, overpowered Hardesty, seized Lewis and Crawford, and marched them down to the scene of their crime—the corner of Seventh and Ohio streets where the City National Bank was located. A large bonfire crackled and lept, lending a hellishly carnival atmosphere to the night. Some of the mob began to chant: "Burn them! Burn them!"[33] It was a sentiment that seemed to find favor with a majority of the mob. But the leaders prevailed, and the lynching proceeded in a more "orderly" fashion, as the *Fort Worth Gazette* would later describe it. A telegraph pole there served as the gibbet; ropes were thrown over the cross bars and nooses fitted around the killers' necks. Boxes were stacked underneath the pole, and both men were made to stand on those makeshift platforms, nooses around their necks and hands tied behind their backs. But they were not hanged right away. The crowd leered, jeered, and taunted. Kid Lewis was not intimidated. He never quivered. He jeered right back at the blood-lusting vigilantes, trading insults and curses with them. The Kid nursed a sizeable wad of chewing tobacco, and from time to time he would squirt a stream of tobacco juice at one of his tormentors. His range and accuracy proved so impressive that he kept even the most rabid of the jackals at a respectful distance. He stood there in his high-heeled boots; stood there on his makeshift, packing-box scaffold in the carnival brilliance of the bonfire; stood there in his red flannel shirt and his black trousers—a tableau at once as colorful as it was macabre and indelible.[34]

When somebody asked him if he didn't want to pray, the Kid snarled: "Pray? You _____ you, when you come to Hell I will meet you at the gate with a Winchester. Go ahead and pull that rope you _____!"

His only request was that somebody tell his father that he had "died nervy."[35] He did.

The mob hanged Kid Lewis first.

But Foster Crawford was another story. He alternated between bravado and cowardice. In fairness to Crawford, however, he had just watched his fellow bandit strangling to death; that while awaiting his turn at the same fate, Lewis's limp body dangling right in front of him, Lewis's noosed neck elongated and twisted, his facial features grossly contorted, and his dead eyes bulging from their sockets—a grisly spectacle. And not only that, there also was the howling, leering crowd surrounding him, free to satiate its lust for raw flesh and hot blood.[36]

Moreover, the veneer of civilization imposed by the teachers of morality had been worn mighty thin in the Old South, even thinner perhaps in Texas after almost a century of continual bloodshed and violence: the Texas Revolution, the Civil War, the mean times of the Reconstruction years, the Indian confrontations, the ongoing hate-fueled racial atrocities along the Rio Grande border, and finally, the brutal crimes perpetrated on the fringes of the westward advance by an influx of hardcase outlaws drawn to the lawless frontier. Is it any wonder that the average citizen in that time and place had become emotionally calloused and inured to violence and killing—had come to accept violence as a normal, almost an inevitable, part of everyday life?

The mob leaders were at the fore in all this, but more vicious were their followers, the body and brawn of the mob. They were the ones who taunted and jeered and chanted "Burn 'em! Burn 'em!" And, most likely they would have had not the leaders vetoed it. Until now the followers might have been the downtrodden, the ignored, the outcasts of society, but now they *belonged*. As part of a mob they were finally empowered. They who had been the powerless were now enforcing on someone else their own standards, and those standards were good and righteous. They who had been the nobodies of society were suddenly elevated and exalted, transformed into the noble dispensers of justice and the guardians of communal values. After all, hadn't the mob leaders and the prominent of the community unanimously said so? For one brief time, they, the lesser of society, were finally vindicated and were now the executors of power rather than its victims; and for once in their boring existence, they were doing something exhilarating, something really important![37]

Then there were the spectators, probably more numerous than the mob leaders plus their henchmen. Even if they didn't actively participate in the lynching, still their role was an important component of the mob and its psychology. Their numbers and their presence—all watching with approval—gave encouragement and validation to the mob, conveying to the mobsters a heady sense of social prominence and noble purpose that they had never felt before.[38]

The unfettered pagan engorgement was not limited to the lynching site. As news was telegraphed to area towns across northwest Texas, spontaneous celebrations erupted. In Seymour, some fifty miles to the west, where less than a year earlier renegade sheriff Joe Beckham gunned down the new Motley County sheriff, George Cook, a cheering crowd put on an impromptu "anvil chorus." Gunpowder was coated atop anvils and then exploded by sledge hammer blows, all to the whooping delight of the spectators. As the *Wichita Daily Times* described it: "The anvils were booming all the time Crawford and Lewis were being lynched."[39]

In the end, Crawford claimed it was Lewis who killed the cashier. Then he begged for whiskey; he got it, and then begged for more. Then he promised that if they would spare him he would lead them to a hidden stash of ten thousand dollars' stolen loot. But the mob was in no mood to play games. Finally, he was reduced to incoherent babbling in English, Spanish, and Comanche. But before he reached that point he spotted his old boss, Burk Burnett, in the mob and summoned him. Crawford and Burnett had an extended conversation, the content of which would later be the subject of considerable debate. In any event, Crawford confessed his sins of thievery (although denying the murder of Frank Dorsey) and begged Burnett to save him from the mob. When that failed, Crawford, apparently angered by Burnett's refusal to interfere with the mob's mission, attempted to kick Burnett. According to one account, Burnett pulled his pistol intending to bring the proceedings to an abrupt halt, but he was dissuaded by a friend who told him that "it wouldn't be right to disappoint the folks who are here to hang him."[40]

Among the spectators that night, there happened to be a vagrant sixteen-year-old boy who would, years later, become the most well known citizen in all of West Texas. His name was Amon Carter—the same man who would become the flamboyant publisher of the *Fort Worth Star-Telegram* and who would become world-famous as "Mr. West Texas," the Texan who played cowboy for America from the 1920s until his death in 1955.

A native of nearby Wise County, Texas, Carter had heard hushed mutterings about the planned lynching of a couple of bank robbers in Wichita Falls—a sensational event that the spirited, though dead-broke, country boy was not about to miss. Young Amon hoboed the next boxcar headed for Wichita Falls, arriving there just in time to witness the final act. Many times thereafter he told and retold the story of what happened that night. When he arrived, Crawford and Lewis were already noosed and standing on packing-crate platforms. He witnessed the hanging of Kid Lewis and then the exchange between Burk Burnett and Foster Crawford, which, according to Carter, culminated in Crawford kicking Burnett in the stomach, after which Burnett responded by kicking the box platform out from under Crawford, leaving him dangling.[41] However, that part about Burnett kicking the platform out from under Crawford sounds suspiciously like an embellishment Carter added much later to dramatize his tale. None of the contemporary accounts of the hanging mention it.

While no thought was ever given to indicting Burnett as a principal of the lynch mob, he nevertheless was present, did have an exchange with Crawford, and did nothing to dissuade the mob leaders from carrying out their purposes. Plagued for years by thieves stealing his cattle, he doubtless was not unduly grieved to see the careers of these two sorry galoots ended. Some years before this lynching, Burnett had shot and killed a man who he claimed had stolen some of his cattle. He was tried and acquitted on his plea of self-defense.[42] And, as will be recounted in a subsequent chapter, in 1913 he would be tried for killing yet another cattle thief. Obviously, crusty old Burk Burnett figured that the only good cow thief was a dead cow thief.

The outlaws were not hanged in the humane manner accorded officially hanged prisoners who are dropped through a trap door and plunge a sufficient distance so that the noose snaps their necks and kills them instantly. The mob leaders simply grabbed the end of the hanging ropes and hoisted the prisoners skyward, causing a lingering death by strangulation. While Lewis was resigned to his fate and died quietly, Crawford died hard—kicking and cursing and praying and fighting the noose. The *Wichita Daily Times* described it this way:

On February 26, 1896—one day after Foster Crawford and Kid Lewis robbed the City National Bank of Wichita Falls and killed a cashier in the process—they were lynched by an angry mob in front of the bank at the corner of Seventh and Ohio Streets. A sketch artist for *The Dallas Morning News* was present and recorded the outlaws dangling from a telegraph pole in front of the bank. The sketch appeared in the February 27, 1896, edition. *(From* The Dallas Morning News*)*

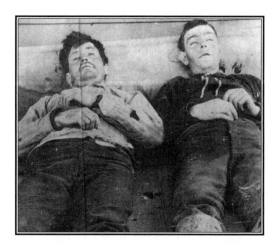

Bank robbers and killers Foster Crawford (*left*) and Elmer "Kid" Lewis are shown here on February 27, 1896, the day after they were lynched in downtown Wichita Falls. *(From the* Wichita Falls Times Record News*)*

He went up on the end of the rope with a curse and a prayer on his lips. He died hard—awfully hard. He tried frantically to fight against the inevitable, and his death writhing caused the mob to melt away like snow before a tropical sun. He was fully ten minutes in quieting down and it looked at one time like he would never give up the ghost. His passing was the end of the chapter.[43]

The blood-lust of the vigilantes finally sated by this hideous spectacle, the mob slowly dissolved into the night. About daylight the next morning, two men came and cut the ropes and carried the bodies to the local funeral parlor. One of those men was Wichita County constable Tom Pickett, a friend and future bodyguard for Burk Burnett. We shall hear much more of Tom Pickett in a later chapter.

At this point we might well pause to ponder a puzzle. Consider that for a large segment of the population, watching a lynching was considered festive entertainment better than even a rodeo. There was little public outcry, and no antilynching legislation had been enacted. Yet, there were vigorously enforced penal laws prohibiting professional prizefighting on the books in forty-four states (including Texas), and when in 1896 Dan Stuart proposed to hold a world heavyweight championship boxing match between Fitzsimmons and Maher in Texas, a firestorm of protest erupted.

The *Wichita Times* writer who ended his story (as quoted above) by concluding that Foster Crawford's passing was "the end of the chapter" was mistaken. Or maybe it was the end of one chapter. But, if so, the lynching was only the beginning of another chapter in the evolving story of frontier justice, for it touched off heated debates, recriminations, denials, countercharges, and a series of events that would reverberate down through the history of Texas jurisprudence.

As gripping as is the tale of the bank robbery, the murder of the cashier, the pursuit and capture of the culprits, and the lynching, the story of its immediate aftermath is at least as interesting—and perhaps more instructive for what it tells us of the times and the people and the maturing of our criminal justice system. Plus, contemporary news accounts of the otherwise somber story were frequently leavened by pinches of unintended humor—humorous, at least, to a modern reader.

NEWS COVERAGE OF THE LYNCHING

The news coverage of the robbery, the murder, the capture, and particularly the lynching of Lewis and Crawford provides us with a priceless anecdotal dissertation on late-nineteenth-century frontier journalism at its best—or worst, depending on how one views it. Or, at least at its most typical.[44] *The Wichita Times*, *The Fort Worth Gazette*, and *The Dallas Morning News* just could not get enough of this story. In reporting the dramatic events, *The Fort Worth Gazette* and *The Wichita Times* editors made absolutely no pretense of segregating factual accounts of what happened from their opinions about those goings-on or their assessment of the character (or lack thereof) of the players. And the sensational headlines! The February 27, 1896, edition of *The Fort Worth Gazette*, in breathless hyperbole, stacked six headlines, one on top of the other, in its front-page story: "The Robbers Lynched," then, "Swift Retribution Meted Out to the Murderers of Cashier Dorsey," then, "Within a Few Feet of the Scene of Tuesday's Terrible Tragedy the Outlaws Expiate Their Fearful Deed," then (the author's favorite), "Bodies Dangle Twixt Heaven and Earth," and then two more, the last ending, "Three Hundred Citizens Carry the Plans into Execution in a Firm, but Orderly Manner." So there.

The ensuing story (when the editor finally got through headlining) was a rich and florid blend of facts, opinions, hyperbole, unintended irony, and plain illogic. The article reported that on that occasion, "Judge Lynch . . . opened a special session of court" during which "swift justice . . . was meted out to the two lawless bandits." Members of the lynch mob were then congratulated (in a news story, mind you) on the businesslike way they conducted the lynching: "a crowd of law-abiding citizens," who were "orderly, sober and quiet," went about their noble task. The *Gazette* reported that all had conducted themselves as though "they were performing a sacred duty they owed to a loved friend, to the dignity of the city and to their fellow men."

Although the *Gazette* had just commended the vigilantes for their "sober" demeanor, it nevertheless went on to opine that some of the vigilantes would someday come to "deplore" their acts "in their sober moments." Then, having just applauded the mob for the "law-abiding" manner in which they hanged the outlaws, it observed that in view of the wanton slaying of Dorsey, "it is no wonder they forgot law in their desire for revenge." And having just praised the work of the noble rope wielders, one might expect the *Gazette* to have singled out at least some of the heroes for individual accolades. But not so. The only names noted as being present when the men were hanged were Burk Burnett and his son, Tom Burnett.

Then, too, journalists of the day never passed up an opportunity to take cheap shots at competing newspapers. The editor of *The Fort Worth Gazette* in its February 28, 1896, edition lowered the boom on *The Dallas Morning News*, smugly noting:

> *The Dallas Morning News* of yesterday [Thursday, February 27] had a very good account of the Wichita Falls bank robbery which occurred two days before. It would have been acutely interesting if the public had not already read all about the affair in Wednesday's [February 26] *Gazette*.

The opening shot in the firestorm between those who condoned the lynching and those who condemned it was fired by Texas Lt. Gov.

George Jester, father of future Texas Gov. Beauford Jester. (Governor Culberson was out of state when the lynching occurred, leaving Jester in charge.) When Jester heard what had happened in Wichita Falls, he fired off a scorching telegram to Wichita County Sheriff C. M. Moses.

> Knowing that you were aided in the arrest by the state Rangers, I supposed you were amply prepared to protect the prisoners. . . . Those who participated in taking the law into their own hands committed an act that is unjustifiable, indefensible and should be condemned by all the law-abiding citizens, and constitutes a blot on the county and state.
>
> The only [reason for a lynching] is that justice cannot be obtained before the courts, which is a reflection on the laws of our state, or the citizenship in not enforcing the law. I believe that the defect is more in the latter than in the former.[45]

In reply Sheriff Moses explained that he was out of the county searching for the two outlaws when the arrests were made and did not return to Wichita Falls until about ten o'clock at night, when the lynching party was in progress, at which time it was too late for him to do anything about it. He added that as soon as he returned to town he was overpowered by a "detachment of citizens," disarmed, and rendered "helpless as a child." He claimed that twenty-five men had been deputized to protect the prisoners. (Just where those twenty-five special deputies were when the skullduggery went down, he failed to say, and nobody else since has explained. Also, since the sheriff was out of the county and supposedly knew nothing of what was going on in Wichita Falls until after the lynching was in progress, one wonders just who deputized those twenty-five specials.) In any event, the sheriff continued, "a regiment of soldiers" could not have prevented the lynching. He then told Jester: "The community to almost a man seems to uphold the method employed in ridding the country of these two noted criminals." In closing, however, the sheriff assured Jester that *he* certainly did not "approve or uphold such methods," and that he stood ever ready to "do his full duty in the premises."[46]

One prominent and irate Wichita Falls citizen took issue with Jester. In a rebuttal appearing in *The Dallas Morning News*, Arch D. Anderson told Jester that "the best citizens of the state and county . . . administered justice to the murderers of that noblest of men, Frank Dorsey." He argued that had the law been allowed to take its course there would have been delay after delay, and that the outlaws might have even escaped justice altogether by jail-break or by pardon. In any event, Anderson explained, judges "have very little practical experience dealing with the class continually committing these foul murders . . . [and] are incapable of dictating to the common citizen his duty under such circumstances." Anderson continued his attack on the judicial system as follows:

> When one of these men [Lewis or Crawford] was asked why he lost his grit and allowed himself to be captured alive, he answered that he thought he would be protected by the Texas Rangers and that he knew no jury could be obtained in this county and was sure he would be able to keep the case in court for several months and he knew of no jail that could hold him that long. Now, when we take the history of the past, was he not justified in his conclusions?

Anderson closed with a commendation to those "gallant men" who strung up Lewis and Crawford: "A more becoming sight I never witnessed than when I saw their bodies dangling in the breeze in front of the bank where they committed the foul murder."[47] Anderson neglected, however, to give individual credit to any of those "gallant men."

Those "gallant men" had the overwhelming support of the community. Of that there was no doubt. Stung by criticism from Jester and other outsiders, a citizens' vigilante committee was formed at a public meeting to voice support for the lynching and for all those who had participated in it, as well as to discourage any future depredations from Indian Territory outlaws.[48] The group also called on the border states of Arkansas, Missouri, and Kansas to join them in pressuring the federal government to open up the Indian Territory for settlement, believing, correctly, that once the territory was settled and local governments formed, law enforcement there would significantly curb lawlessness in the area.[49]

Meanwhile *The Dallas Morning News* criticized the vigilante action, while *The Wichita Times* and *The Fort Worth Gazette* wholeheartedly endorsed the vigilantes and their supporters. In an April 2, 1896, editorial the *Gazette* stated:

> The *Gazette* declared the fate of Crawford and Lewis to have been a just one and suggested that it should serve as a warning to outlaws from the Indian Territory to abstain from murder and robbery in Texas. The people of Wichita Falls, in mass meeting assembled, appealed to Congress to establish a civilized government in the Indian Territory, and to exterminate the lawlessness prevailing there.

The Dallas Morning News, however, had a different take on the matter. The day after the hanging, The *News* weighed in as follows:

> It must be regretted that their punishment was not meted out according to law. It matters not how exasperating the offense. . . . Every such example of collective tumultuous and irrepressible violence deprecates the dignity and repute of the state in proclaiming its incapacity to cope with crime and to maintain an orderly administration of justice.[50]

The Dallas Morning News editorial also criticized "the officers who captured the villains" for failing to protect them from mob violence. The *News* also censured *The Wichita Times* for its enthusiastic support of mob justice, in reply to which the *Times* editorialist, soaring to new depths in the debate, fired back this journalistic nugget:

Some narrow-constructed, clay-brained newspapermen most emphatically condemn the action of lynching the robbers who got their just dues at the end of a rope in this city lately. In our opinion, if some of these fellows were swung to the same telegraph pole, the country would be in much better condition.

To which *The Dallas Morning News* editorialist, in returning the volley, quipped: "The [Wichita] *Times* seems to be somewhat high-strung itself."[51]

The Wichitans took another searing broadside from a federal judge in the Indian Territory. In a letter printed in *The Fort Worth Gazette*, U.S. District Judge Constantine Buckley Kilgore of Ardmore, Indian Territory, equated the murder of the bank cashier to the murder of Lewis and Crawford. He wrote:

The motive in one case was plunder; in the other revenge: and the spirit of outlawry was as conspicuous in one case as the other. . . . [Justifying this lynching upon the ground] that the courts of Texas could not be relied upon to enforce the law and punish the criminals . . . was dangerous ground upon which to seek to justify mob violence . . . and the people of Wichita Falls in their . . . malice undertook to shift the odium of these outrages and the responsibility of these crimes on another. . . . The *Gazette* and the people of Wichita Falls insisted that the mob came out of that work whiter than snow. . . .

Judge Kilgore continued his broadside as follows:

On March 2, 1896, there was a called session of the Wichita Falls mob, the purpose of which was to unload on the people of the Indian Territory the responsibility for the wrongs perpetrated by that community, for the inefficient courts and officials of Texas and the uselessness of the "rangers."[52]

The Dallas Morning News and federal judge Kilgore weren't the only ones who took Bill McDonald and the rangers to task for failing to protect the prisoners. Back in Wichita Falls, District Judge George E. Miller filed a vigorous complaint with Governor Culberson, castigating McDonald for abandoning the prisoners when lynch fever pervaded the atmosphere, leaving only jailer Hardesty to protect them. Apparently Governor Culberson referred the matter to his adjutant general, W. H. Mabry, McDonald's superior in Austin, for investigation. When queried by Mabry, the never-self-effacing ranger was not about to accept any blame, not about to brook even the mildest criticism. Running true to form, he attempted to shift all the blame onto Judge Miller, explaining that when the arrests were first made he intended to take the prisoners to the Fort Worth jail so they would be secure, but that Judge Miller told him not to.[53] (McDonald failed to explain just what authority Miller had to give him such orders.) His allegations against Judge Miller were patently absurd since of all the residents of Wichita Falls, Judge Miller was the most vocal about protecting the prisoners from mob violence. Judge Miller, it will be recalled, was the one who protested McDonald's decision to leave town a few hours before the lynching.

Then McDonald insisted that he had done his "whole duty"— that as soon as he had locked up the prisoners in the Wichita County jail his duty ended. If that were true then why did McDonald and his men disperse the lynch mob shortly after the arrests and then spend that first night in the Wichita jail? And McDonald conveniently forgot to mention that he had persuaded Lewis and Crawford to surrender on the strength of his promise to protect them. After raking Judge Miller over the coals, McDonald attempted to portray himself as the scapegoat, lamenting:

> [T]here must always be some one to attach all the blame to and when they cannot find any one else, the poorly paid Ranger,

who dares open his mouth, gets all the blame and some of us can stand a reasonable amount of abuse at long range.[54]

As if that weren't enough, he proceeded to heap the ridiculous atop the absurd. Although none of the mob had worn a mask or made the slightest attempt at disguise, McDonald reported to Mabry that he had failed "to find anyone who knows anything about those who did the hanging except that they were strangers or women in disguise."[55] This from the man who prided himself on being the Sherlock Holmes of frontier detectives. It was painfully obvious that McDonald, who was simply incapable of ever admitting error, was deeply embarrassed by his blunder and certainly didn't want to stir this stinking mess any further. It is also probable that another factor entered into McDonald's refusal to investigate the lynching. Before becoming a lawman, McDonald had owned and operated a lumber yard in Wichita Falls from 1883 through 1885, and he must have known all the leading citizens of that sparsely populated frontier town. Many of these Wichitans, including a former Wichita County sheriff, were involved, in varying degrees, in the lynching. With-out doubt, had McDonald been on the scene when the lynch mob formed, he would have done all in his power to disperse the mob and, if his prior feats were any indication of his effectiveness, he would have succeeded. Still, once the ugly deed was done, McDonald most likely was reluctant to finger his friends and prominent (and otherwise law-abiding) citizens who, after all, McDonald prob-ably rationalized, had been guilty of nothing worse than adminis-tering a crude but effective form of frontier justice to two heinous outlaws and wanton murderers.

Before resuming the narrative, the striking similarities in the back-ground and early years of our two protagonists—Ranger Captain McDonald and District Judge Miller—are simply too remarkable to ignore. Both were born and bred Southerners; both were deprived of their childhood by the chaos, loss, and ruin of the Civil War and its equally horrific aftermath. McDonald was born on a Mississippi plantation on September 28, 1852, while Miller was born on a Mississippi farm on December 10, 1861. Both their fathers, patriots of the Lost Cause, volunteered to serve in the Confederate army, and both fathers were killed in battle. Before either McDonald or Miller reached their tenth birthdays, both had lost not only their society, their way of life, their family fortunes, but also, their fathers. Their homeland was ravaged, relatives scattered to the winds, and for the tattered survivors, bare survival was a daily struggle. The remnants of both families finally straggled to Texas. There, unlike so many other of their contemporaries reared in that same cauldron of bitterness, violence, and lawlessness, both McDonald and Miller somehow grew to maturity as upholders of the law, albeit with interpretations of their duties sometimes differing considerably—as we have just witnessed.

Judge Miller's father was killed in battle in 1865, and in 1870 his mother died. The orphaned boy was sent to live on a farm with his grandfather. Despite all these travails, he managed to attend the University of Mississippi, and in 1884 he received his law degree from Cumberland University. That same year he migrated to Graham, Young County, Texas, where he set up a law practice. Soon he was elected the county attorney there. In 1888 he moved to Wichita Falls where he was elected district attorney, and in 1890 he was elected district judge, serving four two-year terms—a position he held during the events of this story.[56]

As recounted above, when Judge Miller appealed to the mob to reject rope justice and to allow the law to take its course, one mob member vented his frustration with the inefficiency of the criminal justice system. He had a valid point even if it smacked more of a rationalization, rather than a justification, for the contemplated acts of violence. The fledgling frontier justice system was, in fact, a faulty piece of machinery. Many obviously guilty criminals did slip through its net. In the same edition in which it deplored mob justice, *The Dallas Morning News* addressed this issue. The editorial decried numerous instances of injustice it attributed to "loopholes" in Texas penal laws that permitted the guilty to go free. The *News* repeated its criticism of the Texas Legislature for failing to pass certain remedial legislation that the paper had previously advocated. The *News* then said this:

> The instruments and processes of criminal jurisprudence are too cumbersome and complicated. Civilization demands that mob violence be suppressed, but it demands with just as much emphasis that the law punish the guilty, and give to society the protection which government is supposed to guarantee. Until something is done along this line it will devolve upon officers to prevent lynches.[57]

One of most obvious failings of the immature criminal justice system lay in the inordinate number of convictions reversed by the Texas Court of Criminal Appeals. Slavish adherence to hypertechnical rules of practice and procedure inherited from English common law, plus a predilection to make frog's hair distinctions resulted in the appellate court reversing an astounding 68.5 percent of all criminal cases it reviewed in 1900. (That without counting prohibition and liquor convictions.)[58] Shortly after the Wichita Falls lynching, an 1896 Dallas grand jury took the unusual step of voicing its frustration in this public criticism aimed at the Texas Court of Criminal Appeals:

> We cannot refrain from calling attention to the peculiar action of the Court of Criminal Appeals in reversing cases. . . . That court seldom or never looks at facts to see if the party is guilty, but seems to look at some farfetched matter that could not and did not affect the guilt or innocence of the man. Justice seems to be done in the trial court and undone in the Court of Criminal Appeals. . . . It is certainly no part of the law that our high-

est criminal court continuously aids criminals to escape justice and something ought to be done to stop it. . . . Let the Court of Criminal Appeals be compelled to affirm all cases where there is no question about guilt.[59]

Before examining the Texas appellate court's role in reviewing criminal cases, it should first be recalled that the court was never called on to review acquittals, because the state had no right to appeal a finding of not guilty. Only if the defendant was found guilty did an appellate court consider the case. But, the crescendo of criticism swelled to a point that lawmakers in Austin could no longer turn deaf ears to the problem. When the Texas Legislature next met (in 1897) remedial legislation was enacted to reduce the number of appellate reversals of convictions. Under the prior law, the court of appeals reversed convictions if it found almost *any* error in trial court proceedings. Under the new act the lawmakers decreed that certain technical trial court errors were to be "disregarded" on appeal "unless the error . . . was calculated to injure the rights of the defendant." As numerous appellate courts and legal scholars have since observed, the U.S. and state constitutions were never intended to guarantee defendants a *perfect* trial—only a *fair* trial. That postulate, sensible and right as it is, nevertheless raised another thorny issue that the appellate court would have to deal with when considering whether to reverse or affirm a criminal conviction: that is, at what point does an "imperfect" trial become an "unfair" trial. When does a trial error, or cumulative trial errors, gain sufficient evidentiary (and/or inflammatory) weight to prevent a jury from making a rational determination of "guilt beyond a reasonable doubt"? A tough question, and one that poses a terribly difficult burden on an appellate court.

Difficult though the appellate task was under the new legislation, it was nevertheless a step in the right direction—no automatic reversals of convictions on flimsy technicalities. It was also the precursor of modern jurisprudence's "harmless error" rule. Furthermore, the new 1897 Texas legislation went one more step to prevent trial errors from triggering reversals: to assert reversible error on appeal the defendant must have preserved the error by making an objection at the trial court level. Otherwise the error, if any, was waived, and the appellate court could not reverse a conviction on that ground. Still, this legislation would prove to be only the first step toward reining in the reversal-minded Court of Criminal Appeals.[60]

JUDGE MILLER VS. THE MOB LEADERS

Back in Wichita Falls, meanwhile, most folks probably figured this whole unpleasant episode in their history was just that—history. For sure and for certain they hoped so. But George E. Miller was a determined man dedicated to observance of the law, and he was not about to let it slide. When the next Wichita grand jury met on April 28, 1896, Judge Miller forcefully brought the matter of the lynching to its attention. "You must not turn a blind eye to the law," he lectured them. The men who participated in the lynching of Crawford and Lewis were guilty of murder, he continued, and then ordered the grand jurors to do their duty. (Defense lawyers would later turn this lecture to their own uses.) Judge Miller couldn't resist the opportunity to take another jab at McDonald. Although he didn't name McDonald specifically, he did tell the grand jurors, "If they [the peace officers] had done their duty, Wichita County would not have been disgraced by mob law."[61] In the end, the grand jury returned murder indictments against five Wichitans: former Wichita County sheriff F. M. Davis, W. E. Cobb, Dick Quinn, Frank Smith, and Marion Potter.[62] (It will be recalled that a year or so before the lynching, Foster Crawford had threatened to kill cattleman Marion Potter, causing the latter and his family to move away to avoid trouble.) To say that the indicting of these men was not popular with the general populace would be a gross understatement. *The Dallas Morning News* commented:

> [T]he expressions heard on the street would indicate that most
> people of [Wichita Falls] were very indignant at the grand

jurymen and district judge for their action in the above matter. In fact, the feeling appeared to be about the same as it was the evening that Foster [Crawford] and Lewis were taken from jail and hanged.[63]

Still, Judge Miller was determined that these men should answer before a court of law for their actions. Moreover, he refused to set bonds for the defendants pending a trial. But Judge Miller's resolve was undermined by a clever bit of chicanery in which, apparently, even his fellow brethren at the local bar participated. Louise Kelly, a native Wichitan, compiled a revealing account of the whole affair, and it appears in her limited edition book, *Wichita County Beginnings*. She tells it this way: "When the five [murder defendants] came up for a preliminary hearing, Judge Miller was told his wife was in an accident in Graham. While he was away, the Wichita County lawyers selected a temporary [district] judge, C. M. Sherrod."[64]

In those days, when a duly elected judge was temporarily incapacitated or called out of the county on important matters, a "temporary" judge was sometimes appointed by the county bar to attend to routine, noncontested matters. However, it was customary for the temporary judge to defer decisions on serious, contested cases until the duly elected judge returned and could rule on them.

But not so in the matter of the lynching indictees. Instead of continuing the preliminary hearing in these cases until Judge Miller returned, temporary Judge Sherrod grabbed the ball and ran with it. He proceeded with the hearings in all five cases while, according to Kelly, Judge Miller was apparently on a wild goose chase down at Graham. Although the defendants had been indicted for capital murder and Judge Miller had denied them bonds, Judge Sherrod wasted no time in setting a five-thousand-dollar bond for each defendant, and then, *on his own motion*, proceeded to change the venue of each case. The cases against ex-sheriff F. M. Davis, W. E. Cobb, Dick Quinn, and Frank Smith were transferred to Vernon in Wilbarger County.[65] Marion Potter's case was transferred to Gainesville in Cooke County.[66] One can hardly resist the speculation that the temporary judge, in selecting foreign venues for the trials, chose courts he considered "defendant-friendly."

The next edition of *The Dallas Morning News* duly reported what happened next: "A majority of the best citizens of Wichita Falls went to the courthouse and offered to furnish a bond in any sum" for the defendants. In addition, each defendant was furnished a list of all the attorneys in town and instructed that he could select any two lawyers to represent him, all of whom had agreed to represent the defendants "cheerfully without fee."[67]

The district judge in Vernon, G. A. Brown, called the four cases transferred there for trial on August 3, 1896. Each case was called, everybody announced "ready," and all the defendants pleaded "not guilty." A jury was empanelled, but before testimony began each defendant presented a motion to set aside his indictment on grounds that the indictments were void because, the defendants alleged, both Judge Miller and district attorney J. F. Carter had been present when the grand jury that returned those indictments was *deliberating* upon the proposed charges. Although prosecuting attorneys and other witnesses may appear before a grand jury when it is hearing evidence on various matters, when the time comes for the grand jury to deliberate and make its decisions on whether or not to indict, only the twelve grand jurors are permitted to be present in the grand jury room and participate in the decision-making process. Apparently the gist of the motions to quash the indictments was that Judge Miller's grand jury tongue-lashing and exhortations to indict the vigilante leaders was alleged to have been tantamount to him being present during the grand jury deliberations. In any event, Judge Brown lost no time in granting all four motions and dismissing the indictments. Since the defendants' trials had actually begun when he dismissed the indictments, "jeopardy" had attached. Hence, the "double jeopardy" prohibitions in the Texas and U.S. Constitutions prevented the defendants from ever being reindicted or tried for the lynching murders of Crawford and Lewis. The defendants were home free.

Court was adjourned in Vernon and the four defendants, their attorneys, and about three hundred character witnesses for the defendants cheered all the way back to Wichita Falls—according to one Wichita Falls observer: "happy, and I might say, hilarious."[68]

The case against Marion Potter in Gainesville didn't even get that far. It was left to die on the vine, and finally, on June 7, 1897, it was dismissed by the Cooke County district judge on motion by the district attorney on grounds of "insufficient evidence to convict." Just as well, no doubt. As one disinterested newspaper commented, the dismissals of all the lynch mob indictments were a foregone conclusion: "Prosecutors and others were aware that no Texas jury would return a verdict of guilty."[69]

Many years after the lynching, respected newsman Rhea Howard, longtime editor of the *Wichita Falls Times Record News*, left a handwritten note in the newspaper's file on the 1896 lynching. It reads as follows:

> Hanging of Bank Robbers here in Wichita Falls—the following were present at this event. 1. B. F. Crawford [not to be confused with the bank robber, Foster Crawford]; 2. Bob Daggs; 3. C. W. Ward; 4. Henry McCauley—first one to see them; 5. [County] Judge [Edgar] Scurry; 6. C. K. Thomas—went for Rangers; 7. M. G. Talbert—Rancher; 8. Lee McMurtry; 9. Lem Chesher; 10. Sonnamaker; 11. Tony Thornberry.

The note then states that "Marion Potter—went up pole" and that Potter and Jim Avis "put rope over necks" and finally, "F. M. Davis— Ex Sheriff led mob."

It was signed by Howard and dated March 23, 1964.[70]

Judge Miller ended up paying a dear price for his fidelity to the law. When it came time for the next election some two years later, he wisely chose not to seek reelection. When his term expired he moved to Kansas City and began practicing law there. In 1900, however, he was induced to return to Texas. He joined celebrated Fort Worth attorney A. L. Matlock in a law firm renamed Matlock, Miller and Dycus. He continued to practice law in Texas (but never again in Wichita Falls) until his death on April 25, 1922.[71]

When he died, Judge Miller's body was returned to Wichita Falls for burial, and at his funeral service the leading members of the area bar gathered to pay tribute. Many were Wichitans at the time of the 1896 lynchings, and all spoke at the service and, although much of that tribute did seem a bit too little too late, nevertheless they all recalled Judge Miller's heroic 1896 stand against the lynch mob at the Wichita County jail, noting the physical and moral courage he exhibited that day. It was also recalled that shortly before his death he had returned to Wichita Falls to attend a banquet for the ex-judges of the district court. There he gave an address entitled "Ethics of the Profession." One lawyer told the mourners that while Judge Miller had never made much of a financial success in his law practice, "as an attorney and a man, he had mounted to the highest pinnacle in the success of his profession." Another told of Judge Miller's unswerving dedication to the constitution and the written laws of the land, recalling Judge Miller's repeated assertion that "the greatest danger [to our society] lies in the departure of many people from the enforcement of the written law. . . . The only safety of the country [lies] in the written constitution and the written laws and the right of trial by jury."[72]

There was to be an unusual finale for two of the other prominent players in the drama. Several years after the lynching, jailer Frank Hardesty and Arch Anderson (the apologist for those "gallant men," the vigilantes) both drowned when their boat capsized on Lake Wichita.[73]

THE AFTERMATH: REFORM EFFORTS

Although the mob leaders who meted out summary justice, frontier style, to Lewis and Crawford went scot-free with the overwhelming blessings of Wichita Falls citizens, an increasingly vocal minority across the state, incensed by the lawless brutality of the Wichita Falls spectacle, began to make their voices heard in Austin. To be sure, the 1896 Wichita Falls hanging was not the only incident that pressured the Texas Legislature to consider remedial legislation in 1897. Lynching in America hit its peak in the early 1890s; the 1890s also saw the high-water mark for lynchings in Texas.[74] In addition to the Wichita Falls affair, there were several other sensational Texas lynchings that stirred widespread debate. The lynching of William A. Jones in Tyler, Texas, on May 23, 1897, was a classic case of a mob acting because it feared the defendant would be freed due to the failure of the judicial system. (The mob believed Jones's skilled defense attorney would win an acquittal.)[75] For sheer brutality, however, two other northeast Texas lynchings were sadistic nightmares. On December 29, 1895, a black man accused of murdering a white woman was snatched from police custody by a mob of two hundred men. Henry Hilliard was burned alive while tied to a stake on the courthouse square in Tyler, Texas, in front of seven thousand cheering spectators. It took fifty minutes for him to die.[76] Another, earlier, lynching was even worse. On February 1, 1893, some fifteen thousand spectators converged in Paris, Texas, to observe, participate in, and condone the lynching of Henry Smith by torture and burning. Smith, a black man, was accused of raping and murdering three-year-old Myrtle Vance, a white girl.[77] The account of this gruesome spectacle was condemned in newspapers across the country and lent support to the emerging antilynching movement. One Southerner weighing in on the condemnation side of the issue was L. E. Bleckley, Chief Justice of the Georgia Supreme Court, who explained a fundamental truth about lynching:

> There is a widespread opinion among good and fairly sensible people that no guilt whatever is involved in such a killing, except an artificial guilt manufactured by the law. . . . The prevalence of this opinion is the mainstay and support of mob massacre. . . . Mobs are generally actuated by a most intense feeling of right and justice, and it is sympathy with and par-

ticipation in this feeling by the neighboring population which screens the lynchers not only from punishment but in most cases from accusations and trial.[78]

As we have explored earlier, the motivations of individual mob members may be varied and complex—more complex than Judge Bleckley realized when he laid it all off on the psychological satisfaction of a strong gut-justice instinct sated by the infliction of immediate and fitting retribution upon the perpetrator of an egregious wrong while, at the same time, sending out a strong message of deterrence to others who might be inclined to commit similar acts. The craving for revenge intensified when the mob believed that the miscreant, if not lynched, might get away with his crime because of the all-too-frequent misfires of the immature criminal justice system. In addition to other motivating factors, some mob members (such as Marion Potter in the 1896 Wichita Falls lynching incident) undoubtedly had personal axes to grind. To say the least, a potent blend of mixed motives likely seized the psyches of most of the self-appointed executioners.

However motivated, the macabre 1896 hangings in Wichita Falls as well as the horrific brutality of other contemporaneous lynchings in the state caused a growing clamor of protests as more courageous citizens[79] and an increasing number of influential newspapers[80] joined the crusade. In 1897 Gov. Charles A. Culberson called a special session of the Texas Legislature to address these issues. As previously noted, the legislature did pass statutes designed to curb the appellate court's practice of reversing convictions on account of trivial trial errors. Governor Culberson also proposed an antilynching bill to the legislature, his proposal resulting in the passage of a statute entitled "Murder by Mob Violence." The preamble of that act noted that "no adequate law for the suppression of mob violence" existed. Under the new law, if two or more persons "combined for the purpose of mob violence" and in pursuance of such combination willfully took the life of "any reasonable creature," then the defendant, if convicted, must be sentenced either to life imprisonment or death. Also, if any peace officer permitted any person in his custody to be released to a mob, then that officer would be deemed to be guilty of "official misconduct" and removed from office.[81] As a practical matter, however, the 1897 antilynching law did little, or nothing, to curb mob violence in the state. In 1899 the Court of Criminal Appeals seriously limited the law's scope by interpreting the statute to apply only when the lynch victim was forcibly taken from police custody by a mob.[82] Worse yet, it doesn't appear from appellate records that anyone was ever convicted under that statute. It was quite one thing for legislators in Austin to pass a high-minded abstract law; it was quite another thing for local elected officials (trial judges, prosecutors, and sheriffs) to arrest, prosecute, and convict any of their prominent constituents against overwhelming sentiment to the contrary in their counties.

Judge Bleckley was certainly right about one thing: the prevalence and continuation of lynch law depended on the approval and support of the local community. Regardless of whatever antilynch laws might be on the books, lynching people would continue until the local community support and approval was, if not abolished, at least substantially suppressed. That, in turn, would require a monumental shift in public mores and beliefs—a shift that would not come easily or swiftly. In fact, two decades after the Wichita Falls lynching of Crawford and Lewis, a brutal lynching took place only fifty miles southwest of Wichita Falls in the small town of Seymour. On August 8, 1916, Stephen Brown, a black man and a prisoner of Baylor County Sheriff W. L. Ellis, overpowered the sheriff, murdered him, and escaped. He was captured before sundown and promptly hanged on the local courthouse square before a cheering crowd. Then, while the lifeless body was dangling there, they gathered lumber, started a fire, and burned it. Their rage still not sated, the mobsters proceeded to round up every black person in Seymour they could capture. In the ensuing melee, somebody threw a rock that hit a black child in the head. The child died. The next day the mob herded all their captives to the local railroad depot, loaded them on the next outbound train, and deported them. Nobody gave any serious consideration to prosecuting those responsible for either death.[83]

In both the 1896 Wichita Falls lynching of Crawford and Lewis and the 1916 lynching of Stephen Brown in Seymour, prominent members of the community were foremost in the lynch mobs, and none bothered with masks or any other form of disguise, yet nobody was ever convicted of any offense connected with these incidents. In the Wichita Falls incident, however, Judge George Miller did actively pursue criminal prosecutions and was at least successful in pressuring a Wichita County grand jury into indicting six of the mob leaders. Also, as we have seen, the Wichita Falls lynching stirred such statewide publicity and debate that the state legislature did finally pass an antilynching statute at its next session (although that law, as we have also seen, proved ineffective because of a lack of public support on local levels).

On the other hand, the Seymour lynching that occurred two decades later caused precious little outcry by anybody—in the community or elsewhere in the state. Two reasons may be advanced for this disparity of public reaction. First, while Wichita Falls was not a large city, it was one of the larger cities in West Texas and was located on a major railroad line, whereas Seymour was a tiny and remote West Texas village even in 1916. In addition, it was all done so quickly (the killing of the sheriff and the lynching happened the same day) that there was no prior press coverage and no opportunity for eager outsiders to throng into Seymour for the upcoming show. Secondly, and undoubtedly more significantly, was the race factor: the Wichita Falls lynching was white-on-white while the Seymour lynching was white-on-black.

Nevertheless, by 1916 public opinion was beginning to change significantly—even when the lynchings were white-on-black. On May 15, 1916, in the Central Texas town of Waco, a young black man, Jesse Washington, age eighteen, who had been accused of the rape and murder of a white woman, was maimed, castrated, and subjected to prolonged torture before he was burned at the stake and hanged in the presence of a boisterous and remorseless crowd of fifteen thousand spectators, most of whom would, no doubt, have claimed to be God-fearing Christians.[84] Several other white-on-black lynchings had occurred in the Waco area between 1910 and 1916, all of which were unusually gruesome and witnessed by several thousand cheering spectators.[85]

For sheer barbarity, however, the sadistic lynching of Jesse Washington was unsurpassed, and it triggered an avalanche of outrage in state, national, and even international media. The National Association for the Advancement of Colored People and other reform groups descended on Waco and ensured that this travesty of justice would never by forgotten there or elsewhere.[86] That awful spectacle thus galvanized the nation and marshaled support for the antilynching movement. The lynching of Jesse Washington would prove to be a turning point in public opinion: no longer would local leaders publicly support, praise, and encourage the use of extralegal violence.[87] The lynching of Jesse Washington would not be the last lynching in Texas, or in the rest of the nation for that matter, but it greatly accelerated the nascent cultural and intellectual antilynching sentiment and led to a marked decline in the size and frequency of lynch mobs.

The first lynch-free year in Texas was 1925.[88] In the United States, the number of deaths by lynching declined from 230 victims in the peak year of 1893 to 86 victims in 1919. A decade later there were only nine lynchings recorded in the nation.[89]

HIGH NOON IN PADUCAH

"I Kilt Him Purty . . . Real Purty."

Gripping his hot-headed client's arm with all his might, Charlie Coombes whispered a hoarse warning: "You can't kill them all before they get you." Farley Sayers hissed back, "I would die happy, because before those sons-of-bitches could kill me, I would get half a dozen of them!"[1]

Mincing no words, lawyer Coombes reminded his client that—suicidal bravado notwithstanding—nothing in their contract obligated *him* to face a firing squad. Only then did Sayers finally relent, remove his hand from the concealed pistol, and desist from carrying out his threat to shoot not only the trial judge but also his accuser, Burk Burnett, and the well-armed contingent of Burnett's cowboys who were glaring at them from across the courtroom.

The scene: the Knox County District Court in Benjamin, Texas, 1908.

The little town of Benjamin marks the beginning of a distinctly different kind of ranch country—a huge and remote chunk of northwest Texas so sparsely populated that folks still, to this day, call it "the Big Empty"; a dry and windswept land of rough cedar breaks, steep canyons, buttes, mesas, a few cottonwood and hackberry trees in dry draws, and some mesquite-dotted grassy flats. This broken prairie land rolls on westward from Benjamin for seventy miles or so before it runs headlong into the rearing Caprock escarpment defining the eastern edge of the Staked Plains of far West Texas and the Texas Panhandle. Wild things live there—small creatures mostly, such as coyotes and jackrabbits and rattlesnakes—as well as some cattle and still fewer human beings. It is a lonely—yet hauntingly beautiful—country, so vast and sweeping that it dwarfs mere men and horses and cattle, somehow conveying the sense that it is a land that time has passed by, that lies patiently awaiting the return of great prehistoric beasts—inhabitants more fitting to the hushed vastness.

Perhaps it was that harsh and unforgiving place and time that had something to do with forging the steel of two outsized westerners: Burk Burnett and Farley Sayers. Both were ruthless in pursuit of their goals. And neither was a stranger to violence. In retrospect, it seems clear that Burnett, the gruff, rough-hewn old pioneer lion, and the brash, young, and fearless Sayers, the upstart little rancher who dared to challenge him, were locked together in a death-dance for several years before the final curtain fell.

What happened between Sayers and Burnett leading up to their showdown is a fascinating, yet troubling, yarn of unswerving determination and violence played out on that stark frontier landscape. The inevitable confrontation, when it finally came, was a far cry from the traditional Hollywood confrontation played out on the big screen: the fair and square, one-on-one, face-to-face shootout at high noon in the middle of Main Street between a black hat and a white hat. As it turned out, the "high noon" part of that scenario was about the only aspect that followed the script.

At the time of their final confrontation in 1912, Sayers was only thirty-two years of age while Burnett was sixty-four. By then Burnett was a rich and powerful man—a millionaire Fort Worth banker and owner of the huge Four Sixes (6666) Ranch. Sayers and Burnett owned adjoining ranches in the Big Empty—King County, to be exact. However, Sayers's modest 1,280-acre pasture amounted to no more than a wart on an elephant's behind when compared to Burnett's 300,000-plus-acre spread. Nevertheless, it was to prove an exceedingly irritating wart.

BURK BURNETT

Burnett was raised up hard, and in some mean times. Born on New Year's Day 1849 in Missouri, Burk grew up in the midst of pre–Civil War chaos and guerrilla warfare. When he was only ten years of age he witnessed a terrifying spectacle: a band of Kansas Jayhawkers descended on the Burnett homestead one night and burned it to the ground, together with all the family's other assets. It was then that Burk's father, Jerry Burnett, decided to migrate to Texas, and in 1859 the family settled in Denton County, just north of Dallas.[2]

One year in Denton County's frontier school was the extent of Burk Burnett's formal education.[3] Then in 1863, Jerry Burnett, joined the Confederate army, leaving Burk, his oldest son, to care for the family's livestock and crops and to keep a wary eye peeled for marauding Indians. The Kiowa and Comanche, emboldened by the diversion of most able-bodied settlers to Civil War fronts, increased their raids and extended their rampages farther and farther eastward into more settled areas. All in all it was a daunting challenge for a fourteen-year-old boy.

But things soon got worse. In 1863, shortly after his father left for the army, his mother, Nancy Burnett, died of consumption, leaving seven young children dependent on Burk.

Following the Civil War, Jerry Burnett returned home and began gathering stray, wild cattle on the Texas frontier, soon becoming a successful trail driver. In 1867, when Burk was eighteen years of age, with only one year's prior experience as a trail driver, his father put him in charge of a crew of older cowboys trailing 1,700 longhorns up the Chisholm Trail to Abilene, Kansas. Osage Indians

Burk Burnett, pioneer rancher, banker, oil man, and businessman. Around the turn of the century he cobbled together the famous 6666 Ranch covering approximately a third of a million acres in West Texas and the Texas Panhandle. *(Courtesy Special Collections, University of Texas at Arlington Library, Arlington, Texas)*

promptly raided the outfit and stole about twenty horses, leaving Burk's men with only one mount each. Exhibiting a determination that was to become his trademark, Burk was undaunted.[4] His solution to the problem was simply to trail the herd afoot by day (thus resting the few remaining horses), then to ride the horses by night to protect and hold the herd together. That young Burk was able to implement and enforce such a plan on older and seasoned cowboys who were congenitally averse to undertaking any task that could not be accomplished on horseback (not to mention the most unappealing and humbling prospect of proud cowboys being unhorsed and forced to walk all the way to Kansas) says much for Burk's leadership ability and force of character as well as his implacable will to prevail at any cost. They made it to Abilene, herd intact. As one old-timer later grudgingly recalled, "Hell, he would have taken that bunch of cattle through if he had to drag the lead steer by the tail."[5]

His father gave him a share of the profits from that drive, and that was the seed money with which Burk launched his eminently successful career as a cattleman and banker. Burk soon began branding his cattle "6666," and the myth persists to this day that he got his start by winning a large number of cattle as well as a ranch in a poker game—Burk's winning hand being, of course, four sixes.[6] Though not literally true, still the tale catches something of the essence of the man: a daring and coolly calculating gambler.

Those qualities of Burk's character were best highlighted by what happened when Burk and a longhorn herd reached Abilene, Kansas, at a most inopportune time in the fall of 1873: they called it "the Panic of 1873." A nationwide financial crisis caused the bottom to drop out of the cattle market. Burk found himself stuck in Kansas with a large bunch of cattle that he could scarcely give away. Financial ruin seemed inevitable.[7]

In an odd and most ironic twist of fate, Burk struck a deal with his old nemesis, the Osage Indian tribe, to secure grazing rights on its reservation. (We may safely surmise that Burk Burnett discreetly refrained from calling attention to the remuda that the Osage had stolen from him not so many moons ago.) At any rate, having secured the grazing rights, Burnett retreated southward with his herd and rode out the 1873–1874 season on Osage grasslands. When he again took them to market in Abilene in the fall of 1874, the cattle market had recovered considerably, plus the cattle were in good shape, plus their value was enhanced by an additional year's growth. Bottom line was, instead of suffering a financial disaster, Burk returned to Texas with a $10,000 profit in his saddle bags.[8]

Burk then adopted another strategy that demonstrated his business acumen, a practice soon copied by other cattle drivers. He bought only steers, then fattened them for market before heading them north to Kansas.

However, the times were changing, and the days of successful cattle drives to Kansas were drawing to a close. Ever attuned to financial trends, Burk saw the future, and it lay to the west. Therefore, after Col. Ranald S. Mackenzie's army soundly thrashed the Comanches and Kiowas in 1874 during the battle of Tule Canyon in the Texas Panhandle, banishing them to reservations in Oklahoma, Burnett bought about thirty-five thousand acres of cheap land (twenty-five cents per acre) south of the Red River and just north and west of Wichita Falls, Texas.[9] Of course, Burk and other

Fearsome Comanche war chief Quanah Parker, son of Chief Peta Nocona and a white captive, Cynthia Ann Parker. After being defeated by Col. Ranald S. Mackenzie and his troopers in 1874 at the battle of Tule Canyon in the Texas Panhandle, Quanah adjusted to reservation life and became a close friend and business associate of cattle barons Burk Burnett, W. T. Waggoner, C. T. Herring, and others who leased reservation lands with Quanah's assistance. *(Courtesy Panhandle-Plains Historical Museum, Canyon, Texas)*

wealthy cattlemen were not limited to owned acreage. Their herds also grazed over thousands of unfenced acres of free range.

But the free-wheeling days of the open range were numbered. A steadily increasing stream of settlers began to trickle into West Texas, plus a fellow named Glidden invented the devil's own device: barbed wire. Many of the big cattlemen saw only doom and gloom ahead. But Burk Burnett and a few others saw another opportunity to reap huge profits—another vast and untapped open range. It lay to the north, just across the Red River in the Territory. The Comanche, Apache, and Kiowa Indian Reservation encompassed hundreds of thousands of acres of lush grasslands—a large chunk of which, located in the southern part of the reservation, was referred to as the "Big Pasture" by the cattle barons.

Staggered by a devastating drought in the early 1880s, Burnett and other cattle barons such as Dan Waggoner, E. C. Sugg, J. P. Addington, and C. T. Herring began pushing their herds across the Red River and onto the reservation. Never mind that they hadn't bothered with troublesome details, such as first obtaining formal grazing leases from the federal government. They went about "making themselves at home, building corrals and fences and establishing camps" with the cooperation of the Indians.[10] The cattlemen found themselves growing very fond of their former enemy. Those bitter foes the Indians had suddenly become important allies.

Thus began the courtship of the Indians by "the Big Five," Burk Burnett being the point man. Junk beads, calico, and an occasional jug of cheap rotgut would not do. Diamond stick pins, pearl-handled revolvers, and fun expeditions to Fort Worth, Dallas, and Washington, D.C., were the ticket. Plus, free beef and some cash. Quanah Parker, the last great Comanche chief, was the principal recipient of the Big Five's largess, although several lesser chiefs were also wooed. Quanah was put on the cattlemen's "payroll" for unspecified services at fifty dollars per month while four lesser chiefs received twenty-five dollars per month cash.[11] Later, Burnett decided that a leader of Quanah's stature deserved better digs than a primitive tee-pee, so he constructed an impressive "Comanche White House" on the banks of West Cache Creek for his new friend: two stories consisting of twenty-two rooms (including a separate bedroom for each of Quanah's several wives and their fifteen children), all of which featured fancy furnishings. At the time, it was the only permanent structure between Fort Sill and the Texas border.[12]

On one occasion, however, the Big Five's courtship almost cost Quanah his life. In 1885 Dan Waggoner financed a holiday excursion to Fort Worth and lodged Quanah and Chief Yellow Bear in a modern hotel that featured such high-falutin' and unaccustomed conveniences as gas lights. When, after being properly wined and dined, Quanah and Yellow Bear retired for the evening, they simply blew out the light as was their custom back on the reservation. As a result the "bad air" asphyxiated Yellow Bear during the night and almost killed Quanah as well.[13]

Despite that mishap, the courtship proved highly successful for all members of the Big Five club, and Burnett ended up with three hundred thousand acres of choice grazing land. At first, it cost only gifts, small amounts of "payroll" cash, and all the beef the Indians could eat. Later, the federal government objected to the practice of allowing the Indians themselves to lease their reservations and

The "Star House"—the mansion that Burk Burnett built in 1893 for his Co-manche friend, Quanah Parker, no doubt as a token of Burk's appreciation for Quanah's assistance in helping Burk secure, at a very favorable rate, a grazing lease lasting for almost a quarter of a century and covering about three hundred thousand acres of Oklahoma Territory grasslands. The two-story, twenty-two-room structure was located near the foot of the Wichita Mountains and was the only permanent structure between Fort Sill (Lawton, Oklahoma) and the Texas border. Because U.S. Army generals' rank was denoted by stars, Quanah had gigantic white stars painted on the roof of his "Star House" to underscore the fact that a chief lived there. *(Courtesy Panhandle-Plains Historical Museum, Canyon, Texas)*

threatened to terminate the leases. But Burnett was not about to lose this bird's nest on the ground. In 1889, he loaded up his Indian protégé and headed straight to Pres. Benjamin Harrison's office in Washington, D.C., where he and Chief Quanah persuaded the president to continue the lucrative leasing practices.[14] The leases were renegotiated, however, and the cattle barons were required to pay six and a half cents per acre and to make their payments to individual members of the tribes. Still, it was a cheap lease indeed.

The cattle barons were happy. Quanah Parker was happy. The old chief benefited personally from his association with the cattlemen far more than other members of the tribes. The fact that gifts and favors to Quanah smacked of outright bribery seemed not to have bothered anyone. As Bill Neeley, one of Quanah Parker's biographers, explained, "ethics and morality had no place in the business world in the late nineteenth century."[15]

By 1900 the federal government was under ever-increasing pressure from land-hungry settlers, merchants, and traders to open the Oklahoma Territory for settlement. After all, they argued, the Indians were doing very little to put these lands to any productive use, and why should a handful of cattle barons be allowed to enrich themselves while thousands of hardworking poor folks sat on the sidelines watching the rich get richer? Thus the battle was joined, and the lineups of the competing teams were curious indeed: the feds and the nesters versus the cowboys and the Indians—bedfellows most strange and yet symbiotic, to understate the matter. In 1900 the secretary of the Interior ordered the cattlemen to vacate the reservations. Fortunately for Burnett and his cohorts, Theodore Roosevelt had just ascended to the presidency in 1901 after the assassination of Pres. William McKinley. Unlike the stodgy old McKinley, the old Rough Rider and former Dakota cattleman was just the kind of vibrant, open-collared go-getter who could talk—and understand—Burnett's frontier cowman lingo. Burk took full advantage of the situation. Accompanied by Texas Senator Joe Weldon Bailey, he bypassed the Secretary of the Interior and went straight to the top, laying out the cowmen's case to the president himself—pointing out how ruinous it would be to throw these big outfits off their leases with no place to go with their large herds. He appealed for sufficient time to make necessary arrangements either to effect an orderly liquidation of their herds or to find other pastures. He found a sympathetic listener in President Teddy and won a two-year extension.[16]

The cattle barons continued to court the genial president. In January 1905 Chief Quanah Parker was dispatched to ride (in full Comanche regalia, of course) in President Roosevelt's inaugural parade.[17] Later, in 1905, the Big Five invited their favorite president to a Wild West-style wolf hunt in the Oklahoma Territory. As they

The cream of West Texas and Oklahoma pioneers were on hand in 1905 to escort Pres. Teddy Roosevelt on one of his most famous outdoor adventures—a wolf hunt in the Oklahoma Territory. Jack Abernathy, standing center, was notorious for his ability to catch wolves with his bare hands. Standing (*left to right*): A. W. Bivins, Capt. Bill McDonald, Abernathy, S. B. Young, S. B. (Burk) Burnett, Roosevelt, and L. M. Gillis. Comanche Chief Quanah Parker is kneeling in front of Bivins and McDonald. Seated (*left to right*) are two unidentified soldiers, R. L. More, Guy Waggoner, Cecil Lyons, Dr. Lambert, and D. P. (Phy) Taylor. *(Courtesy Panhandle-Plains Historical Museum, Canyon, Texas)*

expected, it was just the kind of adventure the vigorous Rough Rider couldn't resist. In eager anticipation of a mounted chase, Theodore Roosevelt arrived, as westerners of the day might have put it, "full of beans and rarin' to go." The hunt proved a great success, high-lighted by noted wolf-catcher Jack Abernathy displaying his unique method of capturing wild wolves alive: He would chase the wolf on horseback until he finally came abreast of the tiring beast. Then, still riding full speed ahead, he would bail off his horse and bulldog the animal, whereupon, with his bare hands, he would clamp the wolf's jaws together and then wire them shut. Meanwhile, the Big Five and their entourage were spurring deep and riding frantically just to keep up with the hard-charging Abernathy, the beleaguered wolf, and the exuberant president of the United States of America. Of course all the prairie Caesars and their staunch ally, Chief Quanah Parker, were in the chase and on hand throughout the expedition to ensure that the president received royal treatment. Roosevelt was much impressed, his robust appetite for action-adventure sated—at least for the time being.[18] (Afterward he invited Abernathy to Washington, D.C., saying he wanted Jack to see if he couldn't wire shut the jaws of some of the president's least favorite and most vocal senators.)

One way or another, the extension to vacate was stretched from two to five years, and it was 1905 before the last 6666 critter was chased back across the Red River into Texas. For almost a quarter of a century Burnett had the benefit of almost three hundred thousand acres of lush Oklahoma Territory grassland for a pittance. It was the foundation of his fortune.

But Burnett was not done yet. Always ahead of the curve, he foresaw the end of the cheap Indian leases long before he was finally forced off the reservation. By the time he finally lost the Big Pasture lease in the Oklahoma Territory in 1905, he had already moved westward once again and purchased huge hunks of West Texas real estate for a few dollars per acre. In 1900 he completed the purchase of the 141,000-acre "8" Ranch in King County, and in 1902 he bought the 108,000-acre Dixon Creek Ranch in Carson and Hutchinson counties in the Texas Panhandle.[19] Over the next few years, Burnett kept aggressively acquiring adjacent lands so that his cattle empire swelled to nearly a third of a million acres. Headquarters was at Guthrie, the county seat of King County.

Burnett was blessed with more than his share of native intelligence, business acumen, determination, and the steel nerves of a river-boat gambler shoving in his whole stash on a nine-high bluff. He displayed uncanny foresight in making financial investments. And besides all that, he was lucky as hell. By the 1920s all those lands he had purchased around the turn of the century began sprouting oil and gas wells like toadstools in a swamp. Meanwhile, in 1900, Burk moved to Fort Worth, where he lived for the rest of his life and where he ventured into other profitable enterprises, which included becoming a director and principal stockholder of the First National Bank of Fort Worth.

Whether dealing with Indians, cattle thieves, nesters, other cattlemen, or U.S. presidents, Burk Burnett repeatedly displayed an unswerving determination to expand and to have his own way, and his steel will was edged with a certain ruthless disregard for the impact his deeds had on others—even his own family.

Burk's first marriage, to Ruth B. Lloyd, ended in divorce. In 1892 he married Mary Couts Barradel, a well-educated and refined widow. Unfortunately, after a few years their relationship also soured. In view of what happened later, Burk's next move sounds suspiciously like a strategy to avoid an expensive, and perhaps a socially embarrassing, divorce battle. He filed a petition in a Fort Worth court alleging that Mary was insane, suffering from a "hallucination" that Burk intended to kill her. It can safely be surmised that Burnett, always tight with a penny,[20] abhorred the idea of anyone divesting him of a large chunk of his fortune. It also does not seem a far-fetched speculation that, considering Burnett's tremendous wealth, prestige, and power in Fort Worth, he might not have experienced too much difficulty in persuading a local judge to sympathize with his predicament and thus agree that Mary was insane. In any event, the court declared that Mary was, in fact, insane. As it turned out, subsequent events cast doubt on the court's finding. But to give credit where due, Burk didn't have his wife shipped off to some dreary public insane asylum. Instead, he had her confined to a comfortable home in Weatherford, Texas, and there the unwilling patient languished from 1911 until Burnett died in 1922. The day after he died, Mary escaped. Then she hired a lawyer and had herself declared legally sane. Also, since Burk had cut her out of his will entirely, she filed a successful will contest suit and thus obtained half of Burk's $6 million fortune—$6 million being the equivalent of approximately $72 million in 2006 dollars. (When Mary died, she left most of her $3 million to Texas Christian University in Fort Worth. As one reporter observed: "She probably found no small satisfaction in leaving her money to a university to which her husband had declined to contribute.")[21] Burk also cut his son, Tom Burnett, his only surviving child, out of his will (except for a relatively modest annual stipend) on account of Tom's unexplained "filial misconduct."[22]

Burk Burnett never wasted any sympathy on, or showed any mercy toward, thieves of any kind, as we saw in the previous chapter when Burk watched with approval while a mob lynched Lewis and Crawford in downtown Wichita Falls in 1896. His first violent encounter with a cattle rustler occurred in the summer of 1879 in Clay County, just east of Wichita Falls. A rustler named Jack King, "a man with bad habits, and a terror on the frontier,"[23] smeared his brand over Burk's brand on about twenty steers. Burk cut the cattle out of King's herd and drove them home. The next day King, accompanied by cohorts Pat Walford and Jim Garrison, showed up at Burk's place and announced his intention to retrieve the steers. In the ensuing encounter Burk fired off three or four rounds, and King fell dead with a bullet hole in his head. His two henchmen decided to let the matter drop and rode off. Burk was tried in the Clay County District Court for murder, but he was acquitted on his plea of self-defense.[24]

FARLEY SAYERS

At the turn of the century, Farley Sayers was twenty years of age, born July 11, 1879. His parents owned a small ranch in the western part of King County near Burnett's sprawling empire.[25] Sayers, however, was determined to build his own ranching empire. Trouble was, Farley lacked both capital and backers. Plus, by the turn of the century, there wasn't much cheap land left for settlement. Most of the big spreads had already been put together (and not infrequently at the expense of small ranchers, farmers, nesters, and squatters) during the 1870s, 1880s, and into the 1890s. By the time the big cattle barons made their fortunes, they were disinclined to tolerate young upstarts making aggressive land plays, or anybody else exhibiting loose branding practices. (Never mind that only a few years earlier, this was exactly the way many of them had seized and stocked their cattle kingdoms.)[26] By the 1890s, the cattle kings had abandoned this laissez-faire attitude, and they got downright persnickety about other folks' branding habits.

The tale is told that some years after Burnett and Dan Waggoner had established their cattle empires, Waggoner dropped in for a visit at Burnett's 6666 Ranch. Burnett insisted Waggoner stay for dinner, assuring Waggoner that he would serve him "something that he had never eaten before." But when nothing was set on the table that appeared to be exotic, Waggoner reminded Burk he had promised that something he had never eaten before would be on the menu. "Oh, there is," Burk smirked. "Taste a piece of your own beef!"[27]

However, it cannot be denied that cattle rustling posed a major problem for the big ranches. In 1877 Burnett was one of the pioneer North Texas cattlemen who met at Graham, Texas, to form an organization dedicated to combating cattle thieving, which had become endemic on their ranges. The organization would become known as the Texas and Southwestern Cattle Raisers Association (T&SCRA), a quasi-legal group that to this day vigorously pursues cow country outlaws.

Meanwhile, young Farley Sayers was determined, come hell or high water, to make his own mark as a cattle baron, and he did not intend to be denied his dream. During the first twelve years of the new century Sayers must not have gotten much sleep because he was relentless in pursuing his goal. During that time, by hook or crook, and by unflagging industry, he did manage to acquire some property, including two sections of land (1,280 acres) right in the heart of Burnett's ranch. It is also very probable that he acquired, by means other than purchase, some of Burnett's unbranded calves. Sayers thus became a thorn in Burnett's side, and Burnett, the proud and the powerful, was not inclined to countenance disrespect, much less outright thievery, from any man—especially from a young whipper-snapper with the audacity to challenge him openly.

Even as a youngster, Sayers displayed a rambunctious, rowdy streak bordering on open defiance of anyone in authority, all of which resulted in numerous clashes with local lawmen. Although all of his youthful offenses were misdemeanors (none of which resulted in convictions), the mold was cast, and an ever-widening rift developed between Sayers, the son of nesters, and the cattle barons who dominated cow country lawmen. One eminent trial lawyer of the day, Charles Coombes, later expressed an opinion that peace officers and prosecuting attorneys "hounded [Farley Sayers] into becoming an outlaw."[28]

Coombes recalled one youthful incident that illustrated Sayers' fiery temperament as well as his utter fearlessness. Once, when Coombes was serving as district attorney of the 50th Judicial District, he was working with a King County grand jury in Guthrie. Noontime came and the grand jury foreman asked to be excused briefly to attend to some personal business matters. When he returned later that afternoon it was obvious he had been in a fight. "He was the most bruised and bloodiest person, not to be seriously injured, I have ever seen," Coombs recalled. Naturally the grand jury was inquisitive, but the foreman, who was a strong and robust man, at first declined to give any account of the matter. Finally, however, he relented and told the grand jurors that he had gone to see Farley Sayers about a business difference. The encounter immediately grew heated. Sayers was mounted on his horse at the time, while the grand jury foreman was standing beside the horse. The foreman grabbed Sayers by the leg and told him he was going to pull him off his horse and beat the hell out of him, whereupon Sayers whipped him about the head and face with his lariat until he turned loose. The grand jury wanted to indict Sayers, but the foreman wouldn't have it. "No," he said, "I brought it all on myself. I was the aggressor. He simply defended himself, as he had the right to do. Besides, I am a grown, matured man, while he is yet a boy." Lawyer Coombes concluded that Sayers had found at least "one just man."[29] Many others in King County did not view Farley as a bad man, at least not in the early years, for he was elected a King County commission-

Charles E. Coombes was a pioneer West Texas lawyer, a preeminent defense attorney. He later moved to Abilene, Texas, where he served as mayor from 1923 to 1927. After retirement he penned a narrative account of some of his most colorful trials in his book, *The Prairie Dog Lawyer*. *(From the* Abilene Reporter News, April 14, 1923)

er. Obviously he was popular with the "little folks," whose clique opposed the big cattlemen headed by Burk Burnett. To rub more salt into the cattle barons' wound, Sayers, as a county commissioner, also served as a member of the county's board of tax equalization, which set ad valorem tax values on all the lands in the county (including Burnett's Four Sixes Ranch).

Two incidents, both occurring in 1907, probably marked the turning point in Farley Sayers's life. First, on August 17, he was accused of stealing some unbranded calves from the 6666 Ranch. Farley found a remote box canyon on his ranch (adjacent to the Four Sixes) and fenced off the entrance end. Then, apparently, with the assistance of a 6666 cowboy named Roy Berry, he drove four or more of Burk Burnett's cows and their unbranded calves into this trap, separated the calves from the cows, and then drove the cows back home to the Four Sixes, leaving the unbranded calves in his trap for several days to be weaned. However, before the weaning process was complete, 6666 line rider Charlie Hart noticed the mother cows, bags swollen with milk, pacing back and forth along the fence that divided the Four Sixes from Farley's ranch. The cows were bellowing and bawling, obviously trying to reunite with their calves. Charlie Hart notified King County Sheriff William "Bill" McCarren of these suspicious circumstances, and McCarren and several 6666 cowboys then discovered the unbranded, unweaned calves in Sayers's box canyon trap. The hungry calves were also bawling and pacing back and forth.[30]

A. C. "Arb" Piper, a retired Four Sixes cowboy, recalled that when he first started cowboying for the Sixes in about 1929, the rotting trap fences that Sayers had erected to block off the blind box canyon were still evident. A.C.'s younger brother, Waylon "Toar" Piper, also an old-time 6666 cowboy, remembered seeing the remnants.[31]

Secondly, on September 5—less than a month after Sayers was accused of stealing the unbranded calves from the 6666 but before an indictment was returned against him—Farley had a run-in with Sam Graves (one of the Four Sixes cowboys who had discovered Burnett's unbranded calves). A heated argument ensued. Lawyer Coombes tells the story this way:

> Sayers discovered that his accuser was armed while he was unarmed, so he said, "Lay aside your gun and I will fight you any way you want to fight, with knives or fists, or if you will let me go get my gun, I will shoot it out with you." Graves refused. Then Sayers said, "All right, if you are a damn coward you will shoot me in the back."
>
> As he rode away Graves shot him through his right shoulder with a soft-nosed bullet, knocking him from his horse. Indictments against Sayers for cattle theft and against Graves for assault with intent to murder followed. I was employed to defend Sayers and prosecute Graves.[32]

Graves, apparently, was not the only 6666 hand to try to kill Sayers. According to A. C. Piper, it was common knowledge that another 6666 hand, Lee Oldham, also took a potshot at Sayers, but missed.[33]

Sayers and Roy Berry, a 6666 cowboy, were both indicted and summoned to trial for the theft of four of Burk Burnett's unbranded calves. The alleged theft occurred in King County and indictments were returned by a King County grand jury, but the trial was held in Benjamin, county seat of neighboring Knox County, on a change of venue.[34] Coombes filed a motion to sever the cases, which was granted, and Coombes managed to get Berry tried first because, according to Coombes, the case against Berry was much weaker. He anticipated being able to enlist considerable jury sympathy for Berry, and, of course, a prior acquittal of Berry would only enhance Farley's chances of an acquittal. The crafty Coombes also had another trick up his sleeve in maneuvering the prosecution into trying Berry ahead of Sayers.

First, however, Coombes had a more pressing problem. One of the most difficult tasks a trial lawyer faces is dealing with emotionally distraught clients. And Sayers was, according to Coombes, more than a little distraught when he came to trial—he was outraged. He came to court armed with a pistol concealed under his left arm. Meanwhile, Burk Burnett brought to court an armed garrison consisting not only of 6666 cowboys but also other cattle barons of the area. Coombes's first task was to ensure that a full-scale war did not break out before the trial could get under way. This proved to be a very difficult task indeed.

It was during a recess in the trial that the episode described at the beginning of this story occurred. Farley became so enraged at District Judge Dickson and Burk Burnett that he threatened to draw his concealed pistol and kill them both on the spot. Coombes realized that it was no empty threat, noting that Sayers was "instantaneous on the draw, quick on the trigger, never missed a shot, never knew fear, and when enraged was a most dangerous man." It was at that point that Coombes warned Sayers of the inevitable and lethal consequences of any rash act, and Sayers retorted that he didn't care—would "die happy" because he could kill half a dozen of "those SOBs" before they nailed him.

Sayers was finally dissuaded when Coombes reminded him that such a move would bring certain death upon both of them, and that he had no hankering to play sacrificial lamb just to satisfy Sayers's rage for vengeance.[35] Coombes finally got possession of the pistol, and the trial proceeded.

A large jury panel was called, and both companion cattle theft cases (the case against Roy Berry and the case against Farley Sayers) were to be tried *out of the same panel*. Berry, due to Coombes's finagling, was tried first. According to Coombes's account, most of the potential jurors had strong prior dispositions—some leaning strongly for the prosecution (read, "big ranchers") and some leaning strongly for the defense (read, "nesters").

It was during jury selection in the Berry case that Coombes executed a bold and risky strategy, not anticipated by the other side or even by the two lawyers who were assisting him (A. J. Fires and Coombes's brother, W. N. Coombes). Coombes used all ten of his peremptory "strikes" to eliminate potential jurors whom he knew *leaned strongly toward his side*, gambling that he could win the Berry case without them. The gamble paid off: the jury found Berry not guilty.

Thereafter, the original jury panel was reconstituted, *excluding*, however, the twelve jurors who served during the Berry trial, but *including* the ten defense-oriented jurors whom Coombes had struck from the Berry jury plus the prosecution's ten "cut-backs," all of whom were returned to court for jury selection in the Farley Sayers trial. The prosecution lawyers, Jack Glasgow and I. H. Burney, took the bait Coombes had so daringly dangled before them. Glasgow and Burney were no neophytes. District Attorney Glasgow was known as "the silver-tongued orator of the Brazos," and I. H. Burney, Burnett's hired gun from Fort Worth, was characterized by Coombes as "one of the greatest and meanest trial lawyers I ever met." They assumed that Coombes would cut these same ten potential jurors (whom they also recognized as probably being defense-oriented) just as he had done in the Berry case, concluding that Coombes must have cut them for personal or political reasons, and thus would *also* cut them again in the Sayers case. So the prosecution did *not* strike these ten defense-oriented jurors whom, otherwise, they surely would have cut. Coombes, of course, did *not* strike them this time, resulting in all ten ending up on the jury, thereby giving Sayers a very long leg up in his case.

In addition, Coombes managed to slide one "sinker" juror past the prosecution. By chance, several weeks before the trial, Coombes had overheard one of the potential jurors make a telling remark to a third party. Burk Burnett was in town that day, and the potential juror upon seeing him had told his friend (within earshot of Coombes) the following: "There is old man Burnett. He stole a steer from me about twenty years ago, and I was never able to do anything about it."[36]

Naturally, therefore, when this fellow showed up on the jury panel, Coombes was very hopeful he would make the final cut. When lead prosecutor I. H. Burney examined the panel he was rigorous in trying to disqualify every juror who did *not* know Burnett. He made the mistake most trial attorneys make at one time or another—he assumed something that was not supported by known fact. He assumed that anybody who knew Burk Burnett would have a favorable opinion of him, and thus be a favorable juror. So when the potential juror who had said Burnett had stolen his steer admitted that he knew Burk Burnett and had known him for twenty years, Burney failed to inquire whether he had a bias in favor of, or a prejudice against, Burnett. Coombes, of course, tippy-toed around the issue when he questioned this prospective juror and eagerly accepted him. Coombes thus figured he had at least one juror in his pocket. If true, that meant his client was, at least, insulated from a conviction.

The case against Farley for stealing Burnett's four unbranded calves was a circumstantial evidence case. Nobody saw him steal the calves. Nobody saw him herd the 6666 cows and their calves into his box canyon trap. Nobody saw him separate the cows from their calves and then drive the cows back home to the 6666 range. After the unbranded calves were discovered in Farley's trap, the King County sheriff and some of Burnett's cowboys clandestinely monitored the site hoping to witness Farley return and exercise some control over the calves. In Coombes's account of the trial, he does not mention any testimony indicating that Farley returned to the box canyon trap or that he was otherwise seen having anything to do with the calves. However, another account does contend that Farley showed up one evening and pitched some grass hay into the trap to feed the calves.[37] After spying on Farley's corral for several days, Sheriff McCarren finally let the bellowing 6666 cows go back into Farley's box canyon trap, whereupon at least some of the calves "mammied up" with the cows. The gist of the prosecution's case against Sayers was this: if one of Burnett's mother cows allowed one of the unbranded calves to suckle her, then it must be her calf (and thus owned by Burnett), and this, coupled with the fact that Burnett's calf was discovered in Farley's corral, constituted strong circumstantial evidence that Farley Sayers had stolen it.

But Coombes was able to cast some doubt on this evidence. On cross-examination, some of the state's witnesses admitted that some of the mother cows would not permit any of the calves in Farley's corral to nurse them. The cowboys and the sheriff who set up on Farley's canyon trap hoping to catch Farley coming back to it (while the calves were still penned there) may have unwittingly contributed to this crack in the state's case because this delay may have completed the weaning process for some of the calves, meaning that some of the cows would have refused to let a calf nurse them. Coombes also produced some rancher "experts" who testified that sometimes (although infrequently) a cow will permit a calf that is not her own to suckle her. Nevertheless, it permitted Coombes to argue that you can't prove the ownership of a calf simply by proving that a particular cow allowed that particular calf to nurse her—certainly not proof "beyond reasonable doubt" sufficient to send a man to prison.[38]

Four Sixes cowboy Sam Graves astride old Hub, a famous cutting horse that won a cutting horse contest at age twenty-two. In 1907 Graves shot an unarmed cattle-rustling suspect, Farley Sayers. He was later convicted of assault with intent to murder. *(Courtesy of Eakin Press)*

The wily Coombes also took advantage of other mistakes of the prosecution, mistakes that might be summed up under the heading of "overplaying your hand." No one likes bullies—including juries. Any jury will resent attempts to coerce it into a verdict. Yet the prosecution and Burk Burnett packed the courtroom with 6666 cowboys plus the owners of other big ranches, all in a show of support—a heavy-handed move, bordering perhaps on arrogance. Also, in view of the jurors, the Sixes cowboys rode into Benjamin each day with their .30-30 rifles scabbarded in their saddles. In his jury argument Coombes made the cattle barons pay for their arrogance:

> I did not fail in my argument to call attention to their presence [referring to the neighboring ranchers Burnett had summoned to pack the courtroom] and the power of their combined wealth and the malice against the defendant shown by their united effort to impress the jury. I called them cattle barons who had left their ranches and homes to attend the trial in a body to influence the decision of the jury.

Another favorable circumstance was that the defendant [Sayers] was county commissioner of the county [King] from where these cattle barons came and, during his term of office as commissioner, was on the Board of Equalization that had assessed their lands and cattle for purposes of [ad valorem] taxation. These facts came out during the trial. So, in my argument, I asked, "Do these cattle barons want to send the defendant to the penitentiary to get rid of him, since they are unable to defeat him at the polls?"[39]

Perhaps the prosecution's worst mistake was calling Sam Graves to the stand. This opened the gate wide for Coombes to inform the jury that Graves had previously shot an unarmed Sayers in the back. This testimony was legally admissible for the purpose of demonstrating Graves's bias against Sayers, thus impeaching his credibility as a witness. It also opened the gate for the scorching attack Coombes made in his final jury argument:

> Why such an array of armed men? Why did these witnesses bring their high-powered guns with them? Are they preparing to kill the defendant, *as one of them tried to do* [referring to Sam Graves shooting Sayers]? Will they shoot him in the back or will all of them train their guns on him at the same time and give him no show for his life?[40]

In the end, on October 17, 1908, Sayers was acquitted of stealing the 6666 calves. Coombes then turned his attention to the attempted murder case against Sam Graves. Although an attorney in private practice, Coombes had been hired by Sayers to assist the district attorney in prosecuting this case.

Trial testimony substantiated Coombes's account of what happened. Sam Graves did, following a heated exchange between the two men at a roundup on the adjacent Pitchfork Ranch, shoot Farley Sayers in the back as Sayers rode away. In summarizing the testimony, the appellate court wrote:

When defendant shot Sayers, Sayers's horse ran to a tree between 100 to 250 yards away. Defendant followed after within about 100 to 60 yards of Sayers, who was on the ground and lying with his head on his brother's knee, and holloed [sic] to [Farley's brother] to get out of the way, and let him finish the son of a bitch, when the brother stated not to shoot anymore, as he would be dead in 15 minutes, and the defendant turned and rode off.[41]

According to the record, Farley then turned to his brother and said that he did not mind dying, but he hated to be shot in the back when he was unarmed.

But Farley Sayers did not die. He would live—live to be shot once again in the back. And, ironically, his brother would live to regret that Farley did not die that day.

At his trial, Graves pleaded self-defense. He testified that during his exchange with Farley just prior to the shooting, Farley had cursed him and had threatened to kill him. He did not deny that he shot Farley as he was riding away from him. However, he contended, implausibly as it must have seemed to the jury, that while Farley was riding away from him, Farley "leaned forward as if to dismount and made a movement with his right hand as if to draw a weapon from his bosom." The fact that Farley was unarmed at the time was not disputed at the trial.[42]

In reviewing the trial on appeal, the Texas Court of Criminal Appeals noted that threats to kill, standing alone, do not afford a justification for killing the maker of the threats; that to perfect a self-defense plea, the defendant must go further and show to the jury's satisfaction that the victim "by some act then done [immediately before he was killed] manifested an intention to execute the threat."[43]

The case against Sam Graves for assault with intent to kill Farley Sayers was tried at Anson in Jones County, Texas, on a change of venue. The Jones County jury was not convinced that Sayers had attempted to draw a nonexistent pistol (or made any movement that could have been construed as an effort to draw a pistol) before Graves shot him, and therefore found Graves guilty and sentenced him to two years in the penitentiary. However, on appeal, the Texas Court of Criminal Appeals reversed the conviction, finding that there was a technical defect in the trial court's instructions to the jury. The case was sent back to Jones County for a retrial. Once again the jury found Sam Graves guilty, but this time assessed no prison time. The jury let Graves off with a fine of approximately two thousand dollars—which was promptly paid by Burk Burnett. Graves got off with only the annoyance of having to endure two trials.[44]

At this point the anger that Farley Sayers harbored against Burk Burnett turned to rage—an emotion no doubt echoed by old Burk Burnett when the jury acquitted that young upstart, cattle-thieving Sayers.

After the trial, lawyer Coombes gave his client a bit of free advice— without doubt the best advice Sayers ever got. He reminded Farley that he had succeeded in accumulating sufficient property to become independent, and that the wise thing for him to do would be to move out of this hostile environment, go farther west, and make a fresh start. He pointed out that even though there was much bad blood between the two of them, Burk Burnett would probably pay him more than his land was worth just to get rid of him. Coombes ended his "Dutch uncle" lecture to Farley with this prophetic advice: "If you remain in his pasture, some day the issue of life or death will arise and Captain Burnett will kill you."

But headstrong Farley was never a very good listener. He replied: "Never, Goddamn him. He can't beat me to my gun."[45]

Shortly thereafter, Farley was indicted yet again for cattle theft (though not of Burnett's cattle), and again Coombes represented him. "I am positive he was innocent of this charge," Coombes later wrote. The venue of this case was changed to Motley County where a jury again found him not guilty. Their trip to Matador (county seat of Motley County) was truly memorable and furnishes further insight into Sayers's devil-take-the-hindmost nature. Coombes and his brother, W. N. Coombes, rode with Sayers to Matador. Coombes remembers:

> Automobiles were then few and far between. Sayers owned a Cadillac with carbide lights. The roads were not built for automobiles. A part of the journey was after night. The lights would not work and we sped down narrow lanes with square corners and sudden curves. When we reached the ranch territory where there was no regular road, Sayers drove at a more reckless rate of speed. My brother would cuss him a while and then beg him a while, but neither did any good. Every once in a while Sayers would take a drink of liquor and drive a little faster. At one point I skylighted something in the road ahead.
>
> "Yonder is a big steer lying in the road," I cried.
>
> "Hell, I'll just run over him," Farley replied. He speeded up, the steer jumped, and we missed him about an inch.
>
> When the case was over, Farley came by the hotel and told me he was ready to take me home. I flatly refused.[46]

Soon he was the target of still another cattle theft indictment and was put to trial. The prosecution proved that Farley had sold some of his own cattle, but also included in the herd was a steer jointly owned by two other men. The prosecution called one partner to prove ownership, and then proved that Farley had sold the steer himself and pocketed all the proceeds.

But when the defense had its turn at bat, Coombes put the *other* partner on the stand, and he testified that Farley had not stolen the steer, but instead, with his permission had sold the steer and sent him a check for the proceeds—and the still uncashed check was introduced into evidence. Yet, with all this, the jury hung up—nine for conviction and three for acquittal. In his memoirs, Coombs commented that by this time the prejudice against Farley had become "so deep-seated you could cut it with a knife. . . . It began to appear impossible for Sayers to have a fair and impartial trial, and this particular case manifested that grand juries would indict him without sufficient evidence."[47]

What also became apparent was that whatever sympathy Farley previously enjoyed from at least a portion of the community had just about evaporated. What happened next undoubtedly bankrupted Farley's remaining reserves of support.

Farley Sayers's mother was deceased, and, near the time of these events, his father died. The headstone in the Dumont cemetery in King County for Joel F. Sayers indicates he died November 25, 1910. The elder Sayers owned a small spread in King County, and Farley was determined to buy out the interests of his siblings (two brothers and two sisters), and thus add the family ranch to his own holdings. However, one sister and an older brother, J. D. "Lellar" Sayers, balked. Thwarting the hot-tempered Farley's demands, of course, guaranteed a full-blown family feud between Farley and his older brother.

The brothers' feud, and its intensity, came to Coombes's attention while he and Farley were awaiting the jury's decision in Farley's third cattle theft trial. Coombes, together with a friend of the older brother, tried to mediate the dispute and thus prevent further trouble. Finally they arrived at a tentative agreement whereby the sister and Lellar would sell their interests to Farley, and Coombes promptly drew up a contract to reflect the terms of the agreement. Coombes, Lellar, and Farley were all present in Judge Boulden's law office in Matador when the proposed contract was read to them. Both brothers agreed it was correct. But when it was presented to Lellar to sign, he refused. Farley immediately jumped to his feet and threatened to kill Lellar unless he signed the contract. Still Lellar refused, saying he would sign it only after his sister had approved and signed it. At that, the trouble erupted again. Finally, the men were separated and Lellar mounted his horse and rode off with the contract to find his sister. Coombes once again gave his wayward client good advice.

> Farley, I have defended you for years in all of your difficulties, and I have cleared you from all criminal charges, and I am sure I will get you out of the one now with the jury, but you have become an outlaw and have made up your mind to kill your brother. If you kill Lellar, do not come to me to defend you because I will not do it.[48]

Unfortunately Farley again turned a deaf ear to good advice, and equally unfortunately, the sister refused to sign the contract. Consequently, Lellar also refused to sign it.

Infuriated, Farley rode to his family's ranch located a few miles from the little village of Dumont to confront his sister. Apparently she still refused to sign the contract, because Farley left there even more enraged and tracked Lellar down. He found him in the cotton gin yard at Dumont. Lellar had just loaded four bales of cotton on a wagon and was sitting on the wagon seat talking with friends when Farley rode up. Lellar was not armed—but Farley was. He had a .30-30 Winchester rifle. "We had just as well settle this trouble now as any other," Farley declared as he leveled down on Lellar. Lellar shielded himself behind another man, a King County farmer named A. S. Bass. "If you don't get out of the way, I will kill you both," Farley shouted. The human shield dropped to the ground. Lellar threw up both hands, but Farley shot him anyway. The fatal shot entered Lellar's right shoulder, traveled through his body, and exited just under his left shoulder. At this Lellar exclaimed, "He has killed me." Farley threw down his Winchester and ran to catch his brother. He and Bass succeeded in catching Lellar before he fell, and they held him in their arms as he died. The date was November 25, 1911. Ironically, it was exactly one year to the day since the feuding brothers' father, Joel Sayers, had died.[49]

True to his word, Charles Coombes refused to represent Farley when the inevitable indictment came down charging Farley with murdering his brother.[50] But Farley secured the services of A. J. Fires, who had assisted the Coombes brothers in the celebrated defense of Farley in his first cattle theft trial in Benjamin. Although bond was at first denied, Fires (on appeal) succeeded in getting bail set. Farley made the bond and was freed, pending trial.

ENTER TOM PICKETT, HIRED GUN

At this point, another larger-than-life character was about to appear on the scene: one who was destined to play a central role in this drama, a character we previously met in the story of the lynching of Kid Lewis and Foster Crawford. His name was Tom Pickett, and he was a renowned gunman and former lawman who was reputed to have killed several men—all "in the line of duty." Pickett had previously worked as a cowboy for Burk Burnett on his Wichita County Four Sixes Ranch and for Dan Waggoner on the sprawling Waggoner Ranch west of Wichita Falls, Texas, during the 1880s and early 1890s. He began his law enforcement career when he was elected Wichita County constable in 1894. Thereafter, he was reelected several times and served in that capacity until 1912.[51] While a constable in Wichita Falls, he was a member of Ranger Sergeant Sullivan's posse that ran Indian Territory outlaws Joe Beckham, Hill Loftis, Kid Lewis, and Red Buck Weightman to ground in the Suttle Creek dugout in December 1895, killing Beckham and wounding Weightman.[52] Kid Lewis may have dodged ranger bullets that day but, as we have seen, his days were numbered, and few. As previously noted, Burk Burnett and Tom Pickett were among the spectators who witnessed the 1896 lynching of Lewis and Crawford in Wichita Falls. After the hanging, it was Tom Pickett and another who cut the ropes, let the bodies down, and then hauled them off to the undertaker.[53]

A. J. Fires of Childress, Texas, was a bull-dog frontier defense lawyer. He represented Farley Sayers, who had been indicted for killing his own brother. Ironically, he later represented Burk Burnett, who had been indicted for killing Farley Sayers. *(Courtesy Panhandle-Plains Historical Museum, Canyon, Texas)*

A. C. Piper, the longtime 6666 cowboy previously quoted, still remembers Tom Pickett well. He became acquainted with Pickett a number of years after the incidents of this story, when both were working for the Four Sixes. (Piper began working for the Sixes in 1929.) Piper observed, "He was about as crude an old SOB as you ever met," a comment that, coming from a veteran 6666 cowboy, speaks volumes. Piper recalls Pickett bragging about his killings while a constable in Wichita Falls. He laughed and told about killing black men (that's *not* what Pickett called them) after running them under houses. Pickett explained that their eyes would "shine like a cat" in the darkness, and therefore he had no trouble shooting them "square 'tween the eyes."[54]

Frank McAuley, a retired King County rancher, recalled his uncle, C. L. "Charlie" Dowding, another early-day 6666 cowboy and later King County commissioner, telling him much the same thing about Pickett. "Everybody was afraid of Tom Pickett." After he retired from cowboying for the Sixes, Dowding worked up enough nerve to run for county commissioner against the incumbent commissioner Tom Pickett. Dowding won. Pickett didn't take it lightly. He filed a suit contesting the election, but that didn't work. Dowding then feared that Pickett might attempt to ambush him, so he took care to be well armed and on guard at all times. For example, when Dowding drove a country road at night and came to a gate that had to be opened, he would always turn off the automobile lights before getting out to open the gate: Pickett just might be lying out there in the darkness waiting to ambush him in the lights of the car while he was opening the gate.[55] But Pickett apparently did not take Dowding lightly either. A. C. Piper said that after the election, he heard Pickett grumbling about Dowding: "I'd kill the SOB but he's got a pistol like mine—'cause I've seen it."

Stanton Brown of Benjamin, a Knox County native who served as the Knox County tax assessor-collector for a number of years, still recalls stories about old Tom Pickett. He remembers Wade House, who worked for years on the McFaddin Ranch in Knox County, telling tales about Pickett. One story he related must have occurred about the time of the showdown between Burk Burnett and Far-ley Sayers in 1912, for House recollected that the incident occurred when he was a very young man. (House was born in 1899.)

House told the tale this way: One day Pickett showed up at his place on horseback. Well aware of Pickett's reputation, House was much impressed. So that Pickett wouldn't have to dismount, he ran out and opened a gate for him. Pickett hadn't said a word. To make conversation, the young House remarked that they had been having some trouble with cattle rustlers, and wondered aloud what they ought to do. Pickett took his time replying as he hand-rolled a cigarette. He rode on through the gate, finished rolling his Bull Durham, licked it shut, fished a match out of his pocket, lit it with a flick of his thumbnail, and took a big draw. Then he turned back to House, squinted down at him, and replied: "Well, sonny boy, just shoot the first bastard you catch and leave him lay so's the rest'll get the word." And rode off.[56]

After the Farley Sayers matter was settled, Burk Burnett kept Pickett on his payroll as a full-time bodyguard. Why would Burnett need to hire a full-time bodyguard? Both McAuley and the Piper brothers agreed: fear of retribution. "You didn't put together a block of land as big as the Four Sixes in them days without stepping on a lot of toes," McAuley observed. He remembered his uncle Charlie Dowding telling him that Burnett had run a lot of little people off their homesteads during those first years when he was putting the Sixes together. Dowding, who ran a wagon for the Sixes for about thirty years, told McAuley that Burnett was mighty careful even when he journeyed from his home in Fort Worth and came to Guthrie. Dowding recalled that when he would go up to the company commissary store on the ranch, Burnett would barely crack the door open in order to identify the visitor and make sure he was unarmed. Only then would the door be opened.[57]

Although A. C. and his brother Toar Piper didn't start working on the Sixes until 1929, a number of years after the ranch had already been put together and seven years after Burnett's death, they remembered hearing the old stories. "Burk was afraid of a lot of people," A. C. Piper said. "Old man Burnett, he wasn't what you'd call a model citizen himself." The Piper brothers both voiced the opinion that in those days when the big ranches were being formed, the cattle barons, as A. C. put it, "blowed out a lot of nesters, run off a lot of nesters—all that sort of thing—starved 'em out. . . . They was a lot of stuff went on in them days, I guess. It was pretty damned hard to get anything done [that big] and be really honest about it all." Toar added, "In those days all the big ranches were put together that way."[58]

FARLEY SAYERS'S VENDETTA AGAINST BURK BURNETT

That Farley Sayers became consumed by an overwhelming obsession to kill Burk Burnett after the 1907–1908 incidents and trials cannot be doubted. Sayers failed to take Charles Coombes's sound advice to liquidate, move on, and make a fresh start. And he failed to heed Coombes's warning that if he did not move on, then someday Burnett would surely kill him. But retreat was not in the vocabulary of hot-tempered, fearless, and determined Farley Sayers. Instead, for the next several years he went around voicing threats to kill Burnett to anybody who would listen. He even offered to pay others to kill

Burnett. Of course it did not take long for all these threats to reach Burnett's ears.

Such was the volatile situation when, in 1912, he pulled a daring ("foolhardy" might be a better adjective) stunt that practically guaranteed swift retribution from Burnett. What Sayers did wasn't exactly illegal, although it did violate a sacred cow country code, and undoubtedly it was intended as a clever strategy to enable him to safely steal more Burk Burnett cattle. To make matters worse, Sayers did it blatantly, rubbing Burnett's nose in it.

The big ranches of that day (and most even to this day) make it a policy never to sell off any of their branded mother cows unless they are going directly to the slaughterhouse or can at least be shipped to a distant market for sale. To discourage theft and to prevent any confusion of ownership, the big ranchers didn't want any of the other ranchers, settlers, or, for that matter, anybody else in their area to run any mother cows bearing their brand. Such policy ensured that if any cow bearing a 6666 brand were found on somebody else's ranch in the area, the Sixes would know—and could prove—that she was the property of the 6666 Ranch.

During the spring of 1912, the Four Sixes culled some of their older, branded cows and sent them to Fort Worth to be marketed by Burnett's commission agent, the Cassidy Southwestern Commission Company. Somehow Sayers got wind of it and followed the cattle. Sayers thus managed to buy a train-car load of branded 6666 cows. He promptly reloaded the cows and had them shipped back to Paducah, Texas, where Sayers was to take delivery at the train station and then drive the critters back to his ranch—just across the fence from Burnett's outfit. (Paducah was the closest rail outlet to Farley's ranch near Guthrie.)

Somebody at the Cassidy Commission company realized what was about to happen and alerted Burnett.[59] To say that old Burk flew into a towering rage when he learned that cows wearing the 6666 brand and now legally owned by Farley Sayers were about to end up in Sayers's pasture just across the fence from the Four Sixes, has to be a gross understatement. As longtime Four Sixes ranch manager George Humphreys later stated: "After that, Farley Sayers could have just gotten all the 6666 cows he wanted and claimed they were his, bought by him in Fort Worth."[60] (Not to mention the fact that a lot more of Burnett's unbranded calves might soon be discovered in Farley's pasture grazing beside Farley's 6666 cows.)

Burnett didn't intend for that to happen, however. The same day he got the "heads-up" call from Cassidy, Burk caught the next train for Paducah, hesitating only long enough to stick a "forty-plus" six-shooter in his pocket, and when the train reached Wichita Falls he added the fearsome Tom Pickett to his arsenal.[61] They arrived in Paducah before the cattle shipment did. Farley's 6666 cows were due to arrive in Paducah on May 23, 1912.

On the morning of that same day, Farley and four of his hands rode into Paducah intending to take delivery of the carload of 6666 cows when the train arrived.[62] But the train hadn't yet arrived when they got there, so Farley and his cowboys ambled over to the Goodwin Hotel to wash up and take their noon meal there. What they didn't know was that Burnett, Pickett, and Burnett's brother-in-law, Jim Barkley, were waiting in the lobby of the Goodwin Hotel. Burnett and Pickett quietly followed Sayers into the washroom.

Sayers's checkered career ended abruptly right there. He was shot down and killed in the washroom of the Goodwin Hotel just before noon on May 23, 1912.

THE KILLING OF FARLEY SAYERS

In typical frontier reporting style, the next edition of *The Paducah Post* gave its take on the incident.

> Bible scripture warns that "He who sheds another's blood, his blood by others shall be shed," and this prediction held literally true in Farley Sayers' case, for he, too, was to die less than six months later [after killing his own brother]—murdered *unsuspectingly* as he washed his face in preparation for the noonday meal at a hotel here in Paducah.[63]

Immediately after the killing, Burnett wasted no time in calling for help. He called his Fort Worth lawyer, Sidney Samuels, and, even though Samuels was in the middle of a trial, Burnett demanded that he drop everything and come to Guthrie. Samuels wanted to know what could be so urgent as to stop a jury trial in the middle. Burk's reply was as follows: "I've had occasion to take a hand in the killing of Farley Sayers, and his hide is hanging on the corral fence. I want you to come out here immediately!"[64]

However, the next day Burk changed his mind about strategizing with Samuels at the ranch headquarters in Guthrie and instead caught the train back to Fort Worth where he closeted himself with a premier Fort Worth defense attorney, W. P. McLean, Jr. After consulting with his attorney, Burnett issued the following self-serving press release:

> I regret very much, especially at my age, of having any trouble, but it was absolutely unavoidable, as will be shown at the trial by the evidence of witnesses whose veracity cannot be questioned. Had I known that Mr. Sayers was at Paducah, I would have done everything in my power to avoid meeting him.[65]

Several of his assertions were to come under serious question by later events, statements, and testimony.

Meanwhile, a hurriedly assembled Cottle County grand jury separately indicted both Burk Burnett and Tom Pickett for murder. Venue was transferred to Seymour in Baylor County, approximately eighty miles to the southeast, but still within the 50th Judicial District.[66] This meant that the same district judge and district attorney would be players in the upcoming trial drama. And a grand drama it would be.

THE MURDER TRIAL OF BURK BURNETT

The presiding judge, the Honorable Jo A. P. Dickson, a well-respected jurist, had a colorful past himself. Before earning his law license,

Judge Jo A. P. Dickson presided over the 1913 murder trial of Burk Burnett in Seymour, Texas. Before admission to the bar, Dickson was a fearless frontier law-man, serving fifteen years as a deputy sheriff, first of Young County and later of Baylor County, Texas. Picture on the left depicts Dickson as he appeared at the time of the Burnett trial. At right, how he appeared years later. *(Author's Collection)*

Dickson had a notable career as a peace officer.[67] At age thirty-five, Dickson obtained his law license, and in 1896 he was elected district attorney of the 50th Judicial District, where he served with distinction. Later he was elected district judge, a post he held when the Burk Burnett murder case was called to trial.[68]

Standing six feet, three inches tall, Dickson was an imposing figure as well as being a no-nonsense jurist who kept a tight rein on trial participants and courtroom spectators alike: no outbursts were tolerated. Proper courtroom decorum and civility were further ensured by the fact that Judge Dickson took no pains to hide the .45-caliber pistol he toted and ostentatiously placed on top of the judge's bench when he called the court to order.[69]

To no one's surprise, Burnett didn't spare the horses when it came to putting together an all-star defense team to defend himself and Pickett. His "dream team" was headlined by two real heavy-weights—two of the most famous criminal defense lawyers in all of West Texas and the Panhandle at that time—J. F. Cunningham, Jr., of Abilene and A. J. Fires of Childress. Fires, it will be recalled, had been representing Farley Sayers, who was under indictment for murdering his own brother when he himself was killed. In a judicial switcheroo, neither condemned nor considered unsportsmanlike conduct in that day, Fires followed the money trail and changed allegiances: he hired himself out to Burnett to clear him for killing his recently deceased client Sayers. Burnett's team also included noted trial attorney I. H. Burney of Fort Worth and Rowland Brown of Paducah, as well as J. H. Glasgow and D. L. Kenan, the latter two of Seymour. "Silver-tongued" Jack Glasgow was renowned for his theatrical talent. Colorful J. F. Cunningham, however, was the lead defense attorney. Beginning his career in 1888 as a frontier prosecutor, Cunningham had quickly found his true niche in the legal profession as a criminal defense trial lawyer. And he was truly a superstar in his time and place.[70]

Against this mighty array of legal talent, the state's team paled—considerably. It was headed by the young and relatively inexperienced 50th Judicial District Attorney Isaac Ollin Newton of Seymour, who was assisted by the Baylor County attorney, Bert King of Seymour, and J. Ross Bell of Paducah, the Cottle County attorney. The first question to arise was which defendant to try first: Burk Burnett or Tom Pickett? By agreement of both defendants, as well as the state, it was decided that Burnett would be tried first— which, for reasons we shall soon explore, certainly gave the defense in both cases a huge advantage.

The murder trial of Samuel Burk Burnett for the killing of Farley P. Sayers was called on Monday morning, July 22, 1913, in a hot, stifling Seymour, Texas, courthouse.[71] (Seymour, incidentally, holds the dubious honor of being the hottest spot in Texas history, the thermometer hitting a record high of 120 degrees on August 12, 1936.) The only air-conditioning in those days was afforded by hand-held cardboard fans—"funeral home fans" they were called because, typically, they were distributed, free of cost, by the local funeral home (with logo imprinted) to all courthouses, schools, churches, and other public meeting facilities in the area. Judge Dickson directed that ice water be made available under the shade of trees on the courthouse lawn, and announced at the opening of the trial that the ladies of

J. F. Cunningham, Jr., of Abilene, Texas, earned a reputation for being the preeminent lion of the criminal defense bar in that area. He was the lead attorney defending Burk Burnett when he was tried for the murder of Farley Sayers in 1913. *(Courtesy of Southwest Collection/Special Collections Library, Texas Tech University, Lubbock, Texas)*

the Pieran Club would serve dinner there (at a modest charge) for the benefit of the local library. And so, the searing heat and crowded conditions notwithstanding, the whole affair proved to be more exciting, more entertaining than any circus or rodeo—the most sensational event in many a day in that neck of the woods.

News accounts in *The Baylor County Banner* (published in Seymour) depict a festive atmosphere. The Burnett family made a grand entry into town, greatly impressing the country editor. The *Banner* reported that Burk Burnett arrived for trial in a special railroad car, an "Orient Receiver," and that the other members of the Burnett family arrived in style in four Pierce-Arrow automobiles. S. B. Burnett, Jr., arrived in a red Pierce-Arrow, and Tom Burnett, Burk Burnett's oldest son, motored to town in his gray Pierce Arrow "all the way from Fort Worth to Seymour . . . making the trip in six hours, the last twenty-five miles on the rim." Apparently after Tom arrived, he managed to get his tire fixed because the *Banner* went on to report that "some diversion was created by Tom Burnett's musical auto horn on his palatial Pierce-Arrow. He gave the town a thorough serenade Tuesday night." Other Burnett family members on hand were Clyde and Tib Burnett, nephew and brother, respectively, of Burk Burnett, as well as Jim Barkley, Burk's brother-in-law.

The July 25, 1913, edition of *The Baylor County Banner* noted, "The two $30,000 hotels of the city are crowded to capacity in taking care of witnesses." Cots were installed in all unoccupied spaces. The weekly paper, obviously awed by such an impressive array of cow country royalty, then listed the cast of Burk Burnett's friends and supporters.[72] In addition, Burk subpoenaed about 150 witnesses, most of whom were the elite of West Texas ranch-centered society, called to attest to the "good character" of Burnett and/or the "bad character" of Sayers. Bringing up the rear on the witness list were a few commoners: two whose occupation was listed as "drummer" (as traveling salesmen were then called), plus J. W. Boyles of Knox City, who was described as a "piano man," and Henry Chalk of Quanah, Texas, who was denominated an "auto driver." Finally, at the bottom of this impressive heap was plebeian Jim Randel of Fort Worth, "laborer."

Trial testimony established these uncontradicted facts: Burk Burnett, Tom Pickett, and brother-in-law Jim Barkley arrived at the Goodwin Hotel at about nine-thirty that fateful morning and seated themselves in the lobby. At about eleven-thirty Farley Sayers and four of his cowboys (Walker Morgan, Willie Evans, Walter Edwards, and Fred McDonald) entered the hotel lobby, passed through it, and went to a public washroom intending to scrub off some trail dust before taking their noon meal. (The "washroom" was not a restroom, its sole purpose being to allow customers to freshen up. There were three wash basins on the back wall low enough so that if a guest bent over to wash his face in the basin, his face would be lower than his hips.) As they passed through the lobby, Sayers failed to notice Burnett (one source said that was due to Burk holding a newspaper in front of his face), and none of them knew Pickett.[73] Shortly after the Sayers group reached the washroom, Burnett and Pickett arose and followed them inside. They entered by pushing open the swinging door. A cotton buyer, J. P. Watkins, was standing

The Baylor County Courthouse in Seymour, Texas, as it appeared in 1913 during the Burk Burnett murder trial. The ornate old courthouse was torn down and replaced in 1967 by a more modern, albeit much less impressive, structure. *(Author's Collection)*

just inside, or just outside, the washroom entrance—but with a view of the interior—when Burnett and Pickett entered.

Either Burnett or Pickett fired one shot at such close range that it set Farley Sayers's shirt on fire. It was a clean heart shot. The bullet hit him in the back portion of his left side and then traveled diagonally at a slightly upward path through his body and exited on his right front side. The bullet then plowed into the wall just above the next wash basin. (See the accompanying photographs, which were admitted into evidence at the trial.) Sayers fell dead instantly. Burnett then ordered the survivors out of the washroom—an order that was obeyed by one and all with great alacrity. (Walter Edwards later testified that upon receiving Burk's command, he departed the washroom "right pert" and didn't slow down for about two blocks.)

The state called Sayers's employees Walker Morgan (whose father, J. M. Morgan, had previously served as district judge of several area counties, including Cottle, King, and Baylor), Fred McDonald, and Walter Edwards, plus J. P. Watkins the cotton buyer, all of whom had been either in, or just outside of, the washroom when the fatal shot was fired. Basically, their testimony was consistent.

McDonald and Edwards testified that they and Sayers were bent over separate basins washing their face and hands when Burnett and Pickett came through the washroom door behind them. A shot rang out, and they saw Sayers fall; his face was wet and his wet hands were raised in an upward position in front of his face. No threats were uttered; in fact, nothing was said by any of the parties before the shooting. None of these witnesses saw Sayers make any move to draw a weapon. In fact, none of the state's witnesses knew whether or not Sayers was armed at the time, and none of them saw any pistol in Sayers's hand or on or about his body.

Walker Morgan, who had been sitting on the steps of the washroom at the time, testified that Burnett and Pickett both pulled pistols *as they entered* the washroom. The fatal shot was fired immediately after they entered. Morgan said that although he did not see Sayers at the instant he was shot, he did see him fall with his wet hands up in front of his face; that he did not see Sayers "make any play to defend himself." Cotton buyer J. P. Watkins also added that just after the shot was fired, he saw Burnett with a "smoking gun" in his hand. The *Fort Worth Star-Telegram* reporter covering the trial telegraphed this back to his editor:

> Burnett, Barkley and Pickett were in the hotel lobby when Sayers and four of his companions arrived for dinner; that Sayers and two of them went into the washroom; Burnett started through the washroom door and a quick shot was fired; Burnett and Pickett were seen after the shooting with guns out, but no one testified as to what Sayers was doing at the time of the shot.[74]

Dr. Alexander testified he examined Sayers's body. He described the wounds as stated here and as shown in the photographs introduced into evidence and here reprinted.

The last sight Farley Sayers ever saw—the wash basins in the washroom of the Goodwin Hotel in Paducah, Texas. Farley was bending over washing his face when Burk Burnett and Tom Pickett entered the washroom and shot him once, fatally. *(Official court records*—State v. S. B. Burnett, *Cause No. 1100, Baylor County District Court)*

The matter of whether Sayers was even armed at the time of his death was the subject of some curious testimony. The state called the investigating officer, T. A. Freeman, a Cottle County deputy sheriff at the time, who testified he had examined Sayers's body on the washroom floor shortly after he was killed but found no pistol in his possession. After the state rested, however, the defense called an out-of-county sheriff—Motley County Sheriff Ed Russell—who testified that just after the shooting he had examined Sayers's body and discovered a .25-caliber automatic pistol in Sayers's right pants pocket. Russell then produced the pistol, and it was introduced into evidence on behalf of the defense. Why he had never turned this crucial piece of evidence over to the investigating officer before the trial, or, for that matter, why he never bothered to mention his discovery to the state, was not explained. Burnett's friend, Paducah banker John Richards, also took the stand for the defense and told that immediately after the shooting he met Burnett in the street and

Burnett told Richards to get Sayers's gun. Richards went on to testify that he was present shortly thereafter when Motley County Sheriff Russell found and secured Sayers's pistol. Although this tale has a distinctly suspicious odor to it, still, in light of Sayers's past threats and violent episodes, it does seem unlikely that Farley would have gone anywhere unarmed. (However, it would also appear that even if Sayers was armed with a .25-caliber pistol, that fact alone amounted to strong circumstantial evidence that he was *not* anticipating a shootout. A .25-caliber weapon just does not have the knockdown and incapacitating power of a .44- or a .45-caliber weapon. Shooting an armed man with a .25-caliber pistol leaves open the very real possibility that, even if the victim sustains a mortal wound, he may nevertheless be able to retaliate with a return shot before collapsing.)

Nobody, however, not even Burk Burnett when he finally took the stand, testified that anybody ever saw a pistol in Farley's possession before he was killed.

After the state rested its case, the defense paraded twenty-nine witnesses to the stand, all testifying to Sayers's bad character and to threats they had heard Sayers make against Burnett. Some admitted, however, they had never communicated these threats to Burnett before the shooting. (Relevancy query: How could Burnett have felt threatened by threats that he never heard?)

King County resident Ed Herndon testified that in 1909 Sayers had offered him five hundred dollars to kill Burnett. Henry Chalk, "auto driver" of Quanah, stated that when he was in Guthrie in October 1907, he ran into Sayers in front of the Lasater store (a company commissary owned by the Four Sixes Ranch). Sayers was holding a shotgun, apparently hoping to ambush Burnett. Chalk said he persuaded Sayers to give him the gun and go home. (That bit of testimony seems highly suspect in view of Sayers's character and history. Can we really believe that the violent, volatile, fearless Farley Sayers would be dissuaded from his purpose to kill Burnett and then persuaded to turn over his weapon meekly to an "auto driver"?) Nevertheless, it was beyond dispute that Farley was obsessed with killing Burnett and would have done so at any time if he had had

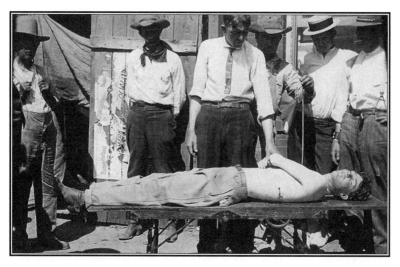

Farley Sayers, laid out shortly after having been shot and killed by Burk Burnett and his bodyguard, Tom Pickett, in the washroom of the Goodwin Hotel in Paducah, Texas, May 23, 1912. The gentleman standing on the left with his thumbs hooked in his galluses, calmly observing the corpse, is none other than Tom Pickett himself. Pickett later bragged, "I kilt him real purty." Sayers was shot once, fatally, through the heart. The entrance wound is shown here on his left side. It traveled at a slightly upward angle and exited just above his right nipple at a point indicated by the rod held by the third man from the right. *(From official court records*—State v. S. B. Burnett, *Cause No. 1100, Baylor County District Court)*

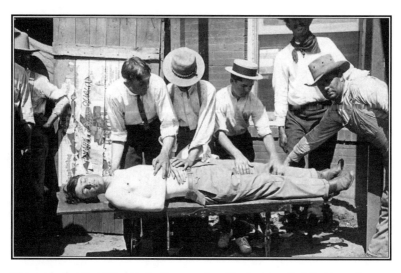

The single shot that killed Farley Sayers entered his body on the left side, as shown in the preceding photograph, and exited his body just above his right nipple, as depicted above. *(From official court records*—State v. S. B. Burnett, *Cause No. 1100, Baylor County District Court)*

the opportunity, that he had freely aired his threats to kill Burnett to many people in the area, and that Burnett was aware of the threats and his peril.

W. N. Coombes, the lawyer brother of Charles E. Coombes, gave some devastating testimony on behalf of the defense. (As mentioned earlier, W. N. Coombes and A. J. Fires both assisted Charles Coombes in 1908 when he successfully defended Farley against an accusation that he had stolen four of Burnett's unbranded calves.) W. N. Coombes testified that after the cattle theft trial, his former client, Farley Sayers, came to his office one day and inquired of Coombes how he could kill Burnett "and get away with it."

It didn't help the state's case when Judge Dickson overruled the prosecution's "irrelevancy" objection and allowed the defense to introduce testimony that Farley had recently gunned down his own unarmed brother. (As a practical matter, though, the Court's ruling didn't really hurt the prosecution since, without any doubt, all the jurors had already heard about this sensational incident from street talk.) From a strictly legal standpoint, this testimony was properly allowed by Dickson so that the defense could prove that Sayers was the kind of man who was more than capable of carrying out his threats of violence, and that therefore, Burnett, when he was told of those threats, was justified in fearing for his life. This, in turn, put a lot of water under Burnett's self-defense paddle.

A very revealing highlight was the reading of a deposition given by Miss Jewel Winter. Miss Winter, then twenty-five years of age, testified that, for about four months during the spring and summer of 1909, she lived with and was a housekeeper for Sayers and his wife. She recounted a conversation with Sayers when she accompanied him to Guthrie to buy a pair of slippers for his little daughter:

> [O]n our way back he told me that after Sam Graves shot him, that he . . . and his wife [laid in wait at] Burk Burnett's office and they tried to get a chance to shoot him through the windows, and Sayers told me that Burnett kept his window shades down and they never could get a chance to see him, and he said

that his wife's sister tried to keep his wife from going, but that his wife had so much nerve that she wanted to kill Burnett the same as he did. We were on our way from Guthrie to Sayers' home and there was a cow dead at the left of the road and Sayers said that it was Burnett's cow and that he killed it. . . . I also heard Sayers say at different places and at different times that he would kill Burnett if he could get a chance.[75]

Tom Pickett, under indictment for the same killing, did not testify, nor could he have been compelled to do so by the prosecution.

Burk Burnett did testify; he was the last defense witness. Burk told the jury this: He took the train from his hometown of Fort Worth and detrained in Paducah, and then traveled by car to his ranch headquarters in Guthrie. The purpose of his trip was to keep a promise made to his old friend Tom Pickett—a promise to give Pickett a pony of his choice from the 6666 remuda. That, he said, was why he stopped off long enough in Wichita Falls to entrain Pickett.

Conveniently, Burk omitted any mention of the carload of 6666 cows just purchased by Farley Sayers—6666 cows that, at the very moment of Farley Sayers's death, were riding the rails to Paducah, tagged for delivery to one Farley Sayers. Nor did he volunteer any reason why he and Pickett loafed around the Goodwin Hotel lobby from nine-thirty that morning until Sayers and his party finally arrived two hours later.

Burk testified that many people had warned him of Sayers's threats to kill him—two, in fact, within twenty-four hours of their fatal confrontation—and that these threats caused him to fear for his life.

He contended that he did not know Sayers was in the hotel washroom when he and Pickett entered; didn't even know Sayers was in town that day. It was only when he and Pickett entered the washroom that he recognized Sayers and, according to Burnett, Sayers immediately recognized him, and "made a play as if to draw a gun." Burnett admitted that he never saw a pistol in Sayers's hand or even on his person before drawing his own pistol and firing the fatal shot. Nevertheless, he insisted that he *believed* Sayers was attempting to draw a gun and therefore it became necessary to kill him in self-defense.

Burnett was on the stand for less than ninety minutes, and if the news accounts are anywhere near accurate, the prosecution's cross-examination was something less than exhaustive. Apparently the prosecution failed to ask some interesting questions: If Burnett really had no idea that Sayers was anywhere in the vicinity, then why were both he and Pickett armed? Why did they wait in that hotel lobby for two hours that morning? How come neither he, Pickett, nor brother-in-law Jim Barkley noticed Farley and his retinue of four cowhands when they entered the hotel lobby and passed right in front of them en route to the washroom? Wasn't it strange that Burnett and Pickett, who had been sitting in the lobby for two hours, suddenly jumped up and headed for the washroom immediately after Sayers passed them headed in that direction? Did Burk really expect the jurors to believe that he had no idea that Farley Sayers was in Paducah that day— the very same day that, according to Cassidy Commission's alert to Burnett, a shipment of 6666 cows Farley had just bought were to arrive by rail in Paducah? If he really feared for his life as a result of Farley's threats, then why didn't he file criminal charges against Sayers and let the law handle it? Or if, as he claimed in his initial press release, he would have "done everything in my power to avoid meeting him," then why did he and Pickett both get up and stalk Sayers into the washroom, thus ensuring a confrontation? If Sayers was really "making a play" to pull a gun on Burnett, then how come none of the other occupants of the washroom saw it? In fact, wasn't it strange that none of the other occupants even noticed Burnett and Pickett until after the fatal shot was fired? Wasn't that circumstantial evidence of stealth and purpose on the part of Burnett and Pickett?

Anybody can climb on the witness stand and concoct any kind of tale that suits the teller's purpose. But objective physical evidence is what it is, and (unless afterward tampered with) it doesn't change or lie. Moreover, it tells its own story, let the chips fall where they may. In this case the forensic evidence simply didn't comport with

Burnett's account of what happened in that washroom, especially in view of other undisputed testimony.

Physical evidence: There were three wash basins in the washroom. Farley Sayers was washing in the far left basin as viewed from the entrance to the washroom. The entrance was only a few feet to the rear of the basins so that anyone entering the room would do so behind and very close to anyone who was already in the process of washing his face and hands in any of the basins. None of the wash basins had mirrors above them. It was undisputed that just prior to the entrance of Burnett and Pickett, Sayers was bending over the basin washing his face and hands. It was also undisputed that just prior to the shooting, nobody—not Sayers or his cowboys nor Burnett or Pickett—uttered a word. Taking into account all those undisputed facts, it would appear most unlikely that Sayers was aware of anybody coming through the door behind him. The other occupants of the washroom testified that the first time that they were aware of the presence of Burnett and Pickett was after the shot was fired.

Physical evidence: Sayers's shirt caught fire at the place of the entrance wound indicating that the fatal shot must have been fired mere inches from his body—a fact much more consistent with the prosecution's version that the assassin sneaked up behind Sayers and shot him unaware, than with the defense version that Sayers somehow recognized Burnett and was in the act of attempting to draw a weapon when he was shot.

Physical evidence: The location of the entrance and exit wounds on Sayers's body evidenced the trajectory of the bullet and Sayers's posture at the time the shot was fired. As it clearly appears from the photographs in evidence, the fatal bullet hit Farley in the back of his left side about four inches below the nipple line, and then traveled diagonally through his body (shattering his heart), exiting his front right side some three inches above the nipple line.

After exiting Sayers's body the bullet struck the washroom wall a few inches above the middle basin. Sayers's cowboys, Morgan, McDonald, and Edwards, all eyewitnesses, all testified that just before the shooting they saw Sayers bending over the left basin *with his head down* washing his face and hands. Again, the physical evidence and undisputed testimony (of every witness other than Burnett) is consistent with the state's version of the event: that Sayers hadn't a clue his killer was approaching, that he was bent over the basin, head somewhat lower than his hips, with his hands in the bowl in the act of washing his face, when the killer sneaked up behind him, placed the pistol on the lower *back* part of his left side, and triggered a heart shot that exited on the upper *front* part of his right side.

The physical evidence proved that the bullet, after exiting Sayers's body, continued on its same downward trajectory until it hit the wall at a low level just above the middle wash basin—all consistent with the state's contention that Sayers was bent over with his face and hands in the wash basin when he was shot. It seems highly unlikely that if Sayers was in that posture, he would somehow also have been in the act of attempting to draw a weapon. (The defense didn't counter with any rebuttal evidence—either forensic evidence or testimony—but relied solely on speculation in its final jury argument that the bullet's downward path after it exited Sayers's body and hit the center basin wall probably was due to the slug having been deflected by hitting a rib or collar bone while still inside the body.)

Judge Dickson gave the jury a lengthy set of written instructions. The guts of the court's charge lay in the court's self-defense definition and resulting instructions:

> [Y]ou are charged that a person who is violently attacked or against whom hostile acts or demonstrations are made is not bound to retreat to avoid the necessity of killing his assailant.

Judge Dickson's "no duty to retreat" instruction accurately reflected the Texas self-defense law of that time. It was a departure from the English common law's doctrine, which held that a person who was assailed and thus put in fear of death or serious bodily injury was nevertheless required, if at all possible, to flee from the attacker and thus avoid a confrontation. He was required to "retreat to the wall" behind his back before resorting to lethal force to repel his adversary.[76] Although the English common law was the bedrock of early American jurisprudence, this "duty to retreat" business didn't sit well with pioneers: the notion that a true man should tuck tail and run when threatened was alien to the hardy souls who conquered the wilderness. In a 1921 U.S. Supreme Court opinion written by the venerable Justice Oliver Wendell Holmes, the English "duty to retreat" standard was rejected in favor of the "stand your ground" rule.[77] Reflecting the mood of frontier America, Justice Holmes explained that "a man is not born to run away."[78]

However, after that decision, Texas as well as the rest of the nation reverted to the old common law "duty to retreat" rule, reflecting a change in our communal mores. In addition, the Texas law made it clear that "verbal provocation" alone would not justify any use of force.[79] Yet in 2007 the Texas Legislature beat a partial retreat from its "duty to retreat" standard when it enacted the "Castle Law," that term harking back to the old adage that "every man's home is his castle." Under the present version, a person may use lethal force to protect himself or herself and family from an intruder in his or her home, automobile, or workplace.[80]

Judge Dickson, in his instructions in the Burnett case, went on to tell the jury that a person is entitled to protect himself from apparent danger of deadly force whether that *perceived danger later proves to be real or not*. Moreover, if the person reasonably feels threatened by "apparent danger" (of death or serious bodily injury), then he is entitled to counter with deadly force to protect himself. He doesn't have to wait for his adversary to get off the first shot (and then hope he misses) before blasting away. Still, the court emphasized that *prior threats alone*, however serious, were not tantamount to a judicial declaration of an "open season" to kill Farley Sayers; that serious threats must also have been accompanied by *some immediate overt act* on the part of the victim evidencing an intent to carry out those threats. Then and only then is a person entitled to shoot his adversary and claim self-defense.

In his initial press release, Burnett promised to produce numerous witnesses whose "veracity could not be questioned," and he made good on that promise. Undoubtedly the jury was much impressed— "dazzled" and "overwhelmed" might be more appropriate—by the number and prominence of Burk's character witnesses. (Undoubtedly the jurors were also much impressed by Sayers's violent and lawless character.) However, there was another promise Burk made in his press release that he did not keep: he promised to produce respected and credible defense witnesses who would testify that the killing of Farley Sayers during the washroom encounter was "absolutely unavoidable" in order for Burk to save his own life.

The only witness—prosecution or defense—who testified he saw Sayers do *any* overt act in furtherance of his threats to kill Burk was Burk Burnett himself. Thus, the ultimate *legal* issue for the jury's consideration boiled down to this: did Farley Sayers, just prior to being shot, really see Burnett approaching him from the rear and then "make some play," which Burnett could reasonably have interpreted as an attempt to draw a pistol? Therefore, Burnett's legal defense ultimately rested on his testimony alone—testimony not only uncorroborated by any other witness, but also at odds with the physical evidence.

That may have been the narrow *legal* issue that the jury was instructed by Judge Dickson to address. But was it the issue the jurors considered?

To give due credit to the outclassed prosecution, in final jury arguments the state's lawyers did point out that Burk's defense rested solely on his own self-serving assertion that he saw Sayers "make some play," which he interpreted as an effort to draw a weapon—a movement nobody else observed—and that Burnett's version of the incident was at odds not only with the forensic evidence but also with the testimony of the other occupants of the washroom. But, in the end, it was clear that Burnett was never in any real jeopardy of being convicted. Not only did he have the best lawyers that money could buy, but by 1913 the rich, powerful, and influential Burnett enjoyed the overwhelming support of nearly everybody who was anybody in West Texas. Plus, he was the beneficiary of two provisions of the unwritten frontier code of justice that still retained considerable potency in cow country even after the turn of the century—both of which were perceived as almost surefire defenses on which a defendant could hang his Stetson in a murder trial. First was the "The-sorry-SOB-deserved-a-damned-good-killin'-anyhow" defense. If ever a deceased fell squarely into that category, it would have been Farley Sayers—he who was a known cattle thief and the rustler of Burk Burnett's livestock; he who, motivated by greed, had only months before slaughtered his own unarmed brother; and he who had repeatedly threatened to kill Burk Burnett if he had half a chance. The other applicable tenet of that unwritten code held that if a man was rash enough to go about threatening to kill another, then he could expect those threats would be taken literally and seriously by any westerner, and therefore, he shouldn't expect that his adversary would give him an even break on the draw when next they met. As one old-timer put it, "In those times, if you made open threats to kill somebody, you pretty well signed your own death warrant."[81] Consequently, frontier juries were not inclined to unduly concern themselves with the issue of whether or not the deceased really was or was not armed "when he got his'n." Furthermore, both adversaries were aware that juries of that day were loath to convict in feud-related murder cases. When a man learned that his life had been threatened, he knew he'd better act quickly and effectively for he realized full well that no fear of conviction would likely deter his opponent.

The case had taken a week to try and went to the jury at five-thirty Friday afternoon, July 25, 1913.

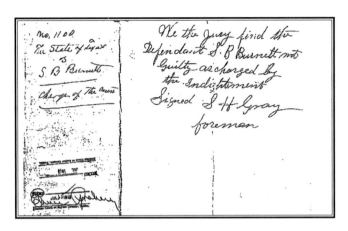

Jury verdict of "not guilty" was returned by a Baylor County District Court jury on July 25, 1913, in the murder trial of Burk Burnett for the killing of Farley Sayers. The indictment against Tom Picket was then immediately dismissed. *(From official court records—State v. S. B. Burnett, Cause No. 1100, Baylor County District Court)*

THE VERDICT

Judge Dickson's lengthy jury instructions consisted of nine, single-spaced, legal-sized pages of legalese. It takes a modern-day, college-educated layman seventeen minutes to silently read that charge, without pausing to ponder the meaning of the numerous provisions. Simply put, there is no way that a 1913 country jury could have retired, organized itself, elected a foreman, read, considered, and understood (much less debated) the court's charge, voted, notified the bailiff, and then returned into court all within the *twenty-three minutes* it took this jury to return with a verdict. The verdict itself came as no surprise to anyone: "not guilty." Thereupon District Attorney Newton moved that the indictment against Tom Pickett be dismissed on grounds of "insufficient evidence," and it was. Pandemonium broke out—and the celebration began.

The August 1, 1913, edition of *The Baylor County Banner* wrapped up its coverage of the Burk Burnett murder trial under the headline: "Burk Burnett Comes Clear." The *Banner*'s report was the usual mixed bag of factual reporting blended in with the editor's personal views. Nevertheless, the *Banner*'s wrap of the case probably gives us the most accurate analysis—a true picture—of how the public in general, and the jury in particular, really viewed the case. After reporting details of the trial, the editor reflected as follows:

> There seems to have been pretty general satisfaction over the verdict. To the average mind it seems evident that Sayers was not trying to draw his gun, and it is probable that he never knew what killed him. But he had been making lots of threats and Mr. Burnett had undoubtedly been much wrought up by the continual peril in which he was placed. The character of Sayers was another extenuating circumstance. The barbaric manner in which he had killed his brother was enough to make anybody think that the world is not much worse off by his having left it. Mrs. Sayers had sued Mr. Burnett for killing her husband, he had compromised the suit by paying her $8,000.00, and that was probably more than Sayers was worth.[82]

Meanwhile, the victory celebration waxed ever more jubilant, spearheaded by a procession of the Burnetts' four new Pierce-Arrows. The Pierce-Arrow, the Cadillac of its day, even in 1913 cost $7,000 new. The luxurious seven-passenger touring sedans all came equipped with musical horns that could be adjusted to play several different notes in whatever sequence desired. The Burnett family took advantage of this last feature on that joyous evening of July 26, 1913, when they were parading up and down the streets of Seymour. They all adjusted their musical horns to play three or four recognizable notes from a well-known hymn of the day, the words to which were:

> *Oh, happy day!*
> *Oh, happy day!*
> *When Jesus washed*
> *My sins away!*[83]

"Not Guilty!" That was the verdict of this Baylor County District Court jury in Seymour, Texas, on July 25, 1913, after deliberating only twenty-three minutes at the conclusion of the murder trial of Burk Burnett for killing Farley Sayers. Top row (*left to right*): Dan Goodwin, R. N. Bills, S. T. Brown, Dan Black, H. E. Heathington, and Joe Chambers. Bottom row (*left to right*): G. R. Buck, S. H. Gray, J. A. Dunlap, Joe Lankford, Will Nichols, and R. L. Eddleman. Baylor County Deputy Sheriff Green stands to the left facing the jury. *(From the* Fort Worth Star-Telegram, *July 26, 1913)*

> State of Texas
> X. P. Sayers No. 1071 In the Dist. Court of
> Geo. Texas
> Now comes the State by her Dist Atty
> and files this motion to dismiss
> above entitled cause
> for the Reason the defendant is
> dead
> District Atty. 50th Judicial District of Tex
> Isaac O. Newton

Beating a murder rap the hard way: District Attorney Isaac O. Newton filed a motion to dismiss the murder indictment against Farley P. Sayers for the killing of his brother, L. D. Sayers, "for the reason that the defendant is dead." He got that way as a result of having been shot by Burk Burnett and his bodyguard, Tom Pickett, in 1912 in the Goodwin Hotel in Paducah, Texas. *(From official court records—*State v. Farley Sayers, *Cause No. 1071, Baylor County District Court)*

And so ends the story of the violent vendetta between the old lion and the brash upstart . . . or does it? Two questions have been debated through the years.

First, was it murder or self-defense? The jury obviously bought into the self-defense theory when it acquitted Burk Burnett. Or, perhaps the jury *used* self-defense as an excuse to reach the desired verdict of acquittal. Both of the weekly newspapers (although supporting Burnett) obviously didn't believe the self-defense story—at least, not self-defense as defined by statutory Texas law. *The Paducah Post:* Sayers was "murdered *unsuspectingly* as he washed his face." *The Baylor County Banner:* "it seems evident that Sayers was not trying to draw his gun. . . . It is probable that he never knew what killed him."[84]

Charlie Coombes, in his memoirs, made this comment:

Just as Farley was raising his hands full of water to his face, Burnett pushed inward the swinging door with his left hand, and with his "forty some odd" [pistol] cocked in his right hand, placed it against the side of his victim, and, without warning, fired, blowing a very large hole through him and killing him instantly.

In my opinion, he [Burk Burnett] was not even in jeopardy [of being convicted by a jury]. I do not blame him for killing Sayers, because had he not done so, sooner or later Sayers would have killed him.

Still, Coombes ended his account of the affair with this melancholy reflection:

Thus the career of a West Texas boy who was hounded from mischief to desperation, murder and death ended.[85]

A. C. Piper, the longtime 6666 hand, didn't work there during the Burnett-Sayers war, but he did, in later years, come to know

Tom Pickett and visited with him about the incident on several occasions. Piper, in his 1999 interview with the author, recalled Pickett making this comment about the killing of Sayers: "Hell, we had to get rid of him. He was up there [at the hotel in Paducah], and we [he and Burk Burnett] decided it was a good time to do it—kill him while he was up there."[86]

Pickett gave a similar account to another longtime 6666 hand, the much-respected ranch manager, George Humphreys, who also served as King County sheriff. Humphreys, like Piper, was not employed by the ranch at the time of the 1912 killing of Sayers. (He started working for the Sixes in 1918.)[87] Pickett, however, was still around and he gave Humphreys an account similar to that which Pickett related to Piper. In a 1969 oral history interview, Humphreys said that Pickett verified that somebody from Cassidy Commission Co. alerted Burk to Farley's purchase of the 6666 cows, and that Burk headed for Paducah the same day, stopping in Wichita Falls just long enough to let Pickett climb aboard. Humphreys also verified the fact that both Burnett and Pickett witnessed Sayers and his group enter the Goodwin Hotel lobby and head for the washroom. "Wonder why the son-of-a-bitch didn't look around?" Burk mused. Pickett told Humphreys that he and Burk then followed Sayers into the washroom and killed him.[88]

The statements of both Humphreys and Piper (both quoting Pickett in separate conversations) flatly contradict Burk's testimony that he had no idea Sayers was anywhere in the vicinity when he and Pickett entered the washroom. Also, contrary to Burk's trial testimony, in neither of Pickett's later accounts of the encounter did he contend that Sayers appeared to be drawing a pistol just before he was shot.

The second question to be considered is, who really killed Farley Sayers? This is the question that has caused the most debate. Perhaps what follows should be evaluated in light of this fact: after the kill-

George Humphreys began cowboying for the 6666 Ranch in 1918 and
worked his way up the ladder until he
was named ranch manager, a position
he held until his retirement in 1970.
He also served as sheriff of King
County from 1928 through 1948.
(Courtesy of Eakin Press)

ing of Sayers on May 23, 1912, Tom Pickett never returned to his
Wichita Falls law enforcement career. He stayed instead on Burnett's payroll at the 6666 Ranch in Guthrie for the rest of his life.

Burnett, under oath, took sole responsibility for firing the fatal
shot. Why would he have done so if he hadn't actually pulled the
trigger? Trial tactics. Burnett was well known and powerful, both
politically and financially. Pickett was relatively unknown and had
no influence except what Burnett provided. Plus, everyone knew
the background of the Burnett-Sayers feud, and most probably felt
that Sayers had been stealing Burnett's cattle for years, and then
openly, and repeatedly, had threatened to kill Burk Burnett. On
the other hand, Sayers had never made any threats against Pickett.
Therefore, it was obvious that Burnett stood a much better chance
of "coming clean" before a Baylor County jury than did Pickett.
Plus, if he succeeded, then that would kill the Pickett indictment.
Conversely, if Pickett had been tried first and had claimed he shot
Sayers in self-defense (with Burnett at his side, mind you), and the
jury had *convicted* him, then Burnett would really have been in a
tight spot when his trial was called.

(In passing it should be noted that under Texas law, then and
now, both Burnett and Pickett would have been equally guilty of
murder, regardless of who actually pulled the trigger, if the evidence

demonstrated that they both, acting together, entered the washroom, pistols in hand, with the common purpose and intent to kill Farley Sayers and succeeded in doing so.)[89]

In the oral history taken from George Humphreys, he said that Pickett once recounted the confrontation to him, and said that both he and Burnett entered the washroom, pistols in hand, with the intent to kill Sayers, but that he, Pickett, was the "back-up" gun, only there to assure the plan was a success even if Burk missed his shot.[90]

However, most folks still believed that Pickett was the real triggerman. For openers, why would a rich man hire an experienced killer as a hit man, and then decide to take it upon himself to kill a deadly enemy when his hired gun was standing right there? Frank McCauley recalled that his uncle, Charlie Dowding, who knew Burnett and Pickett well and was himself a 6666 cowboy, always believed that Pickett was the man who solved Burnett's problems with Sayers.[91] C. M. Randall, another longtime Baylor County resident and one who found himself on the jury panel at Burnett's 1913 murder trial (he wasn't selected as a juror, however), in his oral history had this to say: "Burk admitted that he killed Sayers, but everyone knew that Pickett had killed him."[92] Jack Jones, the resident historian of Baylor County, wrote in his September 15, 1988, weekly historical column for *The Baylor County Banner*:

> Years later, Burnett is said to have confided in some extremely close friends that he didn't kill Sayers at all, but that Tom Pickett did, and that he, Burnett, admitted to the crime because he felt that he could come clear easier than Pickett.

Carmen Taylor Bennett writing in *Our Roots Grow Deep—A History of Cottle County*, says this:

> I suppose no one will ever know for sure who actually killed Farley Sayers . . . but the majority of the people to whom I have talked are not convinced that Mr. Burnett killed Farley Sayers. . . . The theory advanced was that Mr. Pickett fired the

fatal shot, but Mr. Burnett assumed the blame. True, it was the Burnett brand that had been menaced; he was not a man who was ordinarily involved in trouble, but was highly respected among cattlemen; and he was actually justified in any anger he might feel, for a man's brand ranked next to his children as an immediate extension of himself. Not only was Mr. Pickett an able gunman, but he would have less justification for the act. . . . I have been told in many interviews [that Pickett was] the killer of Mr. Sayers. I visited recently and at length with one of Farley's cousins, a Mr. McWhorter, and he nodded assent and seemed to agree with Richard Bolt that the deathbed confession of Tom Pickett was true.[93]

Moreover, Burnett's own words uttered shortly after the shooting when he telephoned his lawyer, Sidney Samuels, seems to imply he was not the actual triggerman. He said to Samuels, "I've had occasion to take a hand in the killing of Farley Sayers."[94]

When Sayers was killed in 1912 in the Goodwin Hotel in Paducah, Elmer Petty was a seventeen-year-old cowboy on the Pitchfork Ranch, which adjoins Burnett's 6666 Ranch on the west. When he was twenty-six, he quit the Pitchfork, moved to Paducah, and opened a barbershop only a short distance from the Goodwin Hotel. Cowboys from far and wide made Elmer Petty's barbershop their headquarters for sixty years. In 1983, when Petty was eighty-eight years old, he told this story to another old-timer, C. Warren:

I knew S. B. Burnett. He gunned down Farley Sayers in 1912 in the wash room in an old hotel here in Paducah. . . . The 6666's had a bunch of cattle at the Fort Worth market and Farley Sayers bought a carload of them cows and moved them back to his ranch. He had six or seven sections between the Forks and the Sixes. He stole lots of cattle, Farley did. He didn't steal from the little fellow.

Burnett's case was transferred to Baylor County and he came clear. You couldn't beat that money. A lot of people don't believe that Burnett killed him, but he taken the rap. They think a policeman from Wichita Falls killed him. The policeman was working for Burnett.

Walter Edwards was about 17, (I cowboyed with all them Dickens [County, Texas] Edwards) and [he] was working for Farley and was in the washroom. He was a witness in the case. When one of the lawyers asked him what he done when the shootin' started, he said: "I tried to climb the wall!"[95]

Substantiating the latter account is that of retired 6666 cowboy A. C. Piper. Toward the end of Pickett's life, he reminisced about his early days—recollections that often included the tale of the demise of Farley Sayers. Piper, in his oral history, states that Pickett himself reiterated the tale several times, each time telling that he was the one who actually pulled the trigger on Sayers. And every time Pickett repeated the story, he ended it with the same statement:

I kilt him purty.
I kilt him real purty.[96]

THE RETURN OF
HILL LOFTIS—AS TOM ROSS

Leaving His Outlaw Past Behind?

Lawman-turned-outlaw Joe Beckham was killed by a ranger-led posse on December 27, 1895, in the Suttle Creek gun battle in the Oklahoma Territory. Three other outlaws escaped into a roaring "blue norther" blizzard late that night. As we have seen, two of the three—Red Buck Weightman and Elmer "Kid" Lewis—came to violent ends within three months of the encounter. But what about the fourth outlaw—Hill Loftis?

Less than two months after the dugout duel, a Wilbarger County, Texas, grand jury convened in Vernon and returned an aggravated robbery indictment against Loftis for the December 26, 1895, armed robbery of Alf Bailey's store.[1] An arrest warrant was promptly issued. The Wilbarger County sheriff offered a twenty-five-dollar reward for Loftis's body—breathing or otherwise—and the Texas Rangers listed him in their "Most Wanted" book. (The rangers called it their "Book of Knaves.")[2] But the elusive Hill Loftis could not be found. For the next seven years the rangers and other lawmen searched high and low for him, but in vain. And, some thirty-three years later, when the curtain finally fell on his incredible and violent journey through the southwest frontier, the finale would not feature a gun battle with lawmen or a neck-tie party thrown by an angry mob.

While Hill Loftis was every bit as nervy and fearless as his cohorts Red Buck and Kid Lewis, there the similarity ended. Loftis was no crude, ignorant, illiterate, inarticulate, psychopathic killer. In fact, he was intelligent, likable, and charismatic, and, at least to his friends and family, he was warm, generous, and loyal. Yet beneath the surface there always lurked something dark, dangerous, and . . . enigmatic.

HILL LOFTIS, A.K.A. TOM ROSS: THE EARLY YEARS

Born on a cotton farm on June 11, 1872, in Monroe County, Mississippi, Hillary U. Loftis was the fourth of six children of Samuel Jameson Loftis and wife, Jane Loftis.[3] He was twenty-three years old at the time of the Sutters line camp shootout, but he had been on his own since he left his Mississippi home at age thirteen and headed west to Texas.[4] By the fall of 1889, seventeen-year-old Hill Loftis was a working cowboy on the sprawling W. T. Waggoner Ranch, which straddled the Red River.[5] At age nineteen his appearance was striking: he had grown into a muscular man standing five feet, nine inches tall and weighing 160 pounds, and he had "flashing black eyes that could pierce through a man like cold steel." His most unusual feature, however, was his head. He had a "peculiarly shaped skull," which caused some to call him "Buffalo Head." Others referred to it as a "watermelon-shaped head."[6] However one chose to describe it, it was a unique physical feature that was just about impossible to disguise or hide—and a decided liability for an outlaw on the dodge.

Cattle czars like W. T. Waggoner and Burk Burnett typically located their headquarters on deeded ranches in northwest Texas, but as we have noted, they leased huge chunks of lush grazing lands for pennies per acre from the Indians north of the Red River in the Indian Territory ("Oklahoma Territory" after 1890). If we add the acreage leased from the Indians just north of the Red River to deeded lands lying south of the river, the Waggoner Ranch controlled about 500,000 acres and carried as many as 60,000 head of cattle.[7] By the time Hill Loftis was twenty years old, the Waggoners had put

Outlaw Tom Ross. His real name was Hillary U. Loftis. He was convicted of the 1923 murder of Texas & Southwestern Cattle Raisers Association inspectors Dave Allison and H. L. Roberson in Seminole, Texas. *(Courtesy Nita Stewart Haley Memorial Library, Midland, Texas)*

him in charge of their Suttle Creek line camp right in the middle of a mighty rough and tumble piece of real estate.[8]

After the Civil War the Red River borderlands became a haven for thieves, murderers, bootleggers, and others Walter Prescott Webb called the "social debris" of the era.[9] Law enforcement was mighty puny in northwest Texas and almost nonexistent in the Indian Territory. Except in certain circumstances, Texas lawmen were not authorized to cross over the state boundary to conduct investigations or make arrests—another circumstance that encouraged borderland banditry. Of that time and place, one observer made this cogent comment:

> In this environment, the general public developed a high tolerance for anyone who could survive the daily perils of life. This appreciation for the self-reliant man included even the outlaw, especially if he were daring and successful. . . . This psychology . . . allowed gunslingers and feudists to become heroes.[10]

Moreover, in the beginning, cattle thievery was widespread and not yet taken very seriously. In that more relaxed milieu, a contemporary of Hill Loftis recalled that as a Waggoner cowboy he got his first lesson in stealing cattle: "We drifted cattle picking up everything we could, shoving all the fat ones and the stolen ones toward the Red River."[11] Ramon Adams, another early-day puncher, later reflected that "mavericking" was common even among the big cattlemen during those times. Rounding up larger, unbranded calves and adding them to one's herd was not only common, but relatively risk-free—certainly not as risky as altering the brand on a neighbor's critter. It was not unusual for the boss man to order his hands to "get out and rustle up a few mavericks," especially during the winter months when big calves missed in the spring and fall brandings were, like ripe fruit, there for the picking.[12] It was in this environment that the young and parentless Hill Loftis came of age.

Frank L. Campbell, who later became a Texas & Southwestern Cattle Raisers Association inspector at the National Stockyards in St. Louis, knew Hill Loftis when he first hired on as a cowboy for the Waggoner Ranch. Years later he recorded this recollection of young Hill Loftis: "In those days he was a good enough young fellow, and I had nothing against him until he got in with a certain outfit of bad men. He was a lively youth, fond of fun and a bright one."[13]

How and under what circumstances young Loftis fell in with a band of outlaws led by the cold-eyed, vicious killer Red Buck Weightman will likely never be known. Apparently it was sometime in the fall of 1895 when Loftis joined Red Buck's gang. Shortly thereafter, Red Buck, Kid Lewis, Joe Beckham, and Hill Loftis went on their Christmas week crime binge.

After Loftis's 1896 Suttle Creek dugout escape, the next reported sighting of Hill Loftis occurred about May 1, 1899, in the Jarilla Mountains in eastern New Mexico Territory. Eddy County New Mexico Sheriff Cicero Stewart and a posse were on the trail of four horse thieves (Dan Johnson, James Knight, Samuel Morrow, and Charles Ware) when they encountered and arrested a man identifying himself only as Ross. Although the man was known to have been in the company of the rustlers previously, Stewart finally released him because he could not positively identify him or prove that he was part of the gang. Little did Sheriff Stewart realize that he had just turned loose a much sought-after desperado whose real name was Hill Loftis.[14]

That same man, now calling himself Tom Ross, next surfaced in 1902 in the remote sand-dune landscape along the West Texas–New Mexico Territory boundary in the southern Staked Plains (Llano Estacado) northwest of Seminole, Texas, and just east of Lovington, New Mexico, where he purchased 2,560 acres of land.[15] Even in 1902 it was such a wild and unsettled borderland that a wanted man would be difficult to locate and capture there.

Some folks in that lonesome place on the southern Staked Plains apparently suspected that "Tom Ross" might have had a past. But in those days frontier folks tended to mind their own business, for it was considered bad manners to get too damned curious about someone's past. "Live and let live" was the way they looked at it. An anonymous bit of humorous verse went something like this:

> *What was your name in the States?*
> *Was it Thompson or Johnson or Bates?*
> *Did you murder your wife?*
> *Did you flee for your life?*
> *Oh, what was your name in the States?*[16]

Humor not being the long suit of the Texas Rangers, they were not amused by such doggerel: Loftis remained a headliner in the Rangers' "Book of Knaves." Strangely enough, Tom Ross gave positive indications that he wanted to turn from his outlaw past and go straight—even become a family man. He settled down as an ordinary rancher on his small spread, and he found himself a wife—his childhood sweetheart, Miss Lillian "Trixie" Hardin, a twenty-two-year-old visually impaired woman (she was almost blind) from a fairly prosperous family. He had known her when her family lived in the North Texas town of Wichita Falls—Waggoner Ranch country. Later, the family moved to New Mexico Territory's unorganized Lea County just across the state line from Tom Ross's ranch. On January 24, 1904, in the little town of Gomez in nearby unorganized Terry County, Texas, "Tom Ross," now age thirty-one, married Miss Hardin.[17] They returned to Tom's Gaines County ranch and settled down.

But there was still that troublesome matter of the outstanding Wilbarger County armed robbery indictment; there was still that outstanding arrest warrant for Hill Loftis, and the Texas Rangers were on his trail.

THE SAND DUNES SHOWDOWN WITH RANGER CAPTAIN ROGERS

In 1904 the Texas Rangers finally got a credible tip that Hill Loftis had changed his name to Tom Ross and was hanging out along the Texas–New Mexico Territory border. In Vernon, the Wilbarger County sheriff, Johnnie Williams, who had campaigned on a promise to capture Hill Loftis, also heard the news, and he wanted a part of the action—or at least a part of the credit for a successful manhunt. Sheriff Williams, Martin County Sheriff Charley Toms, and Texas Ranger Capt. John A. Rogers rendezvoused in June 1904, mounted their horses, and launched a manhunt for Tom Ross, alias Hill Loftis. They had information (accurate, as it turned out) that Ross was assisting in a roundup on the Halff Ranch in the dunes of northwest Gaines County, Texas, near the New Mexico line. For some reason, Sheriff Williams dropped out of the hunt. However, Ranger Captain Rogers and Sheriff Toms did, in fact, find and attempt to confront Ross at the roundup site on June 17, 1904, the result of which has often been referred to as the "duel in the sand dunes." The ever-vigilant Tom Ross spied the approaching lawmen and beat a hasty retreat. Captain Rogers got off a shot or two, attempting to kill or wound Ross or Ross's horse. But he missed, and the lawmen's horses were too jaded to give meaningful pursuit. However, that did not end the episode. The real confrontation was yet to come, the details of which differ significantly depending on who is telling the

Texas Ranger Capt. John H. Rogers, one of the "four great captains" who served during frontier times, tried, unsuccessfully, to arrest Tom Ross in 1904 in the sand dunes west of Seminole, Texas. Instead, Ross turned the tables on Captain Rogers, got the drop on him, disarmed him, and then disappeared once again. *(Courtesy Nita Stewart Haley Memorial Library, Midland, Texas)*

tale. What is clear is that a second confrontation did occur, and that the two lawmen came off second-best.

After Ranger Captain Rogers fired those initial shots at the retreating Ross, Rogers and Sheriff Toms returned to the roundup camp and ate supper. Finishing their meal, the lawmen decided to return to the ranch where they were encamped. They needed fresh horses. To get there, however, they had to take the same route that Ross had taken when he had fled from the two officers just a short time before. It did not occur to the ranger captain or the sheriff that this might not be a wise decision. Obviously they underestimated the wiley and fearless Tom Ross—a mistake other lawmen had made before and would make again. Captain Rogers and Sheriff Toms had traveled only a short distance from the roundup site when they rounded a large sand dune and found themselves face to face with the outlaw Ross. Worse yet, much to their dismay—and terror—Ross had a cocked and loaded Winchester rifle leveled on them. But Ross did not shoot them. A greatly embarrassed Texas Ranger captain described the confrontation to his superiors in his next monthly report. He related that Ross "throwed down" on them, and then continued:

> We immediately jumped from our horses. As I fell to the ground he fired at me. About the same time I hit the ground I slipped and hurt my back. I felt confident that I was ruined. He kept me covered with the Winchester, giving me no opportunity to draw my pistol or even to get a hand on it. Advancing with the Winchester coming all the way to me as I lay on my back with my hands up, and in spite of all I could do or say it looked as though he would kill me, saying that I had tried to murder him an hour and a half previously. Finally he said he would not kill me, but only for the regard of some cowman that had ridden up meantime. He took my pistol from me and unloaded it, returning it to me empty. He also relieved me of the balance of my ammunition. [The] capias [warrant] for his arrest he kept.[18]

Sheriff Toms also gave an account of the episode, and it placed Captain Rogers in an even less favorable light. According to Sheriff Toms, Ross shot the reins off the captain's bridle and then told them (Rogers and Toms) to throw down their guns, which they did. Captain Rogers fell off his horse and began to yell, "I'm shot, I'm shot." Sheriff Toms said, "You'd better get up or you will be shot." Ross threatened to shoot Rogers but was talked out of the notion by Billy Connell, the Halff Ranch wagon boss who had, meanwhile, ridden up on the confrontation. Ross unloaded the lawmen's pistols, pocketed the cartridges, and then returned their weapons.[19]

Ranger Captain Rogers ended his report of the incident to his superior, Texas Adj. Gen. John Hulen, on a contrite note, one completely out of character with the Texas Rangers' usual bluster and braggadocio. He confessed:

It is very humiliating to me, this being the first report of this kind in 22 years of service, but I feel that to have made fight under the condition, being out of range of effective work with a pistol and having a man with a Winchester thrown down on me, I would better have attempted suicide.[20]

Meanwhile, Tom Ross wheeled his horse around and, as night fell, disappeared into the sand dunes, taking with him the rangers' warrant for his arrest. The rangers soon sent out a four-man scouting party to scour the Staked Plains all along the Texas–New Mexico border.[21] They even staked out and watched Ross's ranch home, all to no avail. They concluded that the elusive outlaw "might be out of state."

Along about this time the weekly newspaper in nearby Brownfield, *The Terry Voice*, carried this interesting report in its July 15, 1904, edition:

16 Texas Rangers located Tom Ross lately, and went away empty. We did not learn whether any shots were exchanged . . . but the Rangers are said to have found him practicing with his guns, and it may be that his marksmanship was more or less suggestive of the propriety of their retiring without him.

Salt in the wound of the prideful Texas Rangers.

In his authoritative thesis on Ross, author James I. Fenton casts doubt on the authenticity of this report, suggesting that it might simply be a tardy, though embellished, account of the previous sand dunes encounter. Fenton adds: "Regardless, this account is suggestive of the Rangers' failure to handle Ross in the high-handed manner that had become their trademark in a colorful, though ignoble, part of law enforcement."[22]

In any event, the cagey outlaw had once again thumbed his nose at Texas law enforcement officers in general and at the Texas Rangers in particular. The resulting grudge would only grow and fester with time. And, having twice been fired on by the rangers, Tom Ross nursed a festering grudge of his own.

ANSWERING THE VERNON INDICTMENT

Time passed and nothing more was heard from Tom. Then one day, some two years later, a strange thing happened: Tom Ross calmly strolled into Martin County Sheriff Charley Tom's office in Stanton, Texas—and surrendered. He agreed to return with the sheriff to Vernon in Wilbarger County to face the ten-year-old indictment against him for the Christmastime 1895 armed robbery of Alf Bailey's store and post office. Ross made bond on May 28, 1906, and was released pending a trial scheduled for September 1906.[23]

Hill Loftis, now Tom Ross, duly appeared in Vernon to face trial in September. But first his lawyer, L. P. Bonner, had a preliminary motion to present to the court: a "Motion to Quash the Indictment." While the indictment duly charged that Loftis had, at gunpoint, taken from the *possession* of Alf Bailey a long list of enumerated items stolen on that occasion, still, lawyer Bonner complained, it failed to add the magic words—the allegation that Alf Bailey "was then and there the *owner*" of those items of stolen property taken from his possession. The trial judge considered the motion and granted it, thus dismissing the indictment against Hill Loftis.[24] In frontier Texas criminal jurisprudence, courts insisted that indictments be couched in the long and convoluted legalese so beloved by lawyers of that day, and that all the old common-law archaic and arcane formalities of pleading practice be strictly adhered to. Otherwise the indictment would be dismissed before trial, or, if a conviction were had based on such a faulty indictment, it would be reversed on appeal. However, even if an indictment was dismissed on account of a technical flaw, the prosecutor usually could (and still can) go back to the grand jury and obtain a new and revised indictment and proceed to prosecute the defendant—*usually*, that is, but not always. Worse news yet for the Texas Rangers: since more than five years had passed since the date of the offense, the five-year statute of limitations on robbery barred any reindictment of Loftis for the Alf Bailey robbery. Hence, Hill Loftis/Tom Ross, descended the steps of the Wilbarger County courthouse a free man.

Still, if Tom Ross thought he would start over with a clean slate, he was mistaken.

While the law might have been satisfied, old grudges lingered. Peace officers, with considerable justification, thought that Ross had beaten the system while flouting both the law and mocking the officers sworn to enforce it. Similarly, it was no secret that the fearless and combative Ross never let go of a grudge. And so the stage was set; the actors were motivated.

TOM ROSS, THE RANCHER

With his legal affairs straightened out, Hill Loftis, as Tom Ross, reunited with his family and returned to his ranch along the border of Texas and the New Mexico Territory. Even in 1906 it was yet a remote and unsettled land. For example, Gaines County, where the eastern portion of Ross's ranch was located, was not even organized as a county until 1905, with tiny Seminole as the county seat. Four years later, in 1910, only five hundred people called Gaines County home, three hundred of them residing in Seminole. Mind you, Gaines County was, and still is, a huge chunk of real estate—fifteen hundred square miles, give or take, being about fifty miles wide, east to west, and thirty miles long, north to south. New Mexico did not obtain statehood until 1912, and Lea County (the New Mexico county that joined Gaines County, Texas, on the west and where the western portion of the Ross ranch was located) did not become an organized county until 1917. Truly it was one of the last frontiers of the Old West.

For the next seventeen years Tom Ross prospered. The personable Ross made many friends, and most old-timers agreed he had far more friends than enemies.[25] He seemed, at least, to have left his outlaw past behind for good. A daughter, Bessie, was born to him and Trixie, and Ross increased his land holdings so that his spread covered 7,689 acres straddling the state line.[26] (He received his mail at Knowles, New Mexico Territory.) As ever, in the dry desert of far West Texas (annual rainfall average only about seventeen inches per year), water holes were few and far between. Ross therefore began drilling water wells on his ranch and erecting windmills to provide stock water. Since there were few fences dividing properties in those days, this enabled Ross to use considerably more than his deeded 7,689 acres of range. Plus, in addition to simply raising cattle and selling off the year's calf crop each fall, Ross engaged in buying, selling, and trading cattle the year round, traveling frequently to various markets and occasionally even to markets as distant as the national stockyards in St. Louis, Missouri.

Mary Whatley Clarke was a young, single school teacher who lived a few miles from the Tom Ross ranch when she began teaching in a small rural school in 1920. She became well acquainted with Tom and his family. Years later she would pen reminiscences of Ross:

> He was a good neighbor and this was what counted in that lonely country. His name was Tom Ross and the apple of his eye was his little black-eyed daughter Bessie. . . . When school opened Ross would sometimes come by my aunt's house and take us to school. . . . [Once] Tom invited my aunt's family and me for supper in his home. He prepared a delicious meal consisting of sour dough biscuits, tender steak and rich cream gravy. He was an interesting talker and the evening passed quickly and pleasantly. On other occasions he would send over some freshly killed beef or a dressed turkey.[27]

Clarke added that she and all the other neighbors had heard rumors of Tom's outlaw past. That, she said, plus the fact that Ross "could hit a quail on the wing with a six shooter," caused all the neighboring ranchers to be wary of him.[28] "They tried to be good neighbors with Ross and not have any trouble with him," she said. Nevertheless, Tom was noted for his generosity. Old-timers agreed that Ross would "give his last penny to a widow or orphan."[29]

Other reports attest to the fact that Ross was sociable, likeable, and generous. He donated funds to a local church and to other community projects, such as the building of the first jail in Seminole. In 1908, Tom and Trixie even joined, and were baptized in, the First Baptist Church of Seminole,[30] but when the preacher castigated them for allowing young people to dance in their home, Tom balked. The preacher and his flock responded by "churching" Tom and Trixie out of the congregation for "conduct unbecoming a Christian."[31] But the dancing continued.[32]

Nevertheless, Tom Ross, the former fugitive from justice, had come a long way within a relatively short time. And his fortunes continued to rise, as did his status in the community. He now had several hired hands to help with ranch chores. He bought a nice home in Seminole where the family lived during the winter months. In 1908 he was awarded a contract to operate a fourth-class post office out of his ranch house.[33] In 1913 Ross bought a new Model T Ford. Furthermore, unlike many frontier cattlemen, his generosity was underscored by the fact that he often helped small nesters who, shortly after the turn of the century, began trickling into the county, attempting to eke out a living from farms in that bleak, dry, and desolate land.[34] The charismatic former outlaw thus cultivated quite a following.

However, he was not loved by everyone. On several occasions during these good years, his hair-triggered temper emerged from the dark side, overrode his good judgment, and got him into trouble. During these seventeen years (1906 to 1923) Ross was charged with three misdemeanors: once for fighting in a public place, then for assaulting another with a pistol, and finally for carrying a concealed weapon.[35] These resulted in small fines.

In 1912 he got into a more serious scrape with one Jack Russell, a local rancher. Ross contracted with Russell to buy Russell's calf crop, to be delivered to Ross the next fall when the calves were weaned. Ross then gave Russell $750 as down payment with the balance to be paid on delivery of the calves. Soon, however, Ross changed his mind and demanded that Russell return his $750. Russell refused. In response, the pugnacious Ross pulled a pistol on Russell and forced him to go to town, cash a check, and return the $750 to him.[36]

Russell, in turn, responded by filing criminal charges against Ross, and Ross was eventually indicted on two counts of armed robbery in the Eddy County District Court in Carlsbad, New Mexico.[37] Ross hired a New Mexico lawyer, Col. E. P. Bujac, to represent him, and the lawyer finally worked out a deal whereby Ross would return the $750 to Russell, plead guilty to a lesser charge, and pay a $500 fine plus court costs—no jail time to be served, however. As part of the deal, the more serious criminal charge was dismissed.[38] Although he escaped this mess relatively unscathed, Ross, predictably, was disgruntled with the outcome, and when Bujac presented his fee statement to Ross in the amount of $500, Ross flatly refused to pay his lawyer. "Far too much," Ross grumbled, adding that he could have cut as good a deal himself.

Undaunted, Bujac responded by suing his former client for his fee in the district court in Carlsbad.[39] The next problem was how to get Ross physically served with the court's citation and a copy of the petition, a necessary predicate to going forward with the lawsuit. The Eddy County sheriff was afraid Ross would shoot him if he tried to serve the papers on him. Finally, Bujac hired a private citizen—a man who hated Tom Ross—to serve the papers. The process server eventually accomplished this task by waiting until Ross showed up at a Carlsbad saloon. He then entered the bar with a 10-gauge sawed-off shotgun leveled on Ross and forced Ross to accept the papers. Within the hour Ross showed up at Bujac's office and paid the fee.[40]

As the last two incidents clearly demonstrate, Ross still believed in the frontier custom of resolving disputes by resorting to intimidation, violence, and gunplay. After all, personal vindication of wrongs was a part of the culture of the Old West, and he still clung to those old ways. Even into the 1920s he carried two six-shooters on his person at all times, and a .30-30 rifle concealed in the bedroll he carried with him whether traveling by car or by horse. Ever watchful and wary, Ross never permitted a lamp to burn in his home after sundown, would never sit by a window, and whenever he entered a room he would sit only with his back to the wall. Occasionally during the day Tom would climb the windmill tower near his ranch house and carefully scan the surrounding plains.[41]

BANK ROBBERY IN A SANDSTORM: SEMINOLE, 1912

In 1912 a spectacular crime occurred in Seminole, and a lot of folks in those parts suspected that Tom Ross was involved. If so, his reformation (if he truly had reformed) suffered a serious relapse. It all happened about two-thirty one cold, winter afternoon—February 15, 1912, to be exact. A bone-chilling blue norther had swept through that dusty, desert plateau of a village, kicking up a blinding sandstorm that chased most folks inside and reduced visibility to near nil. Out of the storm two masked riders appeared on the street that led to the First National Bank of Seminole. They rode to the rear of the bank, dismounted, and tied up their horses. When the pair entered, six-shooters drawn, there was only one person inside—the assistant teller, John Haney. It didn't take the disguised duo but a few minutes to scoop up $3,500 of the bank's cash, lock Haney in the vault, and disappear—headed westward—back into the sandstorm. In that day and time, $3,500 was not an inconsiderable sum. The bank heist had gone off without a hitch, as did their escape. The pair (and/or an associate) had cut the telephone lines coming into Seminole from the west, thus precluding local lawmen from alerting other area officers along their westward escape route. The robbers had also taken the precaution of stashing fresh mounts west of Seminole.

Gaines County Sheriff F. F. Lord rounded up a posse shortly after somebody finally discovered what had happened, and the sheriff and his men spurred out after the pair, trailing them into the

New Mexico Territory where, near Hobbs, some fifty miles west of Seminole, the posse lost the trail in the sand dunes. They returned home empty-handed and dejected. Only one piece of inculpatory evidence was ever discovered along the robbers' escape route. It was a Stetson hat with the name "Henry Clay McGonagill" stenciled on the sweat brim. McGonagill was a world-class steer roper and a small rancher in that area. He was also a close friend of Tom Ross. Although Ross and McGonagill were widely believed to have been the culprits, there was never sufficient evidence to bring them to trial. And the money was never recovered.[42]

Meanwhile, as the years passed, even this remote land and its inhabitants were slowly but inexorably being dragged into the twentieth century. Telephone lines began to link even the rural areas with the rest of the world, and cow trails were being graded into roads traversable by Model T Fords. In 1917 the Santa Fe Railroad extended its rails southward from Lubbock to Seagraves, only eighteen miles north of Seminole, and the next year the Texas and Pacific Railroad extended its line northward from Midland to Seminole.

Changes were not limited to physical advances; society itself was evolving. Tom Ross himself, as we have seen, bought a Model T automobile in 1913, and he made use of telephones and rail travel. But Tom Ross—the inner man, both the dark side and the bright side of him—seemed not to have changed at all.

ENTER FEARLESS DAVE ALLISON, LAWMAN

In the early 1920s, lawmen began receiving an increasing number of complaints of cattle rustling in West Texas.[43] In 1922, two cattle inspectors from the powerful Texas and Southwestern Cattle Raisers Association (T&SCRA), William Davis "Dave" Allison and Horace L. "Hod" Roberson, began to suspect that Tom Ross had reverted to his old outlaw ways and was responsible for at least some of the thefts. They were determined that this time Ross would not slip through the net. Both were rough-and-tumble frontier lawmen; both were fearless survivors of more than a few gun battles; and both had several notches whittled on the handles of their six-shooters.

Allison, then sixty-one years old, had been in law enforcement most of his adult life.[44] But, before he managed to get himself elected sheriff of Midland County, Texas, in 1888, he had already earned respect as "a cowboy of the old school." At age twenty-seven, he was the youngest sheriff in the state of Texas. After serving in that capacity for twelve years, he went on to become a sergeant in the Texas Rangers, a lieutenant in the Arizona Rangers, top bodyguard and chief of security for a Mexico mining mogul, chief of police of Roswell, New Mexico, a West Texas constable and deputy sheriff, a U.S. Deputy Marshal, and an inspector for the Texas and Southwestern Cattle Raisers Association. Following his death, the *St. Louis Post-Dispatch* had this to say:

> Dave Allison had been a man of much experience in gun fights. Though according to repute he was inclined to peace, as Sheriff and Ranger he had found it necessary to engage in many hand-to-hand combats. It is of record that during his 12 years as Sheriff of Midland County he never went after a man he did not get, though as a rule he took his prisoners alive. Men sought by Sheriff Allison knew his reputation for coolness in emergencies, and he was not an officer to be resisted by men who cared to keep their hides intact.[45]

Although Allison was generally a well-respected lawman who had proved his effectiveness by subduing, capturing, and, when necessary, killing some of the worst desperadoes on the frontier, still his record was not without a blemish or two. For openers, Allison was bad to gamble—a vice in which his enthusiasm apparently greatly exceeded his skill.[46] After serving twelve years as sheriff and tax collector for Midland County, he resigned under suspicion that he may have gambled away some of the county's tax funds. Despite a sizeable shortage in these accounts (about $10,000 according to one source),[47] he was never charged with embezzlement. Allison did, however, plead guilty to a gambling charge about that time. Later he was fired as an Arizona Ranger for running up excessive gambling debts. Still later, when he was Roswell's police chief, he was indicted for attempting to bribe the district attorney. When a number of sheep were poisoned in the area, sheepmen accused certain cattlemen of the offense. Allison, ever the champion of cowmen, apparently offered a sum of money to the DA in exchange for favorable treatment of his friends. When put to trial, Allison admitted offering a bribe to the official, but the jury bought into his story that it was all a part of his personal "sting" operation designed to determine if the local DA was on the take.[48]

Allison had also been indicted and tried for murder in connection with the killing of Pascual Orozco, Jr., a Mexican Revolutionary general turned outlaw, and four members of his bandit gang. Orozco was a fellow Revolutionary war general with Pancho Villa in the successful effort to overthrow Mexican President Porfirio Díaz in 1911. However, after the Mexican Revolution, Orozco turned full-time bandit and raided, robbed, and killed on both sides of the border. Finally he was charged in the United States with violation of the U.S. neutrality laws, and a warrant was issued for his arrest. U.S. citizens along the border were outraged by the bloodshed, and the focus was on Orozco. Allison and other lawmen received reports in late August 1915 that five Mexican bandits were on a raid south of Sierra Blanca, and on August 30, 1915, a posse led by Allison trapped the bandits in the High Lonesome Mountains in the Van Horn Range and killed all five. It turned out that Orozco was one of the five. There were four bullet holes in his body.

Although most border inhabitants cheered the news of Orozco's demise, still many of Mexican ancestry on both sides of the border regarded Orozco as something of a hero. They raised an outcry, and the Mexican government joined in.[49] All this resulted in indictments against Allison and his men.[50] They were tried in Van Horn, Culberson County, Texas, but, to no one's surprise, were all acquit-

Dave Allison, T&SCRA inspector, was
murdered by Tom Ross and Milt Good
on April 1, 1923, in Seminole, Texas.
(Courtesy The Cattleman *magazine)*

ted. One unsubstantiated report had it that Allison and his men shot
and killed Orozco and his men after they had surrendered,[51] but
Allison and his men swore that the Mexican bandits were all killed
during the battle.[52]

Whatever blemishes might have been on Allison's record,
there remained no doubt that Allison was a fearless lawman. During those years, George S. Patton, Jr., who later gained fame as a
general in World War II, was a U.S. Army lieutenant stationed on
the U.S.–Mexico border. He and Allison became friends. Patton said
of Allison: "He was a very quiet-looking old man with a sweet face
and white hair. He is the most noted gunman in Texas."[53]

In 1922, when the events of this story began to unravel, Allison was a paid inspector for the T&SCRA, but he also held a badge
as a deputy U.S. Marshal and as deputy sheriff of Garza County,
Texas, the latter two being nonsalaried positions.

ENTER DEADLY "HOD" ROBERSON, LAWMAN

Dave Allison's fellow T&SCRA inspector, H. L. "Hod" Roberson,
shared some of Allison's qualities and character traits: Roberson was
also fearless, determined, dangerous, and a deadly gun hand. How-

ever, Roberson, then age forty-eight, a handsome six-foot, 247-pound fellow with brown hair and haunting brown eyes, was very different from Allison in many ways.[54] Folks, even in the law enforcement and ranching communities, were sharply divided when it came to their opinions of Roberson. More than a few assessed Roberson as a vindictive, hot-tempered, arrogant, and self-righteous man who got downright nasty when he didn't get his way. Unlike Allison, he was loud, boastful, and given to voicing intemperate threats. However, that said, it must also be noted that Roberson was an effective lawman and an implacable foe. If lawmen (as well as outlaws, for that matter) are viewed within the context of their time and place, their actions, attitudes, and demeanor can better be understood. The early twentieth century Rio Grande borderland was no place for the weak or the meek. Roberson had proved himself to be up to the task of confronting and conquering some of the worst hard cases of that era—hard cases of both Mexican and Anglo descent.

Roberson was unique in another aspect. Unlike most westerners of the day Roberson didn't touch liquor, didn't smoke, dip snuff, or chew tobacco, and even refused a social cup of coffee. And he always "kept himself perfectly groomed."[55]

Roberson was born November 11, 1874, in Guadalupe County, Texas, and, like many frontier lawmen, started his career as a cowboy. Later he served about a year in the U.S. Army and fought in the Spanish-American War in the Philippines campaign.[56] He also worked as a railroad conductor for a time.[57] On October 11, 1911, he joined the Texas Rangers, serving under Capt. John R. "Border Boss" Hughes along the Rio Grande east of El Paso. Roberson had been a ranger for less than two months when he killed his first Hispanic. At the little village of Calero some five miles east of El Paso, he and two other rangers witnessed a saloonkeeper ejecting some belligerent celebrants from his tavern. Roberson waded into the fray and ended up shooting one of the drunks to death. Thereafter he was tried and acquitted on his plea of self-defense, testifying that the deceased had pulled a knife on him.[58] In April 1914 Roberson was promoted to the rank of sergeant. Two months later he was once

H. L. Roberson, T&SCRA inspector, was murdered by Tom Ross and Milt Good on April 1, 1923, in Seminole, Texas. *(Courtesy* The Cattleman *magazine)*

again indicted for murder. He and another ranger, Private Ira Cline, rode into Marfa to serve a warrant on Carlos Morales Wood, the editor of a Spanish-language newspaper. Somehow that encounter also ended up in a fatal shooting scrape. Both Roberson and Cline were tried and acquitted on their plea of self-defense. They had both shot the editor, they testified, after he had drawn a gun on them.[59] Shortly thereafter, on September 1, 1915, Roberson resigned from the Texas Rangers to take a much higher paying job as foreman of the huge million-acre T. O. Ranch just south of the Rio Grande in Old Mexico. Roberson put together a force of twenty-five gunmen to protect the ranch from Mexican raiders. Not long thereafter, Mexican bandits led by one of Pancho Villa's captains captured Roberson and several of his men. They, no doubt, expected to be executed before sundown, but for reasons not completely clear, they were released a few days later, whereupon they lost no time scrambling back across the Rio Grande into the United States. Roberson was enraged over the incident. A number of unarmed Hispanics soon turned up dead—some murdered in their sleep. Uncorroborated legend has it that Roberson had exacted his revenge. Whatever the truth of the matter, the net result was that Roberson gained the reputation of being a bitter, deadly, and unforgiving enemy.[60]

Roberson's reputation as a violent and dangerous man with a hair-trigger temper was soon enhanced by another incident that almost put him behind bars for quite a spell. The owners of the T. O. Ranch had contracted with an El Paso County rancher named Foote Boykin to pasture a herd of T. O. cattle on Boykin's ranch near Sierra Blanca, Texas. (Sierra Blanca is now the county seat of Hudspeth County. However, until 1917 Hudspeth County was a part of El Paso County.) The owners sent word to foreman Roberson to bring the cattle from Mexico across the Rio Grande to Boykin's ranch. At that time Roberson and Boykin had never met. On January 15, 1915, Roberson and his hands crossed the border with the cattle and penned them overnight at the railroad corral at Sierra Blanca, intending to drive them on to Boykin's ranch the next day. Meanwhile, Boykin had been notified that the cattle were on their way, so early the next morning he and a fellow rancher named Tom Cross got to the railroad pens before Roberson and his hands arrived. Since the pasturage agreement was on a per-head basis, Boykin needed to get a count on the T. O. cattle. He and Cross went into the pens and began counting the cattle. Also present were Ira Norton and his two sons, William and James. While this was going on, Roberson, accompanied by two of his cowhands, Elmer Dumont and a nineteen-year-old kid named Walter Sitter, rode up. Not knowing either Boykin or Cross, Roberson immediately demanded to know what the hell they were doing in the lot with his cattle.

It is undisputed that Roberson was armed with a Winchester rifle and a pistol, and that neither Boykin, Cross, nor the Nortons were armed, except that Boykin did have a pocket knife. It is also undisputed that immediately upon Roberson's arrival, a heated argument flared between Roberson and Boykin, ending only when Roberson, still mounted on his horse and inside the cattle pen, drew his pistol and shot Boykin (who was afoot) three times, killing him on the spot.[61] Boykin, by the way, was no shrinking violet. He stood six feet, three inches tall and was said to be "all man, all time," and

The legendary Texas Ranger Capt. John R. "Border Boss" Hughes. Both Dave Allison and H. L. Roberson served as sergeants in the Texas Rangers under Captain Hughes's command shortly after the turn of the century. *(Courtesy of the Texas Ranger Hall of Fame and Museum, Waco, Texas)*

he refused to be intimidated by Roberson's bluster and threats. Nevertheless, he unwisely failed to heed the old common-sense axiom: "Never take a knife to a gun fight."

Subsequent testimony by Cross and the three Nortons (the youngest being a fourteen-year-old boy) was fairly consistent: The proud and overbearing Roberson didn't bother with polite preamble when he rode up and saw Cross and Boykin in the pen with T. O. cattle. "What the hell are you doing there?" he demanded.

"Counting cattle," Boykin replied.

Roberson ordered him out of the pens. Boykin refused to get out.

Roberson: "You will, you son-of-a-bitch."

Boykin: "You call me a son-of-a-bitch; you are a son-of-a-bitch."

Roberson then started to open the gate into the pen. Boykin walked toward the gate, whereupon Roberson pulled his Winchester from the saddle scabbard and pointed it through a panel in the gate. Boykin called him a coward, pointing out that he was not armed. Roberson scabbarded the rifle and said, "I can clean you without anything."

Boykin then climbed the fence between them. Roberson demanded that Boykin take back his "son-of-a-bitch" epithet. Boykin replied: "You called me one first; you take back the one you called me, and I will take back the one I called you."

But that wasn't the answer Roberson was looking for. In response, Roberson (still mounted) grabbed his lariat and lashed Boykin (sitting on the fence) across the shoulders. Boykin responded by grabbing the rope, jerking it out of Roberson's grip, and throwing it into the pen, no doubt thereby richly seasoning it with fresh cow manure.

Roberson: "Goddamn you, hand me that rope."

Boykin: "I'm not doing any such of a thing."

At this point, Tom Cross, attempting to defuse a potentially lethal showdown, retrieved Roberson's rope and handed it to him. Roberson, however, was not to be placated. After dropping the rope over his saddle horn, he drew his pistol and hit Boykin on the hand, causing him to jump off the fence into the cattle pen. Roberson rode around to the far gate and entered the pen, still mounted. Then he uncoiled the rope and lashed Boykin twice—once on his hand and then across his head. The enraged Boykin charged the still-mounted Roberson, pocket knife in hand. (Roberson would later testify that Boykin stabbed his horse behind the shoulder with the pocket knife. One of the Nortons insisted that Boykin did not have his knife in hand when he charged the mounted Roberson.)

Whether because Boykin stabbed the animal in the shoulder or because he was startled by Boykin's angry charge, the animal whirled away from Boykin. That's when Roberson again pulled his pistol and, as the horse whirled away, shot backward over his shoulder. Fortunately for Boykin, the shot went wild and missed him. Unfortunately for Roberson's young cowboy, Walter Sitter, an innocent bystander, the wild shot did not miss him. He suffered a mortal wound and soon died. Walter Sitter was the son of Joe Sitter, an ex–Texas Ranger and an acclaimed U.S. Mounted Customs Inspector.

But Boykin was a far piece from being out of harm's way. The determined Roberson wheeled his horse around and kept firing, hitting Boykin three times: once in the right side of his back, once in his left side, and finally in the chest. Tom Cross and the three Nortons would later swear that Roberson fired five shots, the last one being a coup de grâce blast to Boykin's chest after Boykin, already hit twice, was lying prostrate on the ground. Roberson and his surviving cowboy, Elmer Dumont, would later testify that Roberson fired only *four* shots and that Roberson did not shoot Boykin after he was felled. Fourteen-year-old James Norton would later testify that just before Roberson shot the prostrate Boykin the final time, he heard Tom Cross yell to Roberson, "Don't shoot him anymore." The Norton boy then continued: "Roberson told Cross to shut up or he would give him some of the same." After firing the final shot, Roberson hung his spurs deep in his pony's belly and departed as fast as the startled animal could carry him—leaving Boykin and Sitter lying dead in the cattle pen. However, he soon had second thoughts about running, and he surrendered. Shortly thereafter Roberson was released on bond pending trial.

INDICTED FOR MURDERING BOYKIN AND BYSTANDER

A grand jury in the 34th Judicial District Court of El Paso County, Texas, indicted Roberson for murder—twice: once for killing Foote Boykin and once for killing the hapless Walter Sitter.[62] The Boykin case was called for trial first during the November 1915 term of the El Paso County District Court.

The principal witnesses were the six surviving eyewitnesses to the killings: Tom Cross and the three Nortons for the state and Roberson and his cowboy, Elmer Dumont, for the defense. The testimony of the state's eyewitnesses is summarized above. For the defense, Elmer Dumont didn't do much to help the Roberson case except to insist that Roberson fired only *four* shots, not *five*, during the incident, and that he did not shoot Boykin after the latter was down. The state would also call two other eyewitnesses: James Burns and Will Bartzer, two travelers who had happened to get off the train near the cattle pens at Sierra Blanca shortly before the shooting began.

Roberson, of course, while not denying the killing, had a very different take on the encounter. According to Roberson's version, he merely had inquired what Cross and Boykin were doing in his pen of cattle, and that was when Boykin got hostile and told him that it was "none of his damned business" and began cursing him, calling him a "son-of-a-bitch." He said that he then asked Boykin not to call him that. After that, Roberson claimed he tried to break off the hostile encounter but that Boykin persisted in abusing him, all of which eventually led to the rope whipping and then to the fatal confrontation when Boykin, in an attempt to unhorse him, ran at him and stabbed his horse just behind the shoulder. Roberson also flatly denied that he fired more than four times and insisted that he did not shoot Boykin after Boykin was down.

Although H. L. Roberson was not a wealthy man by any stretch, he was represented by the crème de la crème of Texas criminal defense lawyers of that day: Moore and Harris of El Paso, the fearsome and unrelenting I. H. Burney of Fort Worth, T. J. Newton of San Antonio, and Martin and McDonald of Austin. C. C. McDonald of that firm was recognized as one of the outstanding trial lawyers of Texas. Although the state didn't have quite the star power of the defense, it did have able representation: Leigh Clark, district attorney, and E. B. Hendricks, assistant attorney general, plus two El Paso firms—Lea, McGrady and Thomason, and Hudspeth, Dale and Harper. Also aiding the prosecution was R. E. Thomason, mayor of El Paso, who later served West Texas as a congressman and finally as a U.S. District Judge. Claude Hudspeth was also at one time a congressman from West Texas. (Hudspeth County, Texas, was named for him.) Still, an unassailable truth should be noted here: consummate politicians do not necessarily make consummate trial lawyers. They may be first cousins, but there is a world of difference between the two. He who has mastered the art of appealing to a wide slice of the populace on election day may well fall flat on his face in front of a jury. And, of course, vice versa.

At any rate, the money to hire this awesome array of legal firepower had to have been considerable in amount, and it had to have come from somewhere—obviously from somewhere other than Roberson's limited money pouch. Best bets were his employer,

Leonard Pence, one of the owners of the T. O. Ranch, and his former (and future) employer, the Texas & Southwestern Cattle Raisers Association.

A FOUL ODOR: THE MURDER TRIALS OF HOD ROBERSON

To the surprise of absolutely no one, when Roberson finally took the stand he claimed he killed Boykin in self-defense. Contrary to the testimony of Cross and the Nortons, he denied that he had fired the final shot after Boykin was already on the ground. Then Roberson, who by all accounts reveled in his reputation as an unforgiving man killer absolutely devoid of fear and trepidation, uttered some words that must have nearly choked him to death. He told the jury: "I shot because I was afraid for my life." This, mind, when Roberson was mounted on his horse and armed with a Winchester rifle and a pistol and Boykin was standing on the ground armed, at best, with a pocket knife.

Nevertheless, relying on the frontier's almost surefire self-defense plea, he went on to testify that he had been warned by his friends that "the Sierra Blanca bunch" was out to get him. True enough, Roberson would not have won any popularity contests in Sierra Blanca. A popular Sierra Blanca cowman named Brown Pascal had previously been the foreman of the giant T. O. Ranch. The owners, however, were apparently seeking a meaner, tougher gun hand to deal with border ruffians, outlaws, and hard cases. They fired Pascal and hired Roberson, which did not endear him to the locals. But whatever resentment the community might have harbored over the replacement of Pascal by Roberson, it seems unlikely that it would have ignited assassination-level fever, particularly regarding Cross and Boykin, neither of whom was related to Pascal. Roberson did produce another witness (one who was not an eyewitness to the shooting) who claimed that Boykin had previously threatened to kill Roberson and that Roberson had been warned of Boykin's threats.

However, it would seem that the importance—even the relevance—of that supposed threat must have been undermined in the jury's eyes when Roberson had to admit on cross-examination that he didn't know Boykin, had never met him before that fatal encounter, and didn't even find out whom he had killed until after Boykin was already dead. Furthermore, if either Cross or Boykin had any serious notion of slaying Roberson it would seem preposterous to believe that they would undertake that chore armed with only a pocket knife. Finally, since Roberson was mounted, while Cross and Boykin were afoot, if he really "feared for his life," as he claimed, then couldn't he have easily taken himself out of harm's way by simply riding away? Maybe so, but, as we have already learned, the "no duty to retreat" provision was a pivotal part of the Texas self-defense statute.[63] Hence, from a strictly legal standpoint, Roberson could assert a self-defense justification for killing Boykin—but only if Roberson believed he was fending off a lethal attack. Still, under the circumstances (and even given the jury's frontier values), the jury must have wondered, as a practical matter, why he didn't just turn and ride away. The jurors must have also wondered whether the high-tempered Roberson hadn't provoked the whole incident in the first place. Plus the jury must have considered the fact that Roberson wasn't dealing with a killer, a desperado, or a cattle rustler. Boykin was a legitimate and respected rancher and family man. Moreover, since he had contracted with Roberson's boss to pasture T. O. Ranch cattle on his ranch, he had a legitimate reason to be inside the railroad pens counting cattle.

Two disinterested witnesses corroborated the prosecution's version of the incident. James Burns and Will Bartzer, who had just gotten off the train at Sierra Blanca, testified that they heard both Boykin and Roberson cursing each other just before the killing. Burns testified:

> [W]e noticed the men quarreling at the stock pens. We went over there, and I heard Boykin call Roberts [sic] a dirty coward for pulling a gun on him when he knew he was unarmed.

Both men testified that Roberson struck Boykin over the head with his rope and only then did Boykin run toward the mounted Roberson, who commenced shooting. Neither man saw a knife in Boykin's hand as he charged Roberson, although they admitted on cross-examination that he could have been holding one.[64]

During the trial Roberson's past record of violence was explored, at least to a limited extent. Under the Texas law of evidence, the state, during a criminal trial, is not ordinarily permitted to offer (or even allude to) evidence of other prior crimes committed by the defendant. The underlying rationale is that a defendant is entitled to be tried for only the crime charged against him in the indictment. Otherwise a jury might be tempted to convict him simply on account of past bad acts, thus destroying the defendant's presumption of innocence until he is proven by the state to be guilty beyond a reasonable doubt of the specific crime for which he was indicted. There are, however, exceptions to that rule. For instance, if the defendant elects to take the stand to testify, his credibility may be impeached by proof that he was previously convicted of (not just charged with) a felony or convicted of a misdemeanor involving "moral turpitude" (e.g., theft, forgery, and so forth, but not misdemeanors such as public intoxication or simple assault). The defense may also inadvertently open the door for the state at least to intimate to the jury that the defendant has been guilty of past violent acts even if no final conviction resulted. This happened during Roberson's murder trial when his lawyer put several character witnesses on the stand who testified that they knew Roberson's reputation for being a "peaceable and law-abiding" citizen. This testimony opened the door for the prosecution to test the witnesses' knowledge of the defendant's reputation as a peaceable and law-abiding citizen. However, this line of questioning must adhere to a very precise and prescribed manner, to wit: the cross-examination question must be framed as follows: "*Have you heard* that . . ." (the defendant committed some specific act that is inconsistent with him being a "peaceable and law-abiding citizen"). The prosecution must then accept the witness's answer whether it be in the positive or in the negative. If it is in the negative, the state cannot go further and offer proof that the specified violent act actually did occur.[65] However, even if the witness denies hearing about such an incident, it usually heists a very large red flag in a juror's mind.

In the Roberson case, an appellate court opinion later summed up the "have you heard" cross-examination of the defendant's character witnesses as follows:

> The appellant's reputation as a peaceable and law-abiding man was in issue. Several witnesses testified in his favor. . . . Some of these witnesses testified on cross-examination that they had heard of previous trials of appellant for murder, and that they had heard of his killing outlaws, claiming to have heard of his killing as many as four men. . . . The attorney for the appellant stated that appellant had killed at different times two Mexicans, and on trial of each case a verdict of acquittal was instructed. An inquiry was made as to whether the witnesses had heard of appellant killing a Negro porter and throwing him off the train, to which there was a negative answer. Inquiry was also made with reference to whether the witnesses had heard of his killing some Mexicans, described as "four old Mexicans." [The defendant's character witnesses also made negative replies to this last inquiry.][66]

It didn't take the jury very long to dismiss Roberson's self-defense contention, and, after only two hours of deliberation, the jury, on December 5, 1915, returned with a guilty verdict to which it affixed a twenty-year sentence.

The manner in which Roberson's attorneys and henchmen succeeded in getting Roberson's jury conviction overturned is enough to turn stomachs. First, they timely filed a rather bland motion for a new trial. Under Texas law, the trial judge then has a specified number of days to consider and rule on a defendant's motion for a new trial. If the judge allows the deadline to pass without making a specific ruling on the motion, then the motion is automatically over-ruled by operation of law, and the sentence stands. The day before that deadline ticked away, Roberson's lawyers filed an amendment to their motion for a new trial—a bombshell that caught the prosecution flat-footed. Roberson's lawyers alleged that one of the jurors who had voted to convict Roberson had previously been convicted of a felony and had failed to disclose that fact in the jury selection process. Under Texas law, any person who has previously been convicted of a felony is absolutely prohibited from serving on a jury. Attached to the amended motion was an affidavit purporting to have been signed by one of the jurors, a fellow named A. J. "Blondy" Martin. In that affidavit Martin stated that he had lied to the court during the jury selection; that his real name was Sidney Burch; and that in 1900 he had been convicted of a felony in the Indian Territory, namely stealing a hog.

Roberson's attorneys did not bother to bring Martin/Burch in person to the hearing to testify in support of their motion, but relied solely on the affidavit. Since it was the last day of the mandated period for the trial judge to rule on this motion, the prosecution leaned on the judge to make the defense physically produce its witness for examination, or, at least, to keep the court in session until midnight while they sent lawmen all over El Paso in a frantic search for the missing juror. Just before midnight on December 14, 1915, when no Martin/Burch could be found, the trial judge granted Roberson's motion for a new trial and thus overturned Roberson's conviction.

Although the damage was already done, the enraged prosecutors did not give up the search for Martin/Burch. Turned out he had hastily departed town, leaving no forwarding address. Nevertheless, some four months later one of the lawmen finally tracked him down and arrested him on his father's farm in Kansas, and then dragged him back to El Paso, where Martin proceeded to recant and tell quite a tale of skullduggery.

No, he admitted, his name was not Sidney Burch. Yes, his name was really A. J. Martin. No, he had never been convicted of a felony. Yes, he had lied in his affidavit, although he claimed he was so drunk when he signed that piece of paper he didn't know what it said. According to Martin's account of that fateful day, a man who had a gun and a badge and claimed to be a law officer had taken him to an El Paso hotel room and plied him with free liquor for hours. Sometime after the deadline had passed he was given eighty-five dollars and told to get out of town but not to worry—that "everything would be covered up." But, as it turned out, not covered up very well. On June 16, 1916, an El Paso grand jury indicted Martin for perjury.[67]

If the actions of Roberson's lawyers and henchmen in this judicial farce stank to high heaven, the action of the trial judge was equally malodorous. When one party files a motion with the court (such as a motion for a new trial), then it is up to the moving party to come forward with credible testimony to support the allegations contained in the motion. Here the Roberson camp came forward at the eleventh hour with only a highly suspicious affidavit. Even more suspicious was the fact that the Roberson faction failed to produce the body of that affiant, put him on the stand, and make him substantiate the defense allegations under oath. Still worse, the trial judge let the defense get away with it. In that courtroom the scent of an unholy collusion was unmistakable.

After all, Martin/Burch was Roberson's witness, and supposedly his team knew his whereabouts. Instead, the judge put the burden on the prosecution to run the defense witness down and to produce him before the court within a few hours, and when the prosecution failed to do so, the judge proceeded to grant the defense's motion and thus overturn the jury's verdict. Any fair-minded judge would have told the defense: "If you want me to seriously consider dumping a jury verdict, then you find your witness, bring him here, and put him on the stand, make him testify, and subject himself to cross-examination. Otherwise, your motion is overruled." The trial judge's impartiality was later impugned further when he overturned still another jury verdict finding Roberson guilty and then transferred a retrial to a Texas county where the influence of the T&SCRA was dominant.

On November 30, 1916, Roberson was retried in the same El

Paso County court. This time the jury found Roberson guilty—not of murder, but of manslaughter—and sentenced him to five years in the pen. Roberson appealed that conviction to the Court of Criminal Appeals in Austin. In a lengthy opinion, the court reviewed the trial court proceedings, found no reversible error, and affirmed the jury's verdict. But Roberson's battery of attorneys wasn't through yet. They pleaded with the appellate court for a rehearing. The court allowed it, and upon rehearing, the court was persuaded to overturn the conviction and send it back to the trial court for a third trial.

Why? Well, explained the appellate court, the trial court failed to instruct the jury that Roberson's possession of the pistol with which he shot Boykin was lawful. Under Texas law, it was unlawful for an ordinary citizen to carry a pistol. However, there were several exceptions to that law, including one that permitted a "traveler" (that is, one traveling outside his home county) to lawfully carry a pistol for his protection. Since Roberson, at the time of the shooting, was a "traveler" as defined by the statute, his possession of the lethal pistol was lawful.

But what did that have to do with the case at hand? First, from what record we now have, the prosecution, during the trial, had not made an issue of whether Roberson's possession of the pistol was lawful or unlawful—nor should it have. Second, what difference did it make? Roberson was being tried for murder. He was not being tried for unlawful possession of a pistol. Did he, or did he not, intentionally and with premeditation kill Boykin? Stranger still, in its brief "revised" opinion reversing the conviction on such narrow ground, the appellate court completely failed to discuss what relevance, if any, the lawful or unlawful possession of the pistol had on the jury's decision to convict or acquit Roberson. Was the court really saying that since Roberson's possession of his pistol was lawful, it therefore gave him a legal right to shoot anybody who came within his gun sights? Even if the trial court should have told the jury that Roberson's possession of his pistol was lawful, was the failure to so instruct the jury so significant that it should have resulted in a reversal of the conviction? Can we really believe that had the jury been told that Roberson's possession of the lethal pistol was lawful, that information would have caused the jury to change its verdict from "guilty" to "not guilty"?

In any event, there was a distinct odor about that reversal—and it sure wasn't the scent of roses in springtime. Could the fact that the Texas and Southwestern Cattle Raisers Association had clout aplenty in Austin (the seat of the Court of Criminal Appeals) have had anything to do with that strange about-face?

The appellate court's decision also afforded Roberson another important advantage. During Roberson's second trial the jury had the choice of finding him guilty of first-degree murder (two years to life in the pen or death by hanging) or manslaughter (two to five years) or, of course, not guilty. When the jury in the second trial found him guilty of manslaughter, it necessarily—by implication—found him not guilty of first-degree murder, which meant that under the "double jeopardy" prohibitions in the Texas and U.S. Constitutions, Roberson could never again be tried for, nor convicted of, *first-degree murder* for killing Boykin. The most any subsequent jury could do upon retrial was to find him guilty of manslaughter.[68]

So the case went back to the El Paso court for a third trial. Once again an El Paso jury found Roberson guilty of manslaughter and, on November 10, 1919, assessed his punishment at two years. Roberson and his team were still not satisfied, however. Once again they filed a motion for a new trial in the trial court, and once again the El Paso district judge granted the motion, thus giving Roberson a fourth bite at the apple. Not only that, but the trial judge decided to change the venue for the fourth trial to Austin in Travis County—a decision that, no doubt, elated Roberson and the Texas and Southwestern Cattle Raisers Association, since it gave them a decided home-field advantage. There were more than two hundred organized counties in the state of Texas at that time, and therefore, when the trial judge (who had already overturned two jury verdicts of "guilty" against Roberson, the Court of Criminal Appeals in Austin having overturned the third guilty verdict) decided to change the venue from El Paso County to another county, he had many choices.

Of these multiple choices, he selected Travis County—the one county where the T&SCRA and the Texas Rangers had the most clout. It was also a place where nobody knew the deceased Foote Boykin—a courtroom five hundred miles distant from the place where Boykin lived and died.

"Step into my parlor, said the spider . . ."

Considering the loaded dice, it was not all that surprising when, on June 21, 1920, a Travis County jury found Roberson not guilty, thus finally putting an end to the judicial farce. It had been almost five and a half years since that January day when Roberson killed Boykin.[69] The murder case against Roberson for the killing of the young, hapless Walter Sitter was never called for trial.

It is also most interesting to note that on May 8, 1916, while Roberson was still under indictment for two murders and some four years *before* he was finally acquitted of the murder of Boykin, the Cattle Raisers Association helped Roberson obtain a commission as a "Special Texas Ranger" and then hired him as a cattle inspector for the association. All of Roberson's salary was paid by the association.[70] At any rate, Roberson kept his badge and continued working for the association, and he was still an association detective when he and Allison commenced their pursuit of Tom Ross in 1922.

"TOBACCO JAKE" BALLARD

The bad blood between Roberson and Tom Ross didn't just happen overnight—it had a history. Ross had a cowboy friend of many years who went under the colorful moniker of Jack "Tobacco Jake" Ballard. Tobacco Jake first surfaced in Vernon in 1906 to support Ross (perhaps as a witness?) when Ross was cleared of the old 1895 Alf Bailey robbery charge. And Ross never forgot a friend—or forgave an enemy. According to Bob Beverly, who was the Midland County sheriff in 1923 when the Seminole killings occurred, Roberson had been pursuing cow thieves in the area of Motley and Dickens counties several years before when he crossed paths with Tobacco Jake. For reasons unknown, that encounter went way south of cordial: Roberson took a shot at Tobacco Jake, but missed. In reply, Tobacco Jake sprinkled Roberson's hind side with birdshot from a shotgun.[71] According to another old-timer, S. T. "Davy" Burk, Roberson responded to this little indignity by framing Ballard for cattle rustling and shipping him off to the pen for a three-year vacation. Burk contended that Roberson himself stole a calf from the Flying A Ranch, killed it, and then buried the hide in Tobacco Jake's pasture, later "discovering it" and blaming Jake. "Never was a dirtier fellow existed than old Roberson," Burk concluded.[72]

A search of the official records of the Motley County District Court of Matador, Texas, reveals that in November 1912 J. N. Ballard was indeed convicted of stealing a calf from the Matador Ranch. The state produced a witness named John Southworth who swore that one evening he was on a hill on the Matador Ranch when, with the aid of field glasses, he witnessed Jake Ballard and his friend John Law rope a yearling calf and drag it across the Matador boundary fence onto Ballard's pasture. The next day the sheriff and others went to Ballard's place where they found the hide and head of a recently butchered yearling matching Southworth's description of the calf. Southworth, however, did not positively identify the hide. Later, they found a fresh beef carcass in the possession of John Law. Both Law and Ballard were tried and convicted, and both were sentenced to two years in prison. Both appealed, but the convictions were upheld by a divided appellate court. The dissenting judge found that the state's case depended on circumstantial evidence, and that the trial court should have instructed the jury on the law of circumstantial evidence.[73]

Later, as we shall soon see, Tom Ross would allege that Roberson killed Ballard. However, official Dickens County death records in Dickens, Texas, reveal that Jake Ballard died in the town of Spur in Dickens County, Texas, on June 18, 1927, more than four years after Roberson's death. At any rate, whatever was the exact nature of the 1912 incident or incidents, it was the beginning of the bad blood not only between Jake Ballard and Roberson, but also between Tom Ross and Roberson.

Jake Ballard blows his "hound-calling horn" (made of a cow horn), summoning his hounds for a hunt. The crusty old Dickens County, Texas, small-time cattle operator was a friend of Tom Ross and shared with Tom a deep hostility toward T&SCRA inspector H. L. Roberson. Apparently Roberson played some part in getting Jake Ballard convicted of stealing a Matador Ranch calf in 1912 and having him sent to the pen for two years. *(Courtesy Motley County Historical Museum)*

Years afterward, Western historian J. Evetts Haley described Roberson as "an ambitious man who spread it around that he was going to get Tom Ross."[74]

ENTER MILT GOOD, OUTLAW

So far we have talked of three fearless gunmen with roots in the nineteenth-century Western frontier: Hill Loftis, a.k.a. Tom Ross; Dave Allison; and H. L. Roberson. But before the tragic paths of these three crossed, another pistol-packing cowboy appeared on the stage. His name was Milton Paul "Milt" Good, age thirty-four.[75] Milt Good was born near Tularosa, Lincoln County, New Mexico, on March 17, 1889, but soon moved with his family to West Texas. His father, Isham J. Good, as well as his uncle, John Good, were reputed to be "man killers,"[76] while his cousin, Walter Good, was one of those killed during a New Mexico feud involving the always-controversial cattleman Oliver Lee.[77] Milt grew up looking at cattle from between a horse's ears. He tried his hand at ranching for a while, but hard times in the cattle business due to the 1917 drought wiped him out. Shortly thereafter, however, he did score a spectacular success: in 1920 at Shreveport, Louisiana, Milt won the world's steer-roping championship.[78] However, in those days winning rodeo championships didn't put much butter on your bread, and Milt had to seek more profitable endeavors. Still, he continued to rope steers. Trouble was, Milt began swinging a pretty wide loop—a lot wider than the law allowed—and he wasn't very particular about whose brand was on the steers he roped. Meanwhile, he settled on the south plains of West Texas in the Brownfield area southwest of Lubbock and northeast of Seminole. Sometime along about then he met Tom Ross.

June 14, 1922, turned out to be the beginning of the end for all the players, although the end came much sooner for some than for others. That was the day Dave Allison received a tip that Milt Good was driving a sizeable herd of cattle branded "L F" across West Texas.[79] Now why, Allison wondered, would Milt Good be moving a big herd of L F cattle across country? L F certainly wasn't Milt Good's brand. At least Allison needed to make a clarification as to the brand: if the L F brand was on the right side of the cattle, then it meant the animals were owned by (or at least had been owned by) the Littlefield Cattle Company of Texas. However, if that brand was on the left side of the critters, then it denoted ownership by G. B. Armstrong of the Four Lakes Ranch in New Mexico.[80] It was possible Good had bought these cattle from one of the ranchers, but, in light of his financial circumstances, that seemed unlikely. Perhaps some other cattleman had bought the cattle and hired Milt Good to straw-boss the cattle drive to the buyer's range. Still, it all seemed mighty suspicious to Allison. Further investigations including personal interviews and examinations of bank mortgage records on cattle owned by these ranches heightened Allison's suspicions. He wired cattle inspector Roberson down at Midland for assistance. The pair met in Lamesa the next day and rattled off in an old Model T Ford in search of the herd. Locating a herd of cattle on the vast

Milton Paul "Milt" Good who, in concert with Tom Ross, killed T&SCRA inspectors Dave Allison and H. L. Roberson. Good and Ross were convicted of both murders. Good, former world champion steer roper, is pictured here while serving his prison sentence, all "duded up" and getting ready for the annual prison rodeo. *(Courtesy Nita Stewart Haley Memorial Library, Midland, Texas)*

sweep of millions of West Texas acres of rangeland was no simple or quick task. Finally, they determined that the herd had been watered on the sprawling Higgenbotham Ranch. At ranch headquarters, Allison and Roberson borrowed cow ponies and eventually encountered the cattle in question about twenty-five miles south of Lamesa, Texas, and it was indeed a large herd, 516 head to be exact. Sure enough Milt Good, assisted by two cowhands, Allen Holder and Pete Kyle, was in charge of the drive.

The inspectors immediately conducted an inquisition of Good. His answers ranged from the evasive to the patently false, so Roberson and Allison arrested Good and his two hands on the spot. Further investigation revealed that 485 of the 516 head of cattle belonged to the Littlefield Cattle Co., and the other 31 head had been stolen from eight other individuals. Indictments against Good and his two cowhands, charging them with cattle rustling on a grand scale, were soon returned in four Texas counties: Hockley, Lynn, Dawson, and Terry.[81] Good made bail and was released pending trials.

As a result of the bust, Allison and Roberson achieved near-hero status with the Cattle Raisers Association and its supporters. Good, on the other hand, called Allison a lot of names, but none of them was "hero." Bitter over the indictments, he confronted Allison on the steps of the Midland County Courthouse not long thereafter. Both were armed and ready. A bloodletting was prevented only when then-Midland County Sheriff Bob Beverly physically separated the two. He said, "Neither one of you men will kill me, and I won't let you kill each other."[82]

Allison, meanwhile, decided he would cash in on the acclaim he received over the Good indictments by running for sheriff of Garza County. Although Allison was a paid inspector for the T&SCRA, he conveniently also held a commission as an unpaid deputy sheriff of Garza County. Since the association was a private organization, its inspectors had no official law enforcement authority to make arrests or conduct official investigations. To remedy this problem, the powerful association leaned on federal and state officials (primarily U.S. Marshals and county sheriffs) to give its inspectors badges and swear them in as unpaid deputy U.S. Marshals or, as in Allison's case, deputy county sheriffs. Outlaws and others who were not supporters of the association derisively referred to these gratuitous badge-wearers as "pistol deputies."

"Pistol deputy" Dave Allison had been commissioned as a deputy sheriff by Will Gravy, sheriff of Garza County. Sheriff Gravy was therefore understandably peeved when his "honorary" deputy up and ran against him in the next election. When he defeated Allison in a runoff, Gravy responded by taking Allison's badge. Allison had nothing to worry about, however. Thanks to the cattleman's association, Allison soon sported another gratuitous badge, this one as an unpaid deputy U.S. Marshal.[83]

THE GATHERING STORM: CATTLE DETECTIVES
BEGIN PURSUIT OF TOM ROSS

When Milt Good was arrested and indicted for cattle theft in 1922, it had been twenty-seven years since Hill Loftis/Tom Ross had been involved in the 1895 Alf Bailey store armed robbery in Wilbarger County, Texas, and twenty years since he had bought ranch land

Midland County, Texas, Sheriff Bob Beverly, affectionately known as "the cowboy sheriff," was well acquainted with the principal characters and the facts surrounding the April 1, 1923, bloodbath in Seminole. Prior to that episode he once prevented a shootout between Dave Allison and Milt Good. *(Courtesy Nita Stewart Haley Memorial Library, Midland, Texas)*

west of Seminole and appeared to have quit the outlaw trail. Still, Allison and Roberson suspected that Ross was somehow involved in the theft of the 516 head of stolen cattle that Good was caught driving; in fact, Roberson believed that Ross was the leader of a gang that was responsible for an upswing in cattle rustling along the Texas–New Mexico border.[84]

Did the inspectors have any hard evidence that Tom Ross was indeed the ringleader of a large-scale cattle-rustling operation? Or did they merely suspect he might be—a suspicion based on his past record and accentuated by the bitter resentment Texas lawmen (and particularly the Texas Rangers) harbored against Tom Ross because he had, in their view, thumbed his nose at law enforcement and gotten away with it? Plus there was that personal (and mutual) grudge between Roberson and Ross on account of the Tobacco Jake Ballard incident. The *Roswell* [New Mexico] *Record* later observed that "bad feelings had existed between these men [Allison, Roberson, and Ross] for years."[85] What part did these old feelings play in Roberson's belief that Ross was rustling cattle, or his determination to nail Ross one way or the other? These questions will forever be the subject of speculation.

According to subsequent testimony, during the fall of 1922 and the early spring of 1923, Roberson, in particular, and Allison, to a lesser extent, made several "intemperate remarks" to the effect that they were determined either to send Ross to the penitentiary or to kill him. Of course it didn't take long for such talk to reach the ears of the proud, fearless, and vengeful Tom Ross.

But the cattle inspectors could not link Ross to Milt Good and the 516 head of stolen cattle—or to any other cattle thefts. In the inspectors' defense, however, it must be stated that in that time and place, and under those circumstances, making a cattle-theft case— one that would stick—against Tom Ross wasn't easy. Old rawhides in the cow country were still mighty tight-lipped, especially around strangers or nosey badge-wearers. A man's past, they firmly believed, wasn't anybody else's business. Plus, there was a strong undercurrent attitude: "Maybe he is, or was, an outlaw—but he's *our* outlaw," so leave him be, at least as long as he's not stealing cows too close to our range![86] After all, in that raw country, neighbors depended heavily on neighbors. Plus, there weren't too many of Tom Ross's neighbors who had any overwhelming urge to step up and point an accusing finger at the fearsome man. One final point in the inspectors' defense: nobody ever accused Ross of the sin of stupidity. For his part, Ross let it be known that no association inspector would ever set foot on his ranch and live to tell about it.[87] The inspectors grew ever more frustrated.

THE NEW MEXICO INDICTMENT: TOM ROSS STOLE FOUR COWS

Finally Roberson caught a break. Tom Ross suffered a painful gall-stone attack and was taken to a Lubbock hospital where he underwent two operations. While Ross was laid up in the Lubbock hospital, Roberson took the uninvited opportunity to visit Tom's ranch. Only two young cowhands, Roy "Alkali" Adams and Tom's brother-in-law, Boone Hardin, were present. Both worked for Ross. After looking through all of Ross's cattle, Roberson discovered four cows belonging to a neighboring rancher, A. Wilhoit. All four bore Wilhoit's brand; none of the brands had been smeared or otherwise altered. The boys told Roberson that the cows were strays and had gotten out of Wilhoit's pasture (about two miles away) through a break in his fence. Nevertheless, that was enough for Roberson, and he persuaded Wilhoit, a member of the Cattle Raisers Association, to sign a complaint against Ross. Roberson promptly took the case to the district attorney at Lovington, New Mexico, and together they persuaded a Lea County grand jury to indict Ross (who was still laid up in Lubbock) for stealing four cows from Wilhoit, two valued at twenty-five dollars each and two valued at fifteen dollars each.[88]

Roberson made his inspection of the Tom Ross ranch on November 11, 1922. Ross later testified that he did not learn about the resulting indictment until after he returned from the Lubbock hospital on December 12, 1922.[89] The indictment alleged that Tom had stolen the Wilhoit cattle on or about October 31, 1922. Ross later testified that the cattle theft indictment charged him with doing what was impossible, since he couldn't have ridden a horse during the two months he was in the hospital. Needless to add, Ross was furious when he got home from the hospital and learned that Roberson had not only come onto his ranch during his absence and without his consent, but that he'd also obtained a cattle theft indictment against him as a result thereof.

In any event, Roberson had his indictment charging Ross with cow theft, albeit alleging the theft of only four cows—hardly what one might have expected from "the king of the cattle rustlers." Furthermore, the case against Ross was purely circumstantial, and, from existent records, does not appear to be all that strong. True enough, four branded Wilhoit cows were discovered on Ross's seven-thousand-acre ranch. However, that's a way yonder south of proving to a jury beyond a reasonable doubt that Tom Ross intentionally stole those four cows. Mere possession of another's property is not sufficient to make a case for theft of that property. The state must prove not only that the defendant possessed the property, but also that he came into possession of the property unlawfully and with the intent to deprive the owner of his property and to convert it to his own use and benefit.[90]

The existent records reveal the following: Tom Ross never confessed he stole those cows; in fact, he was laid up when Roberson claimed he stole them. None of Ross's cowhands ever confessed they stole those cows, either for themselves or for Ross. (In fact, Ross and his hands steadfastly denied any such theft.) No one ever said they saw Ross or his hands steal those cows. No one ever said they followed any horse tracks driving the four Wilhoit cows from Wilhoit's pasture into Ross's pasture. No one testified that Ross tried to sell those Wilhoit cows to a third party or attempted to ship them to market. No one contended that Ross, or anybody else, attempted to smear, obliterate, or alter Wilhoit's brand on those cows. In those days, if a wrangler was desirous of adding a few head of his neighbor's cattle to his own herd, the safest way was not to steal the neighbor's *branded* cows. The aspiring thief waited until the cows' calves were about weaning size and then stole the *unbranded* calves, branded them, and then claimed them. Finally, as this ranch-backgrounded author can himself testify, if a cowman owns a spread of any size, however diligent he may be about keeping his fences in good repair, it seems that never a year goes by without some of his cattle managing to find a hole in, or a wash under, the fence somewhere and thereby end up on a neighbor's pasture. Also it is a near certainty that some of the neighbor's cattle will likewise somehow end up on his range. Typically, in the spring or fall roundup, neighbors' cattle are sorted out from the herd, and all bovines are returned to their proper pastures. To clear the record in this respect, however, it is to be noted that the Ross ranch and the Wilhoit ranch did *not* have a common boundary: they were separated by about two miles. Still, in those days and in that country, fences, if they did exist at all, were usually considerably less than 100 percent cow-proof.

Although Roberson and Allison had secured the New Mexico indictment against Ross, they were concerned that Ross might pull yet another rabbit out of his Stetson and through some legal technicality escape his comeuppance as he had in the 1895 Alf Bailey armed robbery case. Since the four Wilhoit cows were discovered on Ross's ranch and since that ranch straddled the Texas and New Mexico line, the inspectors decided not to rely solely on the New Mexico indictment, thus affording Ross the possibility of dodging a conviction by arguing that if any cattle theft occurred, it had occurred not in New Mexico but in Texas (Gaines County). Allison and Roberson therefore decided to seek an identical indictment against Ross in Gaines County, Texas, for the theft of the same four Wilhoit cows.

The Gaines County district attorney, Gordon B. McGuire, agreed with Roberson and Allison and called a grand jury to assemble at the courthouse in Seminole on Monday, April 2, 1923, to consider the charges. Allison and Roberson would be the key prosecution witnesses before the grand jury.

BLOODY SUNDAY IN SEMINOLE

The Storm Breaks

They all came to Seminole that fateful day. It was April 1, 1923—April Fools' Day. Ironically, it was also Easter Sunday. They all came in anticipation of the opening of the new term of Gaines County District Court. A grand jury was going to be empanelled the next morning to begin its investigations. Cattle rustling was to be the top item on the new grand jury's agenda. The prosecution's two key witnesses were Texas and Southwestern Cattle Raisers Association detectives "Hod" Roberson and Dave Allison, and the targets of their cow-thieving investigation were Tom Ross and Milt Good.

"Hod" Roberson and his wife, Martha, took a leisurely drive that sunny Easter Sunday afternoon from their Midland, Texas, home to Seminole, where they were to rendezvous with Dave Allison at the two-story, wood-frame Gaines Hotel. Roberson was then forty-eight years old. Although he had known Martha Plummer for a number of years, they had been married for only two years. Martha was not a small woman, nor was she a shrinking violet—not by any means. She was, in a word, formidable, and quite up to the task of standing her ground against the blustering, hot-tempered Hod Roberson. Before their marriage Martha had carved out a most remarkable

The Gaines Hotel in Seminole, Texas, as it appeared on April 1, 1923, when outlaws Tom Ross and Milt Good killed T&SCRA inspectors Dave Allison and H. L. Roberson in the hotel's lobby. *(Courtesy of the Gaines County Library, Seminole, Texas)*

career for herself as a registered nurse and a hospital administrator in San Antonio. In fact, she was the first Texas woman to qualify for the American College of Hospital Administration. Apparently she and Roberson were well matched. She took pride in his career as a lawman. In turn, Roberson responded by teaching his wife the finer points of pistol marksmanship, and, as we shall soon see, Martha must have been an apt pupil indeed.[1] It has been speculated that during that sunny Sunday drive up from Midland, they stopped a time or two to practice a bit of target shooting.

Allison, meanwhile, had spent Saturday night alone in a boarding house in Post, Texas, his wife, Lena, having remained at the couple's home in Roswell, New Mexico. That night, sitting alone in his boarding-house room, Dave Allison took pen in hand and wrote Lena a letter that was . . . well . . . mighty strange, to say the very least. What an eerie premonition of doom must have come over him when he began that letter to his wife with these prescient words: "Now for your information and guidance in case of any misfortune to me . . ." Then Dave went on to tell his wife how much money the association owed him in salary and expenses and where to find his five $1,000 life insurance policies. He said he did not know how long he would be tied up in Seminole with the grand jury. Then he ended his letter with this enigmatic farewell: "If the sign is wright [*sic*], I will go on from there [Seminole] to Roswell. Now don't fret . . ."[2]

The sensational crimes that were about to be committed that fateful Sunday were destined to headline newspapers across America, and the resulting trials would later be recognized as a milestone in the history of the criminal justice system in the Southwest. The underlying issue was whether the statutory law, administered in the courthouse, would prevail over the unwritten law of the frontier, which permitted—even mandated—self-redressment of wrongs, especially when the wrong was a public insult to a man's honor.

The drama to ensue would also be the end, or, at least the beginning of the end, for all four of its central characters.

Roberson and Martha, and then Allison, when they all arrived at the Gaines Hotel, found plenty of folks there to visit with. Since Gaines County was one of ten West Texas counties encompassed within one gigantic judicial district—the 72nd Judicial District— several out-of-town court officials, lawyers, and law enforcement officers congregated at the small hotel. In those pretelevision days, court proceedings were of great interest, especially to country folks, so when it came a village's turn to host a session of the district court, it caused quite a stir; it was a major social occasion. Accordingly, the Gaines Hotel was all a-buzz that evening, the center of considerable activity and socializing. The 72nd District Attorney, Gordon B. McGuire of Lamesa, registered for the night. Gaines County Sheriff W. L. Britton stopped by to greet the out-of-town visitors, as did a senior local lawyer, N. R. Morgan, age sixty-nine. (He was referred

Gaines County Sheriff F. L. Britton was a witness to the killing of T&SCRA inspectors Dave Allison and H. L. Roberson. He later appeared as a witness for the state in the murder trials.
(Courtesy The Cattleman *magazine)*

to as "Judge Morgan" out of respect, although he was not an official judge.) Another out-of-town lawyer who registered for the night was George E. Lockhart of Tahoka. Lockhart, a former state senator and a former district attorney, was in town to represent his client, Tom Ross, regarding the cattle-rustling matter. Two prominent local farmers were also present in the hotel lobby that night: Bill Birdwell and William "Billy Bill" Williamson.[3] Six in all—and each a most credible witness.

As was the custom in West Texas hotels, there was a small dining room just off the lobby, and the proprietress (and head cook), Mrs. James Averett, called all to supper sometime around six o'clock in the evening. After the meal, most drifted back to the hotel lobby to smoke, relax, and exchange desultory conversation. Martha Roberson excused herself and climbed the stairs leading from the lobby to her room on the second floor where, clad in her nightgown, she retired with a good book.

Although Ross's lawyer, George Lockhart, arrived too late for supper, the good-natured Mrs. Averett invited him into the dining room and served a late meal. At that point there occurred an incident that would trigger a heated debate in the upcoming murder trials.

While Lockhart was eating, a well-known Seminole resident—and a good friend of Ross—appeared and asked if Lockhart was present. Charley Richards, as it turned out, was more than a friend of Ross—he was also a co-defendant with him in the Lea County, New Mexico, cattle-rustling case involving the Wilhoit cattle. Richards waited until Lockhart finished his meal, then both went outside and had a private conversation. Richards left. Lockhart went back inside the hotel lobby and (according to one prosecution witness) "perceptibly repositioned his chair" inside the lobby.[4]

By eight o'clock the crowd in the hotel lobby had thinned down to eight: Roberson and Allison, Sheriff Britton, District Attorney McGuire, "Judge" Morgan, lawyer Lockhart, and the two local farmers, Birdwell and Williamson. Allison, who had complained of a headache, sat at a table in the lobby with both elbows on the table and his head resting in his hands. Across the table sat Roberson, his chair tilted back so that his head rested against the wall. Roberson and Allison were both armed with pistols. None of the other men, including Sheriff Britton, were armed.

THE BLOOD BATH

At about eight-thirty both Sheriff Britton and District Attorney McGuire suddenly noticed the barrel of a shotgun being pushed through the north door of the lobby. Behind the shotgun was Milt Good and by his side Tom Ross appeared, brandishing two pistols. Neither man was disguised. Without a word, both men opened up, weapons blazing. Nobody knows how many shots were fired in the ensuing fusillade, but estimates were from twelve to twenty. Both Roberson and Allison were hit with the first shots and died almost instantaneously. Even after it was evident that the inspectors were dead, Good and Ross fired additional shots into their lifeless bodies. It appeared that Roberson was Ross's primary target and that Allison was Good's primary target. Meanwhile, all the other men fled in panic during the wild shooting spree—all, that is, except Judge Morgan, who apparently was frozen with fright. No one was hit except

Martha Plummer Roberson, wife of H. L. Roberson, rushed to the murder scene of her husband, H. L. Roberson, grabbed her dying husband's pistol, and managed to wound both of the killers before they could escape. *(Courtesy* The Cattleman *magazine)*

Sketch of a murder scene—the lobby of the Gaines Hotel in Seminole, Texas, just after Tom Ross and Milt Good killed T&SCRA inspectors H. L. Roberson and Dave Allison on April 1, 1923. In the sketch, Roberson's wife, Martha, is ministering to her dying husband. The sketch appeared in the July 22, 1923, edition of the *St. Louis Post-Dispatch* during the trial of Tom Ross for the murder of Dave Allison. *(Courtesy the* St. Louis Post-Dispatch*)*

for Roberson and Allison, although one pistol slug barely missed Judge Morgan, zipping between his arm and his body.

All the survivors knew, recognized, and could identify the shooters: Tom Ross and Milt Good.[5]

The smoke cleared and the shooters undoubtedly thought all the fireworks were over. But they were in for a very rude awakening. While all the men had fled in panic (except the petrified Judge Morgan), one person came flying *into* the room. It was a woman, an unarmed woman. Martha Roberson, hearing all the gunplay in the lobby, leaped out of bed and came tearing down the stairs barefooted and clad only in her night robe. She was horrified by the tableau of terrible carnage. Rushing to her slain husband's side, Martha, a trained nurse, saw immediately that he was dead. The shooters, meanwhile, were departing the lobby. Instead of collapsing in shock and grief, Martha Roberson immediately yanked her husband's sixshooter from its scabbard, but, much to her dismay, she discovered that the handle had been shot off. However, she knew that Roberson also carried a backup pistol, a small-caliber automatic, tucked in his waistband. She seized that gun and headed for the lobby door in hot pursuit of the fleeing outlaws. She was able to fire two shots before the men jumped in their waiting car and made their getaway. She fired twice at them, and she didn't miss with either. One shot hit Tom Ross's metal belt buckle (which probably saved his life), ricocheted, and plowed into his belly fat. The other shot hit Milt Good in the wrist. It was a flesh wound that pierced his wrist and then penetrated the meaty part of his hip. Neither wound was lifethreatening, but both were painful, bloody, and would require medical attention to prevent infection. Martha Roberson later groused: "It was too bad that I had such a small pistol. If only I had had a bigger gun I could have killed him."[6]

But Ross and Good roared off in Ross's Model T Ford. Then there was silence—except for the joined voices of the congregation of the Seminole Methodist Church about a half block from the Gaines Hotel singing an Easter hymn of joy and praise: "He is Risen! He is Risen!"[7]

Milt Good (*left*) and Tom Ross, handcuffed, at their murder trial in Lubbock, Texas, for the murder of Dave Allison. (*Courtesy* The Cattleman *magazine*)

SURRENDER

The outlaws did not flee very far. They drove about thirteen miles northwest of Seminole to the ranch of Soon Birdwell, where they stopped and called Sheriff Britton.

"We want to surrender, Britton," said Ross.

"Who else is with you?" the sheriff inquired.

"Only Milt Good."

"All right," said the sheriff. "I'll come out and get you."

Obviously recalling the 1895 posse that attacked them in Waggoner's dugout as well as the mob that had lynched Kid Lewis and Foster Crawford, Ross asked, "Who'll you bring along?"

"My deputy," replied the sheriff.

"All right," Ross said. "But don't bring a crowd."[8]

As it turned out, a neighboring rancher, Forrest Sherman, volunteered to come to Soon Birdwell's ranch, pick up Ross and Good, and deliver them to the sheriff in Seminole. The trip was uneventful. Sherman recalled that Ross and Good laughed and talked during the trip. One of them said, "Who was that woman that shot us?"[9]

When they arrived, Ross and Good surrendered themselves and their weapons to Sheriff Britton and were incarcerated in the brand-new Gaines County jail. It was a fine jail that the Gaines County citizens were very proud of, since the county's population did not exceed five hundred at that time. Some individual citizens had contributed their own funds toward construction expenses. Ironically, one of the most generous contributors to the building of the new jail was . . . Tom Ross. Ross and his fellow shooter, Good, found themselves to be the very first guests of that new law enforcement facility.

The wheels of justice, just as the mills of the gods, are widely reputed to grind slowly—but not in Gaines County, Texas, in 1923. The criminal justice system of Texas, prodded by the Texas and Southwestern Cattle Raisers Association, put these murder trials on a fast track. The day after the killings, the grand jury at Seminole indicted both Tom Ross and Milt Good for murder. Two separate indictments were returned against each defendant: one for the murder of Dave Allison and one for the murder of Horace Roberson.[10] The next day, April 3, District Judge Clark M. Mullican, on his own motion, changed the venue of all the murder cases to the nearest "big city"—Lubbock, Texas, population approximately four thousand, some eighty miles to the northeast. Ross and Good, still not taking their legal predicament all that seriously, apparently believed they would be allowed to make bond and go free pending the trials. Each filed a writ of habeas corpus. To their surprise, on April 12, 1923, Judge Mullican refused their writs and remanded both to jail. He ordered Ross to stand trial for the alleged murder of Dave Allison on June 18, 1923, with the trial of Good for the killing of Allison to follow immediately thereafter.[11]

It was a significant tactical victory for the prosecution. The prosecution's cases against both defendants were much stronger in the Allison killing than in the Roberson killing. The killing of the relatively low-keyed Allison was calculated to generate considerably more jury outrage than the killing of the bellicose Roberson, who had bragged to several people about how he was going to bring Ross and Good to heel by gun or by gavel, and preferably the former. A prosecution win in the Allison case, plus a severe sentence (hanging, hopefully) would augur well for the prosecution when the Roberson murder trials were called. On the other hand, if the state were put to the test first in the Roberson cases, the outlook was decidedly less sanguine. If either or both defendants were acquitted in the Roberson cases, it would take much steam out of the prosecution before the Allison cases were called. Even if the defendants were found guilty of a lesser offense (such as manslaughter) or meted out a relatively light sentence in the Roberson cases, it would significantly lower the morale of the prosecution and invigorate the defense. Also, in such a small community, news of the outcome would almost certainly be known by future jurors.

THE GATHERING OF THE CLAN

The little town of Lubbock braced itself for the onslaught of court officials, lawyers, lawmen, witnesses, reporters, and crowds of spectators that this high-profile case was bound to attract. The extent of the news coverage itself spoke volumes. In 1923, a time when news reporters for even the largest Texas cities rarely ventured far beyond their respective city limits, major daily newspapers, including the *Amarillo Daily News*, the *Fort Worth Star-Telegram*, and the *Dallas Morning News*, all sent reporters. Even the *Denver Post* and the prestigious *St. Louis Post-Dispatch* sent reporters and gave the story front-page play. The *St. Louis Post-Dispatch* wrapped it all up with a serialized account in three consecutive Sunday supplements.[12] *Post-Dispatch* reporter Robertus Love told the folks back east that the Tom Ross murder trial was "the most important murder trial docketed in the Southwestern country since the twentieth century began." The editor assured his audience that Robertus Love had spent considerable time in West Texas "collecting the facts in a twentieth-century revival of the old wild days in Texas celebrated in song and story." He went on at length to describe how an army of lawmen had descended upon Lubbock to ensure that "old-time Texas gun play" didn't "mar the well nigh perfect record of the proud little city of Lubbock." Reporter Love didn't spare the adjectives or the anecdotes in giving his readers an eyeful of local color. "Titanic Texas isn't what it used to be," he proclaimed. From one unnamed source, Love came up with a quote that turned out to have more meaning and relevance to the case than the reporter intended or understood. His West Texas source (perhaps it was Gaines County Sheriff Britton, who was an unarmed witness to the shooting) was quoted as saying: "Why, we don't even wear guns nowadays when we go to church. Gun play's just about played out [in West Texas]."[13]

Perhaps gilding the lily a bit, reporter Love then shared a pretrial tidbit with his readers, intending, no doubt, to give the folks back home a taste of the not yet totally tamed frontier. He told the following tale: The landlord of the Merrill Hotel, just across the street from the courthouse, rushed into the Lubbock sheriff's office with this breathless report: "Good Lord, Mr. Sheriff, come a-runnin' to the hotel! There's a long-legged, red-headed son of a gun just loped in from the Rio Grande with two guns draggin' the ground, and if you don't come and ketch him quick, he'll kill everybody in town before sundown!" Turned out, however, that the red-headed stranger, "Red" Hawkins, posed no threat to the law-abiding folks; he was a Cattle Raisers Association brand inspector and had accompanied Presidio County Sheriff Jeff Vaughn on the four-hundred-mile trip over dirt roads to help Lubbock Sheriff Bud Johnson keep the peace.[14]

The Lubbock trials proved to be quite a gathering of the clan, a clan composed not only of every association inspector (about fifty in all) but also law enforcement officers from Texas, New Mexico, and Oklahoma (including thirty-two county sheriffs), who arrived not only to keep the peace but also to show support for the prosecution. In addition, many Southwest ranchers, bankers, livestock industry folks, and a good portion of the four thousand members of the Cattle Raisers Association showed up, as well as almost three hundred character witnesses subpoenaed by both sides. And there also came a sizeable contingent of supporters for Tom Ross and Milt Good. Lubbock hotels quickly filled to capacity. The Chamber of Commerce

Lubbock County District Judge Clark Mullican (*right*) and District Attorney Gordon B. McGuire outside of the Lubbock County Courthouse during a recess in the trial of Tom Ross for the murder of Dave Allison. *(Courtesy The Cattleman magazine)*

secured rooms in private homes to accommodate many others, but still, more than 150 spectators found no room at the inn and had to camp out at a city park.[15] Excitement reached a fever pitch as the throngs anticipated an unfolding drama that one writer labeled as an "epic of the Southwest."[16] Although arising out of a tragedy, still, as another observer noted, it provided old friends from across the Southwest an opportunity to gather and "rehash their common past as they danced at night in the streets to the tune of a fiddle."[17]

THE LUBBOCK TRIALS

Also descending on Lubbock was an all-star cast of lawyers for the prosecution and defense. Of course, District Attorney Gordon B. McGuire (himself a witness to the slayings) was the Texas prosecutor in charge of the case, but the Cattle Raisers Association sent its own general counsel, Dayton Moses of Fort Worth, to assist. In fact, Moses, a renowned criminal lawyer, took over as lead prosecutor. Rounding out the state's team were S. C. Rowe of Fort Worth, Lubbock County attorney O. W. McWhorter, and W. W. Campbell and J. E. Vickers, both of Lubbock. The lead lawyer for the defense was the extremely popular W. H. Bledsoe of Lubbock. Bledsoe was a state senator and was generally credited with recently winning legislative approval for the establishment of a new college in West Texas (Texas Technological College, later Texas Tech University) and then seeing to it that the new school was located in his hometown.[18] Assisting Senator Bledsoe were Lubbock mayor Percy Spencer, John Howard of Pecos, Homer L. Parr of Lubbock, and, of course, George Lockhart of Tahoka—one and the same George Lockhart who also had been an eyewitness to the slayings.

The murder trials of Ross and Good were remarkable in a number of aspects, not the least of which was that a lawyer for the prosecution *and* a lawyer for the defense were actually eyewitnesses to the killings. Under modern canons of ethics governing the conduct of lawyers, a lawyer who knows himself to be a material witness in either a criminal or a civil trial must recuse himself as a lawyer in the case and thereby avoid, either voluntarily or involuntarily, putting himself into the position of playing the dual role of witness and advocate. Such, however, was not the case in 1923. McGuire, in fact, not only took an active role in the prosecution but also appeared for the state and testified as an eyewitness to the killings—impartiality, or even the appearance of impartiality, be damned.

District Judge Clark M. Mullican, young, popular, and able, ruled the proceedings with militaristic authority and discipline. Judge Mullican was something of a World War I hero himself. As a U.S. Army colonel, he had commanded a Texas infantry regiment during the bloody campaign in France. Nobody was allowed into Judge Mullican's courtroom without being thoroughly searched for weapons, women included—even Judge Mullican's own wife! Furthermore, Judge Mullican held opposing lawyers' feet to the fire and tolerated no unseemly outbursts, delays, or long-winded legalistic pontifications.[19] Hence, despite a multitude of character witnesses on both sides, Ross's trial took slightly less than two weeks; Good's trial, about one week. The Lubbock courtroom was spacious, having a seating capacity of eight hundred. Still many would-be spectators were turned back at the courtroom door.

Dayton Moses of Fort Worth, lawyer representing the Texas & Southwestern Cattle Raisers Association, was the lead lawyer (assisting District Attorney Gordon McGuire) in the prosecution in Lubbock of Tom Ross and Milt Good for the murder of Dave Allison. Later he led the prosecution in the Taylor County District Court in Abilene, Texas, in the trials of Ross and Good for the murder of Roberson. *(Courtesy* The Cattleman *magazine)*

There were to be four trials. Ross and Good would each be tried separately for the alleged murder of Allison, and then each would be tried separately for the alleged murder of Roberson. The state had little difficulty in convincing the jury that both defendants acted in concert in the killing of the inspectors. Therefore, both would be charged as principals in each killing, and it would not be necessary for the state to prove which defendant actually fired the fatal shot in either death.

It became obvious from the get-go that the trial of Tom Ross (and later the trial of Milt Good) would be a three-cornered affair: The State of Texas and the Texas and Southwestern Cattle Raisers Association versus Tom Ross. The association had been formed in 1877 to eradicate those "Goddamned cow thieves" and had steadily grown in numbers and influence over the years.[20] The legal plight of Ross and Good had been deadly serious before; now, with the high-profile support of the mighty T&SCRA having been thrown behind the prosecution, their fate seemed almost hopeless. Meanwhile, both before and during the trials, the association's official publication, *The Cattleman* magazine, kept up a relentless drumbeat for the vindication of its inspectors and for the noosing of Ross and Good. Just before trial, in its May 1923 issue, for instance, *The Cattleman* ran a page and a half of one-paragraph quotes from its members, weighing in on the Seminole killings. One member wrote: "The Comanche never planned a more dastardly deed than was committed on these two good men."

Even so, the association's high-handed role in the prosecution was not without a negative side. Not everybody revered the Cattle Raisers Association—and its detractors were not all outlaws. To begin with, most of the association's organizers were big cattlemen, men who already had staked out big ranches by making land grabs in the formative years often at the expense of "nesters," as pointed out in previous chapters. There still existed much friction between the "little" farmer or rancher and the cattle barons who dominated the association. Thus the "Goddamned cow thieves" weren't the only ones who had an ax to grind against the association.[21] Moreover, not all the members of the association supported the prosecution in the Tom Ross case. In fact, quite a number refused to join in the support of that action, and some even canceled their membership in protest.[22]

Over the past two decades as a small rancher, a family man, and a good neighbor (at least he was so regarded by many), Ross had attracted a sizeable number of friends and supporters. To many, the charismatic Ross was the champion of the underdog and the little man—a man who would not buckle under to bullies, even if they wore a badge. Too, there was something of the Robin Hood appeal about Ross. Even though he had been—and perhaps still was—a thief, he nevertheless was known as a man who would "give his last penny to a widow or orphan," and, unlike most of the big ranchers of that day, he sometimes went out of his way to help his hard-scrabble "nester" neighbors.

There was yet another underlying factor—subtle and difficult to define—that might prove to be a plus in Tom's favor in the upcoming courtroom battle; that being a curious dichotomy in the American psyche. Americans tend to cheer those steely-eyed, fearless heroes who confront and conquer the villains who threaten the order

J. E. Vickers was a Lubbock lawyer and a member of the prosecution team that succeeded in convicting Tom Ross and Milt Good for the murder of Dave Allison. Vickers also served later as a Lubbock County district attorney. According to Chuck Lanehart, who currently practices law in Lubbock, Vickers had this practical advice for trial lawyers: "If the facts are against you, argue the law. If the law is against you, argue the facts. If both the law and the facts are against you, jump on the opposing lawyer." *(Courtesy of Southwest Collection/Special Collections Library, Texas Tech University, Lubbock, Texas)*

W. H. Bledsoe of Lubbock served as lead defense attorney for Tom Ross at his Lubbock trial for killing Dave Allison. Bledsoe was a popular state senator and was generally given a lion's share of the credit for winning the legislative approval for a new state college to be established in West Texas (Texas Tech University) and then making sure it was located in Lubbock. *(Courtesy of Southwest Collection/Special Collections Library, Texas Tech University, Lubbock, Texas)*

and security of the community. (Think frontier marshals Wyatt Earp and Wild Bill Hickok.) Still, at the same time, there is in the American character an instinctive fondness for individualism and dissent and a distrust of the possessors of power—something that cheers (even if not vocally) the bold, brazen, and charismatic rebel bandit who flouts the establishment and all its rules and who is determined, come hell or high water, to "do it my way." (Think Butch Cassidy, the Sundance Kid, Billy the Kid, Jesse James, and even Bonnie and Clyde.) Sometimes it seems that these two conflicting currents flow simultaneously, even if at different levels, within the same individual psyche.[23] And so, while the cattle association's strident support of the prosecution would prove effective, it nevertheless also triggered a counterpoint blacklash that was playing well in Ross's defense.

Not only that, but much to the chagrin of the association, the press gave some favorable coverage to the personable Tom Ross. He was accessible; he chatted freely and amicably with the reporters; and he was usually good for a quote. When one reporter asked Ross what kind of pistol he preferred, he replied: "I use the automatic pistol. The automatic is to the old six-shooter what lightning is to the wind. The automatic don't jam."[24] Such favorable coverage of Ross riled the association, and some of their representatives undertook to chastise the press. However, Ross's obvious attempts to curry favor with court officials and opposing counsel were not so successful. He made several rather strained, and certainly inappropriate, stabs at favor-currying humor. Once when the prosecution team entered the courtroom and was coming down the aisle to the counsel table, Ross detained a junior member of the team, Owen McWhorter, and said to his wife, Trixie, in McWhorter's presence: "This young man is going to prosecute me. But he is a good boy. He won't be too hard on me. His dad bought some cattle from me last year."[25] Still worse, during a break in the proceedings, he caught Judge Mullican's sleeve and, with an attempt at "jollity," introduced the judge to his thirteen-year-old daughter, Bessie. "Judge," Ross said, "this little girl likes you, and she wants to talk to you."[26]

Throughout the trial, Ross presented an attractive appearance. He certainly did not look like an outlaw, or a killer, or even a cowboy. Dressed in a business suit, white shirt and tie, and neatly groomed, Ross was said to look a lot more like a banker than a criminal. His wife, Trixie, and daughter, Bessie, sat immediately behind him during the trial, and they visited amicably in the presence of the jury and spectators during recesses. He also remained cool and unflappable both on and off the stand during his trial. Even the vigorous cross-examination of the association's man, Dayton Moses, failed to fluster or ruffle his composure. His demeanor during the entire trial seemed more like an interested spectator than a prime candidate for the gallows.

Jury selection was difficult and time-consuming, particularly in view of the limited jury pool in that small community where everyone had already heard much about the killings. Also the state made known that it was seeking the death penalty, and so each juror had to be "qualified" on the death penalty, meaning he had to declare that he had no moral scruples against the assessment of the death penalty in a proper case.[27] One panelist admitted to Dayton Moses that he did have some scruples against assessing a death penalty. Moses asked him if he could think of a case where he would do so. The prospective juror said that he probably could assess a death penalty against a black man who had attacked a white woman.[28] Moses challenged the potential juror, and the judge excused him for cause shown: that is, having scruples against the assessment of a death penalty.

One of the most persuasive arguments of those who oppose the death penalty is that when the prosecution is permitted to "qualify" potential jurors on the death penalty, any panelist who, like the above man, expresses any scruples against the death penalty is excluded. This, they contend with considerable logic, tends to skew the final jury in favor of the prosecution—in effect turning it into a "hanging jury" that is more likely to convict than a true cross-section of the defendant's peers.

Finally, after four days, the lawyers had their jury. Eleven small farmers and one preacher took their seats in the jury box. To reporters, Ross pronounced himself pleased with the appearance of the jury, "even if they hang me."[29] Ross and Lockhart were undoubtedly pleased that the jury was composed of "little" people and no big ranchers or executives.

Then the trial began.

The state's case was simple, straightforward, and loaded with eyewitnesses—credible eyewitnesses. In murder cases, the state, more often than not, has to rely on eyewitnesses whose character is far less than sterling—sleazy companions of the defendant or the deceased, drunken bar chums, co-indictees, ex-convicts, or shady characters who, by their self-serving and prosecution-pleasing testimony, themselves wish to avoid becoming convicts. Here, however, Ross and Good seemed to have gone out of their way to provide the prosecutors with an all-star cast of eyewitnesses whose credibility, just short of the Pope himself, could hardly have been challenged by any man's army of defense attorneys, no matter how skilled.

Neither was "motive" a problem for the state. Whether a juror chose to believe the state's version of motive (to prevent the inspectors from sending the defendants to the pen for cattle rustling), or the defendant's version of motive (self-defense), either way there was motive aplenty. While showing proof of a motive for a killing is not a required hurdle for the prosecution to clear, it is still difficult for most juries to convict a man for murder and hang him or lock him up for life unless the state has offered the jury a reasonable explanation of why the defendant killed the victim. Conversely, if no apparent motive is offered during the trial, jurors are likely to wonder—and thus to develop a "reasonable doubt"—whether the defendant really did pull the trigger.

The state called as eyewitnesses the surviving occupants of the Gaines Hotel carnage—all, that is, except for George Lockhart, who was now representing Tom Ross. That left five to tell the tale, and that tale was direct and consistent: Tom Ross and Milt Good, *sans* disguises, known and recognized by all and with guns drawn, burst through the door of the lobby without warning and, guns blazing, proceeded to slaughter Allison and Roberson.

But that was not all. The state had other damning evidence to share with the jury: namely the cattle theft indictments returned against Ross in Lea County, New Mexico, and Gaines County, Texas, both of which charged him with theft of the same four Wilhoit cows; and worse yet, over strenuous objections from Ross's defense team, the court allowed the state to get into evidence the indictments against Good for theft of the 516-cow herd he was caught driving. These included indictments from four different Texas counties. Throwing the cow-thieving allegations against both Ross and Good into the evidentiary mix was devastating to the defense when the only charge the jury was supposed to consider was the alleged murder of Allison. In order to protect the rights of the accused, the general rule is that the state should not be allowed to bring into evidence (at least not during the guilt-innocence stage of the trial) past crimes of the defendant. Furthermore, even when exceptions to that general rule apply, past crimes cannot be brought to the jury's attention unless the defendant has been *convicted* of those crimes. Here Judge Mullican allowed the state to tell the jury about alleged cow theft crimes that Ross and Good had only been *charged with*—but had *never been convicted of.* (Also recall that Tom Ross, alone, was on trial for murder—not Tom Ross *and Milt Good*—yet the court was permitting the prosecution to parade before the jury allegations that Milt Good may have stolen 516 head of cattle, a crime never laid at Tom Ross's doorstep.) Nevertheless, Judge Mullican's ruling was correct. The introduction of the prior (but yet unproved) allegations of cow thieving against Ross and Good were relevant and material in proving that Good and Ross both had motives to kill the inspectors; that, in turn, being circumstantial evidence tending to show that the killings had been a *premeditated* attack to silence the prosecution's two key witnesses against the defendants. Correct though it was, the ruling allowed the state, in essence, to try Ross not only for murder but also for cattle rustling—both his and Milt Good's. Judge Mullican, as the law required, did instruct the jury not to consider the cattle theft indictments against the defendants for any purpose other than proving motive and premeditation and to disprove self-defense. However, that was probably no more efficacious than throwing a skunk into the jury box and then ordering the jury to disregard the smell.

But there was more—much more in the state's arsenal. The prosecution introduced additional evidence proving that the killings were a part of a premeditated plan. Testimony proved that both

Good and Ross had purchased ammunition shortly before the attack. Particularly damaging was the testimony of a Mrs. Ella Detro, a railway ticket agent at Brownfield, Texas. On the Friday prior to the shooting, Good had bought a ticket in Brownfield en route to Seminole. He had a conversation with Detro at the time he purchased his ticket and told her of his destination and that he was "rearing to go there." When Detro remarked that Good appeared as though he was "looking for trouble," Good agreed, saying, as she put it, that he "did not know but what he was looking for trouble," adding he was going to Seminole "to whip someone or get whipped."[30] Later that day, he hooked up with Ross in Seminole, and they went to Ross's ranch where they spent the remainder of the weekend before returning to Seminole Sunday evening just prior to the shooting.

Defense attorney Lockhart vigorously objected to this highly inflammatory testimony of the railway clerk Detro on the grounds that it was hearsay, that it was a vague and general statement not directed toward either of the inspectors, and that it was not relevant to any issue in the case. Again Judge Mullican overruled a defense objection, allowed Mrs. Detro's testimony, and again he was correct. What the railway clerk's testimony fit squarely into an exception to the general rule against hearsay: any incriminating declaration made by a conspirator during the course of the conspiracy is admissible, not only against the declarant but also against his co-conspirator.

What had gone down in the trial thus far was bad enough from the defense standpoint. But the worst was yet to come. Both widows, Allison and Roberson, took the stand and testified, and did so with telling effect. The spectators and the jury listened in spellbound silence as Martha Roberson recounted the gruesome scene that she encountered when she rushed down the hotel stairs that fateful night: both Allison and her husband already dead, riddled with bullets—the lifeless corpse of her husband still gushing blood from all the wounds. The emotional impact was devastating, bringing sobs from the spectators and barely suppressed tears to the eyes of the jurors. During her testimony, Martha Roberson glared at Tom Ross. He did not return the compliment.[31]

When the state rested its case, it appeared that Ross had effectively backed himself into a corner from which there was no escape. Obviously an "alibi" or "mistaken identity" defense was not an option; neither was "not guilty by reason of insanity." The defense could hardly quibble about the cause of death. And "accident" was completely out of the question. That left only "self-defense" as an out, but in view of the testimony of three eyewitnesses, that appeared to be a pretty slender reed upon which to hang a viable defense.

But Ross took the stand. Predictably, he was unflappable—"as cool and deliberate as he could possibly be."[32] He testified (as did Good during his trial) that there was no prearranged plan to kill either of the inspectors. In fact, Ross contended, they had no idea that either Allison or Roberson was in Seminole that night. They had merely come to town to consult with their attorney, Lockhart, about the cattle theft cases. The first they knew of the whereabouts of the inspectors was when they walked into the Gaines Hotel lobby that night. (Burst through the lobby door, as it were, with loaded guns in both hands.)

As unlikely as that must have seemed to the jury, the state attempted to further rebut the defendant's assertion by showing that Ross's friend (and co-indictee) Charley Richards had come to the hotel shortly before the shooting as a scout for Ross and Good and had a private conference with Lockhart, and that shortly thereafter, when Lockhart returned to the lobby, he moved his chair out of the anticipated line of fire. Of course Richards denied he was a scout, and Lockhart didn't testify. Next Ross told the jury that he had heard about the threats the inspectors had supposedly made to kill him and Good, that he believed those threats and thought Allison and Roberson were the kind of men who could be expected to carry out those threats. Therefore, Ross continued, he was put in fear of his life.[33]

As we saw in the Burk Burnett murder trial, under Texas law (Texas *written* law, that is) a homicide is not justified on grounds of "self-defense" on the basis of prior threats alone, no matter how believable the threats and no matter how much the defendant may have been put in fear for his life. Before the shooter can claim self-defense, in addition to proving his life had been threatened by his adversary, he must further prove that just before the shooting the deceased performed *some overt act or uttered some words* that led the defendant reasonably to conclude that the deceased was about to carry out his threat. Judge Mullican so instructed the jury.

The prosecution produced three very credible eyewitnesses to the killings, including Sheriff Britton, all of whom testified, in effect, that the two brand inspectors never knew what hit them, much less made any effort to draw their weapons before being shot to pieces. Ross, however, when he testified, made at least a nod in the direction of the written law of self-defense. Contrary to the version related by the eyewitnesses, he testified that upon entering the hotel lobby he and Good both observed Allison and Roberson making movements as if to draw their pistols and thus carry out their death threats. Therefore, believing they were about to be attacked, only then, Ross insisted, did they draw their weapons and fire upon the inspectors.[34]

Additional doubt was cast on Ross's claim that he fired only after he observed Roberson make an effort to draw his pistol when Dayton Moses, on cross-examination of Ross, read back Ross's own testimony given only three days after the shootings when Ross and Good sought to have bail set at a habeas corpus hearing. Such testimony, given at a time when Ross was obviously still seething with rage and before he and his attorneys had had much opportunity to map out their defensive strategy, must have sounded distinctly disharmonious to the jury when compared to the self-defense tune the defendant was now singing. At the habeas corpus hearing Ross had not only freely admitted shooting Roberson but had gone on to testify that upon entering the lobby he had drawn his .45-caliber automatic pistol and shot Roberson several times: "I shot at his [Roberson's] heart. I shot at his neck. I shot at his head. I shot twice at his heart."[35]

Could the prosecution have written a better script for its intended swingee?

Still, it is the jury's sole province (and not that of the trial judge or an appellate court) to weigh the credibility of witnesses and thus believe, or disbelieve, all or any part or none of the testimony of any witness. Therefore, weak as Ross's testimony appeared when he (1) denied knowing that the inspectors were present in the Gaines Hotel lobby that fateful evening, (2) denied that he and Good had any prior intent to kill the inspectors even though they burst through the lobby door with weapons cocked and loaded, (3) claimed that Allison and Roberson recognized them as soon as they entered the lobby and immediately attempted to draw their weapons, and (4) claimed that it was only at that point that they concluded it was necessary to draw their own weapons and defend themselves, it nevertheless afforded the jury a legal peg upon which to hang a "not guilty" verdict if, for whatever reason, it chose to do so.

With that obligatory nod in the direction of the written law of self-defense out of the way, Lockhart could now focus on his real defense: self-defense as defined by the unwritten law. To be sure, although the defense team never explicitly referred to the unwritten law, it was an elephant in the room, and furthermore it was the only mount available to Ross if he hoped to ride out of that courtroom as a free man. Under the unwritten law, as we have already learned, threats to kill—nothing more—were deemed sufficient justification to kill the author of the threats. And no overt attempt to carry out those threats just prior to the killing was necessary to perfect that defense. It was left to Tom Ross and his defense team to hope and pray that the old frontier code still retained its potency in the year 1923.

The underlying message that the defense labored to hammer home to the jurors was that Roberson, with his boasts and his threats to kill or conquer Tom Ross, together with his badge heavy arrogance and ungovernable temper and his history of killing anyone who provoked his wrath—even if the victim was, like Foote Boykin, unarmed at the time—had created a "kill-or-be-killed" crisis. Therefore, Ross couldn't afford to wait around until Roberson decided to waylay him at a time and place of Roberson's choosing—without giving Ross fair opportunity to protect his life. Thus a preemptive strike was the only reasonable option left to him. Such an argument was not without considerable common-sense appeal in view of the inflammatory circumstances of this case. Yet the question remained:

would the remnants of the unwritten frontier code be enough to override the clear dictates of the written laws of Texas in this the post-World War I world of West Texas?

At that point the trial turned into a recitation of the threats and other "intemperate remarks" the inspectors allegedly had made against Good and Ross, a retelling of the past violent deeds of the inspectors, and then a duel between opposing character witnesses. Ross testified about the threats. But first he took the opportunity to deny that he had stolen any cattle from Wilhoit, and he denied that he had anything to do with any other cattle-rustling offenses, including the cattle theft charges brought against Milt Good.[36] He also testified about his knowledge of Roberson's reputation for violence, including what he had heard about Horace Roberson killing Foote Boykin, plus the killing of Ross's friend Jake Ballard, plus the killing of several black porters while Roberson was employed by the railroad, plus Roberson's alleged involvement in "lots of other shootings."[37]

Ross also testified that he was aware of Allison's violent past, including the killing of the Mexican rebel leader turned bandit, Pascual Orozco, under questionable circumstances. Then Ross told the jury about the threats communicated to him by a number of men prior to the Seminole incident. "It [the threats] was the general talk all over the country. I got sick and tired of it," Ross declared.[38] Obe Chance, for one, he said, told him that Roberson said that he was going to kill him. Ross said that Obe Chance also told him that Roberson had tried to get him (Obe Chance) to become a witness against Ross.[39] Ross told the jury that while he was in the hospital at Lubbock, Roberson came on his ranch and confronted his cowboy, Roy "Alkali" Adams. Adams testified that Roberson had this to say: "I might not have enough evidence to convict Tom Ross, but I'm going to get him; that he [Ross] was a _____ ." Roberson then told Adams that if he would quit Ross, "he would favor him in every way possible."[40] Adams, of course, had related this conversation to Ross when he returned from the hospital.

Dr. E. Calloway, a Midland doctor, testified that he had warned Ross just prior to the shooting that Roberson intended to kill him.[41]

Dora Burks, who was bailiff of the Lovington, New Mexico, grand jury that indicted Ross in December 1922 for the theft of the four Wilhoit cows, testified that on that occasion Burks visited with both of the cattle inspectors. Allison, he said, told him that Ross was the "brains of all this cattle stealing and that Roberson's going to get him." Burks said he warned Allison, "You boys are going to stir up a lot of trouble." According to Burks, Allison replied, "That won't amount to a thing in the world. Roberson will kill him."[42] C. L. Holland testified that Roberson told him that he would send Ross to the pen or kill him.[43] Ira Norton and Tom Cross, eyewitnesses to the killing of Foote Boykin by Roberson in the Sierra Blanca railroad pens in 1915, took the stand and told the jury a very gruesome story of that event.[44]

John R. Williams of Borden County testified for the defense. He told of an incident that happened while Roberson was transporting a prisoner on a train. During a dispute over seating arrangements, another passenger made some derogatory remark about the Texas Rangers, whereupon Roberson pulled his Winchester rifle and threatened to "beat his Goddamned brains out." He was prevented from carrying out the threat, Williams said, only when other officers restrained him.[45]

Not all of the testimony of the defense's "threat" witnesses could be discounted as coming from biased pals of Tom Ross. Bert Weir, a New Mexican, was no friend of Ross, yet he quoted Roberson as saying that he had "worked up several good cases against different people, but Ross and Good had bowed their necks and seemed unwilling to take their medicine." He said Roberson added that he'd heard of Ross's speed with a gun, but that if Ross were to get him, he would "have to be quick."[46] Jim Griffith recalled talking to the inspectors in January 1923. He said to them, "You fellows are afraid of Ross, aren't you?" According to Griffith, Roberson replied that he was not afraid of Ross and that he "would kill that _____ at the first opportunity."[47] A former Midland County sheriff, W. F. Bradford, testified that he overheard Roberson tell another man that "apparently the only way to get rid of Ross was to kill him or send him to the penitentiary."[48] Coming from another lawman, the quote clearly underlined Roberson's frustration at his inability to bring Ross to heel.

Walter McGonagill testified that Roberson told him that Ross was the leader of a gang of cattle thieves and that he was going to send Ross to the pen or kill him "as the need arose," or "if he wanted to shoot it out, to come down the street with his pistol in hand" and that it didn't make any difference to him if Ross was "awful quick with a gun." According to McGonagill, Roberson added that his "reputation would be complete" in West Texas once he and Allison got rid of Tom Ross and Milt Good "one way or the other." McGonagill also testified that on another occasion he encountered Allison and Roberson in the courthouse in Lovington, New Mexico. Allison, he said, asked what kind of firearms Ross carried. However, McGonagill said that before he could answer, Roberson broke in and said, "We don't care what kind of firearms Ross carries. We're going to kill him."[49] T. C. Henderson of Toyah told of hearing Roberson brag that he had killed thirty-eight men, "Mexicans and all."[50] While most of the defense witnesses focused on Roberson's threats and violent episodes, one witness, E. M. Love of Sierra Blanca, testified that he had been a member of Allison's posse when it cornered Mexican General Orozco. All of the Mexicans including Orozco were killed in the ensuing battle—all except one who surrendered. Love testified that Allison shot and killed the captive although his hands had been in the air for a good ten seconds.[51]

From that point on, the trial turned into a battle between character witnesses. The defense called approximately thirty-five character witnesses who testified that the inspectors had bad reputations as violent and dangerous men who could be expected to carry out any threats they made and that Roberson had made the threats to kill or convict Ross.[52] Several of these witnesses were well-known and upstanding members of their community, such as J. Wiley Taylor, former sheriff, tax assessor, and postmaster from Midland, and County Judge A. M. Walling from Sierra Blanca.

The state, of course, returned the volley by calling just as many witnesses with impressive credentials who testified to the good character and reputation of the inspectors. A *Fort Worth Star-Telegram* reporter observed, "It depended on whether you asked his friend or his enemy what [an inspector's] reputation was."[53] One such witness who testified as to their good reputation was former Texas Ranger Capt. John R. Hughes, Roberson's old boss when he was a ranger. However, one ranger captain was conspicuous by his absence from the prosecution's roster. Although subpoenaed by the state, Capt. John H. Rogers refused to testify against his old nemesis, Tom Ross, recalling that once in the sand dunes of New Mexico, Tom had spared his life while he stared down the barrel of Ross's Winchester rifle.[54]

In addition to testifying that Roberson had a reputation as a "peaceable and law-abiding citizen," the state's witnesses, as if on cue, added that Roberson was a "kind and inoffensive" man. On cross-examination by the defense, however, most admitted that this "kind and inoffensive" gentleman was reputed to have killed several men. Some of the state's witnesses agreed that Roberson did have "some slight reputation as a killer."[55]

Finally it was time for jury arguments.

In his final address, Lockhart tried to exploit sentiment against the cattle association and its inspectors, insisting that it existed mainly for the benefit of prominent stockmen, an approach obviously aimed at appealing to the small farmers on the jury. "There are three parties to this suit," Lockhart told the jury, "the State of Texas, the Cattle Raisers Association backed up by an array of gunmen, and the defendant."[56] He also underscored the self-defense theme, claiming that if Ross had really premeditated the killings that night in Seminole, he would have shot Roberson or Allison through the hotel lobby window with a rifle and then gotten away undetected, with an alibi already in place.[57] He cited Sheriff Britton's testimony to the effect that anybody could view the entire hotel lobby from the outside by looking through the window in the north wall of the lobby.

Dayton Moses closed for the state with a lengthy and emotional appeal. After castigating Lockhart personally for representing Ross and for failing to take the stand as an eyewitness to tell what happened that evening in the lobby of the Gaines Hotel, he zeroed in on his primary target, Ross. "Remove this stigma from the South Plains," he demanded. He told the jury that the assassination in Seminole was murder, pure and simple, and that they should not allow the defense to divert their attention from that fact. He accused the defense of trying to "muddy the waters" by putting the Cattle Raisers Association on trial.[58]

Then the jury retired.

It was not a quick verdict. They were out for twenty-eight hours before returning with a "guilty" verdict with punishment set at thirty-five years in the penitentiary.

Throughout it all, Tom Ross retained his cool, confident demeanor and even joked with his attorneys from time to time. After the jury was excused, one young juror, S. L. Wylie, walked over to Ross before departing the courtroom and shook his hand. He told Ross that they had tried to treat him as kindly as possible, and he was sorry they had to send him up for so long. "Oh, that's all right, son," replied Ross amicably, "you had to do your duty."[59] Another juror, E. T. Daniels, expressed his misgivings over the verdict by sending Ross a large bouquet of flowers.[60] Privately, of course, Ross felt he had been wrongfully convicted. In his view, it was a clear case of justifiable homicide. But then his take was skewed by his bitter animosity toward that braggart bully Roberson as filtered through the lens of his frontier upbringing, which taught the propriety of self-redressment of wrongs. His attorney, Senator Bledsoe, viewing the case more objectively and from a post-frontier perspective, believed that they were fortunate to have dodged the bullet; that thirty-five years to do was a whole lot better than a noose around the neck, and that, from a legal standpoint, his client's position had, at best, always been precarious.[61]

The trial of Milt Good followed immediately thereafter and was almost a replica of the Tom Ross trial. Good's wife and their nine young children, the oldest of whom was only fifteen, were present throughout the trial, which perhaps influenced the jury to shorten Good's sentence. The jury assessed his punishment at twenty-six

Taylor County District Judge W. R. Ely presided over the Abilene, Texas, trials of Tom Ross and Milt Good for the murder of T&SCRA inspector H. L. Roberson. *(Courtesy The Cattleman magazine)*

years in the penitentiary. (It was later speculated that the jury arrived at their odd sentence of twenty-six years by deciding to give Good the same thirty-five-year sentence that Tom Ross received, less one year for each of Good's nine minor children.)[62] Judge Mullican overruled both defendants' motions for new trial and then changed venue of the pending murder cases against Ross and Good for the murder of Roberson to the Taylor County District Court in Abilene, Texas.

THE ABILENE TRIALS

The Abilene trials were presided over by Taylor County District Judge W. R. Ely. The prosecution team was composed of Dayton Moses and District Attorney Gordon B. McGuire plus the Taylor County district attorney, Milburn S. Long, and the previous Taylor County district attorney, W. J. Cunningham. The defense also beefed up its roster. In addition to state senator W. H. Bledsoe of Lubbock and Lubbock mayor Percy Spencer, the defense added two real defense heavyweights: J. F. Cunningham of Abilene and W. P. McLean, Jr., of Fort Worth. However, George Lockhart, Ross's original attorney and an eyewitness to the killings, dropped out of the defense team, doubtless to prevent Dayton Moses from again using him to tar Tom Ross.[63]

Both trials were held during September 1923, and the testimony was essentially the same that was heard by the Lubbock juries. Again, both Ross and Good were convicted. The Abilene jury had a much more difficult time of it, however, when it considered the case against Ross for the murder of Roberson. The jury deliberated for ninety-five hours before agreeing on a verdict. Not one of the jurors held out for a "not guilty" verdict, but one juror held out for a manslaughter verdict, the maximum penalty for which at that time was five years' imprisonment. The other eleven jurors initially voted "guilty of murder" and wanted to assess the death penalty. Finally, they compromised, finding Ross guilty of murder and assessing his punishment at twenty years' imprisonment.[64] Good, meanwhile, received a twenty-five-year sentence for his role in the Roberson murder. Both Ross and Good were enraged, however, when Judge Ely then proceeded to "stack" the Abilene sentences on top of the Lubbock sentences. Both men had expected the Lubbock and Abilene sentences would run concurrently so that the maximum sentence they received in either Abilene or Lubbock would, in effect, be the only sentence they had to serve.[65] But, as a result of Judge Ely's decision, fifty-two-year-old Tom Ross was now looking at a total of fifty-five years of pen time, and thirty-five-year-old Milt Good was staring a fifty-one-year sentence in the face—not an appealing future for either. The Texas Court of Criminal Appeals in Austin affirmed all the convictions, and Tom Ross, for the first time in his life, was looking out at the world through prison bars, and, one would think, with no realistic hope for another free day.

THE END OF A LONG AND WINDING TRAIL

But the Enigma of Tom Ross Remains

The ink had hardly dried on the commitment papers before Tom Ross, Milt Good, and a host of their supporters began bombarding the Texas governor and the Board of Pardons and Paroles with pleas for mercy. However, their repeated pleas failed, even when addressed to Texas Gov. Miriam "Ma" Ferguson, who was famous for her lenient clemency policies. Her refusals have to be credited in large part to the vigorous protests lodged by Dayton Moses and the T&SCRA against any such relief for Ross and Good.[1] The pair became desperate.

Ross finally realized that because of the objections of the Cattle Raisers Association, as well as the enormity of his crimes, his chance of obtaining a pardon, commutation, or early parole at any time in the near future was slim to none. He was fifty-three years old now, and looking at doing another fifty-four years in the pen. He concluded that if ever he were to see the sunlight of freedom again, there was but one recourse left to him: escape.

On Sunday evening, November 29, 1925, Ross and Good, together with two long-term convicts, Clarence Whalen and George Arlington, made good their escape from the Texas prison unit at Huntsville, Texas.[2] Good had secured a position as a prison hospital attendant, which allowed him considerable freedom within the walls. In addition, on that date he was working the night shift. Meanwhile, Ross complained of sickness and was transferred to the hospital ward. (According to prison officials, it was later discovered that he had induced fever by repeatedly inflaming his mouth with generous helpings of red pepper.) In a carefully orchestrated plan, the guard was overpowered and neutralized. (Good maneuvered behind the guard and then knocked him cold with a stick of firewood.) The four cut all prison communication lines and alarm systems. Then, with bolt cutters, they cut their way out of the prison undetected and scurried into a conveniently waiting automobile driven by a never-identified female. The escape was successful. Despite rewards offered by the State of Texas and the Texas and Southwest Cattle Raisers Association, and vigorous efforts on the part of the Texas Rangers and other lawmen, Tom Ross/Hill Loftis was never recaptured. He never spent another day behind bars.

MILT GOOD: RECAPTURE, RETURN, AND FINAL EXIT

Milt Good, however, was soon caught. Shortly after the prison break he had separated from Ross. Although he managed to evade lawmen for almost seven months he was snitched off, apparently by his own brother. Upon returning from a wolf hunt about daylight on June 26, 1926, he was captured near Antlers, Oklahoma, and sent back to his prison home at Huntsville.[3] A little more than a year later, Milt and several other inmates attempted another escape. Good and his pals dug a tunnel under the prison walls. However, a watchful guard, on October 13, 1927, noticed the inmates emerging from their tunnel and gave the alarm. All were captured as they surfaced.[4]

Despite his less than stellar record as a prison inmate, Good and his family and his supporters in West Texas kept besieging the Texas governor for relief. In 1932, despite the continuing protests from the association, Milt was granted extended furloughs to visit his family. Finally, Good succeeded in wrangling a pardon from Gov. Ma Ferguson, who, after an absence from the governor's chair for six years, had regained that office for a two-year term—January 1933 to January 1935. The dates of Ferguson's pardon of Good, and the recitations thereof, are worth noting here. First off, the dates of the pardon raise a question: Gov. Miriam Ferguson signed a "Full and Complete Pardon" (*not* a commutation of his sentence and not a conditional pardon, but a "full and complete" pardon) to Milt Good on November 26, 1934. However, the pardon was not to take effect until January 20, 1935, the day *after* Ma Ferguson's term as governor expired.[5] Stranger yet was why Good was considered a worthy candidate for a pardon: he had been convicted of ambushing two lawmen, had served less than twelve years of a fifty-one-year sentence, and during that twelve years he had managed a successful escape (seven months gone) during which he waylaid a prison guard, and later added an unsuccessful escape attempt to his record.

The "WHEREAS" recitations in Governor Ferguson's pardon of Good are even more interesting and included the following:

> WHEREAS, the District Judge and the District Attorneys and jurors who tried the case now recommend pardon, and the private prosecution have [*sic*] withdrawn their protests of pardon and say that they will approve whatever action is taken for the pardon of the said Milt Good, and
>
> WHEREAS, the various county officials and prominent people of West Texas *who know the facts of the case* now recommend pardon of the defendant, and
>
> WHEREAS, the defendant has a young growing family of daughters who need the support of the defendant.[6]

And so forth.

Volumes might well be written exploring that document—the truth, untruth, or partial truth of its recitations, the suspicious timing thereof, the underlying motivations, the backroom politics (or payoffs or both) involved, and what prompted the Cattle Raisers Association to back off its protests, if in fact it really did. Both Jim "Pa" Ferguson and his wife, Ma Ferguson, routinely mailed out pardons like Christmas cards during their respective terms as governor of Texas. (Humorist Will Rogers reported that Governor "Pa" once sent a pardon to a fellow who promptly wrote him back thanking him for the pardon, but adding that he hadn't been caught yet.) It was widely rumored that the Fergusons, in fact, sold pardons. Recent research tends to confirm those rumors, although the Fergusons also granted many pardons to indigent inmates.[7] At any rate, whatever motivated Governor Ma, on January 20, 1935, the gates swung open, and Milt Good strolled out of the gloom of Huntsville prison into the bright sunlight of freedom, a full and complete pardon for the brutal murders of Allison and Roberson stuffed in his hip pocket.

However, Milt *would* return—and it all had to do with the way Milt supported that growing family. On March 21, 1941, a jury in the district court of Motley County, Texas, in Matador found Milt guilty of felony theft (he stole forty-five joints of oilfield pipe from Humble Oil Company, valued at about $150) and sentenced him to serve two more years in the state prison at Huntsville.[8] At the time of this conviction, Milt was also under indictment for yet another cattle theft charge out of Levelland, Hockley County, Texas.

When they hauled Milt Good back to the pen to serve his second sentence a prison official conducted the usual inmate intake interview. The interviewer concluded his report with this rather elliptical (and thought-provoking) observation: "The subject presents a picture of a spoiled, middle-aged man who has had quite a bit in his time."[9] Truer words . . .

Good served out that sentence and was released. He lived until July 3, 1960, when, at age seventy-one, near Cotulla, Texas, his automobile slipped out of gear while Milt was attempting to open a pasture gate, and it crushed him to death against the gate post.[10]

TOM ROSS: MOST WANTED—ONCE AGAIN

Tom Ross had made good his escape, and he had had plenty of experience in eluding lawmen. It may also be safely assumed that there were not too many lawmen who were overly eager to take on the

Tom Ross, the Enigmatic Outlaw
*(Courtesy Nita Stewart Haley Memorial
Library, Midland, Texas)*

fearsome Tom Ross. Still, his future as a hunted fugitive was not bright. Times had changed: now there were improved communications (telephones and telegraph), improved transportation (automobiles, trains, roads), and more and better-trained lawmen—and courts of law that were to be taken seriously.

In some respects Ross too had changed. No longer was he the wild, devil-take-the-hindmost Hill Loftis of 1895. Now he was the fifty-three-year-old Tom Ross, an old man as outlaws go, an escaped convict burdened with the heavy albatross of two murder convictions hanging about his neck. He would always be hunted, always pursued. Still, the basic Tom Ross remained the same—a determined and dangerous man, and one who could be counted on to battle to the death rather than surrender. His name now was neither Hill Loftis nor Tom Ross. He was Charles Gannon. He headed north, finally landing a job as foreman of the Rimrock Division of the Frye Cattle Company on the Blackfoot Indian Reservation near Browning, Montana. For a time things went well for Gannon.[11] However, he was replaced as foreman of the outfit by Ralph Hayward. For the proud Ross, already frustrated and depressed with his bleak, dead-end existence as a hunted fugitive, his demotion was the last straw. He let his volatile temper get away from him once again. After a brief but heated verbal exchange with Hayward, he yelled: "I have a gun, and I have a notion to kill you; in fact I'm going to do so." With that he emptied his pistol at point-blank range into Hayward's body, killing him instantly in the presence of several cowboys.[12]

TOM ROSS: LIVE BY THE GUN; DIE BY THE GUN

The old outlaw retreated to his bunkhouse. Cooling down, he realized that the game was over. He was forever isolated from his family and his previous life. There would be no escape from pursuing lawmen now—no place left to run, no place left to hide, no life left to live. He burned his personal papers and then sat down and scribbled this cryptic suicide note:

> This fellow is a new man in the cow business. He may be all right among Dagoes but not among cow punchers. Good bye to the world.

With that, Tom Ross, who had lived by the gun, died by the gun. He took his .45 automatic pistol, placed the muzzle against his right ear, pulled the trigger, and ended his life on February 23, 1929.[13] The next issue of *The Cattleman* carried the story of the murder of Ralph Hayward and the suicide of Tom Ross, under a biblical headline that crowed: "The Way of the Transgressor Is Hard."[14]

They shipped his body back to Lovington, New Mexico, for burial, and the funeral attracted the largest crowd ever yet assembled in those parts. His family was there. A host of friends attended as well as a sizeable contingent of his old enemies, no doubt viewing the remains to assure themselves that the feared and hated Tom Ross really was, for sure, dead and gone. As ever, Tom Ross was bigger than life—even in death.

LIFE ENDS—BUT NOT THE STORY

Thus ended the life of Tom Ross. Yet it was not the end of the story. He left a barrel full of questions unanswered and many loose ends dangling. First, a question we have touched on earlier begs further exploration: was Tom Ross's reformation for real?

In 1906 after Ross was cleared of the old 1895 Alf Bailey robbery indictment in Vernon, he returned to his family and Seminole ranch. But did he really quit the outlaw trail once and for all? Or, at some point, did he backslide? Did he become involved in cattle rustling? The 1912 bank robbery? Other crimes? And, if he was rustling cattle as cattle detectives and some of his neighbors suspected, how extensive was his operation? And when did it begin?

A wave of cattle thefts swept across West Texas and eastern New Mexico in the early 1920s, and apparently that's when T&SCRA inspectors Allison and Roberson began suspecting that Ross was responsible for some of those thefts. In fact, as we have seen, they suspected that he might be the kingpin behind it all. They may have believed that, but they came up way shy of marshalling sufficient evidence to prove it. After arresting Milt Good, the inspectors appeared before grand juries in four West Texas counties (Dawson, Hockley, Lynn, and Terry) and obtained indictments against Good and his cowboys for stealing those 516 head of cattle.[15] Obviously, if they had had hard evidence that Ross was a party to the theft, they would have persuaded those grand juries to indict him also.

Allison and Roberson were successful in persuading a Lovington, New Mexico, grand jury to indict Tom Ross for the theft of four of his neighbor's cows—the four Wilhoit cows Roberson found grazing on Ross's ranch in October 1922 while Tom was hospitalized in Lubbock. Testimony subsequently given during the Ross murder trials casts even more doubt on this already wobbly circumstantial evidence case. The weakness of that case was underscored by testimony elicited from Boone Hardin, Tom's brother-in-law and ranch hand, who testified that he had frequently observed Wilhoit's cattle "out of their pasture and roaming at large." Hardin further testified that the four Wilhoit cows found in Ross's pasture by Roberson were strays, and that he had told Roberson that if he would hold off until Tom came home from the hospital "it would be shown that the Wilhoit cattle had not been stolen."[16] Of course, that was testimony elicited from Ross's brother-in-law, thus calling into question its reliability. However, Wilhoit himself testified at the murder trials, and his evidence was not at all helpful to the cattle inspector's case against Ross. Wilhoit testified that at the time Ross was alleged to have stolen four of his cows, he (Wilhoit) only owned a small herd of cows, most his herd having been repossessed by his bank. And when queried about the condition of his boundary fences at the time, Wilhoit answered that they were "like that of other ranches, up part of the time and down part of the time." He further acknowledged that none of the brands on his four cows found on Ross's ranch had been changed, blotched, or altered, and that their calves were still unbranded. He also admitted that when Roberson got his four cows from the Ross ranch, Tom Ross was still in the Lubbock "sanitarium" where he had been ill for some time.[17]

All of which made Roy Adams's testimony in both the Lubbock and the Abilene trials resonate with a ring of authenticity—that being that Roberson told him, "I might not have enough evidence to convict Tom Ross but I'm going to get him. He's a _____."[18]

In a 1945 interview, former Midland County Sheriff Bob Beverly (who was sheriff when this all came down) was asked if he thought Ross stole the Wilhoit cows. Beverly said that he really didn't know, but that he thought Ross was trying to "protect the kids" (apparently meaning his hands: Roy Adams, his brother-in law Boone Hardin, Obe Chance, and possibly others) from theft charges. He continued:

> Tom Ross was trying to get along there. . . . And that rustling come off along the [state] line and, everybody—all them kids, you know, had started out to protect themselves. . . . They had a bunch of cattle and they'd throw things here and there and Tom Ross was favorable to them, and they thought they were under the protection of Tom Ross.[19]

Beverly added that he believed that after the Vernon court cleared Ross in 1906 of the old 1895 robbery indictment, Tom was "trying to go straight."

In the end, it began to appear more and more as if the Wilhoit cow theft indictment was grounded more on enmity than evidence. According to Beverly, the genesis of that grudge between Tom Ross and Hod Roberson was the "Tobacco Jake" Ballard incident in Motley County, which had occurred several years previously. "Tom Ross," he noted, "never buried a grudge—the longer he carried it the bigger it got." Roberson, as his history shows, was himself a world-class grudge holder.[20]

Nevertheless, the lack of sufficient hard evidence to prove up a theft case to a jury "beyond a reasonable doubt" does not necessarily mean that the suspect is actually innocent—not by a long shot. Which brings us back to the fundamental issue: had Tom Ross really given up the outlaw trail completely?

There was, of course, the matter of the unsolved 1912 bank robbery in which Ross was a prime suspect. In addition, some of his neighbors were dubious about his reformation. Noted author John R. Erickson, a fifth-generation West Texan, grew up hearing his family tell tales of the outlaw Tom Ross. His forebearers (the Joe Sherman and Buck Curry families) were pioneer ranching stock who ran cattle in the Gaines County country near Ross's outfit. Erickson's family all agreed that Ross had a wonderful personality, was nice looking, a good dancer, good company, a crack shot, and "was liked and feared by everyone in Gaines County," also noting that "he left you alone if you left him alone, but woe to anyone who angered him!" Nevertheless, they were convinced that Ross never gave up his cattle-thieving ways. Once when they came up missing several big calves, they suspected Ross had stolen them. They were also convinced that during Prohibition days Ross was involved in smuggling bootleg whiskey out of Mexico. And, in 1922 when the body of a bootlegger was discovered in a shallow grave on Ross's ranch with a bullet hole in his head, Erickson's family believed that such was the handiwork of Tom Ross.[21] However, the Gaines County grand jury that investigated the matter subsequently indicted another man—E. C. Lamb, the slain bootlegger's employer—for the murder of the bootlegger.[22] (Lamb died of stomach cancer, however, before being brought to trial.)

Erickson's ancestors, being contemporaries of Ross and also being Gaines County ranchers, obviously were in a position to form cogent opinions as to Ross's guilt or innocence during the two decades prior to the 1923 Seminole incident, and such cannot be dismissed out of hand. Still, what they left behind in family stories were opinions—opinions not supported by hard evidence of any crimes committed by Ross. Other contemporaries quoted in this story, including Midland Sheriff Bob Beverly, believed that Ross was trying to put his outlaw past behind him. Frontier historian J. Evetts Haley devoted a whole chapter in his book *Men of Fiber* to Bob Beverly, characterizing Beverly as a man who "would do to ride the river with." He quotes Beverly as follows:

> [N]o man is all bad and no man is all good, and . . . [sometimes] a man is bad that never had a chance to be good, and many are good because they had no chance to be bad.[23]

Nevertheless, some facts tended to support suspicions that, at least by the early 1920s, Ross may well have slipped back into his old ways. First was the location of his ranch. It was on the boundary between Texas and New Mexico. State officers couldn't cross the state line to make arrests or conduct investigations outside their home state. Plus, even in the 1920s, the South Plains borderland was remote and sparsely populated. All things considered, Tom's ranch was an ideal location for a cattle-rustling operation. Moreover, during the early 1920s Ross made frequent cattle-trading trips to distant markets such as El Paso, Fort Worth, and even Kansas City. Such trips would have provided a convenient cover to dispose of stolen stock. Also, since he was hardly a friend of law enforcement and since he made no bones about his intention to shoot any lawman who trespassed on his ranch, it would have been only natural for lawmen to suspect that rustlers might head for Ross's safe haven and deal him whatever stolen stock they had acquired. (It should here be noted, however, that when Roberson and Allison caught Good and his cowboys driving 516 head of stolen cattle, they were almost a hundred miles from Ross's ranch and headed the other way.)

A couple of other facts tend to bolster the suspicion that Ross was after easy money again in the early 1920s. A terrible drought scorched the Texas and New Mexico rangelands during 1917 and 1918. To make matters worse, following World War I, a period of national deflation occurred in the shift from a wartime to a peace-time economy, which, in turn, seriously depressed the cattle market.[24] Drought coupled with the economic recession may explain why, for four consecutive years (1920 through 1923), Ross, for the first time, failed to pay the ad valorem taxes on his Gaines County ranch.[25]

Contrarywise, it can be argued that if indeed Ross was a rus-tling kingpin during that time, as Allison and Roberson contended, then he certainly should have reaped enough ill-gotten gains to pay his land taxes.

So we come full circle in our inquiry without arriving at a definitive answer. Before Bloody Sunday in Seminole, was Tom Ross living a double life? And, if so, how extensive was his outlawry? How far back did it go? Or, since his reputation as an outlaw was widely known, was he simply a convenient scapegoat to blame anytime a steer was stolen and lawmen didn't catch the thief red-handed? Was he a victim of "the famous outlaw syndrome," where any unsolved robbery that occurred anywhere within a thousand miles of a famous outlaw's known haunts was automatically laid at his doorstep? Or was Ross simply the victim of overzealous, grudge-holding, reputation-hungry lawmen?

THE REAL MOTIVE FOR KILLING THE CATTLE DETECTIVES

All these possible scenarios are prologue for the next questions in the Tom Ross puzzle: why did he and Milt Good kill the inspectors, and why did they do so in the manner they did? The prosecution's contention that Ross killed the inspectors *solely* to defeat the cattle theft charges makes little sense. Ross and Good, undisguised and knowing they would be recognized, killed the officers in front of five credible witnesses and did so without giving them a chance to defend themselves. Why would Ross, who was never accused of stupidity, choose to become the defendant in a bull-stout double-murder case just to defeat a rather weak cattle theft charge? Especially when he had seventeen years of relatively good behavior behind him, having earned the friendship of many in the area (some of whom would undoubtedly have shown up in a jury pool), and having never been convicted of a felony. It appears highly unlikely that all twelve members of any given Lovington or Seminole jury could have been persuaded to find Tom Ross guilty beyond a reasonable doubt of stealing those four Wilhoit cows, and we may reasonably surmise Ross was well aware of this.

Also, as pointed out by Ross's lawyer during the murder trials, if his sole motive for the killings was to defeat the cattle theft charge, then wouldn't he and Good have first set up an alibi for their whereabouts at the time of the shooting, then disguised themselves, slipped quietly into town, stealthily crept up outside the lighted hotel lobby, shot the two inspectors through the window, and then disappeared into the night? The argument was made to bolster the defense's legal self-defense position, to wit: that Ross and Good didn't really know the inspectors were inside the hotel, didn't come there to kill them, and only drew their weapons in self-defense *after* the inspectors had attempted to draw their weapons. But eyewitness testimony and forensic evidence support a different conclusion: that Ross and Good did know the inspectors were in the lobby, did come there with express intent to kill them, and wanted to be identified as the killers. Simply to kill the inspectors and then steal away undetected would have successfully eliminated the threats they posed, but that would have accomplished only half of Ross's goal. The inspectors, particularly Roberson, had insulted and dishonored him publicly. To Ross's way of thinking, in order to redeem his honor and his pride he not only had to kill the inspectors, but also do so openly and without disguise. That the inspectors wore badges mattered not a whit to him; that he would undoubtedly be indicted for murder he must have realized. Also undoubtedly, he expected to be vindicated by the unwritten code of the frontier.

In retrospect, what happened that fateful night of April 1, 1923, in Seminole almost seems inevitable. Obviously, Horace Roberson seriously underestimated Tom Ross. It was also obvious that Roberson was spoiling for a fight; was eager to "make his reputation complete" by bringing down the notorious Ross.[26] Gaines County pioneer Mary Whatley Clarke reported that Roberson had sent word to Ross that if he wanted to shoot it out "to come down the street with a pistol in his hand."[27] Sheriff Bob Beverly, who personally knew all the players, later told historian J. Evetts Haley that Roberson "started more than he could stop." Roberson, he added, "had a pretty bad reputation." Beverly said he himself wouldn't have anything to do with Roberson. According to Haley, Beverly related that shortly before the killings he heard an "old-time rancher," Joe Beasley, advise Allison that he "better not get mixed up in that mess. I know Tom Ross and I know Roberson and that feeling is pretty bad."[28] Roberson was a noted man killer with several notches on his pistol—and proud of them.

On the other hand, the best available evidence indicates that prior to the April 1, 1923, Seminole bloodbath, Tom Ross had never killed anyone. True, two cattlemen of the era, George Cook and Tom Roberts, years later in interviews with Haley, stated that Hill Loftis, while cowboying for Dan Waggoner back in the early 1890s in North Texas and the Oklahoma Territory, killed an unnamed man he caught cutting Waggoner's fence.[29] However, there was never any indictment returned against him, and no newspaper accounts of such a killing have been discovered. Plus, if it really happened, it seems more than likely that it would have surfaced during the Allison and Roberson murder trials. After exhaustive research, contemporary historian James Fenton, who wrote his master's thesis on the life of Tom Ross, could find no proof of such a killing. He concluded, "Contrary to legend, it is unlikely that he had by then [April 1, 1923] ever killed a man."[30]

There were a couple of other significant differences between Roberson and Ross. Unlike Ross, Roberson had quite a mouth on him. He was given to intemperate boasting, bragging about what he had done to his adversaries and what he intended to do to anyone else who crossed him. A really bad habit in the Old West, that. Finally, Roberson wore a badge. Tom Ross didn't. However, as some early pundit observed, sometimes the only way to distinguish a white-hat gunman from a black-hat gunman in the Old West was to turn the bodies over and see which one was wearing a star.[31]

Shortly after his 1935 pardon, Milt Good dictated a brief book to W. E. Lockhart. In *Twelve Years in a Texas Prison*, Good unfortunately declined to go into the details or background of the Seminole bloodbath ("the less that is said about this affair the better it will be for all concerned"), except to add this comment:

> Tom Ross and I were not partners in the ranching business. We were only friends and neighbors. . . . In the trials that followed the killing, Ross and I plead self-defense; and I am still convinced that the plea was justified. . . . Both the inspectors had records as killers and were regarded as dangerous men. . . . We could have run away from this trouble, but we had both been raised in the West and had not been taught to run from anything or anybody.[32]

Moreover, what happened that April night immediately after the killings makes it clear that both Ross and Good believed their gunplay was justified. Neither Ross nor Good made any great effort to escape. In fact, they called the sheriff shortly thereafter, reported their whereabouts, and volunteered to surrender. In the nineteenth-century South it was not uncommon for killers to voluntarily surrender to officers, confident that they would be cleared by a jury of their fellows. Conversely, when a man believed that his life was threatened by another he knew he must act quickly in self-defense, for he knew full well that no fear of the law would operate to restrain his would-be slayer. Statutory sanctions in murder cases had little deterrence value in that time and place.[33]

True, Martha Roberson had winged both the shooters. But still, considering the whole of the circumstances, those superficial wounds could hardly have caused Ross and Good to run up the white flag. After all, neither Ross nor Good attempted to disguise himself or otherwise deflect blame for the killings, and both—Ross particularly—had family and land roots in the area, which they obviously didn't intend to abandon. Plus, as mentioned earlier, while a neighboring rancher was transporting them to jail he reported that both Ross and Good acted normally and occasionally laughed and joked, seeming to take the whole affair rather lightly.[34] They were also surprised when, a few days later, Judge Mullican refused to grant them bail and release them on bond pending trial. It was obvious that neither appreciated the gravity of their legal predicament. In addition, they did not anticipate the active role the Texas and Southwestern Cattle Raisers Association would take in the upcoming murder trials or the considerable influence the association would exert both in and out of court. Both fully expected to be acquitted, or at most to receive lenient sentences.

Viewed from the perspective of our times, more than eighty years later, that expectation seems almost incredible. Viewed, however, from the defendants' perspective as distilled from their background and the cultural values of their early environment, that expectation seemed to make sense.

It can reasonably be postulated that Tom Ross had three motives for killing Allison and Roberson and for doing it in the way that he did. First, it was a preemptive strike made in self-defense; second, and of equal importance to Ross, by openly killing the inspectors, he publicly vindicated his honor; and third, by silencing the inspectors, he would, as a bonus, defeat the cattle-rustling charges, plus put a stop, once and for all, to any further harassment by them.

John Duff Green, a contemporary of Tom Ross, made this thought-provoking comment on the Seminole showdown with Roberson:

> I will never believe that Tom had no grounds for grievance or redress. To say the least, he had been treated shabbily and in an undermining manner that justified an overt redress. . . . His error was not in the act performed, but in the manner of its performance that deprived him of the grounds of justification.[35]

Green's last comment raises an interesting question. How could Tom Ross have settled the score with Roberson in such a way that a West Texas jury would have acquitted him? Re-examining the two Ross murder trials, one can see that, from the defensive standpoint, Ross faced two insurmountable obstacles: Dave Allison and Milt Good.

Allison was at least fairly well-respected as a lawman, and, unlike Roberson, he usually kept his mouth shut. That being the case, when Ross allowed himself to become a principal in the killing of Allison he put himself in a mighty poor position to elicit sympathy from the jury. When tried for Allison's murder his defensive posture was thus reduced to this non sequitur: Roberson was a dangerous, overbearing bully who had repeatedly threatened to kill me, so Milt and I had to kill Allison.

Next was the Milt Good obstacle. When Ross launched the fatal attack in concert with Good, he lost still more ground. Good had recently been caught red-handed with a large herd of stolen cattle, and since Good was a co-principal in the killings, the prosecution could yoke Ross with Good in this major piece of thievery—and the prosecution made the most of it. Didn't much matter that Ross stoutly denied involvement in Good's cattle rustling, and it didn't much matter that the range detectives hadn't been able to turn up sufficient evidence to link Ross to that nefarious activity. Ross still got himself tarred with the same brush in the jury's eyes. The prosecution was therefore able to get the jury to focus on its own scenario:

here we have two major cow thieves who, in order to escape justice for their crimes, slaughtered two dedicated lawmen who were
about to bring them to book. All of this diverted the jury's attention
from the focus the defense preached and upon which its only hope
for exoneration rested—that the arrogant man-killer Roberson and
his repeated threats to kill Tom Ross left a preemptive strike as Tom's
only realistic alternative.

THE TOM ROSS ENIGMA

Still the overriding question remains: Who, and what, was the real
Tom Ross? The answer depended on who you asked. In fact, you
could get about as many different answers to that query as the number of people you interviewed.

As noted above, John R. Erickson's ancestors were convinced
Ross was a certified sociopath who never really reformed at all; that
any acts of apparent kindness or generosity were merely pretenses
to disguise the corrupt inner man. On the other hand, Sheriff Bob
Beverly believed that Ross really did go straight—at least until the
Seminole killings. Years after the killings Beverly reflected, "[Tom
Ross] was a bad one, and still at the same time one of the most like-
able fellows I've ever known."[35]

John Duff Green, who cowboyed with Ross in the early years
when he was still known as Hill Loftis, described Ross as a "whole-
souled, big-hearted fellow . . . an unusually cool, nervy, daringly
brave man and a remarkable shot."[36]

Another contemporary, Byrd Cochrain, had this to say:

Hill [Loftis] had plenty of friends in those days, but he had
more enemies than any one man could handle. He had a superior capacity for loving and hating. For him there seemed to be
no middle ground. Either you were for him or against him. . . .
He [could] neither love too deeply nor hate too violently to
make him regret any excess in either direction. That was certainly Hill, alias Tom Ross.[37]

The young schoolmarm and neighbor of Tom Ross in the 1920s who years later penned an article for *The Cattleman* magazine entitled "Good Man . . . Bad Man?" was horrified by the killings of Allison and Roberson. She nevertheless recalled that Ross was "a hospitable neighbor and friend . . . a jovial, friendly type, and had scores of friends throughout that section of Texas and New Mexico."[38]

Another contemporary, Elizah Deaver Harrington, said this:

> Ross wasn't a very bad man. He was a fighter. You couldn't throw dust in his face that he wouldn't resent it. Ross never did do anything [prior to the Seminole killings] bad enough to amount to anything.[39]

Another, George Cook:

> Tom Ross was a hell of a good man. He caught Bill Sissel stealing a calf—leveled down on him with a 30/30 [but didn't shoot him, just] told him to leave the county.[40]

Another, Hunter Irwin:

> He was a gentleman. He would let worthless people hang around and they'd do things he wouldn't. He befriended the underdog.[41]

Mrs. Hunter Irwin:

> [Ross was a] distinguished looking man of professional appearance . . . fascinating but dangerous . . . brilliant . . . never [did] anything too mean or ornery. I don't know if he was justified [in killing the cattle inspectors], but I believe he did all the things folks said he did.[42]

Milt Good, Tom's cohort in the Seminole killings, later penned his take on Ross:

Tom Ross seemed to possess a dual personality. To his friends he was a kind, lovable man. His door was always open to his friends, but closed to his enemies. He was a big-hearted man who would go the limit for his friends, and gave his last penny to a widow or orphan. His enemies saw only the hard, bitter cruelty in his nature which existed for them alone.[43]

Whatever others may have said about him, in reviewing the life of Tom Ross one thing becomes clear: his character was infected by a virulent strain of violence. It is probably true that Ross never killed another man until the bloody Seminole episode in 1923 when he was fifty-two years old, and it is also true that he released Ranger Captain Rogers and Sheriff Toms unharmed after disarming them (this even though Captain Rogers had just tried to kill him). Still, in a number of nonlethal encounters he exhibited a clear tendency to solve conflicts by resorting to violence—or by threats of violence. Even when he kept a lid on his temper, a Richter-scale jarring eruption seemed always to be a-bubbling, just beneath the surface.

It is interesting to speculate on the cause or causes of his violent temperament. Was Ross's violence-canted mold the result of his early environment? Some authorities teach that a predisposition for violent behavior, as well as the conditions that are appropriate triggers for violent responses, are learned in early childhood.[45] We have only sketchy information as to the character of Ross's parents or his early home life, but we do know he was the product of the chaotic and bloody times in post–Civil War Mississippi. Violence and bloodshed were on the daily menu. The awful and unhealed wounds of that horrific war were exacerbated by the harsh Reconstruction Era lawlessness and oppression. Plus, the South was the home of the merciless "code of honor," which posited that a man's worth was measured by, and depended on, what others thought of him, and that preservation of one's honor was much more important than life itself—his or anyone else's. Better to kill or be killed than to forfeit one's honor and thus be publicly disgraced.[46] Revenge was mandatory.

Another tenet of the code held that if a man's honor were impugned, state-enacted laws and courts were inadequate to redeem his honor. "The law affords no remedy that can satisfy the feelings of a true man," was the dictum handed down to young president-to-be Andrew Jackson by his mother.[47] The story is told that when Jackson was five years old his mother scolded him severely for crying, saying "Girls were made to cry, not boys!" He asked, "What are boys made for?" Her reply: "To fight!" And later, when Andrew was twelve, a much older boy gave him a severe beating. Andrew's uncle wanted to have him charged with assault and battery, but Andrew's mother would have no part of that. "No son of mine shall ever appear as a complaining witness in a case of assault and battery! If he gets hold of a fellow too big for him, let him wait until he grows some."[48] To seek redress through the law was seen as a public confession of weakness—that you had been wronged but that you were not man enough to exact satisfaction on your own.[49] Frederick Nolan, who describes himself as a "grassroots historian," put it this way: "Frontier history is often solidly grounded on an ethic engrained as deeply today as it was then: the belief that a man has to kill his own snakes."[50] A correlative tenet of the code of honor was that if a man did take the law into his own hands and exacted satisfaction for an insult to his honor, no jury should interfere. As one observer noted:

> Almost any thing made out a case of self-defense—a threat—a quarrel—an insult—going armed, as almost all the wild fellows did—shooting from behind a corner, or out of a store door, in front or from behind—it was all self-defense![51]

And, at that time, it probably *was* self-defense given the inexorable way insult led to violence and returned violence in the Old South.[52] Violent family feuds were also common. Before Tom Ross left home he was involved in such a feud: a brother-in-law shot one of Tom's older brothers over a land boundary dispute.[53]

When, in 1885, Ross exchanged his Mississippi home for the

wilds of the northwest Texas–Indian Territory borderland, he hardly improved his environment. His new home was a raw country populated by an abundance of thieves, murderers, bootleggers, gamblers, prostitutes, and other hard characters, many of whom were embittered Southerners displaced by the war—and very few exhibited the slightest interest in being named "Citizen of the Year."

Then, as we have seen, after learning the cowboy trade, young Ross, unfortunately, hooked up with Red Buck Weightman to ride the owlhoot trail. For the next seven years after the dugout encounter, Ross was on the lam, roaming the unsettled western frontier and staying as far away from lawmen and courthouses as he could. Even when he apparently quit the outlaw life and settled down, he did so in another remote frontier where lawmen were few and far between and the rule of law was more of a future ideal than a present reality. In sum, Hill Loftis/Tom Ross spent all his formative years as well as his early manhood on the far fringes of established law and order—places where "the revolver settled more differences among men than the judge."[54]

True enough, the savagery of the Civil War and the lawlessness, violence, chaos, and hate spawned by its aftermath proved a fertile breeding and training ground for outlaws. The James brothers, the Youngers, William P. Longley, and John Wesley Hardin were all graduates of that hard school. But the era also produced stalwart champions of law and order, such as Captain McDonald and Judge George E. Miller. And didn't thousands of other Southern boys come of age during those turbulent years without heading down the crooked trail or feeling compelled to right every personal slight by resorting to violent—often deadly—retribution?[55] Was Ross's barely contained rage the product of heredity or habitat—or both? Or was heredity plus early habitat plus an ill-considered choice by a spirited but immature youth at a critical juncture in his life to blame for his outlaw ways?[56] Was Ross still within the pale of acceptable, civilized, and mature behavior until that bright and adventurous youth, perhaps on a whim, fell in with some of the older Indian Territory hard cases in their fateful Christmastime 1895 rampage of robbery and violence: a bad and irrevocable decision that, for the rest of his life, would haunt, bedevil, and ultimately doom him?

After the Seminole incident, the life of Tom Ross was, for all meaningful purposes, over. He was destined to spend the rest of his life in a lonely prison cell or on the run as a hunted fugitive. In either case he had no hope of returning to his ranch and his home—to Trixie and Bessie. No hope of enjoying his final years among family and friends. He could hide, and he could run . . . but toward what?

In the end, while the brutal bloodbath that snuffed out the lives of Roberson and Allison can never be excused, in retrospect the killings seem so . . . unnecessary, so avoidable. Avoidable, that is, until Roberson's boasts and threats reached the ears of Tom Ross. When Ross heard that Roberson bragged that he intended to "make his reputation complete" by bringing him down "one way or another," and that he would welcome a shootout with Ross, and that it didn't matter what kind of pistol Ross carried because he and Allison were "going to kill him anyway"—then it was no longer avoidable. It was only a matter of when and where. And who went down.

Whatever the merits of the case against Tom Ross for allegedly stealing the four Wilhoit cows, the endeavor by lawmen to bring him before the bar of justice to stand trial could have been, and should have been, handled very differently. In that respect the following undisputed facts should here be recalled: In 1904, almost two decades earlier, Tom Ross had spared the life of Texas Ranger John Rogers in the sand dunes showdown, even when he had Rogers disarmed and in his cross-hairs. This, mind, shortly after Rogers had taken one or more pot shots at the retreating Ross. Two years later, in 1906, Ross quietly walked into Martin County Sheriff Charley Toms's office in Stanton and voluntarily surrendered in order to go back to Vernon and face that old 1896 Alf Bailey armed robbery indictment—a much more serious charge than stealing four of a neighbor's cows that were discovered on his ranch while he was in the hospital. Finally, it was highly unlikely that Ross would attempt to flee and thus avoid facing this indictment. After all, he now had a wife, a child, and a ranch in the Seminole community where he had established residence for almost two decades.

A different kind of lawman—Sheriff Charley Toms of Stanton or Sheriff Bob Beverly of Midland, for example—could most likely have taken Ross to the courthouse without bloodshed. Beverly, it will be recalled, was the lawman who had previously separated Dave Allison and Milt Good on the steps of the Midland courthouse when they were about to "slap leather." Beverly got between the armed men saying, "Neither one of you men will kill me, and I won't let you kill each other."

Beverly's approach to handling hard cases was about 180 degrees opposite from Roberson's. Beverly didn't rely on boasts, threats, gunsmoke, and gore to accomplish his lawman duties, nor did he brag about his exploits or count notches on his pistol handle to nourish an overweening ego. Beverly was a man of quiet courage, and he was wise in the psychology of hardened criminals. More often than not Beverly simply sent word to the subject wherever he happened to be that he was wanted and to come on in and give himself up. Usually, within the course of a few days, the wanted man showed up at his office[57]—just as Tom Ross had done when he surrendered to Sheriff Charley Toms back in 1906.

Noted western historian J. Evetts Haley, in his book *Men of Fiber*, had this to say of Beverly:

> Bob Beverly was . . . a genial, unruffled veteran of adventure [who] summed up the finer qualities of those cowboy peace officers who brought law and order to the cow country. . . . He was a man of quiet courage and impeccable character. Rough life had firmed his nature without hardening his soul. If he did not harbor an element of sympathy for the culprits he gathered in the name of the law, he at least looked upon them with compassion and deep understanding.[58]

Most outlaws, even the worst, thus came to respect Beverly for his underlying sense of fair play as well as for his courage and determination, and therefore Beverly rarely had to resort to gunplay or violence to do his duty.

The killings of Allison and Roberson may be explained, and, from Ross's perspective, may even be understood, if never condoned. But the pointless killing of the Montana ranch foreman, Ralph Hayward, can only be attributed to a frustrated, desperate, and hopeless man who finally had lost whatever remained of his humanity. But how do we explain the good years—his love of family, his generosity and loyalty to friends, his determination to make a life on a hard frontier, and the earned loyalty of so many friends? And how do we explain why he spared the life of Ranger Captain Rogers, a lawman who had just tried to kill him?

And so the enigma of Tom Ross survived the man. Good man or bad man? Dr. Jekyll or Mr. Hyde? A remorseless killer, or a good man with a hair-triggered temper who sometimes let it get out of control—with disastrous results to himself and others? A "whole-souled" fellow—a modern Robin Hood who was generous and loyal to his friends and a champion of the underdog—or a hard case beyond redemption who was clever enough to disguise his true nature for years: a wolf slyly lurking beneath the fleece of a sheep? An unrepentant outlaw, or a kid brought up hard in a lawless frontier and led astray by older outlaws and thereafter forever hounded by reputation-seeking lawmen who never let him redeem himself and live a straight life?

Or, perhaps, some or all of the above? Perhaps, all said and done, the task of analyzing Tom Ross—or any other human being for that matter—is not quite as simple as slotting him neatly into some pre-cut pigeonhole.

FROM GUNS TO GAVELS

Judge Blackstone Ascends

On the fringes of the Western frontier during the last half of the nineteenth century and the first two decades of the twentieth century, the rule of law strained to gain purchase in a harsh environment. In exasperation, one early-day Dallas judge lectured his grand jury as follows: "Gentlemen of the Grand Jury, they tell us that more men are killed in Texas than any other country in the world, and I guess that's a fact, but Gentlemen of the Grand Jury, I tell you that more men need killing in Texas than in any other country in the world."[1]

Even after courts of law were established, it took several decades for Judge Blackstone to completely dethrone Judge Winchester and Judge Lynch, in part, at least, because most westerners still clung to the unwritten laws of the frontier culture, which in turn (and not to put too fine a point on it) borrowed much from the honor code of the Old South. Although the folk laws of the frontier and the code of the South may have been separate and individual things, historians such as C. L. Sonnichsen have admitted that the two are "too similar for easy distinction." Sonnichsen comments:

> In Texas the folk law of the frontier was reinforced by the unwritten laws of the South and produced a habit of self-redress more deeply ingrained, perhaps, than anywhere else in the country. The grievances and abuses of the bad days after

the Civil War gave extraordinary scope for the application of the old ways of dealing justice.[2]

Sonnichsen went on to relate a popular anecdote of the times illustrating the "Texan's code." The tale goes that you can tell where a man is from by his response to being called a liar: if a Texan, he either shoots you or knocks you down; if from somewhere up around Ohio, he waves his fists and shouts, "You're another!"; if from New England, he spits on a grasshopper and calmly remarks, "Well, you can't prove it."[3] In any event, it is generally conceded that much of the violence that erupted in western cattle towns and on the open range (especially in Texas) was transplanted southern violence.[4] In this context then, when we speak of the code of honor of the South, the word *South* refers more to a state of mind than to a geographical place.

Prof. George Stumberg, an esteemed authority on Texas criminal law, commented that the Texas law pertaining to justifiable homicide as applied by the courts and juries of that day amounted to "an implicit system of legalized violent self-redress," provided the defendant could convince the jury "that the killing was in response to a threat against person or property."[5] Jim East, the sheriff in Old Tascosa during the rough and rowdy 1880s, got directly to the point:

Sentiment in the [Texas] Panhandle was strong against sending a man to the penitentiary who had killed a man in combat. . . . It was hard to convict for manslaughter as they would generally plead self-defense.[6]

Furthermore, when threats were made and gunplay became imminent, then—Hollywood myth to the contrary notwithstanding—in the real West, neither gunman expected to be granted an even break on the draw. Most frontiersmen were not cowards, but neither were they fools. Most were human beings who did not intend to get themselves shot. Pat Garrett, for instance, was criticized for killing Billy the Kid without giving him a chance at self-defense. Garrett gave this candid explanation:

I would have utilized any safe place of concealment which might have presented itself—under the bed, or under any article which I might have found. . . . Scared? . . . Well, I should say so. I started out that expedition . . . contemplating the probability of being . . . killed; but not if any precaution on my part would prevent such a catastrophe. . . . I believed that he would make good his threat to "die fighting with a revolver at each ear." . . . I, at no time, contemplated taking any chances which I could avoid by caution or cunning. The only circumstances, under which we could have met on equal terms, would have been accidental, and to which I would have been an unwilling party. Had we met unexpectedly, face to face, I have no idea that either one of us would have run away. And there is where the "square fight" would, doubtless, have come off.[7]

The untamed and dangerous western frontier taught its sons that survival was the ultimate goal, and that lesson number one in the art of survival was the avoidance of unnecessary risks.[8] Tom Ross understood that logic. And he could never get beyond his upbringing, which taught that the law had no poultice sufficient to heal the wound to a man's pride when inflicted by a public insult.

What Ross didn't realize was that times had changed—and changed a lot. The rip-roaring days of the Old West still existed, but now only on that newfangled contraption—the moving picture show. This was not the "Wild West" of the nineteenth century or even of the early 1900s. This was post-World War I, 1923. Indeed World War I had been the great turning point in modern American history. During the war, farm boys from the remotest parts of the country were thrown together with lads from the cities, and together not only did they go through the mechanized slaughter of World War I, but they also saw the bright lights of Paris. (Or, in the words of a popular song of the era, "How ya gonna keep 'em down on the farm, after they've seen Paree?") And none of them, or the nation itself for that matter, ever would be the same again. Meanwhile, the country was being transformed from a horse culture to a modern machine-powered civilization. In 1910 there were two million horse-drawn vehicles in the United States while only 468,500 automobiles were registered. By 1924 the number of cars had jumped to 17.5 million.[9] The seismic shock of the Great War coupled with vastly improved systems of transportation and means of communication—telephones, radios, motion pictures, and national magazines—resulted in a sea change in American values, even in rural areas. One notable change was in the way the general populace now viewed violence. Violence was no longer dismissed as being an inevitable part of everyday life. And no longer was stealing a horse considered a more serious crime than killing a human being. The public no longer believed that threats to kill, alone, automatically excused killings. Popular acceptance of vigilantism and self-help redress of wrongs had, in large part at least, given way to a belief in court-administered justice under statutory laws—even in this Texas–New Mexico borderland country, one of the last outposts of the Old West. But fancy notions about "changing social values" would have been completely alien to Ross's way of thinking even if anybody had bothered to explain such to him. He was still emotionally and mentally rooted in his late-nineteenth-century past—becoming, without ever realizing it, an anachronism from a much more violent and unforgiving time—a time when society not only permitted a man to kill his own snakes, but expected him to do so.

Still, the Lubbock and Abilene juries, in four cases, although finding the defendants guilty of first-degree murder in each, refused to assess the death penalty, instead opting to assess what appear to be relatively light sentences considering the premeditated and ruthless slaughter of two lawmen. Why? The times, the facts in evidence, and the background of the parties suggest three possible explanations for this mitigation, each standing alone or taken in conjunction with the other two: first, the old unwritten laws of the frontier still had some potency; second, some sympathy for, and understanding of, Tom Ross and his perceived dilemma; and third, resentment for the overbearing tactics of the two lawmen, particularly Roberson.

A comparison of the 1913 Burk Burnett trial for the killing of Farley Sayers and the 1923 Tom Ross trial for the killing of Hod Roberson is both interesting and instructive. Both were West Texas murder trials. In both cases the victim had made serious, intemperate, and public threats to kill the defendant, and in both cases those threats were a motive—and probably the primary motive—for the killing. Both defendants admitted they shot the victim with the intention of killing him: yet both, in at least a nod in the direction of the statutory law of self-defense, insisted that just prior to killing they observed the victim make some physical "demonstration" that each interpreted as an effort to draw a weapon. In both cases that testimony was totally without corroboration from any of the eyewitnesses present at the scene. None of the eyewitnesses observed either of the victims make any movement toward a weapon before being killed. Moreover, the physical forensic evidence in each case strongly indicated that the victim never knew what hit him. (In the Burk Burnett case it was later confirmed by his hired gun, Tom Pickett, that he and Burnett had intentionally ambushed and killed Sayers.)

It thus appears that the 1913 West Texas jury in the Burnett trial bought into the old unwritten "legalized violent self-redressment" code when it found him not guilty, while the 1923 West Texas jury in the Ross trial rejected that frontier code and held Ross to the statutory self-defense standard—and found him wanting; found him guilty.

The interesting question thus arises: to what degree, if any, was the tectonic shift in cultural values that occurred in America between the "horse culture" days of 1913 and the post-World War I modern America days responsible for the different verdicts in those two murder trials? To what extent by 1923 had the emerging supremacy of justice under duly enacted laws supplanted the waning potency of the old unwritten codes?

Had the Tom Ross trial for the killing of Hod Roberson occurred in 1913, would the outcome have been the same? Probably so, considering the additional "baggage" Ross carried into that murder trial—that being the basically unprovoked additional slaying of Dave Allison plus the millstone he created for himself by taking on Milt Good as a partner in the killings. But, suppose Dave Allison had not been killed and suppose Milt Good had been nowhere in the vicinity when Ross killed Roberson. Then would the outcome have been different had the trial occurred in 1913—an earlier time when the jurors' mind-set was still attuned to the unwritten code? Roberson's intemperate threats—coupled with his violent past, which clearly indicated that he was very likely to carry those threats to bloodshed—would most certainly have elicited much sympathy for Ross. Still, when it came time for the jury to balance the emotional accounts . . . well, there yet remained Roberson's black-shrouded, weeping widow. And what silver-tongued defense magician could ever make that haunting image disappear? On the other hand, a jury (going against three prior juries) acquitted Hod Roberson for the senseless 1915 slaying of an upstanding rancher, Foote Boykin, when, presumably, Boykin's widow witnessed that judicial debacle in plain view of the jury. If that revised Tom Ross scenario had unfolded in a 1913 West Texas courtroom, it might have been a pretty close horse race.

Similarly, what if the Burnett trial had occurred in 1923 instead of 1913? Considering, on the one hand, the wealth and influence of Burnett and on the other hand the vicious, out-of-control outlaw that Sayers had become—he who not only had stolen cattle from Burnett and who had made repeated threats to kill him, but who also had just slain his own unarmed brother—it is also doubtful that even a 1923 jury would have put such a fine point on the "technical" requirements of the statutory self-defense law. Juries, now as then, and ever hereafter, are not devoid of emotions, and emotional appeal often trumps the law, logic, and the facts. However, by 1923, some jurors might have felt real qualms about putting their stamp of approval on the summary self-help execution of an enemy, however despicable, if they believed that Burnett had hired a hit man and then, guns drawn, together they stalked the unsuspecting victim and shot him in the back.

In the end, the question remains: would the sweeping changes that had occurred in the nation's values and attitudes between the horse-and-buggy times of 1913 and the post-WWI modern America of 1923 have turned the tide in the outcome of the two murder trials if the trial dates had been reversed? Such speculation is fascinating and also is the fodder for endless debates among legal and social historians. Still, those two trials did prove that a radical shift in values had, in fact, taken place during that time frame: the news coverage and contemporary commentaries on those two trials provide irrefutable proof.

In the 1913 Burk Burnett trial, Burk took the stand and, in order to raise a *legal* self-defense issue, testified that just before he shot Farley Sayers, Sayers recognized him and made some effort to go for his pistol. The contemporary observers rejected this version. The editor of *The Baylor County Banner* who covered the Burnett trial in Seymour, Texas, wrote: "To the average mind it seems evident that Sayers was not trying to draw his gun, and it is probable that he never knew what killed him."[10] The editor of the *Paducah Post* (in Paducah, Texas, where Sayers was killed) wrote: "[Farley Sayers] was murdered *unsuspectingly* as he washed his face in preparation for the noon day meal at a hotel here in Paducah."[11]

Charles Coombes, a leading frontier trial lawyer of that day who had represented Sayers in several of his previous brushes with the law, later wrote in his memoirs: "Just as Farley was raising his hands full of water to his face, Burnett . . . placed his pistol against the side of his victim, and without warning, fired."[12]

Still, none of those commentators condemned Burnett for killing Sayers, or for doing so in the manner they described. On the contrary, they approved of Burnett's preemptive-strike style of self-help justice and applauded the jury's verdict of acquittal.

The *Banner* editor:

There seems to have been pretty general satisfaction with the verdict. . . . The world is not much worse off by [Farley Sayers] having left it.[13]

Charles Coombes:

> In my opinion, Burk Burnett was not even in jeopardy [of
> being convicted by a jury]. I do not blame him for killing Say-
> ers, because had he not done so, sooner or later Sayers would
> have killed him.[14]

One noted Southwest historian observed that even in the
second decade of the twentieth century, West Texas continued to
embrace the values and attitudes of the frontier, concluding that
"West Texans continued to resort to violence as readily as frontiersmen of the 1800s, and juries retained the same pragmatic notions of
self-defense as those of the nineteenth century."[15]

It is clear, however, that after World War I a marked change in
the climate of public opinion had occurred—even in West Texas. In
1923, no news account approved of Tom Ross's preemptive-strike
style of self-help justice in neutralizing Roberson, a deadly adversary
who had been threatening to kill him, and none lamented the conviction of Ross for Roberson's murder.

The October 1923 issue of *The Cattleman* magazine commented on the convictions of Ross and Good:

> The lawless days of the West have passed, and it is fitting that
> the measured tread of the fellow officers of Roberson and
> Allison should continuously ring in the ears of those who set
> themselves above the laws of God and man in interpreting the
> paths of right.[16]

And, the *St. Louis Post-Dispatch* reporter who covered the Tom
Ross trials quoted one trial spectator, an old-timer, who perhaps
betrayed just a smidgeon of nostalgia when he opined: "Gun play's
just about played out [in the West]."[17]

That such a radical change in societal values had occurred during that time frame is further attested by the decline in the frequency
of lynchings in the United States. As documented in the conclu-

sion of Chapter Two, the number of lynchings in America dwindled from a total of 230 in 1893 to 9 in 1929. There was a corresponding decline in Texas, and 1925 was the first lynch-free year. During all this time, murder statutes were on the law books of every state, and specific antilynch laws had been enacted by Texas and other states. Yet, as we have seen, those statutes seemed to have had little effect in deterring lynchings. In the end, it was not statutory law but the shift in society's values that finally stopped the lynchings and that finally prevented killers from getting away with murder by pleading the unwritten law.

THE TRANSITIONAL MAN

"Larger than life," dominant, charismatic, keen of mind and wit, daring, fearless, enigmatic, secretive, nervy, generous, cruel, calculating, brutal—all those adjectives and others fail to capture fully the complex character of westerner Tom Ross. No doubt Shakespeare could have penned a dramatic masterpiece using Ross as the model for its central character, whether cast as hero, villain, or somewhere in between. The story of the life and times and the crimes of Tom Ross, fascinating as it is, really does add up to more than the sum of its parts.

To begin with, however one chooses to define him, Ross was a transitional man. His career, in a very real sense, marked the opening and the closing of a door on perhaps the most colorful era of the American Southwest, from the bitter and lawless post-Civil War Reconstruction times until modern America came of age after World War I. The story of his life and times provides a unique laboratory in which students of history can gain revealing insights into the way we were back then and how we got to be the way we are today. To understand what we are, we need to understand what we were. Ross's encounters with outlaws, lawmen, and criminal courts amount to nothing less than a textbook, anecdotal though it may be, about the origin, the development, and the maturation of our criminal justice system during this critical juncture. (There is also an important footnote embedded in that textbook—one that teaches, and documents as well, the gross injustices that happen when over-reaching or overzealous lawmen fail to hew faithfully to their duty of objective professionalism and backslide into personal vendettas or agendas focused primarily on political advancement.)

From his time in the 1880s in northwest Texas and the Oklahoma Territory to his turn-of-the-century days in West Texas and the New Mexico Territory until his 1929 death in Montana, Tom Ross's journey takes us from a land beyond the law to a time and place where, after mighty struggles and sacrifices, the business of dispensing justice and the maintenance of law and order came to be transacted in courthouses. A transition from no law to Winchester law to Lynch law to court-administered law was a bloody trail that progressed, haltingly and painfully, from guns to gavels.

Ross began his adult life as a high-spirited young cowboy on the Texas and Oklahoma cattle prairies and ended his life as an outlaw killer in the frozen Montana wilderness. As a boy he had ridden west to escape the devastation of his post–Civil War Mississippi homeland. As a young man he rode west again to outrun Texas lawmen after his armed robbery spree in North Texas and the Oklahoma Territory. In his fifties, he rode west yet again to elude Texas lawmen after his prison break. But after killing Ralph Hayward in 1929, there was no place left to run. No longer could a man simply mount up and ride west a hundred miles, change his name, and thus escape his past—start all over again with a fresh slate. The Old West that Tom Ross knew had vanished into history.

AFTERTHOUGHTS

The Rule of Law: An
Ongoing Battle

THE BURK BURNETT AND TOM ROSS MURDER TRIALS PROVOKE A COUPLE of final philosophical thoughts on our American criminal justice system. First, shouldn't juries consider the effect their verdicts have on the public? Do we, as jurors, really want to tell John Q. Public that if he believes his antagonist is insufferably worthless, odious, and aggravating, then it is quite all right to hire a hit man and ambush the scoundrel? And what about duly enacted criminal statutes? If you don't agree with a criminal law (such as the law on self-defense) is it OK simply to ignore it: pick and choose which criminal statute you wish to obey? Some recent advocates of "jury nullification" urge jurors to do just that. A slippery slope that—leading right back to the evils of basing verdicts on one's own preferred version of unwritten codes. Either the laws apply to everybody—or to nobody.

And finally, lest we become too smug about our society's triumph of law and order and our collective superiority to the violent ways of the Old West, it will serve us all well to cast an eye on today's newspaper headline—more often than not a stark and sobering reminder that the struggle to achieve justice under established law is an ongoing battle. As long as people are people, there will never be a complete or final victory—a reminder that the veneer of civilization cloaking man's primitive and savage nature is mighty thin indeed. A reminder that, even here in the civilized, law-abiding United States, it takes only a racial incident or a hurricane or some other natural disaster of sufficient magnitude to disrupt law enforcement to trigger widespread thievery, looting, killing, and violence—all of which will rage on until lawmen can regain control. There exists that virulent strain of violence in humankind, and history teaches that it's not much limited by time or place. Furthermore, with men, as with moons, no matter how bright they may shine, there is always that dark side. For humanity, the rule of law, justly administered, is more than just some lofty ideal. It's essential for human dignity and a life worth living.

Moreover, as times change and society becomes ever more complex, the rule of law constantly faces challenges on new fronts. The Internet, for instance, presents legal challenges not dreamed of a few years ago. New laws—both criminal and civil—are required to deal with myriad Internet and public communication issues. How do we keep in balance the need to police antisocial and predatory activities and yet preserve individual rights of free speech?

Meanwhile, another criminal justice debate continues, and will forever continue: what, on the one hand, is the appropriate amount of power and discretion to be granted to police and prosecutors in enforcing our criminal statutes, and, on the other hand, what are the appropriate limitations to be placed on the exercise of that power and discretion? Too much of the former and we drift toward an arbitrary and abusive police state. Too much of the latter and too many criminals will walk the streets and endanger us all. It's a balancing act that requires constant tinkering and refining.

Recent terrorist attacks and threats of future attacks on our nation have created yet another debate over "balance" and yet another challenge to the rule of law in a complex society. A paradoxical dilemma is presented: in order to preserve our civil liberties we must curb certain of our civil liberties. But to what extent? And what safeguards are appropriate?[1] As one commentator put it, "The position of the law in a republican democracy has always been problematical; the law has always seemed too weak in the eyes of some, while to others it has seemed in danger of becoming too strong, of subverting American liberties."[2] In the end it comes down once again to balancing competing goals: maintaining and safeguarding individual rights while at the same time preserving national security and taking criminal predators off the street.

The task of establishing and maintaining the rule of law has never been—nor will it ever be—an easy or a simple one.

CHRONOLOGY

1854 Henry H. Campbell, age fourteen, moves to Texas from his native North Carolina. Later, he serves as a Confederate soldier during the Civil War and is wounded three times. After the war he settles in West Texas where he becomes one of the founders of the huge Matador Ranch with headquarters in what would later become Motley County, Texas. After Scottish investors buy the ranch, he is named ranch superintendent. Disagreements with the Scots, however, lead to his resignation in 1891, and the ill will between them is aggravated when Campbell, against the wishes of the Scots, takes the lead in organizing Motley County.

1859 Burk Burnett, age ten, moves with his family to Denton County, Texas, from Missouri after Jayhawkers burned down their home. In 1863, Burk's father, Jerry Burnett, joins the Confederate forces leaving young Burk to care for the family and farm. In 1867, at age eighteen, he trail-bosses a herd of Texas cattle to Kansas markets.

1866 Bill Jess McDonald, age sixteen, moves with his mother and younger sister from their war-ravaged Mississippi home to Wood County in East Texas. McDonald's father, a Confederate soldier, was killed during the Civil War.

1879 On June 7, 1879, Burk Burnett shoots and kills Jack King, a cattle rustler, on Burnett's Clay County, Texas, ranch. He is indicted for murder but pleads self-defense and is acquitted.

1884   George E. Miller, age twenty-three, armed with a brand-new law license, migrates from his Mississippi home to Graham in Young County, Texas. His father, a Confederate soldier, was killed in the Civil War, and George was orphaned at age nine when his mother died in 1870. Miller is elected district judge in Wichita Falls in 1890, a position he holds in 1896 when Foster Crawford and Kid Lewis rob a bank in Wichita Falls and kill a cashier in the process.

On May 25, 1884, near Mobeetie in the Texas Panhandle, John Pearce Matthews kills a Laurel Leaf Ranch cowboy, James Mankins, by stabbing him in the chest with his pocket knife. Matthews claims it was an accident—the fatal wound being inflicted during a bit of horseplay following a friendly game of "mumble peg." Authorities believe him, and he is not indicted.

1885   Hill Loftis, a.k.a. Tom Ross, age thirteen, runs away from his Mississippi home and heads for Texas where he is hired as a cowboy for the vast Waggoner Ranch in the Red River country along the Texas–Oklahoma border.

1891   On February 5, 1891, Motley County, Texas, is officially organized amidst bitter antagonism between the pro-Matador Ranch faction and the pro-settler faction lead by Henry H. Campbell, former superintendent of the Matador Ranch.

Henry H. Campbell is named the first county judge of Motley County. Joe Beckham, age twenty-one, a former Matador Ranch cowboy, is named as the first sheriff-tax collector of the county, and George Cook is named as one of the first four members of the county's commissioners court.

Texas Gov. James Stephen Hogg makes two appointments that are to play a large role in bringing law and order to northwest Texas. He appoints Bill Jess McDonald as captain of Company B, Frontier Battalion of the Texas Rangers, and W. R. "Billy" McGill as judge of the sprawling 50th Judicial District, which includes the newly formed Motley County.

In December 1891, Motley County Judge Henry H. Campbell files an injunction suit against the Matador Ranch and its officials alleging that the ranch cowboys have systematically run cattle off the settlers' properties in Motley County and chased their stock beyond the distant Matador pasture fences, resulting in a loss of more than 1,600 head of cattle. **District Judge Billy McGill** grants the injunction.

1892   On February 17, 1892, former Matador Ranch cowboy **Jeff Davis Boone** shows up at the Motley County courthouse and confronts **Sheriff Joe Beckham**. In the argument that follows, both pull pistols and wound each other. Beckham's wound is slight. Boone, however, dies from his wound on June 23, 1892. Beckham is indicted and tried for Boone's murder in Floydada, Floyd County, Texas, where he is acquitted.

On November 8, 1892, **John Pearce Matthews**, former Laurel Leaf Ranch cowboy, is elected as the second sheriff of Childress County, Texas.

1893   On January 15, 1893, Motley County **Sheriff Joe Beckham** is arrested in Childress by Childress County Sheriff John Pearce Matthews on a misdemeanor gambling charge.

On June 4, 1893, Motley County Commissioner **George Cook** ambushes and attempts to kill **Sheriff Joe Beckham** as Beckham detrains at the Childress depot. Beckham returns fire. Neither is wounded. Both are indicted in Childress for aggravated assault.

On June 14, 1893, the Motley County Commissioners Court, without lawful authority, declares the office of Sheriff vacant, and then proceeds to appoint **J. L. Moore** the new Motley County sheriff. "Sheriff" Moore and his deputies then arrest **Sheriff Joe Beckham** and his deputies, but not for long. Beckham and his men soon escape custody and proceed to arrest "Sheriff" Moore and his deputies. An all-out civil war was about to erupt in Motley County. **County Judge Campbell** appeals to the governor for help. The governor calls Captain McDonald and the Texas Rangers, who promptly arrive, restore order, and, in effect, put Motley County under marshal law until **District Judge Billy McGill** arrives on August 15, 1893. Judge McGill takes command, appoints his own sheriff (**Billy Moses**), chases the other sheriffs and their deputies out of the courtroom, and declares that "the court is now in session."

On August 18, 1893, **Sheriff Joe Beckham** is indicted for embezzling Motley County tax funds. About a week later, the new Motley County courthouse catches fire and burns down. Beckham is suspected of torching it.

On December 9, 1893, Texas Ranger **Capt. Bill McDonald** and Childress County **Sheriff John Pearce Matthews** settle their grudges in a gunbattle in downtown Quanah, Texas. Both are seriously wounded, but McDonald survives. Matthews dies from his wounds on December 30, 1893. McDonald is indicted for murder.

1894   On May 15, 1894, **Capt. Bill McDonald** is tried by a Quanah, Texas, jury for the murder of Sheriff Matthews and is acquitted.

1895   On May 27, 1895, former Motley County sheriff **Joe Beckham** ambushes and kills the present Motley County sheriff, **George Cook**, at the train station in Seymour, Texas. Cook, who had previously ambushed Beckham at the Childress train station (but missed his shot), had come by train to Seymour to testify against Beckham at his trial there (on a change of venue) for embezzling Motley County tax funds. After killing Cook, Beckham flees to the Indian Territory.

On December 26, 1895, **Joe Beckham** and his new Indian Territory outlaw cohorts, **George "Red Buck" Weightman, Elmer "Kid" Lewis,** and **Hill Loftis** (who would later assume the alias "**Tom Ross**"), hold up Alf Bailey's store near Vernon, Texas.

On December 27, 1895, a posse lead by Texas Ranger **Sgt. W. J .L. Sullivan**, trails the four outlaws to their lair—a dugout on Suttle Creek in the Oklahoma Territory. In the ensuing shootout, **Joe Beckham** is killed. The other three outlaws escape in a blinding blizzard.

1896   On February 12, 1896, a Wilbarger County grand jury at Vernon, Texas, indicts **Loftis, Weightman,** and **Lewis** for the armed robbery of Alf Bailey's store on December 26, 1895.

On February 21, 1896, in a world-title heavyweight boxing match, **Bob Fitzsimmons** KOs **Peter Maher** in a makeshift boxing ring on a sandbar in the middle of the Rio Grande just south of Langtry, Texas, home of the infamous **Judge Roy Bean**. A host of Texas Rangers, including **Capt. Bill McDonald**, who have been dispatched by the

Texas governor to prevent the fight, watch helplessly on the north bank of the Rio Grande as Fitzsimmons takes the title. Boxing promoter **Dan Stuart** and his ally, the wily Judge Roy Bean, have outmaneuvered the Texas governor, the rangers, and the Mexican army. McDonald and his men depart for the Texas Panhandle after the fight—just in time to become involved in the famous 1896 Wichita Falls bank robbery episode.

On February 25, 1896, Indian Territory outlaw **Elmer "Kid" Lewis** and his outlaw companion, **Foster Crawford**, hold up the Citizens National Bank in Wichita Falls, Texas, and, during the holdup, kill cashier **Frank Dorsey**. Both outlaws are captured later the same day by the combined efforts of a citizens' ad hoc posse and **Capt. Bill McDonald** and five of his rangers. The two outlaws are jailed in Wichita Falls. Later that night, McDonald and his rangers disperse a lynch mob.

On February 26, 1896, a Wichita Falls mob storms the jail, seizes the prisoners, **Crawford** and **Lewis**, and proceeds to lynch them. **Burk Burnett** is present at the lynching and has an exchange with Foster Crawford, his ex-employee, before the outlaws are hanged. Over **Judge Miller's** protest, **Captain McDonald** and his men had left town earlier that day and were not present when the mob stormed the jail. Judge Miller's subsequent efforts to have the mob leaders prosecuted prove futile.

On May 4, 1896, Indian Territory outlaw **Red Buck Weightman** is involved in yet another dugout battle in Custer County, Oklahoma Territory. This time he does not escape—killed by Oklahoma lawmen.

1904 On June 17, 1904, lawmen are finally successful in locating **Hill Loftis**, now known as **Tom Ross**. He is working in a cattle roundup along the Texas–New Mexico border between Seminole, Texas, and Lovington, New Mexico. Texas Ranger **Capt. John Rogers** and Martin County **Sheriff Charley Toms** confront Tom Ross in what was to become known as the "duel in the sand dunes." Captain Rogers takes a shot or two at the retreating Ross, but misses. Shortly thereafter, Ross reappears, takes the lawmen by surprise, and disarms them. Instead of shooting them, however, he again disappears into the sand dunes of New Mexico.

1906 On May 28, 1906, **Tom Ross** calmly strolls into the office of Martin County **Sheriff Charley Toms** in Stanton, Texas, and surrenders to face that old February 1896 aggravated robbery indictment still pending against him in Vernon, Texas, for the Alf Bailey store holdup. He makes bond but reappears in Vernon in September 1906 ready for trial. He is cleared of that charge and returns to his ranch west of Seminole where his wife and child greet him. Ross resumes his life, free of criminal charges at last, and prospers as a rancher.

1907 On August 17, 1907, a mighty ambitious young rancher named **Farley Sayers**, owner of a small ranch adjoining the huge 6666 Ranch owned by **Burk Burnett** in King County in northwest Texas, is accused of stealing several of Burnett's unbranded calves, and he is indicted.

On September 5, 1907, after **Farley Sayers** has been accused of stealing Burnett's cattle but before an indictment is returned, one of Burk Burnett's 6666 cowboys, **Sam Graves**, shoots an unarmed Farley Sayers in the back. Sayers survives. Graves is indicted for assault with intent to murder.

1908 On October 17, 1908, **Farley Sayers** is tried for stealing **Burk Burnett's** cattle, but is acquitted.

1910 **Sam Graves** is tried for assaulting **Farley Sayers**. The jury finds him guilty and assesses a two-year prison term. The conviction is overturned on appeal. On retrial in Anson, Jones County, a jury again finds Graves guilty, but this time lets him off with only a $2,000 fine—which is promptly paid by Burk Burnett.

1911 On November 25, 1911, in a dispute over their father's estate, **Farley Sayers** shoots and kills his unarmed brother, **Lellar Sayers**, in Dumont, Texas. He is indicted for the murder but makes bond and is released pending trial.

1912 On February 15, 1912, two masked men hold up the First National Bank in Seminole, Texas. The bank robbers are never apprehended. Some suspect that Tom Ross was one of the robbers.

On May 23, 1912, in the washroom of the Goodwin Hotel in Paducah, Texas, **Burk Burnett** and his associate, **Tom Pickett**, encounter and kill **Farley Sayers**. Both Burnett and Pickett are indicted for murder.

1913 On July 25, 1913, a jury in the Baylor County District Court in Seymour, Texas, finds **Burk Burnett** not guilty of murdering **Farley Sayers**. The murder indictment against Tom Pickett is then dismissed on the prosecution's motion.

On December 10, 1913, lawman **Dave Allison**, then chief of police in Roswell, New Mexico (but formerly sheriff of Midland County, Texas, and later a Texas and Southwestern Cattle Raisers Association inspector), is put on trial in the Chavez County District Court for attempting to bribe the local district attorney. Allison testifies that it is all a part of an attempted sting operation to test the honesty of the DA. He is acquitted.

1915 On January 16, 1915, in a railroad cattle corral near Sierra Blanca, Texas, **H. L. "Hod" Roberson** (a former Texas Ranger) encounters Sierra Blanca rancher **Foote Boykin**, who was in the corral counting cattle. In a heated dispute, Roberson, while mounted, shoots the unmounted and unarmed (well, he did have a pocket knife on him) Boykin four—maybe five—times. In the fusillade, Roberson accidentally kills one of his own cowboys, **Walter Sitter**, age nineteen. Three juries convict Roberson of murder and sentence him to prison terms, but all convictions are overturned. Finally, in a fourth trial held in 1920, he is acquitted. While Roberson is still being tried for Boykin's murder, the T&SCRA hires him as a cattle detective. The prosecution dismisses the murder charge against Roberson for killing Walter Sitter.

On August 30, 1915, a posse of lawmen headed by **Dave Allison** corner ex-Mexican Revolutionary general turned outlaw, **Pascual Orozco**, and four of his fellow bandits in the High Lonesome Mountains south of Sierra Blanca. In the shootout, Allison and his men kill all five bandits. Allison is tried for the murder of Orozco but is acquitted.

1922 On June 14, 1922, T&SCRA inspectors **Dave Allison** and **H. L. Roberson** receive a tip that **Milt Good** of Brownfield, Texas, a friend of Tom Ross, is driving a large herd of stolen cattle across West Texas. The inspectors intercept Good and his cowboys with the cattle herd south of Lamesa. Good is indicted in four counties for stealing 516 head of cattle from area ranchers.

On October 31, 1922, **Tom Ross** is accused of stealing four cows from a neighboring rancher (A. Wilhoit). He is indicted for the alleged theft by a Lovington, New Mexico, grand jury.

1923 On April 1, 1923, **Tom Ross** and **Milt Good** catch T&SCRA inspectors **Dave Allison** and **H. L. Roberson** unaware in the lobby of the Gaines Hotel in Seminole, Texas, and kill both. Roberson's wife, Martha, grabs a gun and wings both of the assassins as they flee the scene. Later that evening they surrender voluntarily to the Gaines County sheriff to stand charges.

In June and July 1923, **Tom Ross** and **Milt Good** are tried in a Lubbock district court for murdering **Dave Allison**, and in September 1923 both are tried in an Abilene district court for murdering **H. L. Roberson**. All trials end in convictions and long sentences for both defendants.

1925 On November 29, 1925, **Tom Ross** and **Milt Good** escape from the Texas penitentiary at Huntsville, Texas.

1926 On June 26, 1926, escaped prisoner **Milt Good** is captured near Antlers, Oklahoma, and returned to prison.

1929 On February 23, 1929, escaped convict **Tom Ross** (now calling himself Charles Gannon) gets into a heated argument with the foreman of a Montana ranch where he is employed. Flying into a rage, he shoots and kills **Ralph Hayward**, who is unarmed. Then Ross retreats to his bunkhouse and turns the pistol on himself, thus ending a long and violent career.

1935 On January 20, 1935, **Milt Good** is unconditionally pardoned by Texas **Gov. Miriam Ferguson** and released from prison.

NOTES

PREFACE

1. Gordon Morris Bakken, ed., *Law in the Western United States* (Norman: University of Oklahoma Press, 2000), xiii–xvi.

2. John Phillip Reid, "Introduction: The Layers of Western Legal History," in Bakken, *Law in the Western United States*, 3–5.

3. Lawrence M. Friedman, "The Law Between the States: Some Thoughts on Southern Legal History," in *Ambivalent Legacy: A Legal History of the South*, ed. David J. Bodenhamer and James W. Ely, Jr. (Jackson: University Press of Mississippi, 1984), 30–46.

4. Bill Neal, *Getting Away with Murder on the Texas Frontier: Notorious Killings & Celebrated Trials* (Lubbock: Texas Tech University Press, 2006.)

5. John W. Davis, *A Vast Amount of Trouble: A History of the Spring Creek Raid* (Niwot: University of Colorado Press, 1995).

6. John W. Davis, *Goodbye Judge Lynch: The End of a Lawless Era in Wyoming's Big Horn Basin* (Norman: University of Oklahoma Press, 2005).

7. Frederick Allen, *A Decent Orderly Lynching: The Montana Vigilantes* (Norman: University of Oklahoma Press, 2005).

8. Gerard S. Petrone, *Judgment at Gallatin: The Trial of Frank James* (Lubbock: Texas Tech University Press, 1998).

9. Steven Lubet, *Murder in Tombstone: The Forgotten Trial of Wyatt Earp* (New Haven: Yale University Press, 2004). The trial lawyer who represented Wyatt, Virgil, and Morgan Earp was Thomas Fitch, a gifted advocate known as the "Silver-Tongued Orator of the Pacific" at a time when declamation was con-

sidered the height of the lawyer's art. He was also one of the best-known legal and political figures on the far West frontier. During his political career he held elective office in four jurisdictions—two states and two territories—and was instrumental in swinging California into the Abraham Lincoln victory column in 1860. He was also a journalist. In Nevada he edited a literary journal called *The Weekly Occidental,* which counted Mark Twain among its contributors. Lubet, *Murder in Tombstone,* 79–82. On the western frontier, lawyers often mixed journalism, public service, private law practice, and other pursuits just to make a living. For more on Thomas Fitch's journalistic career, see Gordon Morris Bakken, *Practicing Law in Frontier California* (Lincoln: University of Nebraska Press, 1991), 13–14. In the 1881 murder trial of Wyatt Earp, Thomas Fitch was able to utilize his journalistic talents as well as his legal skills much to the benefit of Wyatt and his brothers. He took advantage of a gaping loophole in Arizona Territory trial procedure: after the prosecution rested its case, the defendant himself was then allowed to take the witness stand and make a totally unrestricted statement—say whatever he wanted to say, including hearsay and irrelevant assertions—and it was all considered *evidence* on behalf of the defense. He was not even placed under oath. And, best of all, after the defendant had his say, he was not subject to being cross-examined by the prosecution. Wyatt took the stand holding a very long written statement (most likely written, or at least edited and "improved," by Fitch), which he then read to the court. In it he recounted all the prior alleged sins, crimes, and outlawry of the Clantons and the McLaureys and all the threats they had made against him leading up to the gunfight, plus all other information Wyatt and Fitch though might be helpful to the judge—including Wyatt's version of the OK Corral gunfight. No doubt Fitch made generous use of his journalistic and oratorical talents in drafting Wyatt's dissertation. For other accounts of the trial of Wyatt Earp, see Casey Tefertiller, *Wyatt Earp: The Life Behind the Legend* (New York: John Wiley & Sons, 1997); and Casey Tefertiller, "The Spicer Hearing & H. F. Sills," *National Association of Outlaw and Lawman History, Inc.* Vol. XXXI, No. 3–4 (July-December 2007).

10. Richard F. Hamm, *Murder, Honor and Law: Four Virginia Homicides from Reconstruction to the Great Depression* (Charlottesville: University of Virginia Press, 2003), 3.

11. Lawrence M. Freidman and Robert V. Percival, *The Roots of Justice: Crime and Punishment in Alameda County, California, 1870–1910* (Chapel Hill: University of North Carolina Press, 1981), 254.

12. Jake Lule, *Daily News, Eternal Stories: The Mythological Role of Journalism* (New York: The Guilford Press, 2001), 3, 17, 18, 21; Hamm, *Murder, Honor and Law,* 3.

INTRODUCTION

1. Laura V. Hamner, *Light 'n Hitch* (Dallas: American Guild Press, 1958), 115–16.

2. Albert Bigelow Paine, *Captain Bill McDonald, Texas Ranger* (Austin: State House Press, 1986), 154–58.

CHAPTER ONE: DUELS OF THE LAWMEN

1. Sources relied on for the background and career of Capt. William Jess McDonald are as follows: Charles H. Harris III and Louis R. Sadler, *The Texas Rangers and the Mexican Revolution: The Bloodiest Decade, 1910–1920* (Albuquerque: University of New Mexico Press, 2004); Robert M. Utley, *Lone Star Justice: The First Century of the Texas Rangers* (New York: Oxford University Press, 2002); Robert M. Utley, *Lone Star Justice: The Second Century of the Texas Rangers* (New York: Oxford University Press, 2007); Walter Prescott Webb, *The Story of the Texas Rangers* (Austin: Encino, 1971); Virgil E. Baugh, *A Pair of Texas Rangers: Bill McDonald and John Hughes* (Washington: Potomac Corral, the Westerners, 1970); William Warren Sterling, *Trails and Trials of the Texas Ranger* (Norman: University of Oklahoma Press, 1959); Paine, *Captain Bill McDonald*; Madeline Mason-Manheim, *Riding for Texas: The True Adventures of Captain Bill McDonald of the Texas Rangers, as told by Colonel Edward M. House to Tyler Mason* (New York: Rynal & Hitchock, 1936); Harold J. Weiss, Jr., "'Yours to Command': Captain William J. 'Bill' McDonald and The Panhandle Rangers of Texas" (Ph.D. dissertation, Indiana University, 1980). See also, Ron Tyler, ed., *The New Handbook of Texas*, Vol. 4 (Austin: Texas State Historical Association, 1996), 392–93.

2. In 1909 Albert Bigelow Paine undertook to write Bill McDonald's biography. To say that it is an uncritical account of McDonald's life is a gross understatement. Actually it reads more like a ghostwritten autobiography in which McDonald's role in each event is aggrandized—the stuff of pulp western heroes. However, when it comes to his role in the lynching of blacks who had murdered one of his kinsmen, the prose takes a decidedly different tone. Our hero suddenly becomes coy and takes refuge behind the front-man narrator, to wit:

> [H]e [McDonald] was hot-blooded in 'sixty-eight, and the situation was not one to develop moral principles. When, therefore, a mob formed and took the negroes out of jail and hanged them, there is no record of Bill Jesse having distinguished himself in their defense as he certainly would have done in later years. Indeed, it is likely that if he did not help pull a rope that night it was only because the rope was fully occupied with other willing hands.
>
> Paine, *Captain Bill McDonald*, 27.

3. Jeffrey Burton, *Indian Territory and the United States, 1866–1906: Courts, Government, and the Movement for Oklahoma Statehood* (Norman: University of Oklahoma Press, 1995), 121, 152.

4. James L. Haley, *Texas: From the Frontier to Spindletop* (New York: St. Martin's Press, 1985), 249. Although recent historians have branded this legend apocryphal, still, even if it is not the literal truth, it accurately captures an aspect of McDonald's character. There were at least two other documented incidents when McDonald, alone, confronted and faced down angry mobs. Charles M. Robinson III, *The Men Who Wear the Star* (New York: Modern Library, 2001), 247–48. For a brief but balanced account of McDonald's background and early career, including his December 9, 1893, shootout in downtown Quanah with Childress Sheriff John Pearce Matthews, see Utley, *Lone Star Justice: The First Century of the Texas Rangers*, 256–59. For McDonald's career with the Rangers after the turn of the century see Utley, *Lone Star Justice: The Second Century of the Texas Rangers*. There continues to be considerable interest in the history of the Rangers. For example see Paul N. Spellman, *Captain J. A. Brooks, Texas Ranger* (Denton: University of North Texas Press, 2007).

5. Paine, *Captain Bill McDonald*, 165–66; Millie Jones Porter, *Memory Cups of Panhandle Pioneers* (Clarendon, TX: Clarendon Press, 1945), 337–38; John Miller Morris, *A Private in the Texas Rangers—A. T. Miller of Company B, Frontier Battalion* (College Station: Texas A&M Press, 2001), 281–82. Paine's account (as related to him by McDonald) says that Matthews killed a riverboat captain in Louisiana; Porter's account (cited by Morris) claims that the victim was a black man. Porter says that after the killing of Mankins in 1884, Matthews voluntarily returned to Louisiana and succeeded in clearing himself of the murder indictment there. Thereafter, he returned to the Texas Panhandle and reclaimed his proper name under which he was later elected the Childress County sheriff.

6. Capt. W. J. McDonald to Texas Adjutant General W. H. Mabry report dated August 21, 1893, Adjutant General's Correspondence Files (AGCF), Box 401, Folder 429–13, Texas State Archives, Austin, Texas.

7. E. B. Pendleton to Texas Adjutant General W. H. Mabry, letter dated January 28, 1893, AGCF, Box 401, Folder 427–2, TSA.

8. Sergeant J. W. Britton to W. H. Mabry report dated December 11, 1893, AGCF, Box 401, Folder 430–15, TSA.

9. *The Fort Worth Daily Gazette*, December 11, 1893; *The Quanah Chief*, December 14, 1893.

10. Paine, *Captain Bill McDonald*, 166; *The Fort Worth Daily Gazette*, December 11, 1893.

11. James E. & Louise (Beckham) Heidlebaugh, "Sheriff Joseph P. Beckham, son of

Roderic Carroll Beckham and Sarah Bundy," July 19, 1999. MyFamily.com Inc. and its subsidiaries. (Ancestry.com) June 6, 2001. See also Valarie Owen, *Byrd Cochrain of Dead Man's Corner* (Snyder, TX: Feather Press, 1972), 29–30.

12. W. M. Pearce, *The Matador Land and Cattle Company* (Norman: University of Oklahoma Press, 1964), 27.

13. Pearce, *The Matador Land and Cattle Company*, 23–27, 55.

14. C. L. Douglas, *Cattle Kings of Texas* (Fort Worth: Branch-Smith, 1968), 226–27.

15. Pearce, *The Matador Land and Cattle Company*, 7–11, 18–20, 37–39.

16. The account of the organization of Motley County and the resulting political turmoil has been compiled from the following sources: *Matador Tribune*, August 25, 1960; Marisue Burleson Potts, *Motley County Roundup: A Centennial History*, Second Edition (Floydada, TX: Marisue Potts, publisher, 1991), 48; Harry H. Campbell, *The Early History of Motley County*, Second Edition (Wichita Falls, TX: Nortex Offset Publications, 1971), 51–53; Eleanor Mitchell Traweek, *Of Such As These: A History of Motley County and Its Families* (Wichita Falls, TX: Nortex Publications, 1973), 15–17; Pearce, *The Matador Land and Cattle Company*, 56; Wilson E. Dolman III, "Conflicts Over Land: The Settler and the Rancher in West Texas," *West Texas Historical Association Year Book*, Vol. 50 (1974), 61–75; W. M. Pearce, "The Road to Stability: A Decade in the History of the Matador Ranch, 1891–1900," *Panhandle-Plains Historical Review*, Vol. 26 (1953), 29–30. Also see Luke Gournay, *Texas Boundaries: Evolution of the State's Counties* (College Station: Texas A&M Press, 1995), 103; Sammy Tise, *Texas County Sheriffs* (Hallettsville, TX: Tise Geneological Research, 1989), 385; and Bob Alexander, *Lawmen, Outlaws and S.O.Bs., Gunfighters of the Old Southwest, Vol. II* (Silver City, NM: High Lonesome Books, 2007), 250.

17. *H. H. Campbell v. The Matador Land & Cattle Co, John H. Smith, Jesse Baker, A. G. Ligertwood, Lon Barkley*, Cause No. 3, 50th Judicial District Court of Motley County, Texas.

18. Motley County Judge Henry H. Campbell to Governor James S. Hogg, letter dated September 10, 1893, Governor's Papers, Box 301, File 140–230, Texas State Archives, Austin, Texas.

19. Ibid.

20. *The Matador Tribune*, August 25, 1960; Campbell, *The Early History of Motley County*, 52–53. The Matador Ranch, galvanized into action by the initial (1891) and the second (1892) slate of county officers, pulled out all stops for the 1893 election (officers to take office in 1894), and succeeded in getting all its candidates (except for a court clerk) elected to the county offices. However, the settlers rebounded in the next election and swept the slate, and thereafter, from 1896 onward, they had firm control of the county government. Pearce, *The*

Matador Land and Cattle Company, 56; Potts, *Motley County Roundup*, 47–48; Owen, *Byrd Cochrain of Dead Man's Corner*, 31.

21. Duff Green, "Recollections," *The Matador Tribune*, October 9, 1986; Tom Bean, "Joe Beckham, The Outlaw Sheriff," *The [Dickens] Texas Spur*, February 3, 1994; Potts, *Motley County Roundup*, 45; *The State v. Joe P. Beckham*, Cause No. 35, 50th Judicial District Court of Motley County (indicted for murdering Jeff Boone, September 21, 1892).

22. Potts, *Motley County Roundup*, 26–27.

23. *State v. Joe P. Beckham*, Cause No. 193, County Court of Childress County (gambling), February 7, 1893.

24. Potts, *Motley County Roundup*, 46. Another account of the fire says that all the county records were destroyed in the fire. Traweek, *Of Such As These*, 16. However, as will be seen by subsequent events hereinafter related, it would appear that the records did survive the fire—at least the ad valorem tax records.

25. Joe Beckham's swift decline from lawman to outlaw was compiled from the following sources: *The Matador Tribune*, August 25, 1960; *The* [Dickens] *Texas Spur*, February 3, 1994; Potts, *Motley County Roundup*; Traweek, *Of Such As These*; Campbell, *The Early History of Motley County*; Paine, *Captain Bill Mc-Donald*.

26. *The Quanah Chief*, June 8, 1893.

27. Both Beckham and Cook were indicted by a Childress County District Court grand jury in Cause Nos. 173 and 176, respectively, for aggravated assault. Cook was tried on May 30, 1894. A jury found him not guilty. Afterwards, on November 26, 1894, the district court dismissed the indictment against Beckham upon motion from the district attorney giving as grounds therefor: "insufficient evidence."

28. Motley County Judge Henry H. Campbell to Governor James S. Hogg, letter dated September 10, 1893, Governor's Papers, Box 301, File 140–230, TSA; Potts, *Motley County Roundup*, 46; Traweek, *Of Such As These*, 16; Campbell, *The Early History of Motley County*, 52.

29. Campbell, *The Early History of Motley County*, 52; Potts, *Motley County Roundup*, 46; *The Motley County Tribune*, August 25, 1960.

30. McDonald to Mabry report dated August 21, 1893, AGCF, Box 401, Folder 429–15, TSA; Campbell, *The Early History of Motley County*, 52.

31. McDonald to Mabry report dated August 21, 1893, AGCF, Box 401, Folder 429–15, TSA; Paine, *Captain Bill McDonald*, 167.

32. McDonald to Mabry reports dated August 17, 1893, and August 21, 1893, AGCF, Box 401, Folders 429–13 and 429–15, TSA.

33. Tyler, *The New Handbook of Texas*, 4:392; Charles E. Coombes, *The Prairie Dog Lawyer* (Dallas: University Press in Dallas, 1945), 6; Paine, *Captain Bill McDon-*

ald, 31–32, 139–42; Ellis Douthit, "Some Experiences of a West Texas Lawyer," *West Texas Historical Association Year Book*, Vol. 18 (1942), 37–38.

34. Coombes, *The Prairie Dog Lawyer*, 6, 254.

35. *H. H. Campbell v. The Matador Land & Cattle Co., et al.*, Cause No. 3, Motley County District Court. See also, Judge Campbell to Governor Hogg, letter dated September 10, 1893; *Matador Tribune*, August 25, 1960; and Campbell, *The Early History of Motley County*, 52.

36. James A. Gober and B. Bryan Price, *Cowboy Justice—A Tale of a Texas Lawman* (Lubbock: Texas Tech University Press, 1997), 305. Without doubt Sullivan was a fearless, effective, and honest law officer. His contemporaries also gave further insight into Sullivan's character. He was vain in dress and expression, and his outspoken religious convictions led his fellow rangers to dub him the "church fiend." However, his spiritual zeal apparently waned from time to time, and he indulged in spirits of a more earthly variety. On one occasion an extended drinking bout caused McDonald to demand his resignation. McDonald to Mabry reports dated June 23 and July 3 and 4, 1897, AGCF, Box 401, Folders 443–12, 16, and 17, TSA.

37. *The Matador Tribune*, August 25, 1960; Potts, *Motley County Roundup*, 46–47.

38. McDonald to Mabry reports dated August 17, 1893, and August 21, 1893, AGCF, Box 401, Folders 429–13 and 429–15, TSA; Paine, *Captain Bill McDonald*, 166–69.

39. Judge Campbell to Governor Hogg, letter dated September 10, 1893.

40. Coombes, *The Prairie Dog Lawyer*, 9–10. Although Coombes's account accurately depicts the explosiveness of the situation and how McGill adroitly and forcefully handled it, Coombes errs in one detail. Beckham was not in the Motley County District Court when McGill convened it on August 15, 1893. That day, Beckham was McClure's prisoner and they were en route from Quanah to the Matador jail. For related accounts of the incident see *The Matador Tribune*, October 6, 1949; *The Matador Tribune, Old Settlers Edition*, August 28, 1986; and Potts, *Motley County Roundup*, 46–47.

41. *Matador Tribune*, October 6, 1949; *Motley County Tribune*, August 28, 1986; Potts, *Motley County Roundup*, 46–47.

42. Three indictments for misapplication of public money (embezzlement) were returned by the Motley County District Court grand jury on August 18, 1893, in Cause Nos. 17, 18, and 19. On a change of venue, these were filed in the Baylor County District Court under Cause Nos. 541, 542, and 543. Motley County sent over an additional embezzlement indictment on September 11, 1894, which was filed in the Baylor County District Court as Cause No. 567.

43. McDonald to Mabry report dated January 10, 1894 (misdated to read "1893"), AGCF, Box 401, Folder 431–1, TSA.

44. Michael G. Ehrle, *The Childress County Story* (Childress, TX: Ox Bow Printing, 1971), 59–60.

45. Britton to Mabry report dated December 11, 1893, AGCF, Box 401, Folder 430–15, TSA.

46. McDonald to Mabry report dated January 10, 1894, AGCF, Box 401, Folder 431–1, TSA; Paine, *Captain Bill McDonald*, 171–73.

47. *The Dallas Morning News*, December 13, 1893.

48. R. P. Coffer affidavit dated December 30, 1893, quoted in Ehrle, *The Childress County Story*, 59–60.

49. Dick Crutcher affidavit dated January 2, 1894, quoted in Ehrle, *The Childress County Story*, 60–61.

50. Paine, *Captain Bill McDonald*, 169–75.

51. *Quanah Chief*, December 14, 1893, reprinted in *Quanah Tribune-Chief*, December 11, 1918; *Quanah Chief*, January 4, 1894. These reports give a fairly complete and impartial account of the shooting and the wounds inflicted on both McDonald and Matthews.

52. Paine, *Captain Bill McDonald*, 169–75.

53. Sources relied on to compile the account of the McDonald-Matthews duel of December 9, 1983, are as follows: All of the Adjutant General Correspondence Files cited above, Texas State Archives, Austin, Texas; *Fort Worth Daily Gazette*, December 11, 1893; *Quanah Chief*, December 14, 1893; *Quanah Chief*, January 4, 1894; sworn statements of R. P. Coffer and Dick Crutcher and other material quoted in Ehrle, *The Childress County Story*, 59–62; George Webb, interview by Bill Neal, Canyon Texas, *Amarillo Globe-News*, July 17, 1960; sworn statements of R. P. Coffer and other material found in official file in *State v. R. P. Coffer*, Cause No. 293, Hardeman County District Court, Quanah, Texas, 1894; *State v. W. J. McDonald*, Cause No. 273, Hardeman County District Court, 1894; Paine, *Captain Bill McDonald*, 169–75; Morris, *A Private in the Texas Rangers*, 281–82; Weiss "'Yours to Command'"; Bill Neal, *The Last Frontier: The Story of Hardeman County* (Quanah, TX: Southwest Offset Publications, 1966), 67–69.

54. George Webb, interview by Bill Neal, spring 1960. (Feature story appeared in the Sunday edition of the *Amarillo News-Globe* on July 17, 1960.)

55. McDonald to Mabry telegram dated December 10, 1893, AGCF, Box 430–14, TSA.

56. *The Dallas Morning News*, December 13, 1893.

57. *The Quanah Chief*, January 4, 1894; *The Fort Worth Daily Gazette*, December 14, 1893.

58. McDonald to Mabry report dated January 1, 1894, AGCF, Box 401, Folder 431–3, TSA.

59. Ehrle, *The Childress County Story*, 61. See also a pretrial report from *The Fort*

Worth Daily Gazette, May 18, 1894, expressing the opinion that Captain McDonald would "be acquitted beyond any doubt." However, before this opinion was printed, a Hardeman County jury, on May 16, 1894, had already returned a verdict of not guilty. *State v. W. J. McDonald,* Cause No. 273, 46th Judicial District Court of Hardeman County.

60. *State v. R. P. Coffer,* Cause No. 293, Hardeman County District Court. In a sworn statement filed in that case, Coffer said that he "had no animosity toward [Matthews] by reason of the deceased having killed a relative of [Coffer's]"— apparently meaning James Mankins.

61. Ibid.

62. McDonald to Mabry report dated January 10, 1894, AGCF, Box 401, Folder 431–1, TSA.

63. Paine, *Captain Bill McDonald,* 417 (Appendix C).

64. A partial list of his famous cases include the "Murder Society of San Saba," the "Reese-Townsend Feud" at Columbus, the "Conduitt Family Murders" near Edna, the "Orange Race Riot" at Orange, the "Trans-Cedar Mystery" near Athens, the "Hutchinson County Cattle Mutilations Case" in the Texas Panhandle, the "Cherokee Strip Campaign" in Oklahoma, and the "Brownsville Raid" at Brownsville. Morris, *A Private in the Texas Rangers,* 282–83; Paine, *Captain Bill McDonald,* 356–72.

65. Tyler, *The New Handbook of Texas,* 4:392–93.

66. *El Paso Morning Times,* November 7, 1912; Harris and Sadler, *The Texas Rangers and the Mexican Revolution,* 25.

67. Sources differ on the spelling of John Pearce Matthews's name. His gravestone has it "Jo. P. Mathews." However, Childress County historians and other sources spell it "Matthews." Likewise, his middle name is sometimes spelled "Pearce" and other times "Pierce."

68. *Fort Worth Daily Gazette,* June 1, 1895; *The Baylor County* [Texas] *Banner,* September 5, 1929; C. Warren, "Joe Beckham—The Outlaw Sheriff," *Real West* (August 1983), 28–29.

69. Glenn Shirley, *West of Hell's Fringe: Crime, Criminals, and the Federal Peace Officer in Oklahoma Territory, 1889–1907* (Norman: University of Oklahoma Press, 1978), 344; *Oklahoma State Capital,* September 13, 1895, and March 21, 1896; *Oklahoma Daily Times-Journal,* April 4, 1896; Phillip Steele, "The Woman Red Buck Couldn't Scare," *The West* (April, 1971), 20–21.

70. *Oklahoma State Capital,* December 6, 1896; Charles Power Rainbolt, *In Pursuit of the Outlaw "Red Buck"* (Inola, OK: Evans Publications, 1990), 48–49.

71. Alexander, *Lawmen, Outlaws, and S.O.Bs., Vol. II,* 256–57; James I. Fenton, "Tom Ross: Ranger Nemesis," *National Association for Outlaw and Lawman History* [NOLA] Vol. XIV, No. 2 (Summer 1990), 4.

72. *The Dallas Morning News,* December 31, 1895; *The Floyd County* [Texas] *Times,* January 4, 1896.

73. Bill O'Neal, *Historic Ranches of the Old West* (Austin: Nortex Press, 1997), 62–63.

74. *The Dallas Morning News,* December 31, 1895; *The Floyd County Times,* January 4, 1896; Rainbolt, *In Pursuit of the Outlaw "Red Buck,"* 50; Alexander, *Lawmen, Outlaws and S.O.Bs., Vol. II,* 257.

75. Shirley, *West of Hell's Fringe,* 344.

76. Sergeant W. J. L. Sullivan, *Twelve Years in the Saddle for Law and Order on the Frontiers of Texas* (Originally published by W. John L. Sullivan, 1909. Reprint, Lincoln, NE: Bison Books, 2001), 145–48; Shirley, *West of Hell's Fringe,* 341–45; *The Dallas Morning News,* December 31, 1895; Robert K. DeArment, "Bloody Easter," *Old West* (Spring 1994), 14.

77. Sullivan, *Twelve Years in the Saddle for Law and Order,* 148.

78. Various accounts of this incident have identified the creek as "Sutters Creek" or "Suttler's Creek" or "Suttle's Creek." The official name is Suttle Creek, apparently named, despite the spelling variation, for an "Old Greer County" pioneer, B. F. Suttles, who, in the 1880s, settled on an outcropping on the west side of the North Fork of the Red River between Navajoe and Mangum, Oklahoma, where a mountain there bears his name. Alongside Suttles Mountain ran the old Western Cattle Trail to Dodge City. About thirty miles to the south was Doan's Store and Doan's Crossing, where the trail crossed the Red River into Oklahoma Territory via Greer County. Morris, *A Private in the Texas Rangers,* 138–40.

79. Owen, *Byrd Cochrain of Dead Man's Corner,* 36.

80. The location of the dugout on Suttle Creek where the December 27, 1895, shootout between Ranger Sullivan and his men and the four outlaws cannot be pinpointed precisely at this late date. However, it probably occurred at a head-water spring on Suttle Creek approximately as marked on the accompanying map of that area, and just west of the present town of Frederick, Oklahoma.

81. Sullivan, *Twelve Years in the Saddle for Law and Order,* 148–54.

82. *The Dallas Morning News,* December 31, 1895; *The Floyd County Times,* January 4, 1896.

83. *The Dallas Morning News,* February 27, 1896; *Wichita Daily Times,* June 10, 1951.

84. Pearce, *The Matador Land and Cattle Company,* 52; Campbell, *The Early History of Motley County,* 53; Potts, *Motley County Roundup,* 47–48.

85. *State v. Hill Loftis, State v. Red Buck Weightman, State v. Kid Lewis,* Cause Nos. 901, 902, and 903, respectively, in the 46th Judicial District Court of Wilbarger County, Texas.

86. Glenn Shirley, *Heck Thomas, Frontier Marshal* (Philadelphia and New York: Chilton Co., 1962), 139; Bailey C. Hanes, *Bill Doolin: Outlaw O.T.* (Norman: University of Oklahoma Press, 1968), 61.

87. Shirley, *West of Hell's Fringe*, 83–105; Hanes, *Bill Doolin*, 56–59.

88. Hanes, *Bill Doolin*, 61.

89. Glenn Shirley, *Temple Houston: Lawyer with a Gun* (Norman: University of Oklahoma Press, 1980), 255–58; Neal, *Getting Away with Murder*, 106–21.

90. *Taloga* [Oklahoma] *Times-Advocate*, April 17, 1941, et seq. (Recollections of former D County Attorney George E. Black.)

91. Evett Dumas Nix, *Oklahombres* (St. Louis and Chicago: Eden Publishing House, 1929), 143–44; Ramon Adams, *Burrs Under the Saddle* (Norman: University of Oklahoma Press, 1964), 20; and Hanes, *Bill Doolin*, 61–62, 151–52. But see Shirley, *West of Hell's Fringe*, 276, 456.

92. The story of Red Buck's last run is taken from Shirley, *West of Hell's Fringe*, 348–51.

93. "Posse's Guns End Red Buck's Crime Career," *History of Custer and Washita Counties* (Clinton Daily News, 1937); *Arapaho* [Oklahoma] *Argus*, March 5, 1896.

94. Richard S. Graves, *Oklahoma Outlaws* (Oklahoma City: State Printing and Publishing Co., 1915), 98.

CHAPTER TWO: WICHITA FALLS JUSTICE, JUDGE LYNCH PRESIDING

1. The story of the 1896 Wichita Falls bank robbery by Kid Lewis and Foster Crawford, their capture, and their subsequent lynching as set out in this chapter has been compiled from the following sources: *The Fort Worth Gazette*, February 26, 27, 28, March 3, and April 29, 1896; *The Dallas Morning News*, February 27, 28, and May 9, 1896; *The Dallas Semi-Weekly News*, February 28 and March 3, 1896; *Wichita Daily Times*, April 9, 1908; March 21, 1920; March 5, 1950; June 10, 17, 24, and July 1, 1951; *The Wichita Falls Daily Times*, March 21, 1949; Louise Kelly, *Wichita County Beginnings* (Burnet, TX: Eakin Press, 1982), 43–45; Johnnie R. Morgan, *The History of Wichita Falls* (Wichita Falls, TX: Nortex Press, 1971), 87–90; Sullivan, *Twelve Years in the Saddle for Law and Order*, 227–29; Paine, *Captain Bill McDonald*, 199–213; Shirley, *West of Hell's Fringe*, 347–48.

2. *The Dallas Morning News*, February 28, 1896; *Wichita Daily Times*, June 10, 1951.

3. *Wichita Daily Times*, June 10, 1951.

4. Sullivan, *Twelve Years in the Saddle for Law and Order*, 182–84.

5. The tale of the Texas Rangers and their involvement in Dan Stuart's promotion of the Fitzsimmons-Maher championship fight is taken from the account told

by Leo N. Miletich, *Dan Stuart's Fistic Carnival* (College Station: Texas A&M University Press, 1994).

6. *The Dallas Morning News,* February 23, 1896.

7. Paine, *Captain Bill McDonald,* 399–403. (Appendix A to Paine's biography quotes Mabry's February 27, 1896, report of the ranger's role in the Fitzsimmons-Maher affair.)

8. Sullivan, *Twelve Years in the Saddle for Law and Order,* 182.

9. *Wichita Daily Times,* April 9, 1908; *Wichita Daily Times,* March 21, 1920; Morgan, *The History of Wichita Falls,* 87–90.

10. *Wichita Daily Times,* July 1, 1951.

11. *Wichita Daily Times,* April 9, 1908.

12. *The Dallas Morning News,* February 28, 1896.

13. *The Fort Worth Gazette,* March 3, 1896.

14. *Wichita Daily Times,* July 1, 1951.

15. *The Fort Worth Gazette,* February 28, 1896.

16. *Wichita Daily Times,* April 9, 1908.

17. *The Dallas Morning News,* February 27, 1896; *Wichita Daily Times,* July 1, 1951.

18. *Wichita Daily Times,* March 21, 1920; *Wichita Daily Times,* June 10, 17, and 24, July 1, 1951.

19. *The Dallas Morning News,* February 27, 1896.

20. *Wichita Daily Times,* March 21, 1896.

21. *Wichita Daily Times,* April 9, 1908. As to when and where the rangers were notified and how they all congregated at Bellevue and arrived back in Wichita Falls to pursue the fleeing robbers, see Sullivan, *Twelve Years in the Saddle for Law and Order,* 182–84; Paine, *Captain Bill McDonald,* 199–203.

22. *Wichita Daily Times,* July 1, 1951.

23. Ibid.

24. *Wichita Daily Times,* June 17, 1951.

25. *The Dallas Morning News,* February 28, 1896.

26. *Wichita Daily Times,* June 24, 1951.

27. *The Fort Worth Gazette,* February 27, 1896.

28. *Wichita Daily Times,* June 24, 1951.

29. Paine, *Captain Bill McDonald,* 212.

30. *The Dallas Semi-Weekly News,* February 28, 1896.

31. *The Dallas Morning News,* February 27, 1896.

32. *The Dallas Morning News,* February 27 and 28, 1896; *The Dallas Semi-Weekly News,* February 28, 1896; *Wichita Daily Times,* July 1, 1951.

33. *Wichita Daily Times,* June 24, 1951.

34. *The Dallas Semi-Weekly News,* February 28, 1896; *Wichita Daily Times,* June 24, 1951.

35. *Wichita Daily Times,* February 27 and 28, 1896; *The Fort Worth Gazette,* February 26, 27, and 28, 1896; *The Dallas Semi-Weekly News,* February 28, 1896.

36. Psychologist Erich Fromm discusses the unleashing of deeply buried levels of sadism triggered by chain-reaction "frenzy" so intense that mob members go into a state of "ecstatic destructiveness." Erich Fromm, *The Anatomy of Human Destructiveness* (New York: Holt, Rinehart and Winston, 1973), 171–180. Fromm gives a broader discussion of group aggression in the same book: 4, 196, 200, 202–4. After a particularly gruesome lynching in Eastland, Texas, in 1929, an *El Paso Times* reporter put it somewhat more bluntly than Fromm: "After all human passions are but little removed from the jungle state." *El Paso Times,* November 21, 1929. See also John Raymond Ross, "At the Bar of Judge Lynch: Lynching and Lynch Mobs in America" (PhD dissertation, Texas Tech University, 1983), 237–42.

37. Ross, "At the Bar of Judge Lynch," 253–56.

38. Lynch mobs, such as the one that hanged Lewis and Crawford, were formed to execute extralegal violence and are akin to, but not exactly the same as, vigilantism. Usually vigilantism implied established organizations formed to administer justice in areas where regular law enforcement agencies did not exist or were ineffective. As such, vigilantism could be considered a transitional and temporary force in support of law and order. (Trouble was, however, once life was breathed into that monster, the beast often refused to slink quietly back into its lair after its assigned task was done, but instead got completely out of control.) Lynch mobs on the other hand typically occurred in areas where the regular institutions of law and order already existed and were functional, but the mobs formed spontaneously in response to some real or perceived outrage against community standards and were fueled primarily by revenge motivation. Unlike vigilante organizations, however, once a lynch mob's lethal task was accomplished and its blood-lust satiated, the mob usually dispersed. Richard Maxwell Brown, "The Historical Patterns of Violence in America," in *The History of Violence in America,* ed. Hugh Davis Graham and Ted Robert Gurr (New York: Frederick A. Praeger, 1969), 50. The typical lynch mob consisted of three principal groups: the leaders, those that did the lynching, and the spectators. For a discussion of mob composition and the role of the three groups, see Frank Shay, *Judge Lynch, His First Hundred Years* (New York: I. Washburn, 1938), 87–90. Also see David Chapman, "Lynching in Texas" (MA thesis, Texas Tech University, 1973), 15–21.

39. *Wichita Daily Times,* April 9, 1908.

40. *The Dallas Morning News,* February 27, 1896; *The Dallas Semi-Weekly News,* February 28, 1896; *Wichita Daily Times,* June 24, 1951.

41. Jerry Flemmons, *Amon: The Texan Who Played Cowboy for America* (Lubbock: Texas Tech University Press, 1998), 38.

42. On June 7, 1879, in Clay County, Texas, Burk Burnett shot and killed Jack King, whom he accused of smearing his brand over Burk's on about twenty head of steers. *Fort Worth Democrat,* June 8, 1879. He was tried for murder but acquitted on his plea of self-defense. *State of Texas v. S. B. Burnett,* Cause No. 166, Clay County, Texas, District Court.

43. *Wichita Daily Times,* March 21, 1920.

44. For a fascinating study of how newspapers covered sensational crimes and criminal trials during the last half of the nineteenth century, see Richard F. Hamm, *Murder, Honor and Law: Four Virginia Homicides from Reconstruction to the Great Depression* (Charlottesville: University of Virginia Press, 2003). For historians of the culture of the western frontier, and particularly those focusing on journalism in that developing land, instructive and fascinating account is told by David Dary, *Red Blood and Black Ink: Journalism in the Old West* (Lawrence: University of Kansas Press, 1998). He observes at page 63: "There was no clear separation between news and opinion in the early newspapers of the American West. Printers who edited papers thought nothing of including their personal opinions in factual news stories." Other chapters are devoted to topics such as "No Weasel Words," "Town Booming," "Pistol-Packin' Editors," "Death and Religion," and "Hyperbolizing."

45. *The Fort Worth Gazette,* February 28, 1896.

46. *Wichita Daily Times,* April 9, 1908.

47. *The Dallas Morning News,* March 3, 1896; *The Dallas Semi-Weekly News,* March 3, 1896; *Wichita Daily Times,* July 1, 1951.

48. *The Dallas Semi-Weekly News,* March 7, 1896.

49. Eleven years later, Congress did heed the settlers' demands. In 1907 Congress admitted the State of Oklahoma into the Union. The new state included both the old Oklahoma Territory and the old Indian Territory. For an in-depth discussion of the twisted history of how and why it all finally came to be, see Jeffrey Burton, *Indian Territory and the United States, 1866–1906: Courts, Government and the Movement for Oklahoma Statehood* (Norman: University of Oklahoma Press, 1995).

50. *The Dallas Morning News,* February 28, 1896.

51. All of the preceding exchanges between the Dallas, Fort Worth, and Wichita Falls newspapers are quoted in *The Fort Worth Gazette,* April 2, 1896.

52. *The Fort Worth Gazette,* April 2, 1896. (The Wichita Falls Citizens' Committee's heated responses to Judge Kilgore's broadside were all printed in *The Fort Worth Gazette,* April 7, 1896.)

53. Paine, *Captain Bill McDonald,* 211–13.

54. Captain W. J. McDonald to Texas Adjutant General W. H. Mabry, letter dated April 4, 1896, AGCF, TSA. Quoted in *Wichita Daily Times,* July 1, 1951. See also

NOTES

Walter Prescott Webb, *The Texas Rangers* (Austin: University of Texas Press, 1935), 446–47.

55. *Wichita Daily Times,* July 1, 1951.

56. Coombes, *The Prairie Dog Lawyer,* 274.

57. *The Dallas Morning News,* February 28, 1896.

58. Keith Carter, "The Texas Court of Criminal Appeals," 11 *Tex.L.Rev.* 185 (1933), 196.

59. *The Fort Worth Gazette,* April 5, 1896. Texas was far from the only venue where both trial and appellate judges rigidly adhered to all the technicalities of the common law. One Mississippi judge of the era proudly recalled how he had once quashed eighty indictments at one time over a single technicality; J. F. H. Claiborne, *Mississippi as a Province, Territory and State* (Jackson: Power and Barksdale, 1880) 1:482; Reuben Davis, *Recollections of Mississippi and Mississippians* (Boston: Houghton Mifflin, 1889), 104. America inherited its common law from English jurisprudence, and the latter's most esteemed scholar and legal commentator was Sir William Blackstone. It was he who enunciated the fundamental premise of English common law in criminal prosecutions, to wit: "It is better that 99 guilty men should escape, than that one innocent man should suffer." Judge Blackstone's opinion was, no doubt, a reaction to the horrors of the arbitrary Star Chamber injustice that Englishmen had suffered in earlier times. But, in the eyes of late-nineteenth-century western frontier laymen who witnessed large numbers of killers escaping punishment and being loosed on the population, the pendulum had swung too far in the opposite direction. One late-nineteenth-century federal judge sided with the Dallas grand jury that protested appellate courts reversing convictions of criminals on the flimsiest of technicalities. U.S. District Judge Isaac Parker got fed up with the U.S. Supreme Court reversing criminal convictions out of his court. In a public blast at the Supreme Court he railed: "The appellate court exists mainly to stab the trial judge in the back and enable the criminal to go free." On his deathbed, in 1896, he took one final shot at the appellate court: "I would that the law would provide against the reversal of cases unless innocence was manifest. . . . I would have brushed aside all technicalities that do not affect the guilt or innocence of the accused." Fred Harvey Harrington, *Hanging Judge* (Norman: University of Oklahoma Press, 1951), 179–87. See also Robert H. Tuller, *"Let No Guilty Man Escape": A Judicial Biography of "Hanging Judge" Isaac C. Parker* (Norman: University of Oklahoma Press, 2001); and Michael J. Brodhead, *Isaac C. Parker: Federal Justice on the Frontier* (Norman: University of Oklahoma Press, 2003).

60. Art. 723, *The Texas Code of Criminal Procedure*; Gammel, comp., *Laws of Texas*, Vol. 10, 25th Legislature (1897), 17.

61. *The Fort Worth Gazette,* April 29, 1896.

62. The five murder indictments returned on May 6, 1896, in the 30th Judicial District Court of Wichita County, Texas, were as follows: Cause No. 604, Marion Potter; Cause No. 605, Frank Smith; Cause No. 606, W. E. Cobb; Cause No. 607, Dick Quinn; and Cause No. 608, F. M. Davis. Members of the grand jury were: J. C. Hunt, foreman; F. M. Avis, S. M. Butcher, A. A. Honaker, W. C. Heath, F. D. Kildow, R. O. C. Lynch, John Myers, E. A. McCleskey, D. M. Smith, Andrew Weeth, and T. P. Roberts. *Wichita Daily Times*, March 5, 1950.

63. *The Dallas Morning News*, May 9, 1896.

64. Ibid; Kelly, *Wichita County Beginnings*, 45.

65. *The Dallas Morning News*, May 9, 1896. The four indictments transferred to Vernon were filed in the 46th Judicial District Court of Wilbarger County, Texas: Cause No. 940, F. M. Davis; Cause No. 941, Dick Quinn; Cause No. 942, W. E. Cobb; and Cause No. 943, Frank Smith.

66. Marion Potter, Cause No. 3441 in the Cooke County, Texas, District Court.

67. *The Dallas Morning News*, May 9, 1896.

68. *Wichita Falls Record News*, March 21, 1944.

69. *Wichita Daily Times*, July 1, 1951.

70. Handwritten notes of editor Rhea Howard in the *Wichita Falls Times Record News* file on the 1896 lynching of Foster Crawford and Elmer "Kid" Lewis in Wichita Falls, Texas.

71. Coombes, *The Prairie Dog Lawyer*, 274.

72. *Wichita Daily Times*, April 26, 1922.

73. *Wichita Daily Times*, July 1, 1951.

74. David Chapman, "Lynching in Texas" (MA thesis, Texas Tech University, 1973), 90–91; Tyler, *The New Handbook of Texas*, 4:346–47.

75. Ross, "At the Bar of Judge Lynch," 254.

76. Miletich, *Dan Stuart's Fistic Carnival*, 86.

77. *The Dallas Morning News*, January 31 and February 1, 2, and 3, 1893; Tyler, *The New Handbook of Texas*, 4:346–47; Lawrence D. Rice, *The Negro in Texas, 1874–1900* (Baton Rouge: Louisiana State University Press, 1971), 253–54; Anonymous, *The Facts in the Case of the Horrible Murder of Little Myrtle Vance and Its Fearful Expiation at Paris, Texas, February 1, 1893* (Paris, TX: P. L. James, 1893); Ross, "At the Bar of Judge Lynch," 28–32, 120.

78. L. E. Bleckley, "Negro Outrage No Excuse for Lynching," *Forum* 16 (November 1893), 300–302, quoted in Ross, "At the Bar of Judge Lynch," 29.

79. Jessie Daniel Ames was one outstanding example. See Jacquelyn Dowd Hall, *Revolt Against Chivalry: Jessie Daniel Ames and the Women's Campaign Against Lynching*, Revised Edition (New York: Columbia University Press, 1993).

80. The major Texas newspapers consistently beating their journalistic drums against lynching and officials who turned a blind eye to mobsters and their

supporters included *The Austin American, San Antonio Express, El Paso Times, Houston Post, Galveston Daily News,* and *The Dallas Morning News.* In an editorial dated June 28, 1917, the *Galveston Daily News* commented:

> The death of the miserable victim of the mob is not a vital consideration. . . . He probably got what he deserved. . . . The [lynching] offense was not against him. The offense was against the majesty of the law.

On October 13, 1920, *The Dallas Morning News* told its readers this:

> There is no such thing as a citizen too good to be arrested for participation in a mob bent on murder; there is no prisoner so vile to be denied the protection of law while under arrest.

81. H. B. No. 30; Gammel, *Laws of Texas,* Vol. 10, 25th Legislature (1897, special session), 1480.

82. *Alexander v. State,* 40 Tex. Cr. Rep. 395, 50 S.W. 716 (Tex.Ct.Crim.App. 1899). The court held that the act applied only to those who took a prisoner from a law officer but didn't apply to those who only formed a conspiracy to kill the prospective lynch victim or who seized the intended victim when not under arrest.

83. Neal, *Getting Away with Murder,* 228–29.

84. Two recent books have used the 1916 Waco, Texas, lynching of Jesse Washington as a springboard to explore the causes of lynching, including a "historical memory" of "robust culture of violence," as well as the impact and consequences of this ghastly event on the community in which it occurred. William D. Carrigan, *The Making of a Lynching Culture: Violence and Vigilantism in Central Texas, 1836–1916* (Champaign: University of Illinois Press, 2004); and Patricia Bernstein, *The First Waco Horror: The Lynching of Jesse Washington and the Rise of the NAACP* (College Station: Texas A&M University Press, 2005). For earlier authoritative studies of the causes of vigilantism in Texas see Richard Maxwell Brown, *Strains of Violence: Historical Studies of American Violence and Vigilantism* (New York: Oxford University Press, 1975); Richard Maxwell Brown, "The American Vigilante Tradition," in *Violence in America: Historical and Comparative Perspectives,* ed. Hugh Davis Graham and Ted Robert Gurr (Washington and New York: Frederick A. Praeger, and Government Printing Office, 1969); and Daniel T. Williams, comp., "Amid the Gathering Multitude: The Story of Lynching in America, a Classified Listing," Lynching Files, Tuskegee University Archives, Tuskegee University, Tuskegee, Alabama.

85. As noted in the text, from 1910 to 1916 several unusually gruesome lynchings of blacks (including the sadistic lynching of Jesse Washington in the town of Waco) occurred in a seven-county Central Texas area. (The relatively small seven-county area is located in the center of a large triangle with Dallas at the apex to the north, Houston at the southeast corner, and San Antonio at the

southwest corner.) In each instance the lynchings were cheered on by several thousand white spectators. In William D. Carigan's *The Making of a Lynching Culture* (at pages 183–201), the author argues that the reason the inordinate number of these brutal atrocities happened in that particular part of Texas was due to the region's unique eight-decade-long history of violence. That argument seems suspect, however, since Texans of that time living in all of the state's 254 counties (and not just the seven in Central Texas) were all steeped in a "historical memory" of violence and bloodshed beginning with the Alamo, followed by continuing battles with Indians that lasted from before the Civil War until well into the 1870s, and, of course, the horrible and dehumanizing Civil War itself, followed by the tumultuous and lawless Reconstruction era, plus the racial strife and violence along the Texas-Mexico border, not to mention the violence attributable to a post–Civil War surge of outlaws seeking a safe frontier haven. While the seven-county area may have witnessed an inordinate number of white-on-black lynchings during the 1910–1916 time frame, there was at least as much racial violence and bloodshed along the eight-hundred-plus-mile Rio Grande border during that time. See, for example, Charles H. Harris III and Louis R. Sadler, *The Texas Rangers and the Mexican Revolution: The Bloodiest Decade, 1910–1920* (Albuquerque: University of Mew Mexico Press, 2004). It is therefore contended that the concentration of lynchings of blacks in the seven-county area was not so much because of a recalled "memory of violence" unique to its white inhabitants, but rather because of a combination of that region's demographics, economy, geography, climate, and the time and place of the settlement there.

Another recent book, Cynthia Skove Nevels, *Lynching to Belong: Claiming Whiteness Through Racial Violence* (College Station: Texas A&M University Press, 2007), focuses on the inordinate number of racial lynchings in eleven Texas counties along the Brazos River between Waco and the Gulf of Mexico. She notes that a significant number of eastern and southern European immigrants lived in that area and sought to prove their "whiteness" (and thus become bona fide members of the predominant social and political class) by lynching blacks. However, the author recognizes the complexity of the issue; that no single simple answer suffices. She notes:

> [I]n recent decades . . . historians, sociologists, and literary critics have been pondering a host of explanations for such wide-spread and public [racially motivated] brutality. . . . No single explanation has dominated; lynching is a question that seems to give a different answer depending on who is asking and why they are asking the question. Lynching was about economics. It had strong political overtones. There were psychosexual aspects, social repercussions, cultural meanings. It had religious significance, and it was

about gender. And, always, the immediate reason behind any single lynching was simple contingency: a lethal combination of specific social, political, economic, or religious factors that on a particular day in a particular place exploded into horrific violence.

The author of another recent work, Michael J. Pfeiffer, *Rough Justice: Lynching and American Society, 1874–1947* (Urbana: University of Illinois Press, 2004), argues that lynching was an aspect of a larger cultural war between supporters of mob violence and the advocates of due process.

As demonstrated by the two northwest Texas lynching incidents explored in this book (1896 Wichita Falls and 1916 Seymour), there was certainly an inbred inclination on the part of West Texans of that time to resort to violence in resolving disputes and in bypassing the courthouse in order to mete out swift "frontier justice" to suspected criminal offenders. And there was no shortage of racial discrimination there either.

86. Bernstein, *The First Waco Horror.*
87. Carrigan, *The Making of a Lynching Culture,* 189.
88. Tyler, *The New Handbook of Texas,* 4:346–47.
89. Nathan Miller, *New World Coming: The 1920s and the Making of Modern America* (New York: Scribner, 2003), 292.

CHAPTER THREE: HIGH NOON IN PADUCAH

1. Coombes, *The Prairie Dog Lawyer,* 156.
2. Burk Burnett's family history and his first year in the cattle business are derived from Ron Tyler, ed., "Samuel Burk Burnett." *The New Handbook of Texas,* Vol. 1 (Austin: Texas State Historical Association, 1996), 854–55; Peggy Walker, *George Humphreys: Cowboy and Lawman* (Burnet, TX: Eakin Publications, 1978), 47–51; C. L. Douglas, "Cattle Kings of Texas: Burk Burnett of the Four Sixes," *The Cattleman* (August 1970), 99–102; Meredith Martin, "Gunpowder Justice: The Trial of Samuel Burk Burnett for the Murder of Farley Sayers," in *Tales of Texoma: Episodes in the History of the Red River Border,* ed. Michael L. Collins (Wichita Falls, TX: Midwestern State University Press, 2005), 321–40; and Meredith Richards Martin, "Samuel Burk Burnett: Old 6666" (MA thesis, Midwestern State University, 2002), 10–20.
3. Ed F. Bates, *History and Reminiscences of Denton County* (Denton, TX: McNitzky Printing Co., 1918), 76–77.
4. Kelly, *Wichita County Beginnings,* 54; Lawrence Clayton, *Historic Ranches of Texas* (Austin: University of Texas Press, 1993), 19; Martin, "Samuel Burk Burnett: Old 6666," 17–18.
5. Jack Walker, "Four Sixes," *Texas Parade,* Vol. XVI (July 1955), 37.
6. Ibid.

7. Joseph G. McCoy, *Historic Sketches of the Cattle Trade of the Southwest* (Kansas City: Ramsey, Millitt, and Hudson, 1874. Reprint: Washington: The Rare Book Shop, 1932), 227–30; C. L. Douglas, *Cattle Kings of Texas* (Fort Worth: Branch-Smith, 1939), 351.

8. Eugene C. Barker and E. W. Winkler, eds., Vol. V, by Frank W. Johnson, *A History of Texas and Texans* (Chicago: American Historical Society, 1914), 2565.

9. Ernest Emory Bailey, ed., *Texas Historical and Biographical Record* (Austin: Texas Historical and Biographical Record, 1939/1940?), 94; James Cox, *Historical and Biographical Record of the Cattle Industry and the Cattlemen of Texas and Adjacent Territory* (St. Louis: Woodward and Tieran Printing Co., 1895), 532; Martin, "Samuel Burk Burnett: Old 6666," 29–30. The present-day town of Burkburnett, located between Wichita Falls and the Oklahoma border, lies within the ranch. It was originally named "Nesterville."

10. William T. Hagan, *United States Comanche Relations: The Reservation Years* (New Haven: Yale University Press, 1976), 151.

11. Bill Neeley, *The Last Comanche Chief: The Life and Times of Quanah Parker* (New York: John Wiley & Sons, 1995), 190.

12. Morgan, *The History of Wichita Falls*, 47; Neeley, *The Last Comanche Chief*, 197, 199; Gary Cartwright, "Showdown at Waggoner Ranch," *Texas Monthly* (January 2004), 80–81.

13. Neeley, *The Last Comanche Chief*, 197–98; George W. Briggs interviewed by Eunice M. Mayer, June 17, 1937, Granite, Oklahoma, Indian-Pioneer papers, Western History Collections, University of Oklahoma, Vol. 11, p. 173; Douglas, *Cattle Kings of Texas*, 354–55.

14. Mack Williams, *In Old Fort Worth*, "Burk Burnett: Giant of the Frontier," *The News Tribune*, 1977 (Archive Collections, Fort Worth Public Library, Fort Worth, Texas), 68; Terry J. Powell, *Samuel Burk Burnett: A Sketch* (Fort Worth: Graves and Graves, 1916), 1; Zoe A. Tilghman, *Quanah: The Eagle of the Comanches* (Oklahoma City: Harlow Publishing Corp., 1938), 117, 127–28, 160–61; Martin, "Samuel Burk Burnett: Old 6666," 45.

15. Neeley, *The Last Comanche Chief*, 194.

16. Lewis Nordyke, *Great Roundup: The Story of Texas and Southwestern Cowmen* (New York: William Morrow & Co., 1955), 198–200.

17. Cartwright, "Showdown at Waggoner Ranch," 80–81.

18. Ibid. See also John R. Abernathy, *Catch 'Em Alive Jack: The Life and Adventures of an American Pioneer* (New York: Association Press, 1936).

19. Wyman Meinzer and Henry Chappell, *6666: Portrait of a Texas Ranch* (Lubbock: Texas Tech University Press, 2004); Tyler, "Samuel Burk Burnett," *The New Handbook of Texas*, Vol. 1, 855; Martin, "Samuel Burk Burnett: Old 6666," 58–59.

20. Once toward the end of his life, Burk Burnett traveled to Chicago to consult a medical specialist. Two acquaintances were staying at the same hotel, and they noticed that when mealtimes came, Burk would leave the fine hotel where they were lodged and walk down side streets to eat in cheap cafes. Finally, one worked up enough nerve to question him about it: "Here you are one of the richest men in Texas . . . yet at mealtime you go out in sleety blizzard, down a back street to save six bits . . . why?" Burk replied, "I don't need to save money, but I began saving it when I thought I had to save. I wanted to make more money. I got into the habit of saving. . . . The habit stayed with me. . . . I guess it'll hang on till I die." J. Frank Dobie, *Cow People* (Boston: Little, Brown & Co., 1964), 52.

21. Tyler, "Mary Couts Burnett," *The New Handbook of Texas,* Vol. 1, 853; Colby D. Hall, *History of Texas Christian University: A College of the Cattle Frontier* (Fort Worth: Texas Christian University Press, 1947), 186–87.

22. Probate Records, Probate Office of Tarrant County, Texas, *The Estate of Samuel Burk Burnett,* text-fiche, Paragraph 3, Page 3 of "Last Will and Testament," Cause No. 7594, executed on November 24, 1921, filed for probate on July 5, 1922. Arguably, even Burk's rather modest gift to his son (a $25,000 annual allowance for Tom's life out of Burk's $6 million estate) was granted with an ulterior and selfish motive. The will also contained a standard "no contest" clause that provided that should any beneficiary of the will contest its validity and lose, then that beneficiary would forfeit any gift he would have otherwise received under the will. Hence, if Tom contested the will and lost, he would forfeit his annual $25,000 allowance. In view of that, the rather modest testamentary gift to Tom might well be interpreted as a mere insurance premium Burk paid to insure that Tom would not attempt to thwart Burk's postmortem plan. On the other hand, he cut his wife, Mary, completely out of the will, most likely thinking that since he had succeeded in having her declared legally insane, she would be no threat. In this, however, Burk miscalculated. When, immediately after Burk's death, she escaped from her confinement and then succeeded in having her "legal insanity" status reversed, the "no contest" clause presented no impediment to her challenging the validity of the will. Since she was cut completely out of Burk's will, she had nothing to lose by filing a will contest suit, and a lot to gain.

23. *Fort Worth Daily Democrat,* June 8, 1879.

24. *State of Texas vs. S. B. Burnett,* Cause No. 166, Clay County, Texas, District Court.

25. *The Paducah Post,* November 30, 1911; Coombes, *The Prairie Dog Lawyer,* 166.

26. Morris, *A Private in the Texas Rangers,* 93–94, 154, 160. While the big ranchers strongly disapproved of loose branding practices by nesters and small ranchers,

at least some, nevertheless, were not above engaging in a little loose branding themselves when it suited their purposes—as well as otherwise intimidating and starving out the unwanted small folks. Millie Jones Porter, *Memory Cups of Panhandle Pioneers* (Clarendon, TX: Clarendon Press, 1945), 521–25. See also Philip Ashton Rollins, *The Cowboy: An Unconventional History of Civilization on the Old-Time Cattle Range* (Norman: University of Oklahoma Press, 1997), 330–55.

27. R. K. DeArment, "The Gunfights of Pioneer Cattleman: Burk Burnett," *Wild West* (August 2005), 32–33.

28. Coombes, *The Prairie Dog Lawyer*, 153–54.

29. Ibid.

30. George Humphreys, interview by Charles Townsend, July 9, 1969; Tape 1, Southwest Collections/Special Collections Library, Texas Tech University, Lubbock, Texas.

31. A. C. "Arb" Piper and Waylon "Toar" Piper, interview by Bill Neal, Paducah, Texas, October 1, 1999, and December 5, 1999. (Recorded tapes of the interview in possession of the author.) At the time of the interview, A. C. was eighty-five years old and Waylon was seventy-eight. For a detailed discussion of the various methods employed by frontier rustlers to separate unbranded calves from the mother cows, wean, and subsequently steal and brand them, see J. Evetts Haley, *The XIT Ranch of Texas—and the Early Days of Llano Estacado* (Norman: University of Oklahoma Press, 1953), 105–9.

32. Coombes, *The Prairie Dog Lawyer*, 154–155.

33. A. C. Piper, interview by Bill Neal.

34. *State of Texas v. Farley P. Sayers*, Cause No. 50 in King County District Court, and Cause No. 563 in Knox County District Court on a change of venue. (Theft of four unbranded calves from S. B. Burnett.)

35. Coombes, *The Prairie Dog Lawyer*, 156.

36. Ibid, 158.

37. George Humphreys, interview by Charles Townsend. Humphreys says that Sheriff McCarren witnessed Sayers show up at his box canyon corral one evening about dusk and pitch grass hay over the fence for the calves. This would have been another incriminating strand of circumstantial evidence pointing to Sayers's guilt. Coombes, Farley's lawyer at the trial, does not report that testimony to this effect was introduced. Of course, Coombes was representing Farley and may have been biased in favor of Farley. On the other hand, Coombes was present at the trial, and Humphreys's account had to be hearsay since the trial occurred in 1908 and Humphreys didn't begin working for the 6666s until 1918. Another interesting point: Humphreys says that there were ten or twelve unbranded calves discovered in Farley's box canyon corral, and that *all* of the calves "mammied up" with the 6666 cows. However, when Farley Sayers and

Roy Berry were indicted for the theft, the indictment charged them with the theft of only *four* calves. In Coombes's account of the trial, he relates that some of the calves did *not* "mammy up" with the 6666 cows. Such inconsistency leads to the conjecture that although there may have been ten or twelve unbranded calves in Farley's canyon corral, only four of the calves actually "mammied up" with Burk's cows. Another intriguing and unanswered question is this: exactly what role was 6666 cowboy Roy Berry (Farley Sayers's co-defendant) alleged to have played in the theft? In the end, however, these issues didn't matter that much. It is obvious to any impartial observer (on the basis of the record itself) that Sayers really did steal the calves. Coombes himself admits as much when he opens his account of the calf theft trial by stating that he defeated the case against Sayers by trial tactics. (Coombes: "The theft case against Sayers was defeated by strategy.") Coombes, *The Prairie Dog Lawyer,* 157.

38. Coombes, *The Prairie Dog Lawyer,* 159–66.

39. Ibid.

40. Ibid.

41. *Graves v. State,* 124 S.W. 676, 679 (Tex.Ct.Crim.App. 1910).

42. Ibid.

43. The applicable penal statute in effect then, *Article 713, White's Ann.Pen.Code,* provided: "When a defendant accused of murder seeks to justify himself on the ground of threats against his own life, he may be permitted to introduce evidence of the threats made, but the same shall not be regarded as affording a justification for the offense unless it be shown that at the time of the homicide the person killed by some act then done manifested an intention to execute the threat so made."

44. Coombes, *The Prairie Dog Lawyer,* 162; see also J. W. Williams, *The Big Ranch Country* (Wichita Falls, TX: Nortex Offset Publication, 1971), 25–36.

45. Ibid.

46. Ibid.

47. Ibid.

48. Ibid.

49. Ibid, 166–167. In addition to Coombes's account of the killing, also see *The Paducah Post,* November 30, 1911; and Carmen Taylor Bennet, *Our Roots Grow Deep—A History of Cottle County* (Floydada, TX: Blanco Offset Printing, 1970), 34–35.

50. *State of Texas v. Farley P. Sayers,* Cause No. 132, King County District Court; and on change of venue, Cause No. 1071, Baylor County District Court (murder of his brother, J. D. Sayers).

51. Mary Anna Renfro Kearby, ed., North Texas Genealogical Assn., *Pioneers Remember the Past* (Wichita Falls, TX: Nortex Offset Press, 1998), 310–11.

52. See a full account of the dugout encounter in Chapter One: "Duel of the Lawmen."

53. The story of Lewis's and Crawford's ill-fated Wichita Falls bank robbery, their doomed escape attempt, and their lynching has been compiled from the following sources: *The Fort Worth Gazette*, February 26, 27, 28, March 3, and April 29, 1896; *The Dallas Morning News*, February 27, 28, and May 9, 1896; *The Dallas Semi-Weekly News*, February 28 and March 3, 1896; *Wichita Times*, February 27, 28, and March 21, 1896; *The Wichita Daily Times*, April 9, 1908; March 21, 1920; March 21, 1949; March 5, 1950; June 10, 17, 24, and July 1, 1951; *The Wichita Falls Record News*, March 21, 1944; Kelly, *Wichita County Beginnings*, 43–45; Morgan, *The History of Wichita Falls*, 87–90.

54. A. C. Piper, interview by Bill Neal.

55. Frank McAuley, interview by Bill Neal, Knox City, Texas, July 23, 1999. (Interview notes in author's file.) Tom Pickett served as commissioner of Precinct No. 3 in King County, Texas, from 1920 until 1932 when he was defeated by C. L. "Charlie" Dowding, who then held the post from 1932 until 1958. King County Historical Society, *King County—Windmills & Barbed Wire* (Quanah, TX: Nortex Press, 1976), 11.

56. Stanton Brown, interview by Bill Neal, Benjamin, Texas, July 14, 1999, and September 15, 1999. (Interview notes in author's file.)

57. Frank McAuley, interview by Bill Neal.

58. A. C. Piper and Waylon "Toar" Piper interview, October 1, 1999. Both A. C. Piper and Toar Piper stressed that all those events happened a number of years before they began work for the Four Sixes, and what they related in the interview (except for actual conversations A. C. had with Tom Pickett) was based on ranch stories passed down to them plus their general knowledge of those earlier times. They also stressed that all the 6666 ranch managers they worked under were honest, fair, and well-respected cowmen.

59. George Humphreys, interview by Charles Townsend. Humphreys began cowboying for the Four Sixes in 1918 and worked his way up the ladder until he was named ranch manager, a position he held until his retirement in 1970. He also served as sheriff of King County from 1928 through 1948. Peggy Walker, *George Humphreys: Cowboy and Lawman* (Burnet, TX: Eakin Publications, 1978). Another old-time cowpuncher, Elmer Petty, quoted by C. Warren, later recalled the same incident. *Hudspeth County* [Texas] *Herald—Dell Valley Review*, November 27, 1987.

60. George Humphreys, interview by Charles Townsend.

61. Ibid.

62. Ibid.

63. *The Paducah Post*, May 30, 1912 (emphasis added); Carmen Taylor Bennett,

Our Roots Grow Deep—A History of Cottle County (Floydada, TX: Blanco Offset Printing, 1970), 34–35.

64. Clifford Bartlett Jones, interview by David B. Garey II, February 2, March 27, May 15, and June 23, 1968; April 18 and July 10, 1970; February 16, 1971; Southwest Collections/Special Collections Library, Texas Tech University, Lubbock, Texas.

65. *Fort Worth Record*, May 25, 1912.

66. *State of Texas v. S. B. Burnett,* Cause No. 480, Cottle County District Court, and, on change of venue, Cause No. 1100, Baylor County District Court. *State of Texas v. R. T. (Tom) Pickett,* Cause No. 481, Cottle County District Court, and, on change of venue, Cause No. 1099, Baylor County District Court.

67. *The Baylor County Banner,* September 25, 1941; Coombes, *The Prairie Dog Lawyer,* 250. Judge Dickson's father, Robert T. Dickson, was a surgeon in the Confederate army during the Civil War, and three of Judge Dickson's older brothers were killed during that conflict. In 1879, at age twenty, Dickson began his law enforcement career as a deputy sheriff of Young County at Graham, Texas. He then moved to Seymour in 1883 and became a deputy sheriff of Baylor County when it was the westernmost organized county on the northwest Texas frontier. All fifteen of the unorganized counties from Seymour westward to the New Mexico border were attached to Baylor County for judicial and law enforcement purposes, so Deputy Dickson ranged far and wide in those wild and virtually lawless days. Once during this time, Dickson found himself ensnared in the mesh of the criminal justice system. He, together with his brothers, Robert T. Dickson and J. P. Dickson, were indicted by a Baylor County grand jury, all accused of murdering Robert Webb on December 8, 1885, by shooting him with a pistol. Although the criminal file on Judge Dickson's murder case is mysteriously missing from the Baylor County District Court files, the official minutes of the court reflect that all three men were tried before juries in Baylor County and acquitted of the murder charge. *State of Texas v. Jo A. P. Dickson,* Cause No. 263, Baylor County District Court.

68. *The Baylor County Banner,* April 3, 1941. (Obituary of Judge Jo A. P. Dickson.)

69. Tom Craddock, interview by Joe Gibson, Seymour, Texas, August 9, 1971, Reel 1, Southwest Collections/Special Collections Library, Texas Tech University, Lubbock, Texas.

70. J. F. Cunningham, Jr., was wounded during a March 20, 1917, murder trial in the Knox County District Court in Benjamin, Texas, during a wild courtroom shootout wherein his murder defendant client, George Douglas, was killed.

71. The story of Burk Burnett's murder trial for the killing of Farley Sayers has been compiled from the following sources: the official records in the *State v. S. B. Burnett,* No. 1100, Baylor County District Court; *The Baylor County Ban-*

ner, July 25 and August 1, 1913; *Paducah Post,* July 24, 1913; *Fort Worth Star-Telegram,* July 21, 22, 23, 24, and 25, 1913; *Wichita Daily Times,* July 21, 22, 23, 24, and 25, 1913; Jack Jones, "Museum News," *The Baylor County Banner,* July 28, August 4, 11, 18, 25, and September 1, 15, 1988.

72. Notables listed by *The Baylor County Banner* who were in town for Burk Burnett's murder trial included W. F. Connell, Fort Worth banker and one of the wealthiest cattlemen in Texas; Marion Samson and Dan S. Bellows of the Cassidy-Southwestern Commission Co. of Fort Worth; also from Fort Worth, F. J. Meehan, broker and feeder, Judge J. A. Matthews, banker, and H. P Branham, banker; L. F. Wilson, Kansas City cattleman; A. H. Britain and J. T. Montgomery, Wichita Falls attorneys; Gene Mayfield, ranchman of Abilene; W. R. Moore, ranchman; W. M. Moore, attorney of Benjamin; the following from King County: County Judge J. H. Lynn; County Clerk Bud Arnett of the 8 Ranch; J. N. Parramore, cattleman; L. P. Hunsley; J. M. Patterson; H. V. Scott; Dee Hight; C. E. Herndon; J. A. Christian, hardware man; W. L. McLaren, former sheriff; George Martin, ex-sheriff and ranchman; Doug Davidson and Joe Crystal of Guthrie; J. M. Jackson, manager of the Matador Ranch in Motley County; and Harry Daugherty, president of the First National Bank of Jacksboro. Other notables subpoenaed as witnesses for Burk Burnett included J. W. Anderson, Dickens County deputy sheriff; J. L. Backus, Cottle County sheriff; J. M. Barron, Paducah, a cattle inspector; Prince Bowman, Cottle County banker; W. S. Britton, Knox County sheriff; J. R. Christal, Denton, banker; W. D. Davis, ex-mayor of Fort Worth; W. N. Coombes, Dallas lawyer; Ed Harrington, ex-sheriff of King County; Green Harrison, Jayton lawyer; J. M. Hawkins, Cottle County lawyer; Tonk Humphreys, King County sheriff; John J. Richards, Cottle County banker; T. J. Richards, Cottle County cattleman; A. H. Sams, Benjamin banker; Tom Snow, Fort Worth police officer; Ab Stigh, Fort Worth police officer; Fred Surter, Stonewall County sheriff; Joe Swint, Cottle County justice of the peace; John Tullis, Quanah cowman; Amos and Arnett West, Brownwood cattlemen; James M. Whatley, Paducah lawyer, and others.

73. Coombes, *The Prairie Dog Lawyer,* 168.

74. *Fort Worth Star-Telegram,* July 23, 1913.

75. Ibid.

76. Richard Maxwell Brown, *No Duty to Retreat—Violence and Values in American History and Society* (New York: Oxford University Press, 1991), Preface.

77. *Brown v. United States,* 256 U.S. 335 (1921).

78. Quoted in Mark DeWolfe Howe, ed., *Holmes-Laski Letters: The Correspondence of Mr. Justice Holmes and Harold J. Laske, 1916–1935* (2 vols.; Cambridge: Harvard University Press, 1953), I:335–36. See also Thomas J. Kernan, "The Jurisprudence of Lawlessness," *American Bar Association Report* (1906), 451–53, quoted

in Edward L. Ayers, *Vengeance & Justice: Crime and Punishment in the 19th-Century American South* (New York: Oxford University Press, 1984), 342–43.

79. Sections 9.31 and 9.32, *Texas Penal Code*, before the 2007 amendment.

80. Sections 9.31 and 9.32, *Texas Penal Code*, after the 2007 amendment.

81. Tom Craddock, interview by Joe Gibson, Seymour, Texas, August 9, 1971, Reel 1, Southwest Collections/Special Collections Library, Texas Tech University, Lubbock, Texas.

82. *The Baylor County Banner*, August 1, 1913; *Rosa E. Sayers, et al. v. S. B. Burnett*, Cause No. 419, District Court of Cottle County, Texas. Farley Sayers's widow, Rosa Sayers, on behalf of herself and her minor children, sued Burk Burnett in a civil wrongful death suit for damages resulting from the killing of her husband. The parties settled the suit before trial for the sum of $8,000.00.

83. Jack Jones, "Museum News," *The Baylor County Banner*, September 15, 1988.

84. *The Paducah Post*, May 30, 1912; *The Baylor County Banner*, August 1, 1913.

85. Coombes; *The Prairie Dog Lawyer*, 169.

86. A. C. Piper, interview by Bill Neal.

87. King County Historical Society, *King County—Windmills and Barbed Wire*, 311–12.

88. George Humhreys, interview by Charles Townsend.

89. Section 7.02 (a) (2), *Texas Penal Code*.

90. George Humphreys, interview by Charles Townsend.

91. Frank McCauley, interview by Bill Neal.

92. C. M. Randall, interview by Joe D. Gibson, Seymour, Texas, August 4, 1971, Reels 1–3, Southwest Collections/Special Collections Library, Texas Tech University, Lubbock, Texas.

93. Bennett, *Our Roots Grow Deep*, 34.

94. Clifford Bartlett Jones, interview by David B. Garey II.

95. Story written by C. Warren entitled "Crow Flat," appearing on page 4 in the November 27, 1987, issue of *The Hudspeth County Herald—Dell Valley Review*.

96. A. C. Piper, interview by Bill Neal. During the author's interview with Frank McAuley, Knox City, Texas, July 14, 1999, McAuley recalled that when Tom Pickett was on his deathbed, he became mightily concerned about the fate of his soul. He once begged McAuley's uncle, Charlie Dowding, his old King County nemesis, to pray for the forgiveness of his sins—in response to which Dowding shrugged and said: "Aw, hell, Tom, I don't reckon my prayers would get no higher than the ceiling of this room."

CHAPTER FOUR: THE RETURN OF HILL LOFTIS—AS TOM ROSS

1. *State of Texas v. Hill Loftis*, Cause No. 901, 46th Judicial District Court of Wilbarger County, Texas.

2. C. L. Sonnichsen, *I'll Die Before I'll Run: The Story of the Great Feuds of Texas*, reprint (Lincoln: University of Nebraska Press, 1988), 119. The Texas Rangers first published their "Book of Knaves" in 1877 and it was distributed to all ranger captains. By Hill Loftis's time it contained the names and descriptions of about three thousand wanted desperadoes.

3. James I. Fenton, "Tom Ross: Outlaw and Stockman" (Unpublished MA thesis, University of Texas at El Paso, 1979), 2. In his exhaustive and well-researched thesis, Fenton gives the following background on the Loftis family:

> Hillary Loftis's roots go back to the Carolinas in the early 1700's when a distant relative bought land there and began farming. Meager information indicates that the early Loftis family was a family of adequate wealth but of limited education, one having several Negro slaves to bequeath at his death though he was unable to sign the will with anything but an 'X.' The Loftises' story is a familiar one in that as they depleted their lands by planting successive crops, probably cotton, they moved progressively west. By the late 1800s Madison D. Loftis, Hillary's paternal grandfather, had settled in northwestern Alabama's Lamar County, where he seems to have prospered to a degree. Married to the former Susannah York, Madison sired nine children, the eldest of which was Samuel (sometimes called Lemuel) Jameson, who was born in 1827. Samuel served in the Confederate Army during the Civil War as a private in Company E, Twenty-Fifth Alabama Regiment, and was captured by Union forces on November 22, 1863, at Missionary Ridge in Tennessee. He married the former Jane Montgomery, and they had six children born in this order: Emelie (the only girl), Jerome, John, Hillary (born in 1872), Tom and Rod. See Mrs. Jim Dolph Hill to J. I. Fenton, letter, October 30, 1978, Aberdeen, Mississippi, and Confederate Military Service Record of Samuel Jameson Loftis, Dept. of Archives and History, Montgomery, Alabama.

4. *Lovington* [New Mexico] *Leader*, June 29, 1931.

5. Ibid. For more on the history and development of the Waggoner Ranch, see *Vernon* [Texas] *Daily Record*, July 4, 1976, Bicentennial Edition; and John Hendrix, *If I Can Do It Horseback* (Austin: University of Texas Press, 1964), 84–93.

6. Sterling, *Trails and Trials of a Texas Ranger*, 377; Owen, *Byrd Cochrain of Dead Man's Corner*, 43.

7. *Vernon Daily Record*, July 4, 1976; Hendrix, *If I Can Do It Horseback*, 84–93; Bill O'Neal, *Historic Ranches of the West* (Austin: Eakin Press, 1997), 62–63.

8. *St. Louis Post-Dispatch*, July 15, 1923.

9. Walter Prescott Webb, *The Texas Rangers: A Century of Frontier Defense*, 2nd ed. (Austin: University of Texas Press, 1935), 319.

10. Fenton, "Tom Ross: Outlaw and Stockman," 12.

11. Owen, *Byrd Cochrain of Dead Man's Corner,* 23.

12. Raymond Adams, *The Old-Time Cowhand* (New York: Collier Books, 1948), 165; Rollins, *The Cowboy: An Unconventional History of Civilization,* 330–45.

13. *St. Louis Post-Dispatch,* July 15, 1923.

14. Karen Holliday Tanner and John D. Tanner, Jr., *Last of the Old-Time Outlaws: The George West Musgrave Story* (Norman: University of Oklahoma Press, 2002), 153–55; Jeff Burton, *Dynamite and Six-Shooter* (Santa Fe: Palomino Press, 1970), 69.

15. Gaines County Historical Survey Committee, *The Gaines County Story* (Seagraves, TX: Pioneer Book Publishers, 1974), 16. In his subsequent murder trial, Tom Ross testified that in 1902 he filed on three sections of state land and "lived it out." The standard size of a section of land in Texas is 640 acres. Ross's testimony quoted in the *Dallas Morning News,* June 24, 1923.

16. Floyd Miller, *Bill Tilghman: Marshall of the Last Frontier* (Garden City, NY: Doubleday & Co., 1968), 124.

17. Marriage License Records, December 1903 and January 1904 (Vol. 1, p. 20, Martin County Courthouse, Stanton, Texas).

18. "Texas Ranger Papers." Captain John H. Rogers, Monthly Returns, Company C, June 1904, File 2-14, Box 88, Folder 1, Archives Division, Texas State Library, Austin.

19. Fay Eidson Smithson and Pat Wilkinson Hull, eds., *Martin County: The First Thirty Years* (Hereford, TX: Pioneer Book Publishers, 1970), 15–16.

20. "Texas Ranger Papers," Captain Rogers's Monthly Returns, June 1904, Folder 1, State Archives, Austin.

21. Paul N. Spellman, *Captain John H. Rogers, Texas Ranger* (Denton, TX: University of North Texas Press, 2003), 126–29.

22. Fenton, "Tom Ross: Ranger Nemesis," 20.

23. *Texas v. Hill Loftis,* Cause No. 901, 46th Judicial District Court of Wilbarger County, Texas.

24. Ibid.

25. Fenton, "Tom Ross: Outlaw and Stockman," 70.

26. *Fort Worth Star-Telegram,* June 17, 1923.

27. Mary Whatley Clarke, "Bad Man . . . Good Man?" *The Cattleman* (magazine) (December 1971), 43–66.

28. The venerated cow country story-teller J. Frank Dobie even went so far as to describe Tom Ross's marksmanship as follows: "[Ross could] . . . ride a horse at full speed along a fence, hitting every post center." J. Frank Dobie, *Cow People* (Boston: Little, Brown and Co., 1964), 247.

29. Clarke, "Bad Man . . . Good Man?" 43–66.

30. Fenton, "Tom Ross: Outlaw and Stockman," 76.

31. S. E. Ledger, First Baptist Church of Seminole, Texas, April 14, 1913, 83.

32. Hunter Irwin, interview by J. Evetts Haley, Andrews County, November 18, 1936. (Courtesy of the Nita Stewart Haley Memorial Library and the J. Evetts Haley History Center, Midland, Texas.)

33. Post Office Records, Tom Ross's application for a post office, National Archives, Industrial and Social Branch, January 15, 1908.

34. Fenton, "Tom Ross: Outlaw and Stockman," 62–63.

35. *State v. Tom Ross,* Cause No. 79, 106th Judicial District Court of Gaines County, Texas, filed July 24, 1906; *State v. Tom Ross,* Cause No. 21, 106th Judicial District Court of Gaines County, filed May 15, 1908; *State v. Tom Ross,* Cause No. 47, 106th Judicial District Court of Gaines County, filed January 1, 1920.

36. *Carlsbad* [New Mexico] *Argus,* January 31, 1913.

37. *State v. Tom Ross,* Cause Nos. 969 and 970 in the 5th District Court of Eddy County in Carlsbad, New Mexico.

38. James B. McGhee, *Happenings In and Around New Mexico Courts, 1909 to January 1, 1947, Plus an Early One in Texas* (unpublished manuscript), 8–9; Fenton, "Tom Ross: Outlaw and Stockman," 73–75.

39. *E. P. Bujac v. Tom Ross,* Cause No. 1976 in the District Court of Eddy County, Carlsbad, New Mexico, filed April 29, 1914.

40. McGhee, *Happenings in New Mexico Courts,* 9; Fenton, "Tom Ross: Outlaw and Stockman," 73–74.

41. *Lovington Leader,* February 8, 1929; Fenton, "Tom Ross: Outlaw and Stockman," 68–69, 148.

42. The story of the 1912 Seminole bank robbery has been compiled from the following sources: *The Lovington* [New Mexico] *Leader,* February 16, 1912; *The Seminole* [Texas] *Sentinel,* February 17, 1912; *The Lubbock* [Texas] *Avalanche,* February 22 and 29, 1912; and from a paper entitled "A Bank Robbery in a Sandstorm" presented by Jim Fenton to the West Texas Historical Association's annual meeting on March 31, 2006, at Lubbock, Texas. (Manuscript in possession of Jim Fenton, Lubbock, Texas).

43. *St. Louis Post-Dispatch,* July 22, 1923; *The Cattleman,* July, 1922.

44. Most of the background and biographical information on Dave Allison has been taken from Bob Alexander, *Fearless Dave Allison: Border Lawman* (Silver City, NM: High-Lonesome Books, 2003).

45. *St. Louis Post-Dispatch,* July 22, 1923.

46. Thomas H. Rynning, *Gun Notches—A Saga of Frontier Lawman Captain Thomas H. Rynning as Told to Al Cohn and Joe Chisholm* (San Diego: Frontier Heritage Press, 1971), 293; Alexander, *Fearless Dave Allison,* 53.

47. Ex-Midland County Sheriff W. H. "Bob" Beverly, interview by J. Evetts Haley, Midland, Texas, March 24, 1945. (Courtesy of the Nita Stewart Haley Memorial Library and the J. Evetts Haley History Center.)

48. Alexander, *Fearless Dave Allison,* 263–65.

49. Benjamin Heber Johnson, *Revolution in Texas: How a Forgotten Rebellion and Its Bloody Suppression Turned Mexicans into Americans* (New Haven, CT: Yale University Press, 2003), 131–32.

50. *State v. John A. Morine, et al.* (including Dave Allison and nine other named defendants), Cause No. 35 in the 34th Judicial District Court of Culberson County, Texas.

51. *St. Louis Post-Dispatch,* July 22, 1923; *Dallas Morning News,* June 24, 1923.

52. Alexander, *Fearless Dave Allison,* 184–204.

53. Martin Blumanson, *The Patton Papers, 1885–1940* (New York: DaCapo Press, 1998), 298.

54. Most of the background and biographical information on H. L. Roberson has been taken from a sketch contained in Alexander, *Lawmen, Outlaws, and S.O.Bs.,* 221–35.

55. *St. Louis Post-Dispatch,* July 22, 1923.

56. Alexander, *Lawmen, Outlaws and S.O.Bs.,* 222–23.

57. *San Antonio Express,* April 4, 1923.

58. Hughes to AG, December 4, 1911, Walter Prescott Webb Collection, University of Texas, Austin, Texas; Alexander, *Lawmen, Outlaws and S.O.Bs.,* 223.

59. *Alpine Avalanche,* July 2, 1914; Texas Rangers Monthly Report, Co. A, June 30, 1914, AGC; Proceedings of the Investigation of the State Rangers Force, 164.

60. Alexander, *Lawman, Outlaws and S.O.Bs.,* 224.

61. Accounts of the 1915 killing of Foote Boykin and Walter Sitter by H. L. Roberson and the four subsequent murder trials are taken from the following sources: *Roberson v. State of Texas,* 203 S. W. 349 (Tex.Ct.Crim.App., 1917); *El Paso Morning Times,* January 17, 20, November 30, December 2, 3, 4, and 5, 1915; Warren Colquitt, "Beating the Rap," *Paso del Norte* (magazine) (June 1985), 8–12 (courtesy of the J. Evetts Haley Collection and the Haley Memorial Library and History Center); Alexander, *Lawmen, Outlaws and S.O.Bs.,* 221–39.

62. *State of Texas v. H. L. Roberson,* Cause No. 6743 in 34th Judicial District Court of El Paso County, Texas, alleging the murder of Foote Boykin; and *State of Texas v. H. L. Roberson,* Cause No. 6744 in 34th Judicial District Court of El Paso County, Texas, alleging the murder of Walter Sitter.

63. Brown, *No Duty to Retreat,* 26–28, 34.

64. *El Paso Morning Times,* January 20 and December 3, 1915.

65. When the accused puts his reputation in issue by introducing evidence of his good reputation (for any specific character trait), the basis of the knowledge of the witness can be tested on cross-examination through the use of "have you heard" questions. *Rutledge v. State,* 749 S.W.2d 50 (Tex.Cr.App. 1988). In a frog's hair distinction making little sense to anyone except an appellate court, it has been held to be reversible error for the prosecutor to frame his question as "*Did*

you know that . . ." rather than *"Have you heard* that . . ." Rationale being that the "have you heard" question merely tests the basis of the reputation witness's belief that the accused's reputation is good, while a "did you know" question has been held to be improper because the prosecutor thus "asserts the truth of the matter inquired about." Incidentally, even when the question is properly framed, the state must ask that question in good faith and base it on some reliable information that the accused did, in fact, commit the act of misconduct inquired about. For a prosecutor to simply manufacture some terrible act of violence, for example, and use it as the basis of a "have you heard" question would not only subject the prosecutor to a contempt of court sanction, but also would probably result in a reversal of his conviction. When a prosecutor does ask a reputation witness a "have you heard" question based on some alleged incident of misconduct on the part of the defendant, then the defense counsel is entitled to open the prosecutor's file and review his notes and materials to test the prosecutor's good faith belief that such incident did occur. *Texas Rules of Evidence 615.*

66. *Roberson v. State,* 203 S.W. 349, 354 (Tex.Ct.Crim.App. 1918).

67. *El Paso Morning Times,* December 19, 1915, April 23, 1916, and June 17, 1916; Charles H. Harris III and Louis R. Sadler, *The Texas Rangers and the Mexican Revolution* (Albuquerque: University of New Mexico Press, 2004), 456–57.

68. *Roberson v. State,* 203 S.W. 349, 354.

69. *State of Texas v. H. L. Roberson,* Cause No. 18,002 in the District Court of Travis County, Texas.

70. Enlistment, Oath of Service, and Description Ranger Force, H. L. Roberson. May 8, 1916. Special notation, "Cattle Raisers Assn." Texas State Library and Archives Commission, Austin, Texas; Alexander, *Lawmen, Outlaws and S.O.Bs.,* 233.

71. W. M. "Bob" Beverly, interview by J. Evetts Haley.

72. Interview of S. T. "Davy" Burk by J. Evetts Haley, Kermit, Texas, December 16, 1962. (Courtesy of the Nita Stewart Haley Memorial Library and the J. Evetts Haley History Center.)

73. *State v. J. N. Ballard,* Cause No. 119 in the District Court of Motley County, Texas (on a change of venue from Dickens County, Texas), and on appeal, *Ballard v. State,* 160 S.W. 92 (Tex.Ct.Crim.App., 1913); and *State v. John Law,* No. 120 in the District Court of Motley County, Texas (on a change of venue from Dickens County, Texas), and on appeal, *Law v. State,* 160 S.W. 98 (Tex.Ct.Crim. App., 1913).

74. John R. Erickson, *Prairie Gothic: The Story of a West Texas Family* (Denton, TX: University of North Texas Press, 2005), 53.

75. For excellent biographical sketches of the four players in the upcoming drama

(Dave Allison, H. L. Roberson, Tom Ross, and Milt Good) see R. K. DeArment, "Bloody Easter," *Old West* (magazine), Vol. 30, No. 3 (Spring 1994).

76. C. L. Sonnichsen, *Tularosa—Last of the Frontier West* (Albuquerque: University of New Mexico Press, 1960), 18. Sonnichsen commented: "John and his brother Isham [Good] had been close to trouble some time. In the lonesome limestone hills west of Austin they were well, if not favorably, known. There they held their own with the rough characters that haunted the cedar brakes and periodically blasted each other into eternity."

77. Ibid. Walter Good was killed and his body left in New Mexico's White Sands, allegedly as payback for the death of Oliver Lee's close friend, George McDonald. See also Alexander, *Fearless Dave Allison*, 225, 237.

78. Milt Good, *Twelve Years in a Texas Prison* (Amarillo: Russell Stationery Company, 1935), 8–10; Alexander, *Fearless Dave Allison*, 225, 237.

79. Alexander, *Fearless Dave Allison*, 224.

80. *The Cattleman*, July 1922.

81. Ibid; *St. Louis Post-Dispatch*, July 22, 1923; *The Abilene Daily Reporter*, September 19, 1923; Alexander, *Fearless Dave Allison*, 225–30.

82. W. M. "Bob" Beverly interview by J. Evetts Haley; DeArment, "Bloody Easter."

83. *St. Louis Post-Dispatch*, July 29, 1923; *The Abilene Daily Reporter*, September 12, 1923; *The Seminole Sentinel*, April 5, 1923; Alexander, *Fearless Dave Allison*, 230.

84. Fenton, "Tom Ross: Outlaw and Stockman," 89; *The Cattleman*, July 1922; *St. Louis Post-Dispatch*, July 29, 1923.

85. *Roswell* [New Mexico] *Record*, April 2, 1923. See also, *Carlsbad* [New Mexico] *Argus*, April 6, 1923, and *Lubbock Avalanche-Journal*, September 25, 1949.

86. Rollins, *The Cowboy: An Unconventional History of Civilization*, 332–35.

87. *Lubbock Avalanche-Journal*, September 25, 1949.

88. *State v. Tom Ross*, Cause No. 89 in the District Court of Lea County, New Mexico, October 31, 1922, Ross's ranch hands Roy "Alkali" Adams and Boone Hardin, were also indicted for the same alleged theft.

89. *Wichita* [Falls, Texas] *Daily Times*, June 24, 1923; *Abilene Daily Reporter*, June 24, 1923; Alexander, *Fearless Dave Allison*, 233; Fenton, "Tom Ross: Outlaw and Stockman," 94, 146.

90. The offense of "theft" is defined essentially the same in all states. In Texas, for example, Sec. 31.03 of the Penal Code requires the state to prove three elements to make out a theft case: (1) the defendant must have intentionally acquired possession of another's property, (2) done so without the owner's consent, and (3) done so with the intent to deprive the owner of that property.

CHAPTER FIVE: BLOODY SUNDAY IN SEMINOLE

1. Jan Devereaux, "Gentle Woman, Tough Medicine," *NOLA* Vol. XXVII, No. 2 (April-June 2003).

2. Doug Perkins, *Brave Men & Cold Steel* (Fort Worth: Texas & Southwestern Cattle Raisers Association Foundation, 1984), 25–26.

3. *St. Louis Post-Dispatch,* July 23, 1923.

4. *Lubbock Morning Avalanche,* June 22, 1923; *Abilene Daily Reporter,* September 11, 1923; Alexander, *Fearless Dave Allison,* 246; Fenton, "Tom Ross: Outlaw and Stockman," 138.

5. For accounts of the killing of Allison and Roberson, see *The Seminole Sentinel,* April 5, 1923; *The Semi-Weekly Farm News,* April 17, 1923; *Abilene Daily Reporter,* September 11, 1923; *The Cattleman,* May 1923, July 1923, and December 1971; *St. Louis Post-Dispatch,* July 22, 1923; *Fort Worth Star-Telegram,* June 22, 1923; and *Dallas Morning News,* June 22, 1923.

6. *St. Louis Post-Dispatch,* July 22, 1923.

7. Ibid.

8. *Dallas Morning News,* June 22, 1923.

9. *Lubbock Avalanche-Journal,* June 22, 1923; *St. Louis Post-Dispatch,* July 22, 1923.

10. *State of Texas v. Tom Ross,* Causes No. 50 (murder of Allison) and 52 (murder of Roberson) in the 106th Judicial District Court of Gaines County, Texas, and *State of Texas v. Milton Paul Good,* Causes No. 51 and 53 in the same court. Causes No. 50 and 51 were transferred to the District Court of Lubbock County, Texas, for trial as Causes No. 592 and 593, respectively, in the Lubbock court. Causes No. 52 and 53 were transferred to the District Court of Taylor County at Abilene, Texas, for trial as Causes No. 4910 and 4909, respectively.

11. *The Cattleman,* May 1923.

12. *St. Louis Post-Dispatch,* July 15, 22, and 29, 1923.

13. Ibid, July 22, 1923.

14. Ibid, July 15, 1923.

15. *Abilene Daily Reporter,* June 12 and 20, 1923; *Dallas Morning News,* June 18, 1923; *Fort Worth Star-Telegram,* June 17, 1923.

16. *St. Louis Post-Dispatch,* July 15, 1923.

17. Fenton, "Tom Ross: Outlaw and Stockman," 121.

18. Ibid, 122–23; George W. Dupree, "William H. Bledsoe," *Texas Bar Journal* 25 (November 22, 1962), 967–68, 1002.

19. *St. Louis Post-Dispatch,* July 22, 1923; Fenton, "Tom Ross: Outlaw and Stockman," 123–24.

20. Mary Whatley Clarke, *A Century of Cow Business: A History of the Texas and Southwestern Cattle Raisers Association* (Fort Worth: T&SCRA Foundation,

1976), 55; Lewis Nordyke, *Great Roundup: The Story of Texas and the Southwest* (New York: William Morrow and Company, 1955), 245–46.

21. *St. Louis Post-Dispatch*, July 29, 1923. In winding up his account of the Tom Ross trial, Robertus Love, the *Post-Dispatch* reporter, devoted considerable space to tracing the origins and background of the "50-year feud" between the "big" ranchers (read, Texas and Southwestern Cattle Raisers Association) and the little operators and cattle rustlers and how that factor affected the Tom Ross murder trial.

22. *The Cattleman*, June 1923; Fenton, "Tom Ross: Outlaw and Stockman," 115–16.

23. Gerard S. Petrone, *Judgment at Gallatin: The Trial of Frank James* (Lubbock: Texas Tech University Press, 1998), xvii. At that page, Richard Maxwell Brown, in his introduction to the book, makes this cogent comment:

> [I]n both life and legend there is, in counterpoint to the social-bandit, the socially conservative hero of the West, represented, for example, by the frontier marshals Wild Bill Hickok and Wyatt Earp. The aspect of the American mind that values order and security responds to the reassuring myth of the intrepid lawman always besting evil, whereas the social-bandit hero appeals to the instinctive American fondness for dissent and distrust of established power.

24. *St. Louis Post-Dispatch*, July 15, 1923.

25. Weston A. Pettey, "The Seminole Incident" (Unpublished manuscript, Southwest Collections/Special Collections Library, Texas Tech University, Lubbock, Texas, 1978), 18.

26. *Lovington Leader*, June 22, 1923.

27. Fenton, "Tom Ross: Outlaw and Stockman," 130.

28. *Abilene Daily Reporter*, September 10, 1923.

29. *Dallas Morning News*, June 22, 1923.

30. *Lubbock Morning Avalanche*, June 22, 1923; *Ross v. State*, 267 S.W. 499, 501 (Tex.Ct.Crim.App. 1925); *Good v. State*, 267 S.W. 505, 507 (Tex.Ct.Crim.App. 1925).

31. *St. Louis Post-Dispatch*, July 29, 1923.

32. *Lovington Leader*, July 29, 1923.

33. *Ross v. State*, 267 S.W. 499, 500.

34. *Fort Worth Star-Telegram*, June 24, 1923.

35. Weston A. Pettey, "The Seminole Incident and Tom Ross," *West Texas Historical Association Year Book*, Vol. LVI (1980), 139.

36. Fenton, "Tom Ross: Outlaw and Stockman," 147.

37. *Ross v. State*, 267 S.W. 499, 500; Fenton, "Tom Ross: Outlaw and Stockman," 147.

38. *Abilene Daily Reporter,* September 12, 1923.

39. Ibid.

40. Ibid, June 24, 1923.

41. Ibid, September 13, 1923; *Dallas Morning News,* June 23, 1923.

42. *Abilene Daily Reporter,* September 13, 1923.

43. Ibid.

44. Ibid; *Dallas Morning News,* June 23, 1923.

45. *Abilene Daily Reporter,* September 13, 1923.

46. *Dallas Morning News,* June 23, 1923.

47. *Fort Worth Star-Telegram,* June 23, 1923; *Dallas Morning News,* June 23, 1923.

48. *Dallas Morning News,* June 23, 1923; *Abilene Daily Reporter,* September 13, 1923.

49. *Abilene Daily Reporter,* June 24 and September 13, 1923; *Dallas Morning News,* June 23, 1923.

50. *Dallas Morning News,* June 23, 1923.

51. *Dallas Morning News,* June 24, 1923.

52. *Abilene Daily Reporter,* June 24, 1923.

53. *Fort Worth Star-Telegram,* June 23, 1923.

54. Sterling, *Trails and Trials of a Texas Ranger,* 380; Paul N. Spellman, *Captain John H. Rogers, Texas Ranger* (Denton, TX: University of North Texas Press, 2003), 129.

55. *Dallas Morning News,* June 26, 1923.

56. *Fort Worth Star-Telegram,* June 28, 1923.

57. Ibid.

58. Ibid; *The Cattleman,* October 1923.

59. *Dallas Morning News,* June 29, 1923; *Fort Worth Star-Telegram,* June 29, 1923; *Lovington Leader,* July 6, 1923.

60. *Fort Worth Star-Telegram,* July 1, 1923.

61. *Dallas Morning News,* June 29, 1923.

62. *St. Louis Post-Dispatch,* July 29, 1923.

63. *Abilene Daily Reporter,* September 9, 1923.

64. Ibid, September 19, 1923.

65. Fenton, "Tom Ross: Outlaw and Stockman," 165.

CHAPTER SIX: THE END OF A LONG AND WINDING TRAIL

1. *The Cattleman,* October 1923; *The Cattleman,* December 1925.

2. The account of the escape of Ross and Good from the Texas Penitentiary on November 29, 1925, has been compiled from the following sources: *Dallas Morning News,* November 30, 1925; *Fort Worth Star-Telegram,* November 30, 1925; *Abilene Daily Reporter,* December 6, 1925; *The Cattleman,* December 1925;

Milt Good as told to W. E. Lockhart, *Twelve Years in a Texas Prison* (Amarillo: Russell Stationary Co., 1935), 29–30.

3. *The Cattleman,* July 1926; Good, *Twelve Years in a Texas Prison,* 36.

4. *The Cattleman,* November 1927.

5. "Proclamation of Pardon" No. 26637 in favor of Milton Paul Good, appears in the Governor's Executive Record Book, Texas State Archives, Austin, Texas.

6. Ibid. (Emphasis added.)

7. May Nelson Paulissen and Carl McQueary, *Miriam—The Southern Belle Who Became the First Woman Governor of Texas* (Austin: Eakin Press, 1995), 155–66. Also see Norman D. Brown, *Hood, Bonnet, and Little Brown Jug: Texas Politics, 1921–1928* (College Station: Texas A&M University Press, 1984), 270–74; and Kathleen Dean Moore, *Pardons: Justice, Mercy and the Public Interest* (New York: Oxford University Press, 1989), 63. During the years of 1925 and 1926, "Ma" Ferguson's first term as governor, and at a time when the population of Texas was less than a fifth of what it is today, she granted executive clemency to 3,595 convicts. James L. Haley, *Texas—From Spindletop Through World War II* (New York: St. Martin's Press, 1993), 144–47.

8. *State of Texas v. Milt Good,* Cause No. 736 in the District Court of Motley County, Texas.

9. Prison intake interview of Milton Paul Good, No. 97300, taken on June 6, 1941, Texas Department of Corrections records, Texas State Archives, Austin, Texas.

10. DeArment, "Bloody Easter," 19; Alexander, *Fearless Dave Allison,* 262; Doug Perkins, *Brave Men & Cold Steel: A History of Range Detectives and Their Peacemakers* (Fort Worth: Texas and Southwestern Cattle Raisers Foundation, 1984), 27.

11. *Seminole Sentinel,* February 7, 1929; Good, *Twelve Years in a Texas Prison,* 43.

12. *Seminole Sentinel,* February 7, 1929; *Lovington Leader,* February 8, 1929; *The Cut Bank* [Montana] *Pioneer Press,* February 8, 1929.

13. *The Cut Bank Pioneer Press,* February 8, 1929. That same issue carried a very interesting sidebar story, as follows.

> A special to *The Harve Daily News* from Browning, Montana says that it has been quite definitely established that when Gannon [Tom Ross] left Texas he went to Canada and that in a rage one day, at a Canadian cattle camp, he killed a Chinese cook with a club. He then drifted south to the United States and to the Rimrock Ranch of the Frye Company where he had been working.
>
> James Fenton in his thesis, "Tom Ross: Outlaw and Stockman," 189, stated that he researched Canadian newspapers and archives for that period of time but could find nothing to verify the alleged killing of a Chinese cook. He adds, however, "Still, given Ross's low regard for foreign places

and their people and his apparent inability to then control his temper, such a response seems quite likely."

14. *The Cattleman,* March 1929, quoting *Proverbs* 13:15.

15. Perkins, *Brave Men & Cold Steel,* 23. Apparently Milt Good stole the cattle west of Lubbock in Hockley County, Texas, then drove them southeastward through Terry County, then Lynn County, then into Dawson County where Allison and Roberson caught up with Good and his cowboys and arrested them about twenty miles south of Lamesa. Allison and Roberson then obtained grand jury indictments in all four of these counties for the same theft pursuant to Article 13.08 of the *Texas Code of Criminal Procedure,* which provides as follows:

> Where property is stolen in one county and removed by the offender to another county, the offender may be prosecuted either in the county where he took the property or in any other county through or into which he may have removed the same.
>
> It should be noted that while Milt Good et al. were subject to prosecution in any of the four counties, they could have been convicted only once and only in one of the counties for the same theft. It therefore seems rather typical of Allison's and Roberson's somewhat overzealous tactics to have Good indicted in four counties, thus permitting him to be arrested four times and forcing him to post four bail bonds in order to be released pending trial.

16. *Dallas Morning News,* June 27, 1923.

17. *Dallas Morning News,* June 26, 1923.

18. Ibid.

19. Interview of W. M. "Bob" Beverly by J. Evetts Haley.

20. Ibid.

21. Erickson, *Prairie Gothic,* 136–43.

22. *State v. Edd Lamb,* Cause No. 56, District Court of Gaines County, Texas, 1922.

23. J. Evetts Haley, *Men of Fiber* (El Paso: Carl Hertzog, 1963), 38–39.

24. John Allison Rickard, "The Ranch Industry of the Texas South Plain" (Unpublished MA thesis, University of Texas at Austin, 1927), 157–58; *The Cattleman,* month unknown, 1921; Fenton, "Tom Ross: Outlaw and Stockman," 101–102.

25. Gaines County, Texas, Delinquent Tax Roll, Volume for years 1885–1923, pages 6, 7, 15, 28, 37 (Gaines County Courthouse, Seminole, Texas).

26. *Abilene Daily Reporter,* June 24 and September 13, 1923; *Dallas Morning News,* June 23, 1923.

27. Clarke, *A Century of Cow Business: The First Hundred Years,* 146; and Clarke, "Bad Man . . . Good Man?" 62.

28. W. M. "Bob" Beverly interview by J. Evetts Haley.

29. George Cook interview by J. Evetts Haley, June 26, 1937, Hot Springs, New

Mexico. Tom Roberts interview by J. Evetts Haley, Midland, Texas, June 4, 1935. (Courtesy of the Nita Stewart Haley Memorial Library and the J. Evetts Haley History Center, Midland, Texas.)

30. Fenton, "Tom Ross: Outlaw and Stockman," 29.

31. Eugene Cunningham, *Triggernometry: A Gallery of Gunfighters* (Caldwell: University of Idaho Press, 1971), 12–37, 38–65; Paine, *Captain Bill McDonald*, 26–30. See also Weiss, "'Yours to Command,'" 13. Weiss comments, "[Some westerners developed] a taste . . . for mixing outlawry with the work of a peace officer—moving between the two at will."

32. Good, *Twelve Years in a Texas Prison*, 16.

33. Ayers, *Vengeance & Justice*, 269.

34. *Lubbock Avalanche-Journal*, June 22, 1923.

35. John Duff Green, "Recollections" (Unpublished manuscript in possession of Mrs. Joan Green Lawrence, Mineral Wells, Texas, 1988). See also a newspaper article by Duff Green entitled "Recollections," *The Matador* [Texas] *Tribune*, October 9, 1986.

36. W. M. "Bob" Beverly interview by J. Evetts Haley, Midland County, Texas, March 24, 1945, and June 23, 1946. (Courtesy of the Nita Stewart Haley Memorial Library and the J. Evetts Haley History Center, Midland, Texas.)

37. Green, "Recollections," *The Matador* [Texas] *Tribune*, October 9, 1986.

38. Owen, *Byrd Cochrain of Dead Man's Corner*, 6–23.

39. Clarke, "Bad Man . . . Good Man?" 43–66.

40. Elizah Deaver Harrington interview by J. Evetts Haley, Pantano, Arizona, December 15, 1939. (Courtesy of the Nita Stewart Haley Memorial Library and the J. Evetts Haley History Center, Midland, Texas.)

41. George Cook interview by J. Evetts Haley, Hot Springs, New Mexico, June 26, 1937. (Courtesy of the Nita Stewart Haley Memorial Library and the J. Evetts Haley History Center, Midland, Texas.)

42. Hunter Irwin interview by J. Evetts Haley, Andrews County, Texas, November 18, 1936. (Courtesy of the Nita Stewart Haley Memorial Library and the J. Evetts Haley History Center, Midland, Texas.)

43. Mrs. Hunter Irwin interview by J. Evetts Haley, Andrews County, Texas, November 18, 1936. (Courtesy of the Nita Stewart Haley Memorial Library and the J. Evetts Haley History Center, Midland, Texas.)

44. Good, *Twelve Years in a Texas Prison*, 45.

45. John Shelton Reed, "Below the Smith and Wesson Line: Reflections on Southern Violence," in *Perspectives on the American South*, Vol. 1, ed. Merle Black and John Shelton Reed (New York: Gordon and Breach Science Publishers, 1981), 12; Clare V. McKanna, Jr., *Homicide, Race and Justice in the American West, 1880–1920* (Tucson: University of Arizona Press, 1997), 67.

46. Ayers, *Vengeance & Justice*, 9–33; McKanna, *Homicide, Race and Justice in the American West*, 65–69.

47. Ayers, *Vengeance & Justice*, 18; Michael P. Rogin, *Fathers and Children: Andrew Jackson and the Subjugation of the American Indian* (New York: Vintage Books, 1976), 58.

48. Jim M. Perdue, *Winning with Stories: Using the Narrative to Persuade in Trials, Speeches & Lectures* (Austin: State Bar of Texas, 2006), 383.

49. In an exaggerated sense of southern masculinity, any man who refused to wipe out an insult with violence "ain't no man." David Nevin, *The Texans: What They Are—and Why* (New York: Bonanza Books, 1968), 84–87. See also H. C. Brearley in W. T. Couch, ed. *Culture in the South* (Westport, CT: Negro University Press, 1970).

50. Frederick Nolan, *Bad Blood: The Life and Times of the Horrell Brothers* (Stillwater, OK: Barbed Wire Press, 1994), 160–61.

51. Ayers, *Vengeance & Justice*, 18.

52. Ibid.

53. Fenton, "Tom Ross: Outlaw and Stockman," 3.

54. Carl Coke Rister, *Fort Griffin in the Texas Frontier* (Norman: University of Oklahoma Press, 1956), 132.

55. For the impact of the violent and chaotic atmosphere of Reconstruction years on the lives of lawmen (Ranger Capt. Bill McDonald) and outlaws (Bill Longley and John Wesley Hardin) compare Paine, *Captain Bill McDonald*, 26–30 with Cunningham, *Triggernometry: A Gallery of Gunfighters*, 12–37, 38–65; and Joseph G. Rosa, *The Gunfighter: Man or Myth?* (Norman: University of Oklahoma Press, 1969). See also Weiss, "'Yours to Command,'" 13.

56. See Jonathan H. Pincus, *Base Instincts: What Makes Killers Kill* (New York: W. W. Norton & Co., 2001).

57. Haley, *Men of Fiber*, 36.

58. Ibid, 32–33.

CHAPTER SEVEN: FROM GUNS TO GAVELS

1. Darwin Payne, *As Old as Dallas Itself: A History of the Lawyers of Dallas, the Dallas Bar Association, and the City They Helped Build* (Dallas: Three Forks Press, 1992), 12.

2. Sonnichsen, *I'll Die Before I'll Run*, 8.

3. Ibid, 9.

4. Ayers, *Violence & Justice*, 12. See also Charles Sydnor, "The Southerner and the Laws," *Journal of Southern History* 6 (1940), 2–23; Robert Dykstra, *The Cattle Towns* (New York: Knopf, 1968), 112–48; Tery G. Jordan, *Trails to Texas: Southern Roots of Western Cattle Ranching* (Lincoln: University of Nebraska Press, 1981).

5. Brown, *No Duty to Retreat,* 28.

6. James H. East interview by J. Evetts Haley, Midland, Texas, September 27, 1927. (Courtesy of the Nita Stewart Haley Memorial Library and the J. Evetts Haley History Center.)

7. Frank Richard Prassel, *The Great American Outlaw—A Legacy of Fact and Fiction* (Norman: University of Oklahoma Press, 1993), 160. See also Robert M. Utley, *Billy the Kid: A Short and Violent Life* (Lincoln: University of Nebraska Press, 1989), 203; and Leon C. Metz, *Pat Garrett: The Story of a Western Lawman* (Norman: University of Oklahoma Press, 1974), 308–9.

8. For a pithy comparison of Hollywood myth versus the real West, compare cowboy actor-crooner Gene Autry's "Cowboy Ten Commandments," Commandment 1 being: "The cowboy must never shoot first, hit a smaller man, or take unfair advantage," Albert B. Tucker, "B Westerns: An Affective History of the West," *West Texas Historical Association Year Book,* Vol. LXVI (1990), 158; with western historian Johnny D. Boggs's take on the way it really was in the Old West, to wit: "only an idiot would give a murderous opponent the opportunity to draw first." Johnny D. Boggs, *Great Murder Trials of the Old West* (Plano: Republic of Texas Press, 2003), viii.

9. Miller, *New World Coming,* 16, 89, 172.

10. *The Baylor County Banner,* August 1, 1913.

11. *The Paducah Post,* May 30, 1912 (emphasis added).

12. Coombes, *The Prairie Dog Lawyer,* 168–69.

13. *The Baylor County Banner,* August 1, 1913.

14. Coombes, *The Prairie Dog Lawyer,* 169.

15. Bill O'Neal, *The Bloody Legacy of Pink Higgins: A Half Century of Violence in Texas* (Austin: Eakin Press, 1999), 3–4.

16. *The Cattleman,* October 1923, 10.

17. *St. Louis Post-Dispatch,* July 22, 1923.

CHAPTER EIGHT: THE RULE OF LAW: AN ONGOING BATTLE

1. Almost a century and a half ago, Pres. Abraham Lincoln wrestled with this thorny issue before finally suspending citizens' right to writs of habeas corpus during the Civil War, thus allowing the arrest and detention of certain U.S. citizens he deemed to be dangerous to the public safety—a Draconian measure that not even the most aggressive hawk is now advocating. Paul M. Angle and Earl Schenck Miers, eds., *The Living Lincoln: The Man, His Mind, His Times and the War He Fought, Reconstructed from His Own Writings* (New York: Barnes & Noble Books by arrangement with Rutgers University Press, 1992), 417, 546–54.

2. Ayers, *Vengeance & Justice,* 32–33.

BIBLIOGRAPHY

BOOKS

Abernathy, John R. *Catch 'em Alive Jack: The Life and Adventures of an American Pioneer.* New York: Association Press, 1936.

Adams, Ramon. *Burrs Under the Saddle.* Norman: University of Oklahoma Press, 1964.

Adams, Raymond. *The Old-Time Cowhand.* New York: Collier Books, 1948.

Alexander, Bob. *Fearless Dave Allison: Border Lawman.* Silver City, NM: High-Lonesome Books, 2003.

Alexander, Bob. *Lawmen, Outlaws and S.O.B.s: Gunfighters of the Old Southwest.* Silver City, NM: High-Lonesome Books, 2004.

Alexander, Bob. *Lawmen, Outlaws and S.O.B.s: Gunfighters of the Old Southwest. Vol. II.* Silver City, NM: High-Lonesome Books, 2007.

Allen, Frederick. *A Decent Orderly Lynching: The Montana Vigilantes.* Norman: University of Oklahoma Press, 2005.

Angle, Paul M., and Earl Schenck, eds. *The Living Lincoln: The Man, His Mind, His Times and the War He Fought, Reconstructed from His Own Writings.* New York: Barnes & Noble Books/Rutgers University Press, 1992.

Anonymous. *The Facts in the Case of the Horrible Murder of Little Myrtle Vance and Its Fearful Expiation at Paris, Texas, February 1, 1893.* Paris, TX: P. L. James, 1893.

Ayers, Edward L. *Vengeance & Justice: Crime and Punishment in the 19th-Century South.* New York: Oxford University Press, 1984.

Bailey, Ernest Emory, ed. *Texas Historical and Biographical Record.* Austin: Texas Historical and Biographical Record, 1939.

Bakken, Gordon Morris. *Practicing Law in Frontier California,* Lincoln: University of Nebraska Press, 1991.

Bakken, Gordon Morris, ed. *Law in the Western United States.* Norman: University of Oklahoma Press, 2000.

Bates, Ed F. *History and Reminiscences of Denton County.* Denton: McNitzky Printing Co., 1918.

Baugh, Virgil E. *A Pair of Texas Rangers: Bill McDonald and John Hughes.* Washington, DC: Potomac Corral, the Westerners, 1970.

Bennet, Carmen Taylor. *Our Roots Grow Deep: A History of Cottle County.* Floydada, TX: Blanco Offset Printing, 1970.

Bernstein, Patricia. *The First Waco Horror: The Lynching of Jesse Washington and the Rise of the NAACP.* College Station: Texas A&M University Press, 2005.

Blumanson, Martin. *The Patton Papers, 1885–1940.* New York: DaCapo Press, 1998.

Bodenhamer, David J., and James W. Ely, Jr., eds. *Ambivalent Legacy: A Legal History of the South.* Jackson: University Press of Mississippi, 1984.

Boggs, Johnny D. *Great Murder Trials of the Old West.* Plano: Republic of Texas Press, 2005.

Brodhead, Michael J. *Isaac C. Parker: Federal Justice on the Frontier.* Norman: University of Oklahoma Press, 2003.

Brown, Norman D. *Hood, Bonnet and Little Brown Jug: Texas Politics, 1921–1928.* College Station: Texas A&M University Press, 1984.

Brown, Richard Maxwell. *No Duty to Retreat: Violence and Values in American History and Society.* New York: Oxford University Press, 1991.

Brown, Richard Maxwell. *Strains of Violence: Historical Studies of American Violence and Vigilantism.* New York: Oxford University Press, 1975.

Burton, Jeffrey. *Dynamite and Six-Shooter.* Santa Fe: Palomino Press, 1970.

Burton, Jeffrey. *Indian Territory and the United States, 1866–1906: Courts, Government and the Movement for Oklahoma Statehood.* Norman: University of Oklahoma Press, 1995.

Campbell, Harry H. *The Early History of Motley County,* Second Edition. Wichita Falls, TX: Nortex Offset Publications, 1971.

Carrigan, William D. *The Making of a Lynching Culture: Violence and Vigilantism in Central Texas, 1836–1916.* Champaign: University of Illinois Press, 2004.

Claiborne, J. F. H. *Mississippi as a Province, Territory and State.* Jackson: Power and Barksdale, 1880.

Clarke, Mary Whatley. *A Century of Cow Business: A History of the Texas & Southwestern Cattle Raisers Association.* Fort Worth: T&SCRA Foundation, 1976.

BIBLIOGRAPHY

Clayton, Lawrence. *Historic Ranches of Texas*. Austin: University of Texas Press, 1993.

Coombes, Charles E. *The Prairie Dog Lawyer*. Dallas: University Press of Dallas, 1945.

Couch, W. T., ed. *Culture in the South*. Westport, CT: Negro University Press, 1970.

Cox, James. *Historical and Biographical Record of the Cattle Industry and the Cattlemen of Texas and Adjacent Territory*. St. Louis: Woodward & Tieran Printing Co., 1895.

Cunningham, Eugene. *Triggernometry: A Gallery of Gunfighters*. Caldwell: University of Idaho Press, 1971.

Dary, David. *Red Blood and Black Ink: Journalism in the Old West*. Lawrence: University Press of Kansas, 1998.

Davis, John W. *A Vast Amount of Trouble: A History of the Spring Creek Raid*. Niwot: University of Colorado Press, 1995.

Davis, John W. *Goodbye Judge Lynch: The End of a Lawless Era in Wyoming's Big Horn Basin*. Norman: University of Oklahoma Press, 2005.

Davis, Reuben. *Recollections of Mississippi and Mississippians*. Boston: Houghton Mifflin, 1889.

Dobie, J. Frank. *Cow People*. Boston: Little, Brown & Co., 1964.

Douglas, C. L. *Cattle Kings of Texas*. Fort Worth: Branch-Smith, 1939.

Dykstra, Robert. *The Cattle Towns*. New York: Knopf, 1968.

Ehrle, Michael G. *The Childress County Story*. Childress, TX: Ox Bow Printing Co., 1971.

Erickson, John R. *Prairie Gothic: The Story of a West Texas Family*. Denton: University of North Texas Press, 2005.

Flemmons, Jerry. *Amon: The Texan Who Played Cowboy for America*. Lubbock: Texas Tech University Press, 1998.

Freidman, Lawrence M. "The Law Between the States: Some Thoughts on Southern Legal History." In David J. Bodenhamer and James W. Ely, Jr., eds. *Ambivalent Legacy: A Legal History of the South*. Jackson: University Press of Mississippi, 1984.

Freidman, Lawrence M., and Robert V. Percival. *The Roots of Justice: Crime and Punishment in Alameda County, California, 1870–1910*. Chapel Hill: University of North Carolina Press, 1981.

Fromm, Eric. *The Anatomy of Human Destructiveness*. New York: Holt, Rinehart and Winston, 1973.

Gaines County Historical Survey Committee. *The Gaines County Story*. Seagraves, TX: Pioneer Book Publishers, 1974.

Gober, James A., and B. Bryan Price. *Cowboy Justice—A Tale of a Texas Lawman*. Lubbock: Texas Tech University Press, 1997.

Good, Milt. *Twelve Years in a Texas Prison.* Amarillo: Russell Stationery Co., 1935.

Gournay, Luke. *Texas Boundaries: Evolution of the State's Counties.* College Station: Texas A&M University, 1995.

Graham, Hugh Davis, and Ted Robert Gurr, eds. *The History of Violence in America.* New York: Frederick A. Praeger, 1969.

Graves, Richard S. *Oklahoma Outlaws.* Oklahoma City: State Printing and Publishing Co., 1915.

Hagan, William T. *United States–Comanche Relations: The Reservation Years.* New Haven, CT: Yale University Press, 1976.

Haley, J. Evetts. *Men of Fiber.* El Paso: Carl Hertzog, 1963.

Haley, J. Evetts. *The XIT Ranch of Texas and the Early Days of Llano Estacado.* Norman: University of Oklahoma Press, 1953.

Haley, James L. *Texas—From Spindletop Through World War II.* New York: St. Martin's Press, 1993.

Haley, James L. *Texas—From Frontier to Spindletop.* New York: St. Martin's Press, 1985.

Hall, Colby D. *History of Texas Christian University: A College of the Cattle Frontier.* Fort Worth: Texas Christian University Press, 1947.

Hall, Jacquelyn Dowd. *Revolt Against Chivalry: Jessie Daniel Ames and the Women's Campaign Against Lynching.* New York: Columbia University Press, 1993.

Hamm, Richard F. *Murder, Honor and Law: Four Virginia Homicides from Reconstruction to the Great Depression.* Charlottesville: University of Virginia Press, 2003.

Hamner, Laura V. *Light 'n Hitch.* Dallas: American Guild Press, 1958.

Hanes, Bailey C. *Bill Doolin: Outlaw Oklahoma Territory.* Norman: University of Oklahoma Press, 1968.

Harrington, Fred Harvey. *Hanging Judge.* Norman: University of Oklahoma Press, 1951.

Harris, Charles H., III, and Louis R. Sadler. *The Texas Rangers and the Mexican Revolution: The Bloodiest Decade, 1910–1920.* Albuquerque: University of New Mexico Press, 2004.

Hendrix, John. *If I Can Do It Horseback.* Austin: University of Texas Press, 1964.

Howe, Mark DeWolfe, ed. *Holmes-Laski Letters: The Correspondence of Mr. Justice Holmes and Harold J. Laske, 1916–1935.* Vol. I. Cambridge, MA: Harvard University Press, 1953.

Johnson, Benjamin Heber. *Revolution in Texas: How a Forgotten Rebellion and Its Bloody Suppression Turned Mexicans into Americans.* New Haven, CT: Yale University Press, 2003.

Johnson, Frank W. *A History of Texas and Texans.* Edited by Eugene C. Barker and E. W. Winkler. Chicago: American Historical Society, 1914.

Jordon, Tery G. *Trails to Texas: Southern Roots of Western Cattle Ranching.* Lincoln:

University of Nebraska Press, 1981.

Kearby, Mary Anna Renfro. *Pioneers Remember the Past.* Edited by North Texas Genealogical Assn. Wichita Falls, TX: Nortex Offset Press, 1998.

Kelly, Louise. *Wichita County Beginnings.* Burnet, TX: Eakin Press, 1982.

King County Historical Society. *King County: Windmills & Barbed Wire.* Quanah, TX: Nortex Press, 1976.

Lubet, Steven. *Murder in Tombstone: The Forgotten Trial of Wyatt Earp.* New Haven, CT: Yale University Press, 2004.

Lule, Jake. *Daily News, Eternal Stories: The Mythological Role of Journalism.* New York: The Guilford Press, 2001.

Martin, Meredith. "Gunpowder Justice: The Trial of Samuel Burk Burnett for the Murder of Farley Sayers." In Michael L. Collins, ed. *Tales of Texoma: Episodes in the History of the Red River Border.* Wichita Falls, TX: Midwestern University Press, 2005.

Mason-Manheim, Madeline. *Riding for Texas: The True Adventures of Captain Bill McDonald of the Texas Rangers, as Told by Colonel Edward M. House to Tyler Mason.* New York: Rynal & Hitchcock, 1936.

McCoy, Joseph G. *Historic Sketches of the Cattle Trade of the Southwest.* Kansas City: Ramsey, Millett & Hudson, 1874. Reprint: Washington: The Rare Book Shop, 1932.

McKanna, Clare V., Jr. *Homicide, Race and Justice in the American West, 1880–1920.* Tucson: University of Arizona Press, 1997.

Meinzer, Wyman, and Henry Chappell. *6666: Portrait of a Texas Ranch.* Lubbock: Texas Tech University Press, 2004.

Metz, Leon C. *Pat Garrett: The Story of a Western Lawman.* Norman: University of Oklahoma Press, 1974.

Miletich, Leo N. *Dan Stuart's Fistic Carnival.* College Station: Texas A&M University Press, 1994.

Miller, Floyd. *Bill Tilghman: Marshall of the Last Frontier.* New York: Doubleday & Co., 1968.

Miller, George W., Jr. *The Trial of Frank James for Murder.* New York: Jingle Bob/Crown Publishers, 1977.

Miller, Nathan. *New World Coming: The 1920s and the Making of Modern America.* New York: Scribner, 2003.

Moore, Kathleen Dean. *Pardons: Justice, Mercy and the Public Interest.* New York: Oxford University Press, 1989.

Morgan, Johnnie R. *The History of Wichita Falls.* Wichita Falls, TX: Nortex Press, 1971.

Morris, John Miller. *A Private in the Texas Rangers—A. T. Miller of Company B, Frontier Battalion.* College Station: Texas A&M Press, 2001.

Neal, Bill. *Getting Away with Murder on the Texas Frontier: Notorious Killings & Celebrated Trials.* Lubbock: Texas Tech University Press, 2006.

Neal, Bill. *The Last Frontier: The Story of Hardeman County, Texas.* Quanah, TX: Southwest Offset Publications, 1966.

Neeley, Bill. *The Last Comanche Chief: The Life and Times of Quanah Parker.* New York: John Wiley & Sons, 1995.

Nevels, Cynthia Skove. *Lynching to Belong: Claiming Whiteness Through Racial Violence.* College Station: Texas A&M University Press, 2007.

Nevin, David. *The Texans: What They Are—and Why.* New York: Bonanza Books, 1968.

Nix, Evett Dumas. *Oklahombres.* St. Louis and Chicago: Eden Publishing House, 1929.

Nolan, Frederick. *Bad Blood: The Life and Times of the Horrell Brothers.* Stillwater, OK: Barbed Wire Press, 1994.

Nordyke, Lewis. *Great Roundup: The Story of Texas and Southwestern Cowmen.* New York: William Morrow & Co., 1955.

O'Neal, Bill. *The Bloody Legacy of Pink Higgins: A Half Century of Violence in Texas.* Austin: Eakin Press, 1999.

O'Neal, Bill. *Historic Ranches of the West.* Austin: Eakin Press, 1997.

Owen, Valarie. *Byrd Cochrain of Dead Man's Corner.* Snyder, TX: Feather Press, 1972.

Paine, Albert Bigelow. *Captain Bill McDonald, Texas Ranger.* New York: Little and Ives, 1909. Facsimile of original, Austin: State House Press, 1981.

Paulissen, May Nelson, and Carl McQueary. *Miriam: The Southern Belle Who Became the First Woman Governor of Texas.* Austin: Eakin Press, 1995.

Payne, Darwin. *As Old as Dallas Itself—A History of the Lawyers of Dallas, the Dallas Bar Association, and the City They Helped Build.* Dallas: Three Forks Press, 1992.

Pearce, W. M. *The Matador Land and Cattle Company.* Norman: University of Oklahoma Press, 1964.

Perdue, Jim M. *Winning with Stories: Using the Narrative to Persuade in Trials, Speeches & Lectures.* Austin: State Bar of Texas, 2006.

Perkins, Doug. *Brave Men & Cold Steel: A History of Range Detectives and Their Peacemakers.* Fort Worth: T&SCRA Foundation, 1984.

Petrone, Gerard S. *Judgment at Gallatin: The Trial of Frank James.* Lubbock: Texas Tech University Press, 1995.

Pfeiffer, Michael J. *Rough Justice: Lynching and American Society, 1874–1947.* Urbana: University of Illinois Press, 2004.

Pincus, Jonathan H. *Base Instincts: What Makes Killers Kill?* New York: W. W. Norton, 2001.

Porter, Millie Jones. *Memory Cups of Panhandle Pioneers.* Clarendon, TX: Clarendon Press, 1945.

Potts, Marisue Burleson. *Motley County Roundup: A Centennial History,* Second Edition. Floydada, TX: Marisue Potts, publisher, 1991.

Prassel, Frank Richard. *The Great American Outlaw—A Legacy of Fact and Fiction.* Norman: University of Oklahoma Press, 1993.

Rainbolt, Charles Power. *In Pursuit of the Outlaw "Red Buck."* Inola, OK: Evans Publications, 1990.

Reed, John Shelton. "Below the Smith and Wesson Line: Reflections on Southern Violence." In Merle Black and John Shelton Reed, eds. *Perspectives on the American South,* Vol. 1. New York: Gordon & Breach Science Publishers, 1981.

Reid, John Phillip. "Introduction: The Layers of Western Legal History." In Gordon Morris Bakken, ed. *Law in the Western United States.* Norman: University of Oklahoma Press, 2000.

Rice, Lawrence D. *The Negro in Texas, 1874–1900.* Baton Rouge: Louisiana State University Press, 1971.

Rister, Carl Coke. *Fort Griffin in the Texas Frontier.* Norman: University of Oklahoma Press, 1956.

Robinson, Charles, III. *The Men Who Wear the Star.* New York: The Modern Library, 2001.

Rogin, Michael P. *Fathers and Children: Andrew Jackson and the Subjugation of the American Indian.* New York: Vintage Books, 1976.

Rollins, Philip Ashton. *The Cowboy: An Unconventional History of Civilization on the Old-Time Cattle Range.* Norman: University of Oklahoma Press, 1997.

Rosa, Joseph G. *The Gunfighter: Man or Myth?* Norman: University of Oklahoma Press, 1969.

Rynning, Thomas H. *Gun Notches: A Saga of Frontier Lawman Captain Thomas H. Rynning as Told to Al Cohn and Joe Chisholm.* San Diego: Frontier Heritage Press, 1971.

Shay, Frank. *Judge Lynch, His First Hundred Years.* New York: I. Washburn, Inc., 1938.

Shirley, Glenn. *Heck Thomas, Frontier Marshal.* Philadelphia and New York: Chilton Co., 1962.

Shirley, Glenn. *Temple Houston: Lawyer with a Gun.* Norman: University of Oklahoma Press, 1980.

Shirley, Glenn. *West of Hell's Fringe: Crime, Criminals, and the Federal Peace Officers in Oklahoma Territory, 1889–1907.* Norman: University of Oklahoma Press, 1978.

Smithson, Fay Eidson, and Pat Wilkinson, eds. *Martin County: The First Thirty Years.* Hereford, TX: Pioneer Book Publishers, 1970.

Sonnichsen, C. L. *I'll Die Before I'll Run: The Story of the Great Feuds of Texas.* Lincoln: University of Nebraska Press, 1988.

Sonnichsen, C. L. *Tularosa: Last of the Frontier West.* Albuquerque: University of New Mexico Press, 1960.

Spellman, Paul N. *Captain John H. Rogers, Texas Ranger.* Denton: University of North Texas Press, 2003.

Spellman, Paul N. *Captain J. A. Brooks, Texas Ranger.* Denton: University of North Texas Press, 2007.

Sterling, William Warren. *Trails and Trials of the Texas Rangers.* Norman: University of Oklahoma Press, 1959.

Sullivan, W. J. L. *Twelve Years in the Saddle for Law and Order on the Frontiers of Texas.* Lincoln, NE: Bison Books, 2001.

Tanner, Karen Holliday, and John D. Tanner, Jr. *Last of the Old-Time Outlaws: The George West Musgrave Story.* Norman: University of Oklahoma Press, 2002.

Tefertiller, Casey. *Wyatt Earp: The Life Behind the Legend.* New York: John Wiley & Sons, 1997.

Tilghman, Zoe A. *Quanah: The Eagle of the Comanches.* Oklahoma City: Harlow Publishing Co., 1938.

Tise, Sammy. *Texas County Sheriffs.* Hallettsville, TX: Tise Geological Research, 1995.

Traweek, Eleanor Mitchell. *Of Such As These: A History of Motley County and Its Families.* Wichita Falls, TX: Nortex Offset Publications, 1973.

Tuller, Robert H. *"Let No Guilty Man Escape": A Judicial Biography of "Hanging Judge" Isaac C. Parker.* Norman: University of Oklahoma Press, 2001.

Tyler, Ron, ed. *The New Handbook of Texas, Vol. 4.* Austin: Texas State Historical Assn., 1996.

Utley, Robert M. *Billy the Kid: A Short and Violent Life.* Lincoln: University of Nebraska Press, 1989.

Utley, Robert M. *Lone Star Justice: The First Century of the Texas Rangers.* New York: Oxford University Press, 2002.

Utley, Robert M. *Lone Star Justice: The Second Century of the Texas Rangers.* New York: Oxford University Press, 2007.

Walker, Peggy. *George Humphreys: Cowboy and Lawman.* Burnet, TX: Eakin Publications, 1978.

Webb, Walter Prescott. *The Story of the Texas Rangers.* Austin: Encino, 1971.

Webb, Walter Prescott. *The Texas Rangers: A Century of Frontier Defense.* Austin: University of Texas Press, 1935.

Williams, J. W. *The Big Ranch Country.* Wichita Falls, TX: Nortex Offset Publications, 1971.

PERIODICALS

Bleckley, L. E. "Negro Outrage No Excuse for Lynching." *The Forum* 16 (November 1893): 300–302.

Carter, Keith. "The Texas Court of Criminal Appeals." *Texas Law Review* 11 (1933): 196.

Cartwright, Gary. "Showdown at Waggoner Ranch." *Texas Monthly* (January 2004): 80–81.

Clarke, Mary Whatley. "Bad Man . . . Good Man?" *The Cattleman* (December 1971): 43–66.

Colquitt, Warren. "Beating the Rap." *Paso del Norte* (June 1985): 8–12.

DeArment, R. K. "Bloody Easter." *Old West* Vol. 30, No. 3 (Spring 1994): 15–18.

DeArment, R. K. "The Gunfights of Pioneer Cattleman: Burk Burnett." *Wild West* (August 2005): 32–33.

Devereaux, Jan. "Gentle Woman, Tough Medicine." *National Association for Outlaw and Lawman History.* Vol. XXVII, No. 2 (April–June 2003): 7–15.

Dolman, William E., III. "Conflicts Over Land: The Settler and the Rancher in West Texas." *West Texas Historical Association Year Book* 50 (1974): 61–75.

Douglas, C. L. "Cattle Kings of Texas: Burk Burnett of the Four Sixes." *The Cattleman* (August 1970): 99–102.

Douthit, Ellis. "Some Experiences of a West Texas Lawyer." *West Texas Historical Association Year Book* 18 (1942): 37.

Dupree, George W. "William H. Bledsoe." *Texas Bar Journal* 25 (November 1962): 967–68, 1002.

Fenton, James I. "Tom Ross: Ranger Nemesis." *National Association and Center for Outlaw and Lawmen History.* Vol. XIV, No. 2 (Summer, 1990): 4–21.

Kernan, Thomas J. "The Jurisprudence of Lawlessness." *American Bar Association Report* (1906): 451–53.

Pearce, W. M. "The Road to Stability: A Decade in the History of the Matador Ranch, 1891–1900." *Panhandle-Plains Historical Association Year Book* 26 (1953): 29–30.

Pettey, Weston A. "The Seminole Incident and Tom Ross." *West Texas Historical Association Year Book* LVI (1980): 139.

Sydnor, Charles. "The Southerner and the Laws." *Journal of Southern History* 6 (1940): 2–23.

Steele, Phillip. "The Woman Red Buck Couldn't Scare." *The West* (April 1971): 20–21.

Tefertiller, Casey. "The Spicer Hearing & H. F. Sills." *National Association for Outlaw and Lawman History* Vol. XXXI, No. 3-4 (July–December 2007): 16–25.

Tucker, Albert B. "B Westerns: An Affective History of the West." *West Texas Historical Association Year Book* LXVI (1990): 158.

Walker, Jack. "Four Sixes." *Texas Parade* XVI (July 1955): 37.

Warren, C. "Joe Beckham—The Outlaw Sheriff." *Real West* (August 1983): 28–29.

DOCUMENTS

A. COURT CASES

E. P. Bujac v. Tom Ross, Cause No. 1976 in the District Court of Eddy County, New Mexico (1914).

H. H. Campbell v. The Matador Land & Cattle Co., et al., Cause No. 3, Motley County, Texas, District Court (1891).

Rosa E. Sayers, et al. v. S. B. Burnett, Cause No. 419 in the District Court of Cottle County, Texas (1912).

State v. John A. Morine, Cause No. 35 in the District Court of Culberson County, Texas (1915).

State v. Hillary Loftis, Cause No. 941 in the District Court of Wilbarger County, Texas (1896).

State v. Edd Lamb, Cause No. 56 in the District Court of Gaines County, Texas (1922).

State v. F. M. Davis, Cause No. 608 in the 30th Judicial District Court of Wichita County, Texas, and Cause No. 940 in the District Court of Wilbarger County, Texas (1896).

State v. Farley P. Sayers, Cause No. 132 in the District Court of King County, Texas, and Cause No. 1071 in the District Court of Baylor County, Texas (1911).

State v. Farley P. Sayers, Cause No. 50 in the District Court of King County, Texas, and Cause No. 563 in the District Court of Knox County, Texas (1908).

State v. Frank Smith, Cause No. 605 in the 30th Judicial District Court of Wichita County, Texas, and Cause No. 943 in the District Court of Wilbarger County, Texas (1896).

State v. George Cook, Cause No. 176, Childress County, Texas, District Court (1893).

State v. H. L. Roberson, Cause No. 18,002 in the District Court of Travis County, Texas (1920).

State v. H. L. Roberson, Cause Nos. 6743 and 6744 in the 34th Judicial District Court of El Paso County, Texas (1915).

State v. Hill Loftis, Cause No. 901, Wilbarger County, Texas, District Court (1896).

State v. Jo A. P. Dickson, Cause No. 263 in the Baylor County, Texas, District Court (1885).

State v. Joe P. Beckham, Cause No. 173, Childress County, Texas, District Court (1893).

State v. Joe P. Beckham, Cause No. 193, Childress County, Texas, County Court (1893).

State v. Joe P. Beckham, Cause No. 35, Motley County, Texas, District Court (1892).

State v. Joe P. Beckham, Cause Nos. 17, 18, 19, and 20, Motley County, Texas, District Court (1893), and Cause Nos. 541, 542, 543, and 567, Baylor County, Texas, District Court (same four indictments transferred from Motley County to Baylor County on change of venue) (1893).

State v. Kid Lewis, Cause No. 903 in the Wilbarger County, Texas District Court (1896).

State v. Marion Potter, Cause No. 604 in the 30th Judicial District Court of Wichita County, Texas, and Cause No. 3441 in the District Court of Cooke County, Texas (1896).

State v. Milt Good, Cause No. 51 in the District Court of Gaines County, Texas (1923), transferred on change of venue as Cause No. 593 in the District Court of Lubbock County, Texas.

State v. Milt Good, Cause No. 53 in the District Court of Gaines County, Texas (1923), transferred on change of venue as Cause No. 4910 in the District Court of Taylor County, Texas.

State v. R. P. Coffer, Cause No. 293, Hardeman County, Texas, District Court (1894).

State v. R. T. (Tom) Pickett, Cause No. 481 in the Cottle County, Texas, District Court, and Cause No. 1099 in the Baylor County, Texas, District Court (1911).

State v. Red Buck Weightman, Cause No. 902, Wilbarger County, Texas, District Court (1896).

State v. S. B. Burnett, Cause No. 166 in the Clay County, Texas, District Court (1879).

State v. S. B. Burnett, Cause No. 480 in the Cottle County, Texas, District Court and on change of venue, Cause No. 1100 in the Baylor County, Texas, District Court (1911).

State v. Tom Ross, Cause No. 21, District Court of Gaines County, Texas (1908).

State v. Tom Ross, Cause No. 47, District Court of Gaines County, Texas (1920).

State v. Tom Ross, Cause No. 50 in the District Court of Gaines County, Texas (1923), transferred on change of venue as Cause No. 592 in the District Court of Lubbock County, Texas.

State v. Tom Ross, Cause No. 52 in the District Court of Gaines County, Texas (1923), transferred on change of venue as Cause No. 4909 in the District Court of Taylor County, Texas.

State v. Tom Ross, Cause No. 79, District Court of Gaines County, Texas (1906).

State v. Tom Ross, Cause No. 89 in the District Court of Lea County, New Mexico (1922).

State v. Tom Ross, Cause Nos. 969 and 970 in the District Court of Eddy County, New Mexico (1914).

State v. W. E. Cobb, Cause No. 606 in the 30th Judicial District Court of Wichita County, Texas, and Cause No. 942 in the District Court of Wilbarger County, Texas (1896).

State v. W. J. McDonald, Cause No. 273, Hardeman County, Texas, District Court (1894).

State v. J. N. Ballard, Cause No. 119 in the District Court of Motley County, Texas (1912).

State v. J. L. Law, Cause No. 120 in the District Court of Motley County, Texas (1912).

B. APPELLATE COURT CASES

Alexander v. State, 50 S.W. 716 (Tex.Ct.Crim.App. 1899).

Ballard v. State, 160 S.W. 92 (Tex.Ct.Crim.App. 1913).

Brown v. United States, 25 U.S. 335 (1921).

Good v. State, 267 S.W. 505 (Tex.Ct.Crim.App. 1925).

Graves v. State, 124 S.W. 676 (Tex.Ct.Crim.App. 1910).

Law v. State, 160 S.W. 98 (Tex.Ct.Crim.App. 1913).

Roberson v. State, 203 S.W. 349 (Tex.Ct.Crim.App. 1917).

Ross v. State, 267 S.W. 499 (Tex.Ct.Crim.App. 1925).

Rutledge v. State, 749 S.W. 2d 50 (Tex.Ct.Crim.App. 1988).

INTERVIEWS

A. C. "Arb" Piper, interviewed by author, *audio tape* in possession of author, Paducah, Texas (October and December 1999).

C. M. Randall, interviewed by Joe D. Gibson, Seymour, Texas, *audio tape,* Reels 1-3, Southwest Collections/Special Collections Library, Lubbock, Texas (August 1971).

Clifford Bartlett Jones, interviewed by David B. Garey II, *audio tapes,* Southwest Collections/ Special Collections Library, Texas Tech University Library, Lubbock, Texas (February, March, May, and June 1968, and April and July 1970, and February 1971).

Elizah Deaver Harrington, interviewed by J. Evetts Haley, Pantanao, Arizona, *audio tape,* J. Evetts Haley History Center, Midland, Texas (December 15, 1939).

Frank McAuley, interviewed by author, *author's notes,* Knox City, Texas (July 1999).

George Cook, interviewed by J. Evetts Haley, Hot Springs, New Mexico, *audio tape,* J. Evetts Haley History Center, Midland, Texas (June 4, 1935).

George Humphreys, interviewed by Charles Townsend, *audio tape,* Reel 1, Southwest Collections/Special Collections Library, Texas Tech University, Lubbock, Texas (July 1969).

George Webb, interviewed by author, Canyon, Texas, appears in *Amarillo News-Globe,* July 17, 1960.

Hunter Irwin, interviewed by J. Evetts Haley, Andrews County, Texas, *audio tape,* J. Evetts Haley History Center, Midland, Texas (November 18, 1936).

James H. East, interviewed by J. Evetts Haley, Midland, Texas, *audio tape,* J. Evetts Haley History Center, Midland, Texas (September 27, 1927).

Mrs. Hunter Irwin, interviewed by J. Evetts Haley, Andrews County, Texas, *audio tape,* J. Evetts Haley History Center, Midland, Texas (November 18, 1936).

S. T. "Davy" Burk, interviewed by J. Evetts Haley, Kermit Texas, *audio tape,* J. Evetts Haley History Center, Midland, Texas (December 16, 1962).

Stanton Brown, interviewed by author, *author's notes,* Benjamin, Texas (July and September 1999).

Tom Craddock, interviewed by Joe Gibson, Seymour, Texas, *audio tape,* Reel 1, Southwest Collections/Special Collections Library Texas Tech University, Lubbock, Texas (August 1971).

Tom Roberts, interviewed by J. Evetts Haley, Midland, Texas, *audio tape,* J. Evetts Haley History Center, Midland, Texas (June 4, 1935).

W. H. "Bob" Beverly, interviewed by J. Evetts Haley, Midland, Texas, *audio tape,* J. Evetts Haley History Center, Midland, Texas (March 24, 1945).

Waylon "Toar" Piper, interviewed by author, *audio tape* in possession of author, Paducah, Texas (October and December 1999).

George W. Briggs, interviewed by Eunice M. Mayer, Granite, Oklahoma, Indian-Pioneer Papers, Western History Collection, Vol. 11, p. 173, University of Oklahoma (June 17, 1937).

THESES

Chapman, David. "Lynching in Texas." MA thesis, Texas Tech University, 1973.

Fenton, James I. "Tom Ross: Outlaw and Stockman." MA thesis, University of Texas at El Paso, 1979.

Martin, Meredith Richards. "Samuel Burk Burnett: Old 6666." MA thesis, Midwestern State University, 2002.

Richard, John Allison. "The Ranch Industry of the Texas South Plain." MA thesis, University of Texas, 1927.

Ross, John Raymond. "At the Bar of Judge Lynch: Lynching and Lynch Mobs in America." PhD dissertation, Texas Tech University, 1983.

Weiss, Harold J., Jr. "'Yours to Command': Captain William J. 'Bill' McDonald and the Panhandle Rangers of Texas." PhD dissertation, Indiana University, 1980.

LAWS

Laws of Texas, Article 723, Vol. 10, *Texas Code of Criminal Procedure.* Gammel, comp., 25th Tex. Legis. Session (1897), 17.

Laws of Texas, H. B. 30, Vol. 10, *Texas Code of Criminal Procedure.* Gammel, comp., 25th Tex. Legis., Special Session (1897), 1480.

Texas Code of Criminal Procedure, Article 13.08.

Texas Penal Code, Section 31.03.

Texas Penal Code, Section 7.02 (a) (z).

Texas Penal Code, Section 1220.

Texas Penal Code, Sections 9.31 and 9.32.

Texas Rules of Evidence, Rule 615.

White's Ann. Pen. Code, Article 713.

RECORDS

Affidavit of Dick Crutcher dated January 2, 1894. Quoted in Ehrle, *The Childress County Story,* 60.

Affidavit of R. P. Coffer dated December 30, 1893. Quoted in Ehrle, *The Childress County Story,* 59.

Affidavit of R. P. Coffer dated May 16, 1894. *State v. R. P. Coffer,* Cause No. 293, Hardeman County, Texas, District Court.

Texas Adjutant General's Correspondence Files (hereinafter cited "AGCF"), Box 401, Folder 429-15. Report from Captain W. J. McDonald to Adjutant General W. H. Mabry dated August 21, 1893. Austin: Texas State Archives (TSA).

AGCF, Box 401, Folder 427-2. Letter from E. B. Pendleton to Adjutant General W. H. Mabry dated January 28, 1893. Austin: TSA.

AGCF, Box 401, Folder 429-13. Report from Captain W. J. McDonald to Adjutant General W. H. Mabry dated August 17, 1893. Austin: TSA.

AGCF, Box 401, Folder 430-15. Report from Sergeant J. W. Britton to Adjutant General W. H. Mabry dated December 11, 1893. Austin: TSA

AGCF, Box 401, Folder 431-1. Report from Captain W. J. McDonald to Adjutant General W. H. Mabry dated January 10, 1894 (misdated to read "1893"). Austin: TSA.

AGCF, Box 401, Folder 443-12. Report from Captain W. J. McDonald to Adjutant General W. H. Mabry dated June 23, 1897. Austin: TSA.

AGCF, Box 401, folder 443-16. Report from Captain W. J. McDonald to Adjutant General W. H. Mabry dated July 3, 1897. Austin: TSA.

AGCF, Box 401, Folder 443-17. Report from Captain W. J. McDonald to Adjutant General W. H. Mabry dated July 4, 1897. Austin: TSA.

AGCF, File 2-14, Box 88, Folder 1. Report from Captain John H. Rogers to Adjutant General John Hulen dated June 1904. Austin: TSA.

Daniel T. Williams, "Amid the Gathering Multitude: The Story of Lynching in America, a Classified Listing," Lynching Files, Tuskegee University Archives, Tuskegee University, Tuskegee, Alabama.

Fort Worth Public Library, Archive Collections. "In Old Fort Worth: Burk Burnett, Giant of the Frontier." *The News Tribune*, 1977.

Gaines County, Texas, Delinquent Tax Roll, 1895–1923, pp. 6, 7, 15, 28, 37. *Tom Ross*. Gaines County Courthouse, Seminole, Texas.

Governor's Executive Record Book, Pardon No. 26637, *Milton Paul Good*, 26 November 1934. Austin: TSA.

Handwritten notes of editor Rhea Howard in the *Wichita Falls Times-Record News* file on the 1896 lynching of Foster Crawford and Elmer "Kid" Lewis in Wichita Falls, Texas.

James I. Fenton. "A Bank Robbery in a Sand Storm." Unpublished manuscript in possession of James I. Fenton, Lubbock, Texas, 2005.

John Duff Green. "Recollections." Unpublished manuscript in possession of Mrs. Joan Green Lawrence, Mineral Wells, Texas, 1988.

Marriage License Records of Martin County, Texas. Vol. 1, p. 20. January 24, 1904. Marriage of Tom Ross and Lillian "Trixie" Hardin. Martin County Courthouse, Stanton, Texas.

Probate Records of Tarrant County, Texas, Cause No. 7594, The Estate of Samuel Burk Burnett, "Last Will and Testament." Fort Worth, Texas.

S. E. Ledger of First Baptist Church of Seminole, Texas. P. 83. April 14, 1913. Seminole, Texas.

Texas Department of Corrections Records, Prison Intake Interview, *Milton Paul Good*, 6 June 1941. Austin: TSA.

Texas Governor's Papers, Box 301, File 140-230. Letter from Motley County Judge Henry H. Campbell to Governor James S. Hogg dated September 10, 1893. Austin: TSA.

Walter Prescott Webb Collection, University of Texas Library. Captain John R. Hughes report to Adjutant General dated December 4, 1911. Austin, Texas

Weston A. Pettey. "The Seminole Incident." Unpublished manuscript. Southwest Collections/Special Collections Library, Texas Tech University, Lubbock, Texas, 1978.

INTERNET

James E. & Louise (Beckham) Hedlebaugh. "Sheriff Joseph P. Beckham, son of Roderic Carroll Beckham and Sarah Bundy," July 19, 1999. MyFamily.com Inc. and its subsidiaries. (Ancestry.com) June 6, 2001.

INDEX

Page numbers in *italics* refer to illustrations.

* * * * *